The Archaeology of Context

in the

Neolithic and Bronze Age

Recent Trends

Edited by
J. C. Barrett and I. A. Kinnes

Department of Archaeology and Prehistory
University of Sheffield

© Individual Authors 1988
Publisher: John R. Collis
Editor: J. Collis
Cover: E. Moth
Typists: D. Brookfield, T. Simpson
Layout: Russ Adams

Our thanks to the Robert Kiln Charitable Trust for
assistance in the publication of this volume

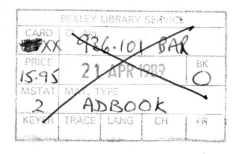

British Library Cataloguing in Publication Data

The Archaeology of Context in the Neolithic and
Bronze Age: recent trends.—
   (Recent trends; v.3).
   1. Great Britain. Prehistoric Antiquities.
   Archaeological Investigation
   IV. Series
I. Barrett, John C. *1949-* II. Kinnes, Ian
III. University of Sheffield *Department of
   Archaeology and Prehistory*
IV. Series
936.1

ISBN 0 906090 31 8

Department of Archaeology & Prehistory
University of Sheffield
Sheffield S10 2TN

Typset at Oxford Computing Services
Printed by H Charlesworth & Co Ltd
Huddersfield
England

Contents

List of Figures

List of Tables

List of Contributors

John Barber	*Scottish Development Department (AM), Edinburgh*
John Barrett	*Department of Archaeology, University of Glasgow*
Christopher Evans	*Department of Archaeology, University of Cambridge*
John Evans	*School of History and Archaeology, Univerity of Wales College of Cardiff*
Andrew Herne	*Department of Prehistoric and Romano-British Antiquities, British Museum, London*
Robin Holgate	*Luton Museum, Luton*
Ian Kinnes	*Department of Prehistoric and Romano-British Antiquities, British Museum, London*
Susan Limbrey	*Department of Archaeology and Ancient History, University of Birmingham*
Ian Máté	*Department of Archaeology and Ancient History University of Birmingham*
R.J. Mount	*School of History and Archaeology, University of Wales College of Cardiff*
Stuart Needham	*Department of Prehistoric and Romano-British Antiquities, British Museum, London*
Francis Pryor	*Fenland Archaeological Trust, Peterborough*
Colin Richards	*Department of Archaeology, University of Glasgow*
A.J. Rouse	*School of History and Archaeology, University of Wales College of Cardiff*
Niall Sharples	*Trust for Wessex Archaeology, Salisbury, Wiltshire*
Marie-Louise Stig-Sørensen	*Department of Archaeology, University of Cambridge*

iii

Introduction

In the public's perception archaeologists dig, but amongst themselves archaeologists assess each other by how much they write. This could lead the more naïve observer into thinking that archaeologists write about the sites they excavate. But, whilst there has been an explosion of archaeological publication, there remains a publication crisis defined precisely by a failure to write up excavations. It seems easier for us, as a discipline, to write about what we think was happening in the Neolithic or Bronze Age (or any other period) than it is for us to publish our excavations. The failing is so general that it must tell us something about the nature of current archaeological practice.

It was Wheeler, normally remembered as an excavator and technician, who deprecated the division between the archaeologist as technician, busy with 'analyses and smudges in the soil' and the humanist 'busy with... vital interpretation'. And yet the divide has remained, contributing towards divisions within the organisation and teaching of the discipline. Indeed the division is enshrined in the positivism of the New Archaeology, for whilst the technician no longer produces the smudges for the humanist to interpret, it is the theoretician who supposedly generates models of the past which are to be technically assessed.

The consequence of this division of labour has been to foster a belief that knowledge about the past is initially gained in the realm of theory and that available archaeological data are simply a means to assess the validity of those theories. However, a disconformity exists between theoretical knowledge of the past which is generalising and unspecific and a practical knowledge of present data which is particular and specific. Given this, it is hardly surprising that we have problems knowing how to manage the abundant data derived from fieldwork and excavation, for these data are often incompatible with highly generalised statements about the nature of the past. We will only resolve this problem when such data are seen to be directly involved in our understanding of the past.

The point we wish to make here, and the reason why we collected these papers together and edited this volume, is simple and we believe uncontentious. Our knowledge of the past derives from the evidence we have available and our theoretical and critical competence in employing that evidence. Our knowledge of the past is not an abstraction that can await support from data of uncertain quality, for here speculation is dressed as theory and the testing is trivial. The human past took place in the context of those material conditions we recover as fragmentary remains today. It follows that our knowledge of the past is itself context specific. The more detailed our understanding of those material contexts and of the way humans act in relation to their material world the better will be our understanding of the past. Theory precedes knowledge in as much as it tells us how to observe the contexts of the past, but knowledge has to be built out of a practical engagement with the details of our evidence. This is what we mean by a contextual archaeology, and it is to that end that this volume is dedicated.

John C. Barrett
Ian Kinnes

1. The Cattleship Potemkin: Reflections on the First Neolithic in Britain

Ian Kinnes

Among the assurances given by V. I. Lenin of the changes to be wrought in post-revolutionary Russia was that there would be 'no more Potemkin villages', the temporary façades of rustic wellbeing organised by Marshal Potemkin to reassure Catherine the Great in royal progress. To this Trotsky responded, as historiographer:

> "They were real, and this is the truth, for which I can cite authorities. The illusion that they did not exist was created by historians, who are the source of most of our illusions about the past". (*Pre-Revolutionary Correspondence*, Vol. 1)

This paper will suggest that both observation and interpretation of fourth millennium bc circumstance in Britain has depended upon the partial perceptions of individual scholars, vulnerable to the disparity of the evidence as much as to the persuasions of the intellectual context. The information sets need to be defined and reviewed towards a realisation of the structure which must exist but is, conceivably, not (yet) capable of formulation.

This essay attempts to clarify the circumstances of the inauguration of food production in Britain. The nature and date of this is basic to an understanding of subsequent developments and is critical, too, to assessment of the formation processes in archaeological thinking which develop received perceptions of the past.

The term 'Neolithic' is regularly redefined and held in question. The central thesis, best outlined by Childe over several decades of progressive work, holds that food production is a prerequisite to the formation of increasingly complex societies. Demonstrations of the relative success of hunter-gatherers (critically in Lee and Devore 1968) have largely served to add sophistication to the argument and reduce the effects of misunderstandings generated by the less able of Childe's successors. The subsidiary or alternative attributes of this classification will be considered in the appropriate contexts below, but, for the moment, some further preliminary remarks are necessary.

The insecure usage of terms such as 'First', 'Early' or 'Earliest' Neolithic can rank as a typical and traditional recognition of confusion of thought and analysis. Notoriously Britain has always lacked the chronological basis provided by the neat artefact bracketing adumbrated in Europe, especially within the spheres of Germanic influence. There the general understanding is that rich ceramic inventories allow of refinement to successive phasing so that even a few sherds, independent of context, should provide more or less precise assignation. The traumatic effect on insular prehistorians should not be underestimated, through from first encounter as under-graduate. The reactions have tended to polarise: phasing is impossible and Neolithic answers must be sought for other questions, or phasing must be imposed, however sparse, intractable or variable the evidence. Whatever, the desire for chronological structure is implicit to both.

There are several themes for assessment. Food production *per se* should be recognised by the appearance of the actual remains of cultivated plants and domestic animals but the effects of this appearance might be taken as an equivalence. By extension and by experience, the artefacts *associated* with food production, an area fraught with danger, might be taken as the durable or accessible component: pottery and certain kinds of flint and stone. By further extension the 'Axe Age' (Kendrick 1925) might be characterised also by distinctive monuments which could again function as alternative by default. Finally, chronology is necessary to an understanding of processes of formation and change and has, equally, come to be seen as assessable information in its own right.

Economy

Direct economic evidence is sparse and the indirect vulnerable to varying interpretation. No large faunal assemblages have been retrieved except from causewayed enclosures and these can hardly be regarded as early. Even then detailed analyses are not yet available from recent excavations although enclosures such as Crickley Hill, Etton and Hambledon Hill along with the Runnymede 'domestic' site should remedy this. All, in preliminary assessment, would seem to be dominated by cattle. This is not necessarily a state that can be extrapolated back over several centuries. Such evidence as exists for the fourth millennium does little more than provide a presence/absence record with an expected confirmation of cattle, pig and caprovine.

The assumption is that these animals were imported breeding-stock from established continental herds. Despite the rarity of late Mesolithic faunal assemblages, it is held that wild cattle and pig were present, caprovines not. This declaration of a separate and external gene pool for the domesticates might be plausible but lacks confirmation. Both Dennell and Rowley-Conwy (1983; 1981) have delineated the potential complexities of domestic animals as an innovation, and Dennell, in particular, has provided a model for cultural preconditioning towards animal herding in late Mesolithic deer management. We can add to this the observation from the same source that even in the temperate zone of continental Europe, a relatively coherent biome, the distinctions between wild and domestic cattle tend to the subjective, at least so long as data is only available for bone size. Should usable faunal assemblages become available for fourth millennium Britain there are further cautions: in particular the conditions of insularity might produce further ambiguity, a circumstance alluded to but not confronted by Woodman (1978) in his perceptive realisation of the role of megafauna in the Irish Late Mesolithic.

Plant remains in context are even rarer than animal bone and the overwhelming proportion of the evidence derives by extrapolation from pollen analysis. The problems here might be characterised by an assessment of the evidence for cereals in pre-elm decline deposits (Edwards and Hirons 1984). Three sites are in Ulster and have produced grains described variously as 'large grass...almost certainly a cereal', 'of cereal type' and so on, with dates pre 3370 ± 170bc (D36: Newferry), pre 3345 ± 85bc (UB 2488: Weir's Lough) and interpolated c. 3800bc (Ballynagilly). The latter two sites provided some indication of contemporary altered forest cover. In association with 'clearance episodes' in western Ireland there is a 'single grain' of *Gramineae* type undated (Dolan) and two *'Triticum* type' with one *'Hordeum* type' between 3895 ± 100bc and interpolated c. 3420bc (UB 2413: Cashelkeelty 1). In Britain there are 'clearance episodes' with two *Hordeum* grains at interpolated c. 3425bc (Machrie Moor, Arran) and several 'cereal grains' at 3870 ± 95bc (Q2394: Soyland Moor, central Pennines) and at interpolated c. 3400–3270bc (Rimsmoor, Dorset).

Setting aside the factor of elm decline, since this must now be detached from inevitable anthropogenic cause (Groenman-van Waateringe 1983; Goransson 1984; Girling and Greig 1985), these records are of considerable interest in apparent confirmation of widespread cereal cultivation in the north and west from the early fourth millennium bc. The climatic amelioration of the late Atlantic seems to be evident first in Ireland, allowing grass growth for most of the year and hence highly favourable to cereals (Barker 1985:202) and this would seem to add valuable support to the argument for precocious agriculture. Evidence for clearance or significant alteration in forest cover is now familiar for the period commonly recognised as Late Mesolithic and has achieved general agreement as to its anthropogenesis, to improve browse for wild ungulates and encourage the spread of understorey food plants (Mellars 1975). This interpretation, whilst plausible, must be seen as a 'good fit' argument appropriate to the recent optimising view of the Mesolithic and the man-animal symbiosis favoured in the developed Higgs school, but it can be held in question (Edwards and Ralston 1984).

The definition of clearance too can be nebulous and might depend upon the presence of charcoal in peat deposits. This is not necessarily anthropogenic, a circumstance explored by Boyd (1982a, 1982b) and Moore (1982).

Where, as in the instances already cited, comparable profiles showing 'clearance' have produced large grass pollen grains, with varying degrees of certainty in identification as cereal, interpretation shifts to small-scale cultivation. It is clear that ancillary information is needed, either in the form of plant remains in unequivocal contexts or by establishing a direct association of pollen and human activity: areas with good preservation of secure contexts such as the wetlands (Pryor, this volume) or river valley deposits (Needham 1985). This is vital not only to resolve the ambiguity of agricultural innovation in the insular scene but has broader implications for post-glacial vegetational history. As Barker (1985) has shown, the distribution of potential cultigens is not fully documented, and modern wild populations might be random residuals of original wide dispersals rather than indicators of domestication core areas. There is, for example, a single record of 'cereal pollen' in an immediately post-glacial context from the Paris Basin but this awaits confirmation from other localities. The general tendency to accept larger grass pollen grains as indicative of grain rather than seed heads must be held in question. We have already seen that the fourth millennium climate was especially favourable to grass and may, indeed, have encouraged exceptional growth. Such considerations are exemplified also by the probability that plantain, rather than being a secure indicator of clearance, could have survived as a glacial relict in coastal and northern upland areas. The evidence is thus ill-defined and prone to subjective interpretation. The implications, of grain — major food resource — cultivation — clearance as a framework in which the conclusion justifies the definition, are manifest. Actual cultigen remains have not been recovered from any context earlier than the Hembury enclosure, apparently of final fourth millennium date, and grain impressions on pottery have no proven antecedence to this. The artefacts of cultivation and plant processing provide no real assistance. Plough or spade use, anyway only rarely documented, cannot be demonstrated before the early third millennium at South Street (Fowler and Evans 1967). Suggestions that developed *sols lessivés* beneath long barrows at Kilham and Dalladies were a product of agricultural activity (Limbrey 1975) have been dismissed by Fisher (1982) in declaring a 'natural' origin under woodland cover. Querns are unknown in Mesolithic contexts and rare on Neolithic sites, largely being retrieved as single finds. Single-piece sickle blades are infrequent and likely to be of relatively late date and no unequivocal example of composite mounting is known although the serrated and primary blades of the Earlier Neolithic (*and* Late Mesolithic) would be appropriate here.

It would appear then that we are in no position to document dietary or subsistence changes in the fourth millennium. There is no question that cultivation and stock-raising were practised over wide areas by the end of the period but the process of their establishment remains unknown. Tendentious interpretation of the evidence, still unfortunately largely derived from pollen analysis, has served the cause badly and urgently demands re-evaluation. It would seem still that an essential intellectual confusion exists about the role of palynology: just like culture history, a primary purpose as chronological framework has been shifted into a function as economic yardstick.

Artefacts

Nominally there should be an attempt to distinguish between continuity and innovation in the artefact record but this begs the question of function *versus* typology or stylistic change. This is well expressed by the flint assemblages: blade or narrow flake production continues throughout the fourth millennium and, where retouched, both light backing and serration are a constant feature. On the broader European scene a comparable pattern exists so that the questions of continuity or innovation cannot be resolved on the insular evidence. Discriminant analysis (Pitts 1978; Pitts and Jacobi 1979) points to a tendency for narrower flakes in the Neolithic but raw material from newly-exploited sources might be influential here. Most tool-types are held in common, unsurprising in assemblages functionally dominated by meat and hide processing equipment. The most obvious contrasts lie in the presence/absence of microliths and leaf-shaped arrowheads and the replacement, in southern Britain at least, of tranchet by ground-edge core tools. The real novelty here is the bifacially-worked leaf arrowhead and this poses its own problems. The form is effectively without insular or continental precedent although the triangular piercing arrowheads known in some Rössen assemblages could provide ultimate inspiration. Occasional leaf points in East Baltic TRB contexts have been seen by some Polish scholars as indicative links with Britain, an effective demonstration of their rarity on the Continent. It may be that such arrowheads are associated rather with social developments in prestige linked to archery and warfare; they are certainly not a clue in the hunt for origins.

The ground or polished axehead is of course the classic denoter of the Neolithic although this precision has foundered in the light of evidence for the technique in 'pure' Mesolithic contexts in Ireland (Woodman 1978). More important here is the means of production, particularly the organised exploitation of mining and quarrying. It is however worth recall that an unknown, but certainly significant proportion of flint (and perhaps stone) axes are, as before, made on surface material. There are no real precursors for quarrying in the Mesolithic: occasional scoops and hollows are simply a natural extension of surface collection. In western Europe there are no mines proven before the mid or perhaps later fourth millennium where they are associated with cultural groups in cousinly relationship to the British: TRB, Michelsberg and Chassey. Again it would seem that we are dealing with social processes not dependent upon diffusion for explanation.

There is one artefact which can claim the status of an early import: the jadeite axe from the Sweet Track is undeniably exotic and has a secure late fourth millennium context (Coles *et al* 1974). By extension single finds of comparable large non-utilitarian pieces might also reflect external contact. From a probable Piedmontane source (Woolley *et al*

1979) jadeite products would appear to circulate widely in western Europe, with cultural boundaries recognisable only in occasional local assigned status as in the major deposits in early Breton ceremonial sites. They are therefore an indicator of contact but not of movement.

Whatever the actual date of initiation, ceramics represent a novel component in the artefactual and technological record. The containers of the Mesolithic are unknown but are presumptively organic. No fired clay component is known previously so that pyrotechnology might represent as much of an innovation as the use of pottery storage, cooking and table-wares. The importance of this should not be exaggerated since the precocity of a limited ceramic range in the frontier context of Swifterbant and Ertebølle-Ellerbek groups demonstrates that the new technique could be accommodated within a processing technology. On current evidence, however, the early pottery in Britain includes thin-walled, refined-fabric burnished bowls and these should be the products of an established ceramic tradition. Whether part of the baggage of colonist groups or shared package, it seems that we must accept that the pottery derives from continental originals. Herein lies the source of much confusion and wasted effort. One thing is clear: plain bowls are common throughout western Europe in post Bandkeramik contexts, representing a broad tradition originally formulated as Western Neolithic by Schuchhardt (1919). Much depends upon classification by negative characteristics: absence of decoration or complex moulding, absence of real form differentiation, but this simplicity is none the less significant. Carination is the most, perhaps only, distinctive feature although its proportional occurrence has yet to be quantified. The generic Grimston-Lyles Hill label (Herne: this volume) effectively disguises both the actual distribution and potential regional variation, and the classification is widely-abused. Accepting that the distribution is almost universal in the British Isles we need to know actual time-depth and range of spatial and chronological variation; neither have been established.

One aspect deserves more detailed investigation, that of a potential role as special form for particular deposition in broadly 'non-functional' contexts. The repeated occurrence of one or more near-complete vessels or particular selections of rim and shoulder sherds in isolated pits begs the question of special status. Equally the systematic primary association of plain bowls with funerary monuments — even those such as Skendleby or Radley built within the currency of decorated styles — suggests a long tradition of perceived value. The interchangeability of bowls and crania hinted at in several contexts and now broadly confirmed at Etton adduces further reinforcement. It is therefore conceivable that, like the leaf arrowhead or *all-over* polished axe, pottery is a symbol and not a reflection or concomitant of changed circumstances. Is it, for example, conceivable that the standard domestic pottery assemblage is a relatively late feature of the insular Neolithic?

The search for European parallels is a familiar component of the literature (summarised in Whittle

4

1977, 1985). There are no agreed sources although western Michelsberg groups provide reasonable cousinly and broadly contemporary linkage. An ultimate origin within the Rössen plain-ware component, as adumbrated by Case (1969) assists lineage but not explanation. Material within the Hazendonk spectrum has been compared to northern Grimston by Louwe-Kooijmans (1976) and there are good correlations although comparison suffers from the problem of matching a good contextual assemblage (Hazendonk) against the somewhat indifferent retrieval of relevant British 'groups'.

Other artefacts are unhelpful. Rare figurines in western Europe find no congeners in Britain at an early date. The bone and antler industry is simple and generalised although broad parallels for the relatively rare (and apparently long-lived) antler combs, objects of unknown use or purpose, exist in the Belgian Michelsberg.

Monuments

Communal works, of whatever nature or purpose, would appear to be a new component of the fourth millennium. So far as structures go, only elements such as the water-edge platforms at Star Carr and, perhaps, Eskmeals indicate co-ordinated labour towards a common end. There are, obviously, two particular categories to consider: causewayed enclosures and mortuary sites, with some further note on domestic structures.

With the exception of Briar Hill (to be considered in the next section), causewayed enclosures have generated radiocarbon dates from the end of the fourth millennium onwards. They have not produced Carinated Bowls. Continental analogues, in both structure and perceived function, are widespread west of the Rhine from Scania to Aquitaine and are largely of the same date-range. Some ancestry has been found in enclosures of developed Bandkeramik and Rössen attribution (Whittle 1985). We can thus show functional or ideological linkage with a wide European cultural spectrum, itself not of common ancestry, and would appear to be dealing with an international phenomenon comparable to that of chambered tomb construction. Major modern excavations at Crickley Hill, Etton and Hambledon Hill have all emphasised the structured 'ritual' base of such sites and this is firmly echoed outside Britain. Added to this, causewayed enclosures are perhaps the classic monuments of an organised landscape whose components are commemorated and, perhaps, controlled by the segmented but integral structure.

For chambered tombs we can abandon the vision of direct introduction of external types, for the earlier stages at least. The effective lesson of recent excavations is that we are dealing with a wide range of formats, united only by the provision of an enclosed space for mortuary purposes. The accompanying or accreted structural components are variable, occasionally functional, often specific embellishment. There is certainly no reason to assume that monuments are a secondary component because of their demands upon the labour budget. Firstly, a number of sites can be shown to begin as small-scale enterprises, easily undertaken by a family workforce. Secondly, and more important, the need for monuments, normally those linked to mortuary or ancestral process, cannot be assigned a status secondary to that of the food-quest. Monuments, clearly, were necessary.

The chronology of both insular and continental traditions is poorly-established and radiocarbon determinations more than usually vulnerable to problems of sampling and attribution. We can, however, point to a firm mid-fourth millennium date for the longhouse-trapezoid mound transform at Passy-sur-Yonne (inf. Carre) and Les Fouaillages (Kinnes 1982), both sites with simple organic chambers and good artefact association within final Bandkeramik grouping. The proliferation of this tradition, and that of elaborate stone structures, throughout western Europe is again cross-cultural, reflecting socio-economic circumstance rather than intricate cross-connections. The frequently-observed correlation of early tomb densities with areas of intensive Mesolithic activity recognises no more than relative survival rates in coastal situations. Any Mesolithic component, and this cannot be discounted, can be argued on better grounds.

Turning to domestic matters, it is notorious that houses remain elusive in Britain. It is perhaps no coincidence that the three major discoveries of earlier Neolithic houses in recent years are all accidental: Ballyglass beneath a court cairn, Balbridie as a dark age hall and Lismore Fields by trial trenching for a Roman road (Ó Nualláin 1972; Ralston 1982; inf. D. Garton). This should be sufficient to cast serious doubts on the methods and purpose of research (or rescue) designs. Only at Fengate has a structure emerged as part of a deliberate approach to landscape history (Pryor 1974).

This rarity has occasioned great agony, if not guilt, to insular prehistorians but should perhaps be put into perspective. Houses are equally, perhaps more, rare in western Europe after the Bandkeramik: we are dealing here with common problems.

None of the British houses certainly pre-date 3000bc and are mainly lacking in specific parallels. The tripartite construction of the large examples already cited (perhaps only partly-recognised at Fengate: inf. Pryor) invokes a structural tradition reflective of an established Neolithic state of stable nuclear family, organised storage and animal accommodation, the latter presumptively but not certainly confined to overwintering of breeding stock.

One further component should be mentioned. The Sweet Track (Coles, Hibbert and Orme 1973) is firmly dated at c. 3200bc and would seem to have built within an altered landscape. Its construction certainly presupposes a specific comprehension of problems of constructon and use. This would, however, seem to tell us more about woodworking as the basic Neolithic craft than the mechanics of received knowledge.

Chronology (Figs.1.1 & 1.2)

It is necessary to reiterate that chronology is fundamental to understanding process and, sadly, that the radiocarbon framework that exists is inadequate and often misleading. Much of this is caused by sampling error at site level and is embellished by a failure to approach the problems as those essentially of context and statistical treatment.

We might begin by reviewing dates for apparent Neolithic activity prior to 3500bc as an example of potential vicissitudes in understanding (Table 1.1). This would seem to offer little comfort to proponents of early 'colonisation' and indeed the main weight of dated material suggests Neolithic activity as firmly established only within the last quarter of the fourth millennium. This poses two problems. The first depends upon the expected, interpreted or actual circumstances of Neolithic inauguration. Can we separate the data — rare finds or few radiocarbon dates — from the process? Whatever process or combination is involved, the various sources of information should reveal similar trajectories of intensification; the numerical increase of sites and expansion of food production should be reflected, even in default of research design, by enhanced visibility and retrieval. Thus the chronological pattern could represent anything from random — as above — to expected intensification. No decision is possible.

On this basis, we are confronted by the second and potentially greater problem. We have already seen that the suggested climatic conditions of the late Atlantic should be more favourable to early agriculture in Ireland than elsewhere, and these can add to the observations on precocious cereal cultivation in Ulster. One of the sites in question here is Bally-nagilly, with an integrated date series from excavated site and from adjacent peat, the two not entirely compatible but near enough, and certainly arguing for the expected components of a Neolithic presence well before 3500bc. ApSimon (1976) has made a thorough review of the contextual integrity of these determinations and, on current evidence, these cannot be held in question. However, no support is forthcoming from elsewhere in the British Isles. Apart from all else, this Ulster enclave must rest firmly in isolation both locally and internationally as a precocious Plain Bowl assemblage. The claims for comparably early activity at Carrowmore (Burenhult 1984) remain questionable and here the contextual doubts expressed by Caulfield (in Burenhult 1984) are compelling.

On present evidence, the pattern of radiocarbon dates might be seen to justify the colonisation mode: from c. 3800 bc several hundred years before the secure establishment c. 3200 of widespread food-production and solid-based society, at which point we have lift-off. Even setting aside the dubious provenance of many dates at home and abroad, the sample size still falls within the range where a bell curve would be normal and hence we are on insecure ground. Only Ballynagilly would fulfil appropriate standards and might be the critical factor lacking; equally, can it be reconciled with the home-base of Woodman's well documented Irish later Mesolithic (1978) or the broader scene of late Bandkeramik Europe? There is, unfashionably, a chronology based upon the typological systematisation of the last century. This alone would suggest that Plain Bowl assemblages at Ballynagilly are unlikely to precede 35–3400bc and, equally, that even if this were so, nigh on a millennium of ceramic conservatism in Ireland would be unparalleled and surprising.

Table 1.1 Radiocarbon dates for Neolithic contexts pre-3500 bc.

Garvin's Track	4330 ± 70 HAR1222	also dated as 2430 ± 70 HAR682
Eaton Heath	4305 ± 60 BM771	?natural feature, association dubious
Abingdon	4070 ± 110 BM349	other dates post c. 3100bc
Boghead	4055 ± 60 SRR690	other dates post c. 3100bc
Knap of Howar	3755 ± 85 SRR347	also dated as 2130 ± 65 SRR452
Briar Hill	3730 ± 70 HAR4072 3590 ± 140 HAR4092 3490 ± 110 HAR2282	note 1
Raisthorpe	3555 ± 145 NPL140	note 2
Broome Heath	3475 ± 115 BM679	old land surface, uncertain associations

Note 1: Critical review in Kinnes and Thorpe 1985; dubious in context and association; other dates third millennium for associated material.

Note 2: Massive post at centre of façade; c.f. anomalous date for comparable context at Street House c. 500 years earlier than others for structure (Vyner 1983).

Some Conclusions

The problems and the difficulties of the evidence have been outlined and it must now be clear that there is little firm information which has not been, or could not be, subject to manipulation towards preconception. The literature is well-known. Much of it is concerned with irrelevancy or speculation in the face of seemingly intractable problems. We might thus find that the unprovable, such as the nature of skin boat required for colonising enterprise, might be given equivalent weight to the affiliations of that which is, or could be, observable.

The chronology depends heavily upon the radiocarbon patterns: neither that for western Europe (Fig.1.1) nor for the British Isles (Fig.1.2) sheds much light but provides a raw text for interpolation. There are no close correlations between the definable, insular, Neolithic and that of mainland Europe except in terms of process — and does this derive from social community, economic trajectory or understandable convergence? The nature of the preceding/ contemporary Mesolithic is largely unknown and certainly only rarely capable of providing understanding of anything other than lithic technology. There is, in effect, an inverse relation-

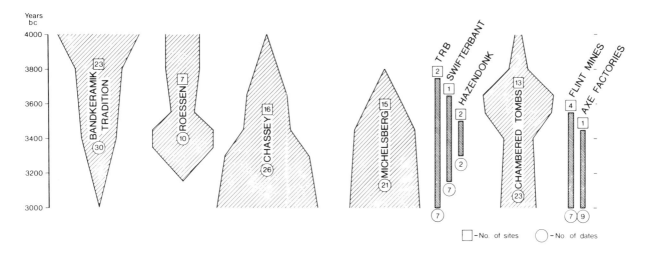

Fig.1.1. Frequency of radiocarbon dates 4000 - 3000 bc (standard deviations in excess of ±150 excluded)

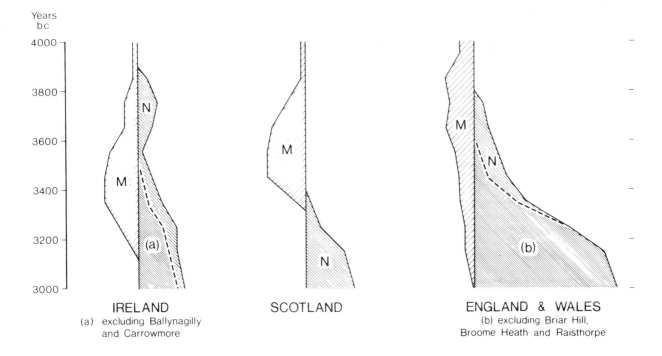

Fig.1.2. Relative frequency of radiocarbon dates for the fourth millenium bc (standard deviations in excess of ±150 excluded).

ship between evidence and interpretation. Some plausible panaceas (as Kinnes 1984, 1985) have been offered in explanation of the inauguration of insular food production but all suffer from the lack of sought-for critical information and the stifling effect of opinion as a substitute for research.

It is probable that appropriate mechanisms are provided for rapid long-distance contact by Mesolithic littoral communities where the better-preserved contexts have evidence for exchange systems in rare materials and for deep-sea fishing, allowing for the rapid transmission of selected traits ahead of full-scale implantation of an entire package. One effect of this is that any given context in the fourth millennium might show any perceived status from 'pure Mesolithic' to 'pure Neolithic'. The critical need is for the excavation of well-preserved sites of human activity with a good range of environmental and economic evidence against which the accompanying artefact record might be tested. At present we do not have the information to disentangle process from circumstances, a situation in which Potemkim villages have traditionally thrived.

References

ApSimon A.M. 1976 Ballynagilly and the beginning and end of the Irish Neolithic. In S.J. de Laet (ed) *Acculturation and Continuity in Atlantic Europe*. Bruges.

Barker G. 1985 *Prehistoric Farming in Europe*. Cambridge.

Boyd W.E. 1982a Sub-surface formation of charcoal and its possible relevance to the interpretation of charcoal remains in peat. *Quaternary Newsletter* 37:6–8.

Boyd W.E. 1982b Sub-surface formation of charcoal: an unexplained event in peat. *Quaternary Newsletter* 38:15–16.

Burenhult G. 1984 *The Archaeology of Carrowmore*, Stockholm.

Case H. 1969 Neolithic explanations. *Antiquity* 43:176–86.

Coles J.M., Hibbert A. and Orme B.J. 1973 Prehistoric roads and tracks in Somerset: 3, the Sweet Track. *Proc. Prehist. Soc.* 39:256–93.

Coles J.M. *et al.* 1974 A jade axe from the Somerset Levels. *Antiquity* 48:216–20.

Dennell R. 1983 *European Economic Prehistory: a New Perspective*. London.

Edwards K.J. and Hirons K. 1984 Cereal pollens in pre-elm decline deposits: implications for the earliest agriculture in Britain and Ireland. *J. Archaeol. Sci.* 11:71–80.

Edwards K.J. and Ralston I.B.M. 1984 Post-glacial hunters, gatherers and vegetational history in Scotland. *Proc. Soc. Antiqu. Scotland* 114:15–34.

Fisher P.F 1982 A review of lessivage and Neolithic cultivation in southern England. *J. Arch. Sci.* 9:299–304.

Girling M. and Greig J.A. 1985 A first fossil record for *Scolytus scolytus* (F.) (elm bark beetle): its occurrence in elm decline deposits for London and the implications for Neolithic elm disease. *J. Archaeol. Sci.* 12:347–51.

Goransson M. 1984 Pollen analytical investigations in the Sligo area. In Burenhult 1984:154–93.

Groenman-van Waateringe W. 1983 The early agricultural utilisation of the Irish landscape: the last word on the elm decline? In F. Hamond and T. Reeves-Smyth (eds) *Landscape Archaeology in Ireland*. Oxford.

Kendrick T.D. 1925 *The Axe Age*. London.

Kinnes I.A. 1982 Les Fouaillages and megalithic origins. *Antiquity* 56:24–30.

Kinnes I.A. 1984 Microliths and megaliths: monumental origins on the Atlantic fringe. In Burenhult 1984:367–70.

Kinnes I.A. 1985 Circumstance not context: the Neolithic of Scotland as seen from outside. *Proc. Soc. Antiqu. Scotland.* 115, 15–58.

Kinnes I.A. and Thorpe I.J. 1986 Radiocarbon dating: use and abuse, *Antiquity* 60:221–223.

Lee R.B. and Devore I. (eds) 1968 *Man the Hunter*. Chicago.

Limbrey S. 1975 *Soil Science and Archaeology*. London.

Louwe-Kooijmans L. 1976 Local developments in a borderland: a survey of the Neolithic of the Lower Rhine. *Oudheid. Meded* 57:227–97.

Mellars P. 1975 Ungulate populations, economic patterns and the Mesolithic landscape. In J.G. Evans *et al.* (eds) *The Effects of Man on the Landscape: the Highland Zone*. London.

Moore P.D. 1982 Sub-surface formation of charcoal: an unlikely event in peat. *Quaternary Newsletter* 38:13–14.

Needham S.P. 1985 Neolithic and Bronze Age settlement on the buried flood-plains of Runnymede. *Oxford J. Archaeol.* 4:125–37.

Ó Nualláin S. 1972 A Neolithic house at Ballyglass, Co. Mayo. *J. Royal Soc. Antiqu. Ireland* 102:49–57.

Pitts M. 1978 Towards an understanding of flint industries in post-glacial England. *Bull. Inst. Archaeol. London* 15:179–97.

Pitts M. and Jacobi R. 1979 Some aspects of change in flaked stone industries of the Mesolithic and Neolithic in southern Britain. *J. Archaeol. Sci.* 6:163–77.

Pryor F.M. 1984 *Excavations at Fengate, Peterborough, England: the first report*. Toronto.

Ralston I.B.M. 1982 A timber hall at Balbridie farm. *Aberdeen University Review* 168:238–49.

Rowley-Conwy P. 1981 Mesolithic Danish bacon: permanent and temporary sites in the Danish Mesolithic. In A. Sheridan and G. Bailey (eds) *Economic Archaeology*. Oxford.

Schuchhardt C. 1919 *Alteuropa*. Berlin.

Vyner B.E. 1984 The excavation of a Neolithic cairn at Street House, Loftus, Cleveland. *Proc. Prehist. Soc.* 50:151–96.

Whittle A. 1977 *The Earlier Neolithic of Southern England and its Continental Background*. Oxford.

Whittle A. 1985 *Neolithic Europe: a Survey*. Cambridge.

Woodman P. 1978 *The Mesolithic in Ireland*, Oxford.

Woolley A.R. *et al.* 1979 European Neolithic jade implements: a preliminary mineralogical and typological study. In T.H.M. Clough and W.A. Cummins (eds) *Stone Axe Studies*. London.

2. A Time and a Place for the Grimston Bowl

Andrew Herne

Preface

The theme of this paper is simply stated. The class of Neolithic pottery known as Grimston is in its present form ill-defined, confused of meaning and of little interpretative value. Grimston/Lyles Hill series pottery is dismantled as a unitary construct. A class of Carinated Bowls is defined and shown to have both chronological and contextual integrity. The depositional contexts of these bowls shows them to have a determinate function as part of a distinctive set of Neolithic social practices. The study of the time and place of the Grimston bowl makes visible aspects of the social transformation that is the Neolithic across Britain and Ireland.

This paper is in the first instance an attempt, through a literary review, to lay to rest a number of persistent misconceptions about Neolithic chronology and pottery. In this respect it is in large part a destructive paper, from which it is hoped new interpretations of the British and Irish Neolithic can be constructed from a tighter chronological framework than has hitherto been recognized. Productive models for the Neolithic of the British Isles demand as a prerequisite a well-grounded chronology, and this paper is intended as a response to that need.

In the text the term 'Carinated Bowl' refers to a class of high quality undecorated open carinated vessels, unless this is stated otherwise. They are characterized by an angular bipartite profile and are distinguished from a category of 'Shouldered Bowls' in which the carination defines an upright shoulder on the upper part of the vessel.

Introduction: 'Neolithic Cultures'

The pottery from Hanging Grimston has a long history in interpretations of the British Neolithic. Menghin (1925) made the first formalization of the bipartite nature of British Neolithic pottery with his definitions of Grimston-keramik and Peterborough-keramik. Schuchhardt (1919) in a seminal work followed by Childe (1932), had already related the first category to the great 'family' of western Neolithic wares common across much of western Europe Despite changes in nomenclature (Leeds 1927; Piggott 1932), subsequent definition of the insular corpus continued to make reference to the possibilities of continental origins and influences (Piggott 1934, 1937, 1954, 1955).

In 1954 Piggott introduced the term Grimston Ware to describe the group of undecorated open Carinated Bowls of fine fabric and finish from the Primary Neolithic of Yorkshire. It is not a part of this paper to discuss in detail the origins and development of the Neolithic paradigm present in 'Neolithic Cultures'. The volume marked the closure of the first period of modern study into the British and Irish Neolithic. The Neolithic pottery corpus at that time derived primarily from two sources: small but significant collections from 19th century excavations and from circumstantial recovery, and larger assemblages from the excavations of the 1920's and 1930's. These latter were primarily those of the southern English causewayed enclosures, but also included that from Lyles Hill in Ireland.

Within the cultural model of 'Neolithic Cultures' the pottery from these newly excavated sites was of crucial importance in underpinning both a chronological and cultural framework for the Neolithic of the British Isles. That this was possible was not merely because pottery was present on most sites, but because it was amenable to classification into identifiable styles and that these different styles were conceived as the material expression of distinct cultural groups. As an explanatory framework for the Neolithic period the cultural model had an added significance for the study of pottery. The production and use of pottery was at the very basis of the meaning of 'Neolithic' since it carried with it implicit assumptions about the nature of settlement, the domestic economy and the establishment of tradition. Classification of Neolithic pottery was at the same time a statement about the establishment and development of the British and Irish Neolithic itself.

Also underwritten in 'Neolithic Cultures' was a secondary theme to that of culture itself, one that was and still is a recurrent feature of insular prehistoric studies. The question of the origin of the British Neolithic was framed in terms of 'settlement', that is, the movement of people carrying with them cultural traditions, both from the continent to the British Isles and to different places within the British Isles. Again, pottery provided the major means for investigating this issue precisely because pottery was perceived as the primary indicator of cultural groups and of relations between them.

Pottery in these two contexts, like settlement itself, had two meanings. It was both the proof of established community and the evidence for its origin. These valuations remain implicit in contemporary Neolithic research so that much interpretation of Neolithic pottery, and of Grimston in particular, arises out of a conflation of the different meanings pottery has for Neolithic explanation.

Regional Trends in Earlier Neolithic Pottery Studies

Beginning in the mid 1950's two developments occured that were to have a major impact on the course of Neolithic studies. Post-war economic recovery and the growth of the interventionist state promoted a massive increase in state-funded excavation. The possibilities arising from the new technique of radiocarbon dating were of a more immediate and obvious relevance. Less evident, at least initially, were any changes to the basic concerns of a prehistoric archaeology. Regional differences in the quality of existing data sets, in the scale of new excavations, or rather of new pottery assemblages, and in the usefulness of C14 led to different regional trends in earlier Neolithic pottery studies following on from the publication of 'Neolithic Cultures'.

The classification of Irish Neolithic pottery by Case (1961) followed only shortly after the publication of the Lyles Hill and Lough Gur assemblages (Evans 1953; Ó Ríordáin 1954). The majority of the material studied first-hand by Case was in fact already known by Piggott in 1954. The classification was framed as a typological sequence. In contrast to the scheme in 'Neolithic Cultures' it was ordered solely on the basis of the large corpus of insular Irish material. A subsequent article (Case 1963) dealt with the cultural relations of this material with that from Britain and the continent. The detailed arguments of these two papers are highly complex, and in effect they presented a chronology and description for the Irish Neolithic as a whole.

Underlying the classification was the traditional cultural framework of 'Neolithic Cultures'. Primary Neolithic settlement was represented by the round-based shouldered bowls of western Neolithic ware (the Lyles Hill ware of Piggott). These were subdivided into the four styles of Dunmurry, Ballymarlagh, Lyles Hill and Limerick, distinguished on the basis of typological developments in rim and shoulder. The unelaborated plain bowls of the Dunmurry style were the sole pottery of an early Neolithic period, and relations with Grimston, Hembury and Breton styles were emphasized. The other 'developed' styles followed in a chronological order of appearance: Mesolithic acculturation was represented by decorated Sandhills Ware, whilst horizons of cultural contact in the late Neolithic period were indicated by Ballyalton Bowls and Carrowkeel Ware.

Early C14 dates (Watts 1960) were in most part easily assimilated into the above model. However Case subsequently modified this scheme as a result of new evidence (Case 1969b). The pottery from Ballynagilly (in ApSimon 1969) was described as having similarities not only with the Dunmurry style but also as having attributes of the more developed Ballymarlagh and Lyles Hill styles (although this was based on an examination of eight rims). The C14 dates for Ballynagilly, supported by other early dates for similar featured pottery from Knockiveagh and Coygan Camp, suggested that all three styles were current in the 4th millennium bc. The effective result was to replace the chronologically sensitive typological sequence with a broadly contemporary stylistic division of uncertain significance. Publication of subsequent discoveries of undecorated carinated pottery reflected this return to generality, as for instance at Knowth and Newgrange (Eogan 1984; O'Kelly et al. 1978).

A full-scale revision of Irish Neolithic pottery has been recently completed by Sheridan (1986). Although her thesis has a thematic concern with the application of exchange studies in social archaeology, it is also a substantive restatement of Irish Neolithic chronology and pottery. Only a number of points are brought out here from this valuable study, many of the themes of which are germane to the arguments of this paper.

The pre-Beaker Irish Neolithic is divided into three phases, defined primarily by the appearance or disappearance of pottery styles and monument types, informed and delimited by a C14 chronology. The pottery of phase 1 (3800–2900bc) is restricted to a style labelled as a 'Traditional Western Neolithic'. Only assemblages dated by C14 to within the above brackets are definitely ascribed to this phase; they can all be described as of either the Dunmurry or Ballymarlagh styles of Case. From the evidence of individual variation within well-preserved vessels Sheridan argues that there is no valid distinction between these two styles defined from sherd assemblages. Affinities with British Grimston pottery are demonstrated and a common ancestry in continental Michelsberg is suggested, although similarities with northwest French material are also mentioned. The discussion is essentially traditional, constrained within the 'Neolithic origin' model of influence and settlement. Contradictions in the received C14 chronologies are not effectively countered, nor interestingly is the original criticism of Hawkes (1935) to the first suggestion of a Michelsberg derivation (Piggott 1934).

Traditional 'Western Neolithic' forms continued into phase 2 (2900 2500bc) concurrent with the appearance of novel decorative styles (elaborate shouldered and unshouldered bowls), coarsewares either within the 'Western tradition' or exotic to it (Carrowkeel) and regionalization of the 'Western' tradition itself (for instance the Lyles Mill assemblage). Traditional forms are now part of more variable, elaborate and decorative assemblages within a wide-ranging 'Modified Western Neolithic' style.

In Scotland, despite an increase in the number of excavations, few new sizeable assemblages outside Orkney have been recovered, such as Fochabers and Auchetagan (Burl 1985; Marshall 1980). Although a number of sites have yielded both significant pottery finds and C14 dates the discussion of sub-Orkney material has relied for its cultural attribution and interpretation on apparently similar sites and finds elsewhere in the British Isles. In general the absence of large indigenous assemblages has paradoxically ensured a continuing debate over such traditional issues as terminological definition, the range of cultural contacts and typological sequence (Atkinson 1962; Henshall 1963 & 1972; McInnes 1969; Scott 1964, 1969, 1977a).

Possible relations with the southern English styles have been a consistent theme, the one-way transfer indicative of the relative paucity of material and the lack of indigenous context from Scottish sites. Relations with Ireland over Lyles Hill pottery and decorated bowls were apparently allowed a greater degree of mutual interchange and movement. The separation of the form G bowl from Lyles Hill ware, in which eastern English connections were emphasized, to the extent of comparing the Auchetagen assemblage with Broome Heath, suggests that the Irish connection was perceived more as one of ambivalence than equivalence. The recent definition of insular groups such as the eastern carinated assemblages and western Rothesay/Achnacree pottery has remained underwritten by Scottish perceptions of cultural peripherality. Current work (Henshall 1983a, 1983b, 1984; Sharples 1982) indicates two solutions to an acknowledged confusion in Scottish pottery studies, a return to generality of cultural attribution and an emphasis on the specificity of particular vessel forms.

The pattern of Welsh studies is structurally similar to that outlined above. Again the existing pottery record was very small, there was a large increase in excavation, and a number of significant new assemblages, although on a small scale. As with Scotland interpretation has been largely dependant upon reference to outside sources. Pottery from Severn-Cotswold tombs was traditionally related to the southern English decorated styles. Much of the remainder is now classified as the 'Irish Sea Group' (Lynch 1969, 1976; Powell 1973) and defined in relation both to Lyles Hill and to Hembury. The material is limited in quantity and its treatment has been confined to the establishment of cultural connection. Nevertheless a number of associated C14 dates has given a sense of regional integrity to this group. As has been apparent elsewhere a broader alignment of this material into the Grimston/Lyles Hill Series is a recent development (Lynch 1984).

Yorkshire and northern England was the original setting for the form G bowl of Piggott (1932) and the Grimston Bowl of the same author (1954). All of this material derived from 19th century excavations, primarily from the burial mounds of East Yorkshire (Newbigin 1937). Although a cultural context in the Neolithic was established, it was limited almost entirely to a non-domestic record. Cultural origins were sought in Britain itself or directly from the continent (Piggott 1955). The existing material provided the basis for future studies, and the subsequent excavation of a large number of barrows and other sites provided the means for a revision of Piggott's cultural framework.

In the same way that Smith (1956) was able to expand Piggott's category of the East Anglian Bowl into the Mildenhall style through the study of new material, so Manby (1958, 1963, 1967) expanded the category of the Grimston Bowl into that of a full Grimston assemblage. In a sense this was the 'domestication' of pottery out of a non-secular context in order to give it full Neolithic status such as a cultural product. It was achieved by the arrangement of a 'degeneration' sequence of bowl forms from the classic fine-ware bowls as represented at Hanging Grimston to slack shouldered and S-shaped forms as at Willerby Wold. By this process degenerate Grimston forms could be shown to be associated with a part of the coarse Heslerton Ware

of Piggott. As a result the distinction between Grimston and Heslerton was rejected, which allowed a larger number of small 'occupation' assemblages to be classified as Grimston. As a by-product the remainder of Heslerton Ware (which included those bowls from round barrows) was hived off as Towthorpe Ware (Manby 1964).

The significance of this redefinition of Grimston into a full pottery assemblage was in the direct support it gave to the interpretation of the Broome Heath pottery as a Grimston assemblage (Wainwright 1972). As a consequence this large and carbon dated assemblage has effectively determined the subsequent treatment of Grimston pottery, as widely defined. This is not least in providing the justification for some of the more recent Grimston assemblages in the north (Manby 1975).

The Hembury Style of the southwest played an important role in the Neolithic explanations of 'Neolithic Cultures', as a pottery tradition directly related to its continental precursors. The excavated material was dominated by that from Hembury itself and from Maiden Castle. Early C14 dates for the former only further established the Hembury or Southwestern Style as a primary component in the Neolithic settlement of Britain, by whichever means this was carried out (Case 1969a; Whittle 1977). Subsequent excavations in the southwest have demonstrated the integrity and homogeneity with only minor variations, of this distinctive pottery style, for example at Carn Brea, Hambledon, Hazard Hill, and High Peak (Smith 1984; Mercer 1980; Houlder 1963; Pollard 1966).

The work of Peacock (1969) on the petrology of pottery in the southwest has forced a rethink of assumptions about the communal nature of a pottery tradition, and led to alternative models for pottery production and distribution (Smith 1974). Unfortunately more recent studies have tended only to emphasize the technical difficulties of the petrographic approach. A number of general points can be made. There is no necessary relationship between fine-ware production and craft organization. Emphasis has been placed on the mechanics of distribution rather than on the purposes of distribution, i.e. that of consumption. Inasmuch as the traditional model has been replaced by a craft and mercantile model, it is still an approach to Neolithic explanation, if only an imposed 'western' view rather than a received 'primitive' one.

The Decorated Styles of the southeast have been given relatively little attention as a total phenomenon since Smith (1956), despite the excavation of a number of sizeable assemblages and the large database already in existence. The pottery typology in Smith (1956) was framed primarily as a regional model, in contrast to the chronological sequence for Ireland in Case (1961). The Mildenhall Style defined in Smith (1956) was more fully described in the Hurst Fen report (Longworth 1960) and Windmill Hill and Abingdon styles also received treatment (Smith 1965; Case 1956; Case and Whittle 1982). Subsequent pottery reports have been mainly concerned with descriptive definition of the different styles and in the establishment of regional connections within style boundaries. Publication of the Broome Heath assemblage (Wainwright 1972) and the recognition of an undecorated Grimston style in the southeast posed considerable difficulties for this regionally-based stylistic framework.

Boundary disputes over assemblage-classification have been a consistent feature, both at the local level and in regional synthesis. For the former the most relevant for this paper are disagreements over whether an assemblage should be classified as in the Decorated Style or not, where the most common alternative in fact has been Grimston rather than 'plain-ware'. These disagreements are indicative of the general difficulties raised by the generic term 'plain-ware' assemblages, as to whether formal characteristics of these assemblages that are in common with decorated assemblages are sufficient for stylistic attribution to decorative styles. Regional disagreements (Kinnes 1978; Smith 1974; Whittle 1977) over the relative extent of styles are underlain by different emphasis of relative chronology and of origin.

C14 dating has been extensively carried out in the southeast. The critical issue has been the way in which a selective treatment of this dating evidence has been instrumental in providing the basis for interpretative frameworks of the Earlier Neolithic in this region, and by extension for the rest of the British Isles. The emphasis on individual and extreme results has led to an effective failure to consider the statistical nature of radiocarbon dating. Primary source criticism is also a rarity, with the result that repetition of argument leads to the reinforcement of received ideas. This is most apparent in the accepted dating of the appearance of decorated styles in the southeast, for which despite the lack of secure and grounded evidence, a 4th millennium background is currently assumed. A literary review of synthetic statements in order of appearance is instructive:

Case (1969a:182–183):
"the apparently very early date of the decorated pottery from Fussell's Lodge.... cautions one against seeing decorated pottery all as Middle Neolithic ".

Wainwright (1972:73):
"the Mildenhall style vessel from the Fussell's Lodge long barrow has opened the possibility that a decorated style may have been current during the last quarter of the 4th millennium bc in southern England ".

Smith (1974b:108):
"the appearance of decorated pottery...can now be placed almost as early as those of the plain Grimston/Lyles Hill and Hembury styles".
(Additional evidence given in support are the early dates from Abingdon, even though the seven dates listed (which ignores one at >4000 bc) are not separable stratigraphically and they average c. 2800 bc).

Whittle (1977:94):
"there are now strong indications that the Decorated Style can be dated as early as the 4th millennium bc on the basis of the radiocarbon dates from Eaton Heath, Fussell's Lodge, Lambourn and Abingdon".
(There is no decorated pottery from Lambourn, the Eaton Heath date comes from a bulk sample from three pots).

Bradley (1984:29):
"plain and decorated wares were used in parallel throughout the late fourth and third millennium".
(The only additional evidence is a bulked date from Spong Hill and one from the Trundle, both with high standard errors (which is also the case for Fussell's Lodge itself).

Table 2.1a shows all sixty-one published dates available up to January 1986 for Decorated Style pottery in the southeast. Central dates only are plotted, to the nearest 100 year interval. Many dates have very large standard errors, and most have only a poor association with the deposition of pottery. Nevertheless given a large enough sample of dates individual random errors can be expected to cancel out and overall patterns should become apparent. The figure shows an approximately unimodal distribution centred on 2750bc, with no good reason for supposing that the pre 3000bc dates represent anything other than random error.

Grimston/Lyles Hill Series, Broome Heath, and Definition

The dominant trend in pottery classification has become one of increased generalization, in marked contrast to such studies as Case 1961. This has been brought about in part by an increase in the sheer variety of new evidence and the lack of recent systematic studies. But the most significant fact was undoubtedly the confusions wrought by the evidence of C14. With a short chronology for the Neolithic, the typological study of pottery was well-suited as a method for the elucidation of Neolithic settlement, cultural origins, contacts and change. With no independent dating evidence, a spurious precision was possible in the charting of the movements of, or contacts between, specific cultural groups. With a long chronology, this explicit cultural model has been less easy to sustain, nevertheless it continues to underly most Neolithic interpretations. The consequences of this, coupled to a consistent mis-use of individual C14 dates, has led to the current confusion over Neolithic pottery and the resort to generalization as an attempt at solution. One other response to uncertainty has been the formulation of a bipartite rather than a tripartite division of the Neolithic period (Smith 1974b: Whittle 1977) *contra* Piggott. In as much as the concept of the Middle Neolithic carried with it in the southeast the appearance of decorated styles (Clark 1966), the loss

Table 2.1 Radiocarbon dates for conventional earlier Neolithic ceramic traditions.

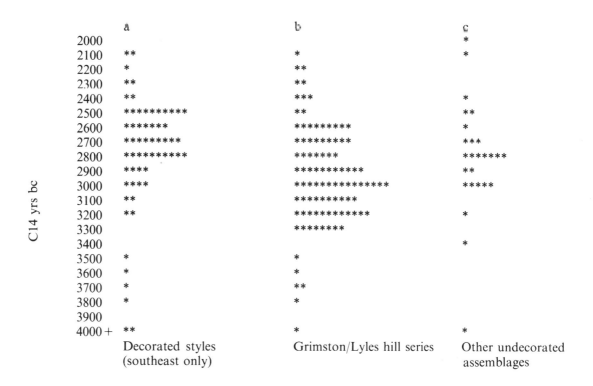

C14 yrs bc

	a	b	c
2000			*
2100	**	*	*
2200	*	**	
2300	**	**	
2400	**	***	*
2500	*********	**	**
2600	*******	********	*
2700	********	********	***
2800	*********	*******	*******
2900	****	**********	**
3000	****	**************	*****
3100	**	**********	
3200	**	***********	*
3300		********	
3400			*
3500	*	*	
3600	*	*	
3700	*	**	
3800	*	*	
3900			
4000 +	**	*	*
	Decorated styles (southeast only)	Grimston/Lyles hill series	Other undecorated assemblages

Table 2.2 British and Irish Neolithic radiocarbon dates, total (pre-2500bc.)

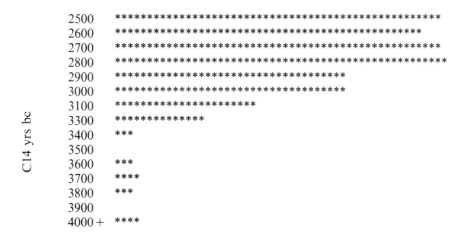

C14 yrs bc

```
2500  **********************************************
2600  *********************************************
2700  **********************************************
2800  ***********************************************
2900  ********************************
3000  ********************************
3100  *********************
3300  *************
3400  ***
3500
3600  ***
3700  ****
3800  ***
3900
4000 + ****
```

13

of this chronological division further exacerbated the temporal fluidity of the perceived ceramic record.

The Grimston/Lyles Hill series was a novel attempt by Smith (1974b) to accommodate both earlier work on undecorated carinated pottery and the recent evidence from Ballynagilly, Broome Heath, and from C14. A similar review was provided by Wainwright (1972) in a discussion of the Broome Heath assemblage itself. This was concerned to provide a background for the cultural affinities and origins of the Broome Heath assemblage. Its traditional approach was hedged in its conclusions because of difficulties over chronological primacy but nevertheless asserted a common relation between Grimston pottery (in Manby's broad sense) and Lyles Hill ware (in Piggott's broad sense) and with cultural traditions across the North Sea.

The contrast in Smith (1974b) between the Grimston/Lyles Hill 'series' and the Peterborough 'tradition' is instructive. The latter term is taken from Longworth (1961) and is employed in order to demonstrate the evolutionary character of Peterborough pottery. This is in contrast to the term 'series' applied to Grimston/Lyles Hill which is employed to indicate the uncertain status of a grouping of regional pottery variants. Their relative chronology is unclear, both for origin and for survival. The implication is that for Grimston/Lyles Hill, an evolutionary sequence is either not known or may not have been present. It may be unfair to note that regional sequences for each variant style were perfectly acceptable prior to C14 dating, and that, in contrast to Grimston/Lyles Hill, there were in the early 1970's (and still are) very few dates for Peterborough pottery.

Smith (1974b) deliberately eschewed an explicit cultural approach to Neolithic pottery, as shown in her discussion of southwest gabbroic ware, but as indicated above this did not necessarily imply a rejection of its principles. Of more importance is that the pottery typologies on which the Grimston/Lyles Hill series was based were themselves a product of cultural model interpretations of the pottery evidence (see references to Manby and Case above). It is the difficulties caused by attempts to integrate these regional cultural models into a C14 chronology based on selective dates that has accounted for the difficulties inherent in the Grimston/Lyles Hill scheme. An approach based on a critical interpretation of C14 and on a functional and contextual treatment of the pottery should result in the dissipation of many of these problems.

Pottery in the Grimston/Lyles Hill series, as conventionally defined, is present at both the beginning and the end of the Neolithic. It is unchanged in form over two (calibrated) millennia, and shows little interaction with any other pottery style or tradition. It is both secular and ritual in function, as both a group of highly distinctive fineware burnished bowls in specific depositional context and large and varied assemblages of a domestic nature from settlement sites. These statements are applicable to most definitions and discussions of Grimston/Lyles Hill pottery. Accounts of Neolithic society based on such statements should be criticised

as both absurd in construction and ludicrous in effect. As an entry into the dissolution of the current state of affairs, a critical re-interpretation of Broome Heath as a site and an assemblage is appropriate, as its publication provided an apparently secure base for contemporary interpretive frameworks.

Broome Heath is the type-site for Grimston pottery in Britain. The reason is twofold: the size of the pottery assemblage; and the presence and range of the C14 dates. The cultural attribution and early date of Broome Heath taken together with those for Ballynagilly ensured a central role for Grimston/Lyles Hill pottery at the beginning of the Neolithic. The mid third millennium dates and settlement status of Broome Heath supported the idea of Grimston/Lyles Hill pottery as a conservative tradition within the cultural milieu of the developed Neolithic. The late date for the site supported other evidence that suggested a long survival of Grimston/Lyles Hill through to the end of the Neolithic.

This apparent usefulness of Broome Heath has hidden the site and its pottery from critical view. Only Louwe Kooijmans (1984) has written:

"a plea is made for alternative interpretations of some basic data, like the Broome Heath C14 dates".

Of the four dates from the site, only those from pits 29 and 40, 2573 ± 67bc and 2629 ± 65bc, are from contexts certainly contemporary with the use and deposition of the pottery assemblage. The date of 2217 ± 78bc is from the surface of the fossil soil (layer 4) sealed below the inner bank of the enclosure. The date of 3474 ± 117bc is from the base (layer 5) of this fossil soil. The published sections record only a gravel bank, an alternative interpretation is that layer 4 is a topsoil dump below this, with layer 5 as the old ground surface. Although Neolithic pottery is recorded from layer 5, it is uncertain if any was in direct association with the dated charcoal. In any case little value can be given to charcoal from such a context not directly associated with cultural material. Although unweathered sherds were recovered from layer 4, this can be accounted for by re-deposition of pottery in the soil or possibly from pits in the line of the ditch. Again there is no good basis for applying the date from layer 4 to pottery found in the layer. On this reinterpretation of the contexts of the C14 dates, Broome Heath instead of a domestic site in use over two millennia, with no discernible change in pottery style, is more reasonably interpreted as an open settlement of pit clusters dated securely to the Middle Neolithic.

If Broome Heath is removed as the key to a long chronology for Grimston pottery, then much of the evidence from other sites for a Grimston survival into the late Neolithic falls apart; either that published before Broome Heath to which it provided confirmation, or that published after Broome Heath to which it lent conviction.

Evidence for a late survival of Grimston/Lyles Hill pottery on C14 evidence alone (e.g. Monamore, Ballyotuag) is not valid, again because it is based on a selective treatment of the total evidence available

(MacKie 1964; Watts 1960). Table 2.1b shows in the same manner as Table 2.1a all 97 dates for Grimston/Lyles Hill series pottery in the British Isles as a whole. The presence of much of this pottery in 4th millennium contexts appears to be assured, reasons for its apparent continuation into the middle of the 3rd millennium are discussed below. Of interest here is that dates post 2500bc are as likely to be a product of statistical error as are the pre 3000bc dates for decorated pottery.

The evidence for direct association with later Neolithic pottery (Developed Peterborough, Grooved Ware and Beaker) is not convincing. Green (1976) interpreted Stacey Bushes with a C14 date of 1830±150bc as a domestic site in which both Grimston pottery and Grooved Ware were in contemporary use. A reinterpretation of the site might relegate most of the excavated features to a natural origin, in which the 'borrow trenches' that provide the C14 date and pottery association can be viewed as tree-collapse structures (see Green 1976, Fig.2.2 and compare to Kooi 1974, Fig.4). Grooved Ware is likely to be contemporary with this phase of activity, Grimston pottery (if indeed it is) is residual only.

The Beaker (and Food Vessel) sherds from the Neolithic mound of Cowlam 57 (Greenwell 1877; Newbigin 1937) have no useful value coming from a site excavated over 100 years ago. Their continued presence in the literature as relevant evidence only made sense in the historical context of a short Neolithic and its cultural survival in 'backward areas', applicable to Scottish instances as well as to other Yorkshire examples given in Newbigin (1937). Criticism of Craike Hill (Manby 1958) as a single-phase occupation with Grimston, Peterborough, Grooved Ware and Beaker on a site with a metre of colluvial stratigraphy, with Grimston as the sole pottery at the base of the stratigraphy, should also recognize the contemporary disciplinary context. The reporting of Beaker sherds from within the mound at Skendleby is well known (Phillips 1935). It is still a unique occurrence and its significance should not be overstated.

In Scotland associations of Beaker sherds with Lyles Hill pottery were claimed for East Finnercy and Loanhead of Daviot (Atkinson 1962). Henshall (1983) has recently demonstrated the lack of evidence for true association at these two sites. The few cord-impressed sherds from within the front of the blocking at Cairnholy 1 (Piggott and Powell 1949), in which a Lyles Hill bowl was deposited, cannot be regarded as definitive evidence.

In Ireland the association of Lyles Hill style pottery with flat-based Kilhoyle pottery in the chamber at Legland (Davies 1940; Case 1961) has little additional support or credence. Whatever the validity of the association of Lyles Hill pottery with sherds of Ballyalton Bowls at Tamnyrankin (Herring 1941; Case 1961) and elsewhere, the dating of these bowls themselves to the later Neolithic is unlikely, contra Case (Sheridan 1986).

Table 2.1c shows for comparison with Table 2.1a and b all 26 C14 dates for undecorated bowl assemblages in the British Isles not classified as Grimston/Lyles Hill. Comparison produces a number of patterns. Much of the undecorated pottery is contemporary with the southeastern Decorated Styles. The majority of the dates in this range are in fact for 'Plain Bowl' assemblages in the southeast. A second component of Table 2.1c covers an earlier range, this includes the early dates for Hembury style pottery. Grimston/Lyles Hill stretches over a longer duration than for all the remainder, even with the latest dates excluded. It is suggested that two chronological distributions are in fact superimposed. The first, and earliest, to be classified as Carinated, or Grimston, Bowls is described in the next section. The second and later distribution is for pottery that is more closely allied in classification and in context to the 'plain-wares' and decorated styles of the middle Neolithic. This pottery is again best introduced from the viewpoint of Broome Heath.

Broome Heath is not a Grimston assemblage. As the current type-site for Grimston pottery this may be a surprising statement. Nevertheless as a preliminary to a treatment of early Carinated Bowls, their relationship if any to the Broome Heath middle Neolithic domestic assemblage should be assessed.

The classic Grimston Bowl first defined by Piggott (1954:114) is of fine fabric and finish, with an open and shallow profile, marked carination and a simple everted and beaded rim. The overall impression is of a bipartite bowl, the lower part of the vessel sharply differentiated from the upper part, with the carination often low on the body. The mouth of the vessel itself is not a dominant feature, it serves only to reinforce the emphasis on simple division.

In contrast the shouldered bowls from Broome Heath have a dominant emphasis on the upper part of the body, the carination is invariably high on the body and is only part of a stylistic and functional complex of shoulder/neck/rim. Rims are elaborate, either expanded or markedly rolled-over. Necks are usually concave and upright so that there are no true open carinated forms. The carination serves only to define a ledge shoulder. These bowls are markedly functional in form, the design focused on successful handling of the vessel mouth. As such the distinction between these shouldered bowls and the more open S-profiled forms at the site must be by context of use rather than mode of use since both show rim elaboration as a functional design feature. Taken together with the small cups and large jar forms the whole assemblage might be regarded as fulfilling an integrated functional and utilitarian domestic vessel repertoire.

In functional terms there is little to separate this assemblage from that at Hurst Fen (Longworth 1960). A concern with decorative style hides a fundamental unity. Both show a range of forms suitable for the storage, preparation, cooking or eating of agricultural and other products.

This expression of functional unity can be extended to other assemblages in the region. Briar Hill should be re-interpreted as a relatively short-lived site c. 2700bc given the weak contexts of the C14 dates for the presumptive fourth millennium phases I and II (Bamford 1985; Kinnes and Thorpe 1986). The pottery report is ambiguous as to the attribution of the material to either the Mildenhall or Grimston Styles. If the Broome Heath and Hurst Fen assemblages have the same chronological and functional context despite an apparent difference in decorative treatment, then the Briar Hill pottery is easily accommodated within the range of variation expressed. In a very different depositional context, hence more problematic for interpretation, is the assemblage at Swale's Tumulus (Briscoe 1956). Referred to by different authors both as Grimston and Mildenhall Style, the choice is essentially artificial. Despite the likelihood of individual selection in the pyre deposit, basic similarities with the above assemblages are evident.

The relationship of middle Neolithic decorated styles to 'Plain Bowl' assemblages is not the concern of this paper. Nevertheless this discussion shows that for undecorated assemblages, to make a choice between Grimston or 'Plain Bowl' according to the presence or absence of shouldered forms or unelaborated rims, is an inappropriate procedure. In East Anglia at least, the functional assemblage common to Broome Heath and Hurst Fen encompasses all middle Neolithic pottery forms, whether decorated or Plain Bowl, shouldered or not. The essential results are that a middle Neolithic functional assemblage can be defined, it fulfills a primarily domestic function, formal variation is a consequence of functional intent and none of these domestic assemblages are Grimston, Broome Heath included.

Carinated Bowls and Regional Developments in Earlier Neolithic Pottery

The argument of this paper is that an initial horizon for the British and Irish Neolithic can be recognized by the common presence across a range of related contexts of the fine Carinated Bowl as typified at Hanging Grimston. Regional patterns and trends in the ceramic evidence are outlined in some detail. A comparison of regional sequences suggests common themes of initial ceramic use and in subsequent developments of ceramic design and function.

The dating to the middle Neolithic of decorated/Plain Bowl pottery in southeast England is already given. The evidence for any Neolithic presence c. or before 3000bc is limited, and should not be overstated. Relevant and acceptable C14 dates are few. Early Neolithic contexts have been assumed rather than demonstrated. In this setting an early horizon marked by pottery distinct from the large and well-known middle Neolithic assemblages is a problematic issue. Possible assemblages for this phase are usually small with only a few vessels represented. This may indicate a real situation as much as a phenomenon of archaeological survival.

Carinated Bowls occur as single finds from pits at Chippenham barrow 5, Cambridgeshire (Leaf 1940) and at Layer de la Haye, Essex, as a near complete vessel c. 250mm diameter (Priddy 1982). A bowl recovered from a Saxon layer at Clapham, London,

must from its condition have come from a primary context (Kinnes pers. comm.). Sherds of similar bowls (c. 200mm dia) occur with those from larger vessels (c. 300–350mm dia) in coarser fabric at Sparham, Norfolk (Healy 1984) and Fengate, Cambridgeshire (Smith 1974a). These two assemblages, the first from a pit context associated with flint debitage, the second from a possible longhouse associated with a blade industry and jet bead fragment (Pryor 1974), show markedly similar attributes of vessel form. Open vessels are both carinated and simple S-profiled, with everted and internally thickened rims. Internal fluting occurs at Fengate. Dating for the latter is ambiguous, 3010 $\pm$ 64bc and 2445 $\pm$ 50bc. Two other dated sites in this area may also be relevant, a pit with carinated pottery at Tattershall Thorpe, Lincolnshire, (Healy pers comm.) dated to 3150 $\pm$ 100bc and the small assemblage from the 'black band' at Shippea Hill, Cambridgeshire, dated to 3000 $\pm$ 120bc and 2920 $\pm$ 120bc (Clark et al. 1935; Clark and Godwin 1962).

Carinated Bowls are a deliberate placement at the non-megalithic linear banked structure with inhumation deposits at Orton Longueville, Cambridgeshire (Brown 1982). Similar pottery is recorded from the Neolithic complex at Grendon, Northamptonshire (Gibson 1985), with dates for the site at 3000 $\pm$ 80bc, 2740 $\pm$ 130bc and 2330 $\pm$ 70bc. Both sites show structural similarities with others further north.

Carinated Bowls are also present at Lion Point, Essex, (Warren al. 1936, Fig.2.5, c. 240mm dia) as are larger open uncarinated vessels (Warren and Smith 1954 Fig.2.2,3, c. 300mm dia). The associations of this material are unreliable, although the context is presumably of domestic status. The coarse-ware vessels (c. 250mm dia) from the hearth-pit at Little Waltham, Essex, (Drury 1978) with a date of 3170 $\pm$ 130bc have similarities with the Essex coast material. An unpublished collection of material recovered from quarrying at North Shoeburyness, Essex, (Kinnes pers. comm.) apparently includes both fine Carinated Bowls and much larger carinated vessels (350 + mm dia). Rims, as in all the instances above, are simple, often beaded or everted.

Most of the pottery discussed above can be distinguished from that represented by the large assemblages at Broome Heath. This is certainly the case for the fine Carinated Bowls such as at Layer de la Haye, but also for most of the remainder that show direct or only indirect association with such bowls. Nevertheless a clear-cut chronological division is neither possible nor necessarily to be expected. Shouldered bowl assemblages in East Anglia (both Hurst Fen and Broome Heath) do show developmental trends from Carinated Bowl assemblages. Decoration is apparently a local (or contextual) option. Across this division there is a tendency towards closure of form, often incorporating a developed rim and carination into upright shouldered/necked vessels. Simple hemispherical cups may well be present in Carinated Bowl assemblages, this form becomes established across size and decorative classes in later assemblages.

In Kent the pottery from the pit at Wingham (Greenfield 1960) shows many similarities with the above material. Associated with the pottery in a dark ashy matrix was an antler comb, a bone point, stone quern and rubber fragments, and a number of conjoining flakes. Seven vessels were represented which appeared to have been deposited as upper parts of these vessels. Rims are internally thickened and flared. Although there are no carinated sherds, fluting is widely present and fabric and finish is very fine. The vessels all cluster around *c.* 280mm diameter. Coarse-ware sherds are absent. The small assemblage from the forecourt of Chestnuts chambered tomb (Alexander 1961) with *c.* six vessels represented is also of fine bowls with simple rims. Decorated/Plain Bowl assemblages in Kent are not well defined, and any developmental model would be premature. Carination apparently continues as a dominant theme, rims generally remain un-elaborated, decoration is restrained. There is more variation in vessel shape. Most sites for these assemblages occur in East Kent (Dunning 1966), and Ebbsfleet represents a very different situation (Burchell and Piggott 1939).

The large rim and shoulder sherd from the upper infill of the Cissbury shaft, Sussex, (Clark and Piggott 1936) is, as drawn, from a fine Carinated Bowl. The small assemblage from New Barn Down, Sussex, (Curwen 1934) may have more similarities with the large decorated assemblage at Whitehawk in that the line of carination on the vessels is of less structural significance. The context of the site is possibly that of a ditch segment fill (causewayed enclosure?). Decorated/plain-ware assemblages in Sussex show formal similarities with Carinated Bowls in the emphasis on open forms and simple rims. Carination is retained, but more as a focus for design than as basis for overall shape. Decoration is a dominant phenomenon as elsewhere in the southeast.

The pottery from the upper infill of a Neolithic shaft at Cannon Hill, Berkshire, (Bradley *et al.* 1976) including both fine Carinated Bowls (*c.* 140mm dia) and larger bowls or jars (*c.* 240mm dia), also of sharp carinated form. Small hemispherical cups are also represented. A date for charcoal from this layer is 3320±110bc. Fine carinated sherds are recorded from the grey ashy fill sealing a cremation deposit in a large pit below the Bronze Age barrow 62a at Bishop's Canning, Wiltshire, (Proudfoot 1965; Kinnes pers comm). Sherds from Carinated Bowls were found in the pre-barrow soil at South Street, Wiltshire, (Ashbee *et al.* 1979) with a pre-barrow date of 2810±130bc. Similar sherds may have occurred in a pre-barrow 'occupation layer' at Ascott-under-Wychwood chambered long barrow, Oxfordshire (Selkirk 1971), with a date of 2943 ±70bc, and again in the 'midden' deposit under Hazelton chambered long barrow, Gloucestershire (Saville 1984bc), with dates of 3020±80bc and 2965 ±80bc (Saville pers. comm.).

Carinated Bowl assemblages are numerically rare in central southern England. Whether this is because of a genuine absence of this pottery as against other preferred forms, an absolute rarity of early presence, or an artificial product of dominant excavation concerns is simply unknown on present evidence.

The argument of this paper is at its weakest here, since there are no secure grounds for the pottery development model applied elsewhere. No attempt is made to resolve these issues in the context of this paper, they do not necessarily deny the validity of the argument, although they do provide an obvious focus for criticism.

The Carinated Bowls from the Sweet Track, Somerset, provide the best dated context for this class of pottery in the British Isles (Coles *et al.* 1973; Coles and Orme 1979, 1984). C14 dates of the wooden structure itself and of the peat sequence directly associated with it give a secure dating for the pottery vessels deposited alongside the track. Seventeen dates are potentially applicable, and an interval around 3200bc is most likely (Orme 1982). The pottery is solely of part or near-complete single vessels, and taken together with the associated finds of a jadeite axe and unpolished flint axe, intentional deposition must be inferred rather than casual loss. Although there is a range of variation between the five reconstructed vessels (all >200mm dia) the group as a whole is markedly similar in fabric, finish, and form. An upright profile is a characteristic local feature.

Carinated Bowls from elsewhere in the southwest have only occurred as part of Hembury or 'Southwestern' Style assemblages. With the exception of three dates from Hembury itself, all but one of the twenty-seven dates from other assemblages have given 3rd millennium results. Hembury is also the only causewayed enclosure with an apparently secure 4th millennium context, but it has been suggested that the dates may be of old timber on the basis of comparable evidence from current work at Maiden Castle (Sharples 1986). If this is accepted then there is little or no evidence other than from the Sweet Track for a 4th millennium Neolithic presence in the southwest, and any discussion of the Hembury style should recognize this state of affairs.

Carinated vessels are a dominant feature of the Carn Brea assemblage from Cornwall, but only as an integral part of a wide range of other forms (Smith 1984). A similar situation occurs in a much smaller assemblage at Hazard Hill (Houlder 1963), and also at Hembury (Liddell 1930, 1931, 1932, 1935), both in Devon. Carinated Bowls are absent from the large assemblage at Maiden Castle, Dorset, (Piggott 1943) and in southwestern assemblages further east. Given the contemporaneity of these sites, demonstrated also by the distribution of gabbroic ware, Carinated Bowls can be seen as a culturally preferred form in the west of the region.

In the virtual absence of demonstrably early pottery there is little basis for understanding pottery development in the southwest. Nevertheless it may be suggested that carinated forms were available as pre-existing models, and that their unchanged survival into broad spectrum middle Neolithic assemblages in the southwest is an alternative, and perhaps more conservative, trajectory to that proposed for the southeast. The conspicuous absence of decoration on Hembury style pottery as a whole, its continuation of simple forms, are in marked contrast to contemporary decorated styles. The elaboration of handle design on shallow open bowls is an apparent exception.

Despite the above limitations two other sites in the southwest may represent aspects of a Carinated Bowl horizon. The pit at Handley Hill, Dorset, (Piggott 1936) excavated by Pitt-Rivers contained a disarticulated skeleton and twelve ox bones sealed below *c.* 1m of chalk rubble. Associated with this deposit and mixed with the rubble was one-third of a fine S-profiled bowl. This is markedly similar to vessels associated with Carinated Bowls in eastern England, and the form would appear to be absent in the large Hembury assemblages from Dorset. The excavation of the passage grave at Broadsands, Devon, (Ralegh-Radford 1958) recovered nine fine ware sherds, in some cases apparently contemporary with early deposition of human bone, in others re-deposited. Carinated sherds are represented.

There are no large Welsh Neolithic pottery assemblages. Nevertheless chronological sequences can be informed by C14 evidence and by contextual association. Only a number of themes are relevant for this paper.

The pottery from the pit in the forecourt of the portal tomb (western chamber) at Dyffryn Ardudwy, Gwynedd, (Powell 1973) is contemporary with the first phase of the site. Four or five Carinated Bowls are represented (all *c.* 240mm dia.). Rims and carinations are simple, sharp and well-defined and fabric and finish are very fine. The pit contained stones and charcoal as well as pottery, the latter deposited as large sherds from the upper parts of vessels. Part of the upper portion of a sixth vessel (*c.* 220mm dia.) was recovered from the forecourt of the eastern chamber. The small rim fragment is rolled-over and the shoulder is rounded. The typological difference between the two pottery groups, with the latter regarded as more 'developed', may simply reflect a site specific depositional sequence.

The small assemblage from Llandegai, Gwynedd, is similar in fabric and form to that from Dyffryn Ardudwy (Lynch 1976). Fine Carinated Bowls are represented, although rims are described as more developed. Again similarities are perhaps best emphasized over differences. The site context at Llandegai is possibly a post-built longhouse, sealed at some stage beneath the outer bank of the henge. A C14 date associated with the pottery is 3290±150bc. A third carinated assemblage was associated with struck flint on the old ground surface beneath the phase one simple passage grave at Trefignath chambered tomb in Anglesey (Smith 1981). A C14 date from this surface is 3100±70bc.

The consistency of these C14 dates has given credence to the date of 3050±95bc associated with the pottery from an isolated pit at Coygan Camp, Dyfed (Wainwright 1967). However the pottery from the pit consists of only 24 sherds from a single coarse-ware pot (*c.* 400mm dia.) associated with charcoal, struck flint, cattle and sheep fragments, hazel-nut shells and a sandstone block. The surviving part shows only an externally thickened and everted rim.

Comparisons of the Coygan Camp pottery can be made with isolated sherds from other Welsh pottery assemblages such as that from the forecourt of the simple chamber at Pant-y-Saer (Scott 1933), and the uncertain context of the pottery from the chamber at Lligwy (Piggott 1933), both in Anglesey. The range of forms and fabrics from these assemblages and a comparison of their contexts with those given above suggests that these are not early assemblages. The same is true for the large domestic assemblage at Clegyr Boia in Dyfed (Williams 1953), where the Shouldered Bowls share the same structural features as those from Broome Heath. Again they are only part of a broad spectrum domestic assemblage, and one in which decorative elements are also present. A similar development from simple carinated forms may be apparent in the uncontexted 'Western Neolithic' pottery from the chambered tomb at Bryn yr Hen Bobl, Anglesey (Hemp 1936).

The recent publication of Gwernvale, Powys, (Britnell and Savory 1984) has produced an important new contextual assemblage. The pottery from the pre-cairn structures is in overall terms a Carinated Bowl assemblage. Nine of the sherds from one vessel came from a pit dated to 3100±75bc. The distribution of sherds from at least four fine Carinated Bowls (*c.* 180–260mm dia.) have been plotted from within the pre-cairn soil and features. The patterns suggest a process of breakage, deposition and disturbance or re-deposition. At least one hemispherical bowl is also represented with a heavy thickened rim. Other heavy rolled rims occur. These vessels are in a quartz fabric distinct from the vesicular Carinated Bowls. There seems no reason to doubt their broad contemporaneity. The structures themselves can be variously interpreted, both as a unitary phenomenon and in relation to the construction of the subsequent cairn. Interpretation is restricted by partial extent of excavation. As an alternative to that given in the report a longhouse oriented east-west and focused on a standing stone may be suggested as one possibility from the visible evidence.

Further discussion of the site and its pottery is not considered here except for one point. The argument that the Gwernvale assemblage supports the concept of an 'English' style in Welsh Severn-Cotswold tombs (Lynch 1984), with its implications of cultural drift and historical sequence, has no basis. On the current evidence for pottery sequences in southeast Wales and southern England, there are no dates or contexts that might suggest a westward movement of Abingdon style pottery.

One further site may be of significance. The simple chamber tomb at Carreg Sampson, Dyfed (Lynch 1975), contained as a sherd deposit on the chamber floor, beneath slate paving, about three-quarters of a large bowl (*c.* 350mm dia.). The hemispherical bowl has a fine fabric and finish, with slightly everted rim and a flattened base.

Earlier Neolithic pottery from Yorkshire is known in small quantity although it is derived from a large number of sites. Many of these are barrows, and most were excavated wholly or partly in the last century. Interpretation of the barrow record has to encompass variability in monumental form, in structural elements, in the condition and disposition of human remains and in the quality of the excavation record. Pottery associated with these monuments cannot be considered in isolation from their manner of use, internal phasing and relative chronology.

At Kilham (Manby 1976), a fine Carinated Bowl was associated with unburnt and burnt part-articulated human skeletal material contained within an embanked linear zone with three axial pits. This primary structure is offset to a rectangular palisade enclosure and its subsequent mound. A C14 date of 2880 ± 125bc for the enclosure is a *terminus ante quem* for the mortuary structure. Plain-bowl pottery occurred in secondary contexts, mostly from above the primary silt in the flanking quarry ditches. At Whitegrounds (Brewster 1985) two Carinated Bowls are associated with part-articulated human bone, a dog skeleton and an amber bead in a linear stone built chamber aligned within a U-shaped embankment. There is a C14 date of 3000 ± 90bc for human bone from the chamber.

Although the evidence at Grimston is weak (Mortimer 1905), two pits define a linear zone east of a façade trench. Part of a Carinated Bowl occurred in one pit, two more bowls were recorded above the other pit, with a fourth from the intervening deposit. Although no human bone was found pig bone occurred both in this zone and in the façade trench. Pottery is recorded from the façade but none survives. A C14 date of 2760 ± 90bc from pig-bone in the façade gives a *terminus ante quem* for the pottery (Pierpoint 1979). Although pottery from façade trenches is a common feature of the Yorkshire barrow series, its relationship to any one phase in a façade life-cycle is in most instances unclear. Where the context is known for certain, as at Willerby Wold and Street House, the pottery is post-façade destruction and is Plain Bowl only. Carinated pottery is not certainly recorded from any façade context, the drawn profile for that at Street House is unconvincing.

The linear embanked zone with crematorium deposit at Willerby Wold (Manby 1963) has no ceramic association. The shouldered plain-ware bowls from the site are in secondary contexts in front of the mound. They are unrelated to dates of 3010 ± 150bc and 2950 ± 150bc for the primary structure. Sherds from similar crematoria at Kilburn and Westow are not informative (Greenwell 1877). Rim sherds of fine open bowls survive from the linear crematoria at Cowlam 277 and Garton Slack 81 (Mortimer 1905). Both these structures appear to underlie round barrows without façade components. There are no details of the pottery associated with a stone/timber enclosure (with C14 date 3080 ± 90bc) and crematorium deposit beneath a round cairn on Seamer Moor (Vatcher 1961; see also Kinnes 1979 Aa6). Two Carinated Bowls and other sherds are associated with a post defined crematorium deposit and boulder enclosure beneath a second round cairn on Seamer Moor (Simpson 1963; see also Kinnes 1979 Aa7 and pers. comm.). There is no pottery directly associated with the primary use of the Street House monument with its square enclosure, embanked linear zone with cremated human bone, and

angled façade (Vyner 1984). The Plain Bowl pottery from the site occurs in a similar context to that at Willerby. The primary monument itself is securely dated to c. 2900 bc. A fine Carinated Bowl is associated at Garton Slack C37 with a single adult cremation and charcoal in a pit with no monumental context (Mortimer 1905).

There are consistent patterns and trends in this evidence. Carinated Bowls where present are associated with primary use and primary phases of these monuments. C14 dates where applicable are universally early. There is a strong association with cremation practice, multiple and mixed skeletal deposition, and simple linear embanked structures. Carinated Bowls are not a feature of subsequent trends in the Yorkshire barrow series (Kinnes 1979), and are replaced by the often closed forms, 'overhanging rims' and minimal decoration of Towthorpe Bowls. There is no necessary relation between the fine Carinated Bowls in the primary structures of early monuments and Plain Bowl sherds in secondary contexts. This undecorated regional style is characterized by wide rimmed open and shouldered bowls, with close functional similarities to the Broome Heath assemblage. Differences between this pottery and that classed as Towthorpe may be overstated given the very small assemblages concerned and rarely comparable site and depositional circumstances.

A non-mortuary context for Carinated Bowls in Yorkshire is not established. Of the small assemblages recorded from pre-barrow contexts, isolated pits and colluvial deposits, only those from Cottam Warren and Rudston Corner Field Site 6 (Manby 1975) are difficult to place in a developed Plain Bowl style. These sites comprise individual pits with varying quantities of cultural material present. Carinated coarseware vessels over 300mm are represented in these contexts.

In Derbyshire, with two exceptions, putative early Neolithic assemblages are simply too small and of uncertain association to be considered. At Aston a Neolithic hearth c. 1m diameter was sealed beneath a presumed Beaker round barrow (Reaney 1968). Approximately 100 sherds of a single Carinated Bowl (c. 350mm dia.) overlay the hearth and 400 carbonized cereal grains. There is a C14 date from the carbonized grain of 2750 ± 150bc. A recent excavation (1984–85) at Lismore Fields, Buxton, (Trent & Peak Arch. Trust 1985) led to the fortuitous discovery of a post and slot construction Neolithic longhouse 15m by 5m in size. The building is oriented east-west, with east entrance, internal partitions and two central hearths. Sherds of Carinated Bowl were present in the structural features and in pits both inside and outside the building. Struck flint and chert and carbonized grain also occured. An adjacent shallow pit with charcoal and sherds is dated to 3270 ± 80bc.

With the exception of the weakly contexted site at Ehenside Tarn (Darbishire 1874), all other Carinated Bowl sites in northern England cluster in the Millfield Basin, Northumberland. Underlying a round cairn at Ford (Greenwell 1877) was a discontinuous layer of burnt earth and charcoal within which was associated cremated human bone, many sherds and struck flint including bifaces, scrapers and flint axe fragments. The surviving pottery represents a number of Carinated Bowls with simple, often rolled-over, rims. A shallow hemispherical bowl is also present.

In the excavation of the Anglo-Saxon site of Yeavering (Hope-Taylor 1977) two adjacent Neolithic bowl-shaped pits were excavated. Pit 30 contained a sandy fill with charcoal, fragments of cremated bone and originally a complete Carinated Bowl. The rim was lost by ploughing, but the shoulder (320mm dia.) is low-slung above a shallow rounded base. Similar sherds occurred elsewhere on the site. The adjacent pit was full of blackened earth and cremated bone. At Old Yeavering henge (Harding 1981) an irregular depression outside the eastern entrance contained a silty matrix and a large number of sherds from a number of carinated vessels.

The excavation of the Anglo-Saxon site at Thirlings (Miket 1976) also uncovered evidence of Neolithic activity. Information is published on pit F366, from which over 400 sherds and a minimum of twelve vessels were recovered. The pottery apparently includes both fine and coarse wares, one carinated vessel with simple rim is given with a diameter of 500mm. Others range from 200–300mm diameter. Both weak and strong carinated forms and one simple closed bowl are represented. A date of 5250 ± 150bc from small charcoal in the pit can be rejected. An adjacent post-pit with similar pottery, including one conjoin, is dated to 3280 ± 150bc.

For northern England as a whole with the exception of a transition from Carinated Bowl to simple decorated rim pottery within mortuary contexts, there is little evidence for pottery sequence. The existing data-base is simply too small. In Northumbria virtually all Neolithic bowl pottery is Carinated Bowl, and there are good grounds for regarding all these assemblages as closely related and early in date. In Yorkshire a Plain Bowl tradition is apparent, but whether part of this material is early and contemporary with the fine Carinated Bowls in mortuary contexts cannot be judged at this stage. There is some evidence that carinated forms, as distinct from plainware shouldered forms, may continue into the middle Neolithic, on one interpretation of the material and C14 dates from Grendon, Aston and Street House. Nevertheless the evidence is very strong for recognition of an early Carinated Bowl horizon in this region.

In eastern Scotland there are a series of sites related by context, C14 dating and by the sharing of a common pottery repertoire (Henshall 1983). The complex pattern of Neolithic structures and deposits at Boghead (Burl 1985) is not easily interpreted. Part of the mound was removed in recent times, and other post-Neolithic activity has resulted in extensive disturbance of the original form. It is possible to reconstruct the site as an unitary round or U-shaped cairn beneath a sand capping, with a central linear space oriented northeast-southwest and focused on the central pit and hollow H. Ancillary areas of *in situ* burning, material deposition and associated stake and post structures occur to either side of this central zone and are covered by construction of the cairn body. Highly fragmented burnt bone, a large sherd assemblage of Carinated Bowls, a small flint and chert assemblage, charcoal and carbonized grain are present in the pre-cairn black layer XIII, and to different degrees in the old land surface, pre-cairn features, cairn mass and in the sand mound cover and intervening sand infill. Within the black layer particular areas of concentration occur for the different classes of material. A series of five C14 dates for the site range from 3081 ± 100bc to 2873 ± 60bc.

The pottery assemblages of over 1000 sherds contains a minimum of 37 vessels (Henshall 1985). Carinated Bowls (250–300mm dia.) of high quality are numerically dominant. Carinations are sharp and occur low on the body, rims are outwardly curved, and may be slightly thickened or beaded. Fluting is common inside and outside the neck and above the rim. Simple bowl forms also occur (*c.* 150mm dia.) and fabric and finishing techniques overall are very homogenous with few exceptions. These latter are sherds from *c.* 5 heavier and coarser bowls.

Elsewhere, Carinated Bowls are recorded from Powsode Cairn at Atherb (Henshall 1983). 19th century records (Milne 1982) suggest a possible pyre or crematoria under a round cairn, with flint arrowheads directly associated with, and pottery adjacent to, the burnt zone. Similar pottery is present at the unpublished site of Midtown of Pitglassie (Henshall 1985; Kinnes pers. comm.). This is a kerb cairn sealing a number of individual cremation deposits, some associated with pottery. There is a C14 date for one cremation of 2990 ± 60bc. At Pitnacree (Coles and Simpson 1965) part of a Carinated Bowl (dia 230mm), other carinated sherds and part of a simple bowl are associated on the old ground surface with a considerable quantity of charcoal, four separate cremation deposits and a C14 date of 2860 ± 90bc. This deposit underlines a small U-shaped cairn enclosing a linear zone bracketed by two postholes containing two further cremation deposits.

The large collection recovered last century from Easterton of Roseisle (Henshall 1983; Walker 1968; Young 1896) closely matches in details of design that from Boghead and was collected from two large pits lined with burnt stone and with much charcoal and wood ash in the fills. Large lumps of fatty matter were recorded from the base of the pits. The 13 + fine fluted bowls (rim dia *c.* 250–300) are a very homogenous group. All are probably of carinated form. Plain Carinated Bowls also occur and possibly simple hemispherical bowls. A number of coarser vessels of divergent form occur in the collection, but given the circumstances of recovery and subsequent storage, the material should not all be considered as a secure closed group.

Possibly related to the above is the small assemblage from below the tripartite passage grave at Tulloch of Assery B in Caithness (Corcoran 1966). 107 small sherds representing a minimum of nineteen vessels are associated with a deposit of charcoal and small fragments of intensely burnt bone. There is a

C14 date of 2890±65bc for this deposit (Sharples 1986a).

Early C14 dates and early contexts can be demonstrated for this pottery style in northeast Scotland. A shallow open carinated form is the most common, and there is a regional emphasis on the production of elegant fluted surfaces. Other forms are restricted to small hemispherical bowls. If lugged bowls are present in these Carinated Bowl assemblages then it is only as a minor secondary element. There are too few non-Carinated Bowl assemblages in the region to provide any comparison of context, date or material. If this lack of evidence is an argument for a continuation of Carinated Bowl into the middle Neolithic, then it is not supported by the current range of C14 dates.

Elsewhere in Scotland the evidence for Carinated Bowl assemblages is slight. They are absent in Orkney and Shetland, and as a corollary the C14 dates for Unstan Bowls places the appearance of this pottery class to the middle Neolithic. Again Carinated Bowls are absent in northwest Scotland and the Hebrides. Plain bowls and undecorated lugged bowls are consistently associated with decorated pottery in chambered tomb deposits as far as can be assessed. There are no early C14 dates and there is no good evidence for early contexts. There is no necessary relationship between these pottery assemblages from the tombs and primary use of the monuments.

The pottery from Auchategan (Marshall 1980) is the only published Carinated Bowl assemblage in the Scottish southwest, since comparable pottery in the Luce Sands collection has no contextual integrity (McInnes 1964). The report argues for two phases of Neolithic occupation within an area of c. 10m by 10m. The evidence for a stratigraphic sequence is however very weak. Structural evidence consists of stone settings and hearths, post emplacements, stakeholes, areas of cobbling and discrete patches of dense charcoal. Alternative interpretations to those given of circular huts and working areas are possible. If the two phase plans are amalgamated then a number of linear arrangements can be made. In addition to the pottery, artefacts of greenstone, flint, pitchstone and quartz, and hazelnut shells and small fragments of bone are all present. A C14 date of 2300±110bc comes from hearth 18. Reservations of this date arise from the shallowness of vertical stratigraphy and the evidence for extensive Bronze Age and post-Roman construction activity on the site. The assemblage comprises over 400 sherds (Scott 1980). Many are sooted, part burnt and abraded. C. 60 Carinated and S-profiled Bowls may be represented. Other forms are virtually absent.

In the interim report on Lochhill (Masters 1973), 180+ sherds from Carinated Bowls are recorded from disturbed contexts and from the undisturbed cairn adjacent to the second phase stone chamber. There is no information on any pottery associated with the first phase non-megalithic linear mortuary zone and associated structures for which there is a C14 date of 3120±105bc. At Cairnholy (Piggott and Powell 1949) 100 sherds survive from the broken fragments of a single carinated bowl (dia.230mm).

This was deposited beneath a clean earth spread in the tomb forecourt and below blocking material. Seventy sherds of an upright bowl with ledge carination and out-turned rim survive from within the blocking material itself.

Taken as a whole the evidence for early pottery in the Scottish southwest is minimal. C14 dates provide little pattern, although there are a few early third millennium dates for contexts with individual decorated of elaborately moulded vessels. Claims for stratigraphic sequences from forecourt deposits such as Cairnholy or Monamore, the latter with C14 dates, have little real value. For Scotland as a whole the only strong internal evidence for an early Neolithic pottery horizon is provided by the Carinated Bowl assemblages in the northeast. In the absence of large assemblages and/or well contexted and dated material any overall sequence for pottery development must be premature.

The overall outlines of earlier Neolithic pottery development in Ireland are now relatively secure, both from the viewpoint of internal typology, the pattern of C14 dates, and the few instances of relative stratigraphy. Since both the argument and the evidence for it are presented in Sheridan (1986) there is no purpose in simple repetition. From the perspective of this paper, fine undecorated Carinated Bowls with a very few other basic forms, define an early Neolithic horizon. The middle Neolithic sees the appearance of specific vessel types in novel forms and decoration, a wider assemblage variability in forms and fabric quality, and a regionalization of particular styles. The carinated form in Ireland persists as a paradigm pottery model, on which decoration is usually restrained or absent although formal elements are commonly exaggerated. The latter effects a modification of the carinated form so that the angular division of the vessel is often transformed into the structural elements of ledge shoulder or cordon.

Within this pattern of development the large highly variable assemblages at Lyles Hill and Lough Gur (Evans 1953; Ó Ríordáin 1954) can be regarded as typical products of these middle Neolithic developments. As highly functional and structured assemblages they compare well with the large decorated assemblages of southern England. If Broome Heath is removed from the class of British Carinated Bowl assemblages, then so is Lyles Hill not a Carinated Bowl assemblage. Neither of the two major descriptive sources for the Grimston/Lyles Hill Series as defined are in fact composed of Carinated Bowls.

Any discussion of these bowls in Ireland must begin with Ballynagilly (ApSimon 1976), despite the fact that the lack of full publication imposes limits to interpretation. The illustrated earlier Neolithic pottery, although divided into two groups on the basis of associated C14 dates, are not noticeably different from each other. Carinated Bowls appear to be exclusively present. The variability in rim form within each group seems as high as that between groups. The fluted sherds in the later group are not sufficient in themselves to suggest any demonstrable change in stylistic development.

Two pits containing pottery, and a hearth associated with pottery, provide four C14 dates between 3795 and 3550bc. These extreme dates are hard to reconcile with others for Carinated Bowls or those for the Neolithic in the British Isles as a whole. If the often quoted early date from Broome Heath is rejected, these four dates stand alone, and their significance should be shelved for the present, as currently unsupported and uninterpretable. Other dates directly associated with pottery from Ballynagilly are more consistent with expectation. Two dates of 3280±125 and 3215±50bc for what may be part of a long-house structure, and dates of 2960 ±90 and 2885±55bc for two pits. Other early dates given for Ballynagilly have no record of associated pottery.

Other C14 dates relevant for Carinated Bowls in Ireland lie in the range given by the later dates at Ballynagilly. In nearly all instances they are from the north of Ireland. A carinated assemblage associated with a hearth at Mad Man's Window (Woodman 1977) has a date of 3145±120bc. Although undated, a sizeable carinated assemblage below passage grave Site L at Newgrange may be from a comparable context to Ballynagilly (O'Kelly et al 1978). It is associated with pits, areas of burning and much charcoal. Cultural material includes charcoal, struck flint and bone (some burnt). Other similar site contexts are those of the hearth site at Dunmurry (Whelan 1938), the scatter of sherds and struck flint at Feltrim Hill (Hartnett and Eogan 1964), Shane's Castle (unpub. Sheridan 1986) where the assemblage includes sharply carinated and fluted vessels, and Tullywiggan (Bamford 1971; Sheridan 1986) where both Carinated and S-profiled Bowls are associated with pits, hearth and struck flint. Some of the pottery at the latter site shows evidence of thermal damage.

Carinated sherds are associated with industrial flint extraction at Ballygalley Hill (Collins 1978). At Langford Lodge (Waterman 1963) carinated sherds and struck flint are associated with a length of ditch, pits or postholes, stakeholes and boulders. The latter may represent the surviving evidence of post and stone settings of a rectilinear structure and can be compared to that at Ballynagilly and at Ballyglass. The longhouse at Ballyglass (Ó Nulláin 1972) may have been intentionally demolished prior to construction of the elaborate court tomb. Rim forms from the house structure are of simple form, although no sharp carinated sherds are present. Five C14 dates range from 2530–2730bc, although whether these are for primary structural elements is not clear.

Also beneath a group of passage graves at Knowth (Eogan 1984) are a series of structures associated with carinated and other plainware pottery. These comprise a large sub-rectangular enclosure with a central area of paving and an offset area of burning and charcoal, two parallel palisade trenches that overly this, possible rectilinear post and slot structures, and areas of pebbling. There is a date of 2902±71bc for one large pit with associated pottery. These structures cannot all be contemporary. The sherds from the enclosure primary fill appear to be from simple Carinated Bowls only, whereas sherds from other (later) contexts include occasional lugs, cordons and exaggerated shoulders.

There is a date of 3060±170bc for the small sample of pre-cairn deposit excavated at the round cairn at Knockiveagh (Collins 1957). This thick dark soil which extended beyond the cairn kerb contained much charcoal, burnt bone, pottery, struck flint and stone axe fragments. Burnt human bone occurred in horizontal scatters within the main cairn mass. An earth bank was stacked around the boulder kerb, and an earthen cover sealed the cairn itself. Pottery was found as distinct concentrations in the pre-cairn soil and in the earth bank. External and internal fluting occurs on a number of the Carinated Bowls represented.

The pottery information from court cairn contexts is highly variable. At Tully (Waterman 1978), small quantities of fine quality sherds (possibly from Carinated Bowls) were associated with cremated deposits over the floor of chamber 1, and with dates of 2940±65 and 2835±85bc. A small carinated assemblage was associated with charcoal and struck flint (some burnt) below the court cairn at Ballymarlagh (Davies 1949) with a date of 3050±50bc (approx, Sheridan 1986). This pattern is repeated at Ballybriest (Evans 1939), where burnt human bone was also recorded from the pre-cairn deposit. Small stone-lined pits also occurred. Hemispherical bowls occur in addition to fine carinated forms. There are two C14 dates of 3095±95 and 2980±80bc. A small group of fine carinated sherds were recovered from the pre-court cairn non-megalithic phase at Ballymackaldrack (Evans 1938; Collins 1976). This is defined by three axial pits and intervening cremation deposits within a stone-walled linear zone. C14 dates for this first phase monument are 3200±90 and 2990 ±50bc. Hemispherical bowls (two decorated) and a decorated closed Carinated Bowl are related to the use of the second phase megalithic monument with single chamber, stone façade and forecourt.

Elsewhere the relationship of Carinated Bowls to other pottery classes in court cairns and to their construction, use and modification is unclear. This is the case with the fine carinated pottery from chamber B at Creevykeel (Hencken 1939), those from chambers I and II at Clontygora Large Cairn (Davies and Patterson 1938), those from the internal pits and chamber deposits at Ballyalton (Evans and Davies 1938) and those from the forecourt and chambers at Browndod (Evans and Davies 1936).

Pre-3000 C14 dates are now available for monuments in the passage-grave cemetery at Carrowmore (Burenhult 1980). No pottery is certainly associated with the initial use of these monuments, and they appear as a regional and chronological anomaly in the early Irish Neolithic. In structural design however they are closely matched by the monument at Ballintoy, Antrim (Mogey 1941), with central megalithic chamber, boulder kerb circle and stone infill. An extensive black charcoal-rich layer which underlies this cairn contains sherds of carinated pottery, struck flint and cremated bone.

There are no C14 dates relevant to Irish portal dolmens, and virtually all associated material cannot be regarded as dating the structures (*contra* Herity 1964). On the evidence of sherd distribution there is reason to regard the plain carinated sherds at Ballykeel (Collins 1965) as primary to the monument, the origin of which is unrelated to the presence of the elaborate decorated shouldered bowls from within the chamber.

A model for the development of Neolithic pottery in the British Isles can be characterized as a movement from simple to complex, from the universal to the particular. The elaboration of functional and stylistic variation is regionally and contextually expressed. Specific trends are the expansion of forms from an initially restricted set and the introduction and extension of decorative design. These archaeological trends can be interpreted from two directions. They are a direct consequence of a greater everyday use of pottery in order to fulfill a wider range of functional requirements in the middle Neolithic. A partition and differentiation in the social contexts of ceramic use may have material expression through stylistic differentiation of individual vessels and ceramic suites.

This general model underlies all regional sequences in Britain and Ireland. A common background to these developments lies in the chronological and contextual integrity of an early Neolithic horizon across the British Isles. The archaeological marker of this horizon, and a consistent feature of its cultural representation, is the fine Carinated Bowl.

C14 Chronology, Archaeological and Social Contexts for the Carinated Bowl

C14 evidence allows a chronological definition of Carinated Bowls and reveals their relationship with an early Neolithic horizon. This is best expressed in graphical form. Table 2.2 shows the total available sample of C14 dates for the British and Irish Neolithic grouped within one hundred year intervals and taken down to 2500bc. There is no common basis from which to accept the validity of the isolated dates prior to 3300bc. A high proportion of these dates are from the single anomalous circumstance of Ballynagilly. Where to denote the beginning of the visible Neolithic on this curve is open to debate. It is useful to break down Table 2.2 into its regional components, as is done in Table 2.3. The most mature curve is that for southeast England and this follows the general statistical outline of Table 2.2. The remainder all show a pickup in dates between 3100 and 3200bc. Given the small sample size regional differences should not be overemphasized. The first appearance of a Neolithic archaeological record across the British Isles as a whole can reasonably be placed within an interval shortly before 3000bc.

As a comparison to Tables 2.2 and 2.3 which show C14 dates from all Neolithic sources, Table 2.4 shows the dating evidence, by region and combined, for those Neolithic contexts with Carinated Bowls. The total column does not match the remainder, as only a single averaged date is recorded for multiple dated contexts. This removes the dominance of such contexts as Sweet Track and Fochabers. Two patterns are apparent. The overall range of dates is highly restricted, and statistically may be limited to the interval 3150–2850bc. The range of dates for each region across the British Isles are all comparable with each other. An horizon for Carinated Bowls, both geographically diverse and temporally limited, is demonstrated.

The practical value of isolating Carinated Bowl assemblages is shown by a comparison of Table 2.4 with that of Table 2.1b for assemblages classified as within the Grimston/Lyles Hill Series. Statistically, chronological definition is improved by an order of 3x. A comparison with Table 2.1a shows that for southeast England, as for elsewhere, the overlap between decorated and carinated assemblages is minimal, if present at all.

Comparing Table 2.4 with Tables 2.2 and 2.3 shows the close relationship of Carinated Bowls with the evidence for the Early Neolithic of the British Isles. Many of the other dated sites of this period, those that show no excavated evidence for Carinated Bowls, can be directly related in terms of structure and depositional process to sites that do show this evidence.

Detailed discussion of the archaeological contexts given above for Carinated Bowls must be limited since to consider these particular sites in isolation is unwarranted and to cover all early Neolithic evidence is beyond the scope of the paper. Carinated Bowls are a frequent occurrence over a wide range of diverse mortuary sites, often as part of burial deposits that appear to be the product of common practices, even if specific structural or monumental forms show local or regional differentiation. Other contexts, whether as sealed surface or as pit deposits, show an expression of commonality with these mortuary sites through the makeup of the deposits and their material content. Single or multiple deposition of characterising vessel segments is one obvious point of identity. Further instances of depositional practice occur from shaft contexts and from the Sweet Track, at the latter matched by jadeite and flint axe placements. Carinated Bowls from settlement contexts are also a consistent occurrence. But as indicated below, the division settlement/funerary hinders rather than assists understanding, this might be shown for example with the cranial fragments from the pre-cairn structure at Gwernvale. To work from this particular instance and interpret the Gwernvale structure as a mortuary house only compounds confusion of interpretation.

The archaeological contexts for the depositional circumstances of Carinated Bowls cuts across conventional divides between the 'domestic' and the 'ritual', between settlement and funerary evidence. This can be understood in two ways. Carinated Bowls may have an appropriate function, with different meanings attached to them and to their use, in these different settings. Alternatively, it is the interpretative categories by which these constructed settings are understood that are inappropriate. The social functions and meanings that may be held by

Table 2.3 British and Irish Neolithic radiocarbon dates by region (pre-2500bc)

C14 yrs bc	Southeast England	Wales and southwest England	Northern England	Ireland	Scotland
2500	*************	*****††††	***	*******	*******************
2600	*************	****††††††††	****	*******	******
2700	*****************	****††††††††	*******	*****	*********
2800	**************	****††††††††	****	******	*********
2900	***********	****††	******	******	********
3000	**********	******†	******	******	********
3100	****	***	****	**	*
3200	*******	****†††	**	***	
3300	****	****††	**	*	
3400	**				
3500	****		*		
3600	*			**	**
3700	*	†		***	**
3800				**	*
3900					
4000+					

† dates on Somerset Levels structures

Table 2.4 Radiocarbon dates for carinated bowls, by region and total.

C14 yrs bc	Southeast England	Wales and southwest England	Northern England	Scotland	Ireland	Total (1 per context)
2500	**					*
2600		†				
2700	*	†	**	*		**
2800	*	†	*			***
2900	****	*††	*	****	***	*********
3000	*****	†	*	***	****	*********
3100	*	**††††	*	**	***	*********
3200	*	******††	**		**	**
3300	*	***			*	****
3400						
3500						
3600					*	*
3700					**	*
3800					*	*
3900						
4000+			*			

* inc. dates on Sweet Track structures
† dates on Sweet Track tree-ring series

24

Carinated Bowls do not neatly divide into two categories of use and sense. Social practices that are referenced through material culture are highly complex and are situated in a lived world that cannot simply be represented as a related set of functional spheres with determined behaviours.

From this position it cannot be assumed that the archaeological record allows in itself any valid statement about the social practices, and meanings involved in the practices, that may surround any particular material circumstance. Social practices are simply not constrained by their immediate setting, in time or in space. As an instance, the funerary record for the early Neolithic is dominated by the evidence for deposits of disarticulated, multiple and usually burnt human bone. These deposits, from similar or from very different archaeological contexts, may have been intended as final deposition, or they may not have been. They may have been the product of long-term or immediate collection of their constituent parts. Different cultural transformations in the meaning and value of this material will have taken place. This may be materially expressed through the construction and destruction of formal enclosures, spaces or buildings, and through burial exhumation and reburial. These different activities may have occurred in a number of settings and over long periods of time. At some points in this process it may be that the activities and their locations bear no resemblance to 'funerary activities' and 'funerary sites' at all. Social practices and meanings about such deposits are not simply those concerned with the appropriate treatment of the dead. They are bound into wider concerns of the agricultural, generational and cosmological cycles, into both material and cultural reproduction of the lived world itself.

It is not therefore surprising that particular components of the archaeological record tend to recur in novel combinations and in very different circumstances. This is the position from which to consider the social context of Carinated Bowls at the beginning of the Neolithic in the British Isles. The chronology, formal definition and archaeological contexts for these bowls has been given in this paper. The problems for interpretation are inherent in the above. One response is to be pessimistic about the possibilities for an adequate understanding of the real past through the interpretation of archaeological evidence. An alternative view is to recognize the possibilities for understanding through a contextually situated approach to the material culture record.

Carinated Bowls are typically vessels of extreme high quality. This is evident from the care spent on preparation of the clays and fillers, on the construction and surface treatment and on firing. Where 'coarsewares' are present, these too are of high quality. As the first pottery present in the British and Irish Neolithic, the apparent paradox of this technical expertise with no previous indigenous ceramic tradition is self-evident. Explanatory accounts have been traditionally those that invoke settlement into these islands from the continent of people knowledgeable in ceramic science and practice. Similar pottery does occur in the same period from the Netherlands and from northwest France. Nevertheless it must be accepted that the archaeological record for this material on the continent is far weaker than that for the British Isles itself. This is so much the case that Louwe Kooijmans (1976) accounts for the carinated pottery from Het Vormer and Hazendonk II by suggesting movement or ideas from Britain, rather than the other way round.

If immediate precursors are not apparent, then perhaps the argument is in fact false, rather than view the absence of comparanda as simply a result of the low scale or attention of archaeological research in these areas. This latter sort of reasoning parallels that which would account for the absence of Linearbandkeramik pottery in Britain simply by the failure to find it. The precision of the main sequence continental chronology is such that when compared with the actual evidence for the beginnings of the Neolithic in the British Isles, there is a credibility gap inherent in the settlement model. The primary Neolithic of the North European Plain is a result of colonization and settlement. For a continuation of this process to have taken place in the British Isles, a hiatus of over 500 uncalibrated years must be accounted for.

Alternative frameworks for indigenous Neolithic origins are now well developed for Denmark (Zvelebil & Rowley-Conwy 1984), the Rhine-Meuse delta (Louwe Kooijmans 1976), and Brittany (Kinnes 1984). The first two have been accepted because they are based on well-defined frameworks of local empirical sequences. The last is accepted because the available evidence contains contradictions for a settlement model application. The reasons why indigenous models have not been traditionally applied to the British Isles are complex and are not considered here. There seems no good reason not to apply such models.

Existing knowledge of the later Mesolithic of the British Isles is extremely limited and highly partial. Overall parameters such as population and economic base can only be modelled on very little evidence. This is equally the case for the early Neolithic, where settlement and economic models invariably make use of data that is either weak, not applicable or absent. A critique of this situation is in Kinnes, this volume. The only valid statement that can be made for the appearance of the Neolithic in the British Isles is that it is recognized solely as a phenomenon of material representation. There is no visible Mesolithic/Neolithic transition (*contra* Bradley 1978), only a relatively rapid transformation in the means and forms of cultural expression. There is no archaeological evidence for economic transition. The formulation of account for 'Neolithicisation' that make use of existing data-sets must necessarily be directed at transformations in the meanings and uses of material culture, and so to the social practices within which these are located.

The Neolithic is a transformation of existing structures, from which only one is perceived, that of material production and reproduction. Material symbols occupy positions within this structure that are contextually situated and highly meaningful, they may be ambiguous and they may be powerful.

The Carinated Bowl is a material symbol; in its production it is a cultural transformation of natural elements; in its use it is both an object in itself and a container for others; its final consumption is a subject for concern since it is inherently ambiguous.

This is a long way from saying how is it made and what is it used for. It is of course true that pots are used as containers and have determinate functions in this sense. But it is through the contexts of use, and the meanings attached to pots as material objects and to pottery as a material category, that significance is located. The very quality of Carinated Bowls, the restrictions on appropriate form, and the contexts of their deposition, mark out this class of objects as meaningful in their own right. The significance of the Carinated Bowl lies in itself as a unique material symbol, rather than as part of a suite of internally differentiated vessels, in which each individual class vessel is situated in a pragmatic context of specific function. The latter instance is applicable to an understanding of design and functional variability in middle Neolithic assemblages, where pots and their uses have become an integrated part of the material and social structures of everyday living. The utilitarian pottery as an undetermined cultural product to become a vehicle via assemblage and design differentiation for representing and producing other sets of structural relationships in the social world.

This is not the case with Carinated Bowls. Their form denies the possibility of differentiation, their manufacture emphasises the value of the product itself. Referring back to the paradox given above, the difficulty in reconciling high quality production with an absence of ceramic tradition is only a problem given a conception of pots as being nothing but containers for utilitarian use. Even assuming that Carinated Bowls did function as vessels for storage and cooking the introduction of novel techniques such as boiling food is not simply the recognition of possibility, but must have affected radical changes in the cultural categories and symbolic boundaries that are built around the consumption of edible food. Given this sort of context, it would not be surprising if the manufacture of such vessels was a carefully controlled procedure, one hedged around with formalized rules and practices, that both made the outcome symbolically safe and pragmatically successful. The introduction of potting and the techniques for it, must almost certainly have been introduced through established networks with the continent, but this is no intrinsic reason for supposing a lengthy interval in the gaining of technical expertise.

As is suggested above, the uses to which Carinated Bowls are put are also likely to be constrained within the sets of meanings that underlie these social contexts. The final treatment and disposal of these bowls is again dictated by their conception as material symbols, as part of the material representation of Neolithic society. The maintenance of reproductive cycles, through social practice, is a dominant interest. Structured deposition of the material symbols of Carinated Bowls, animal bone and human remains can be seen as the material expression of these interests.

In conclusion, the Carinated Bowl defines archaeologically an horizon for the inception of the Neolithic across the British Isles. It is also a material symbol that is given meaning in specific social practices that also define this Neolithic horizon. Both contexts provide a time and a place for the Grimston Bowl.

Acknowledgements

I acknowledge information and assistance, support and criticism from a number of individuals: Jim Hibbs, Ian Kinnes, Stuart Needham, Niall Sharples, Alison Sheridan, Nick Thorpe and Sarah Yates. My apologies to a long-suffering John Barrett, without whom I would never have finished.

References

Alexander J. 1961 The excavation of the Chestnuts megalithic tomb at Addington, Kent. *Archaeol. Cantiana* 76:1–57.

ApSimon A.M. 1969 An early Neolithic house in Co. Tyrone. *J. Royal Soc. Antiqu. Ireland* 99:165–168.

ApSimon A.M. 1976 Ballynagilly and the beginning and end of the Irish Neolithic. In S.J. de Laet (ed) *Acculturation and Continuity in Atlantic Europe*. Bruges, pp.15–30.

Ashbee P. 1966 The Fussell's Lodge long barrow excavations 1957. *Archaeologia* 100:1–80.

Ashbee P., Smith I.F. and Evans J.G. 1979 Excavation of three long barrows near Avebury, Wiltshire. *Proc. Prehist. Soc.* 45:207–300.

Atkinson R.J.C. 1962 Fishermen and farmers. In S. Piggott, (ed) *Prehistoric Peoples of Scotland*. pp.1–32.

Bamford H. 1971 Tullywiggan. *Excavations in Ulster* 1971:24–25.

Bamford H. 1985 *Briar Hill*. Northampton Development Corporation.

Bradley R. 1978 *The Prehistoric Settlement of Britain*. Routledge, London.

Bradley R. 1984 *The Social Foundations of Prehistoric Britain* Longman, London.

Bradley R. *et al.* 1976 The excavation of a Neolithic site at Cannon Hill, Maidenhead, Berkshire, 1974–75. *Berks. Arch. J.* 68:5–19.

Brewster T.C.M. 1984 *Whitegrounds Barrow* 1, *Burythorpe, North Yorkshire*, East Yorkshire Archaeological Committee, Malton, Yorkshire.

Brindley, A.L., Lanting, J.N. and Mook, W.G. 1983 Radiocarbon dates from the Neolithic burials at Balintruer More,Co. Wicklow and Ardcrony, Co. Tipperary. *J. of Irish Arch.* 1:1–9.

Briscoe, G. 1956 Swale's Tumulus: a combined Neolithic A and Bronze Age barrow at Worlington, Suffolk. *Proc. Cambs. Antiqu. Soc.* 50:101–112.

Britnell W.J. and Savory H.N. 1984 *Gwernvale and Penywyrlod: Two Neolithic long cairns in the Black Mountains of Brecknock*. Cambrian Archaeological Monographs No 2.

Brown A.E. (ed) 1983 Archaeology in Northamptonshire 1982. *Northants Arch.* 18:171–172.

Burchell J.P.T. and Piggott, S. 1939 Decorated prehistoric pottery from the bed of the Ebbsfleet, Northfleet, Kent, *Antiqu. J* 19:405–420.

Burenhult G. 1980 *The Archaeological Excavation at Carrowmore, Co Sligo, Ireland*, Excavation Seasons 1977–79, Theses and Papers in North-European Archaeology 9, Stockholm.

Burl H.A.W. 1985 Report on the excavation of a Neolithic mound at Boghead, Speymouth Forest, Fochabers, Moray, 1972 and 1974. *Proc. Soc. Antiqu. Scotland* 114:1–38.

Case H. 1956 The Neolithic causewayed camp at Abingdon, Berkshire. *Antiqu. J.* 36:11–30.

Case H. 1961 Irish Neolithic pottery: distribution and sequence. *Proc. Prehist. Soc.* 27:174–223.

Case H. 1963 Foreign connections in the Irish Neolithic. *Ulster J. Archaeol.* 26:3–18.

Case H. 1969a Neolithic explanations. *Antiquity* 43:176–186.

Case H. 1969b Settlement-patterns in the north Irish Neolithic. *Ulster J. Archaeol.* 28:47–70.

Case H.J. and Whittle A.W.R. 1982 The pottery, Abingdon causewayed enclosure. *Settlement Patterns in the Oxford Region.* CBA Research Report No. 44:26–33.

Childe V.G. 1932 The continental affinities of British Neolithic pottery. *Archaeol. J.* 88:37–66.

Clark J.G.D. 1966 The invasion hypothesis in British Archaeology. *Antiquity* 40:172–189.

Clark J.G.D. and Godwin H. 1962 The Neolithic in the Cambridgeshire Fens. *Antiquity* 36:10–23.

Clark J.G.D, Godwin H & M.E. and Clifford M.H. 1935 Report on recent excavation at Peacock's Farm, Shippea Hill, Cambridgeshire. *Antiqu. J.* 15:284–319.

Clark J.G.D., Higgs E.S. and Longworth I.H. 1960 Excavations at the Neolithic site at Hurst Fen, Mildenhall, Suffolk, 1954, 1957 and 1958, *Proc. Prehist. Soc.* 26:202–245.

Clark J.G.D. and Piggott S. 1933 The age of the British flint mines. *Antiquity* 7:166–183.

Coles J.M., Hibbert F.A. and Orme B.J. 1973 Prehistoric roads and tracks in Somerset 3: The Sweet Track. *Proc. Prehist. Soc.* 39:256–293.

Coles J.M. and Orme B.J. 1979 The Sweet Track: Drove site. *Somerset Levels Papers* 5:43–64.

Coles J.M. and Orme B.J. 1984 Ten excavations along the Sweet Track (3200 bc). *Somerset Levels Papers* 10:5–45.

Coles J.M. and Simpson D.D.A. 1965 The excavation of a Neolithic round barrow, at Pitnacree, Perthshire, Scotland. *Proc. Prehist. Soc.* 31:34–57.

Collins A.E.P. 1957 Trial excavations in a round cairn on Knockiveagh, Co. Down. *Ulster J. Archaeol.* 20:8–28.

Collins A.E.P. 1965 Ballykeel dolmen and cairn, Co. Armagh. *Ulster J. Archaeol.* 28:47–70.

Collins A.E.P. 1976 Doey's Cairn, Ballymacaldrack, County Antrim. *Ulster J. Archaeol.* 39:1–7.

Collins A.E.P. 1978 Excavations on Ballygalley Hill, County Antrim. *Ulster J. Archaeol.* 41:15–32.

Corcoran J.X.W.P. 1966 The excavation of three chambered cairns at Loch Calder, Caithness. *Proc. Soc. Antiqu. Scotland* 98:1–75.

Curwen E.C. 1934 A late Bronze Age farm and a Neolithic pit-dwelling on New Barn Down, Clapham, near Worthing. *Sussex Archaeol. Coll.* 75:137– 170.

Darbishire R.D. 1874 Notes on discoveries in Ehenside Tarn, Cumberland. *Archaeologia* 44:273–292.

Davies O. 1940 Excavations at Legland horned cairn. *Proc. and Reps. Belfast Nat. Hist. and Phil. Soc.* 2S, 1 pt.5:16–24.

Davies O. 1949 Excavations at the horned cairn of Ballymarlagh, Co. Antrim. *Ulster J. Archaeol.* 12:26–42.

Davies O. and Paterson, T.G.F. 1938 Excavations at Clontygora Large Cairn, Co. Armagh, *Proc. and Reps. Belfast Nat. Hist. and Phil. Soc.* 1, 2S:20–42.

Drury P.J. 1978 *Excavations at Little Waltham.* CBA Report 26, London.

Dunning G.C. 1966 Neolithic occupation sites in East Kent. *Antiqu. J.* 46:1–25.

Eogan G. 1984 *Excavations at Knowth* Vol. 1. *Smaller Passage Tombs, Neolithic Occupation and Beaker Activity,* Royal Irish Acad. Arch. Monograph 1.

Evans E.E. 1938 Doey's Cairn, Dunloy, Co. Antrim, *Ulster J. Archaeol.* 1:59–78.

Evans E.E. 1939 Excavations at Carnanbane, County Londonderry: a double horned Cairn, *Proc. Royal Irish Academy* 45C:1–12.

Evans E.E. 1953 *Lyles Hill: A Late Neolithic Site in County Antrim,* Archaeological Research Publications (Northern Ireland), no.2, Belfast.

Evans E.E. and Davies O. 1935 Excavation of a chambered horned cairn at Ballyalton, Co. Down. *Proc. and Reps. Belfast Nat. Hist. and Phil. Soc.* 1933–34:79–104.

Evans E.E. and Davies O. 1936 Excavation of a chambered horned cairn, Browndod, Co. Antrim. *Proc. and Reps. Belfast Nat. Hist. and Phil. Soc.* 1934–35:70–87.

Gibson A. 1985 A Neolithic enclosure at Grendon, Northants. *Antiquity* 59:213–219.

Green H.S. 1976 The excavation of a late Neolithic settlement at Stacey Bushes, Milton Keynes, and its significance. In C. Burgess and R. Miket (eds) *Settlement and Economy in the Third and Second Millennia bc.* BAR 33. Oxford.

Greenfield E. 1960 A Neolithic pit and other finds from Wingham, East Kent. *Archeologia Cantiana* 74:58–72.

Greenwell W. 1877 *British Barrows.* Oxford.

Harding A.F. 1981 Excavations in the prehistoric ritual complex near Milfield, Northumberland. *Proc. Prehist. Soc.* 47:87–135.

Hartnett P.J. and Eogan G. 1964 Feltrim Hill, Co. Dublin: a Neolithic and Early Christian site. *J. Royal Soc. Antiqu. Ireland* 94:1–37.

Hawkes J. 1935 The place of origin of the Windmill Hill culture. *Proc. Prehist. Soc.* 1:127–129.

Healy F. 1984 Farming and field monuments: the Neolithic in Norfolk. In C. Barringer C. (ed) *Aspects of East Anglian Prehistory.* Geo Books, Norwich, pp. 77–140.

Hedges J. and Buckley D. 1978 Excavations at a Neolithic causewayed enclosure, Orsett, Essex, 1975. *Proc. Prehist. Soc.* 44:219–308.

Hemp W.J. 1936 The chambered cairn known as Bryn yr Hen Bobl, near Plas Newydd, Angelesey. *Archaeologia* 85:253–292.

Hencken H.O'N. 1939 A long cairn at Creevykeel, Co. Sligo. *J. Royal. Soc. Antiqu. Ireland* 69:53–98.

Henshall A.S. 1963 *The Chambered Tombs of Scotland* Vol. I. Edinburgh.

Henshall A.S. 1972 *The Chambered Tombs of Scotland* Vol. II. Edinburgh.

Henshall A.S. 1983a The pottery. In J.W. Hedges *Isbister, a Chambered Tomb in Orkney* BAR 115, Oxford.

Henshall A.S. 1983b The Neolithic pottery from Easterton of Roseisle, Moray. In A. O'Connor and D.V. Clarke (eds) *From the Stone Age to the 'Forty-Five.*

Henshall A.S. 1985 The pottery. In H.A.W. Burl, Report on the excavation of a Neolithic mound at Boghead, Speymouth Forest, Fochabers, Morsay, 1972 and 1974. *Proc. Soc. Antiqu. Scotland* 114:1–39.

Herity M. 1964 The finds from the Irish portal dolmens. *J. Royal Soc. Antiqu. Ireland* 94:123–144.

Herity M. 1982 Irish decorated Neolithic pottery. *Proc. Royal Irish Academy* 82C:247–404.

Herring I.J. 1937 The forecourt, Hanging Thorn Cairn, M'Ilwan's Hill, Ballyutoag, Ligoniel. *Proc. and Reps. Belfast Nat. Hist. and Phil. Soc.* 1, 2S:43–49.

Herring I.J. 1941 The Tamneyrankin cairn: west structure. *J. Royal. Soc. Antiqu. Ireland* 71:31–52.

Hope-Taylor B. 1977 *Yeavering, an Anglo-Saxon Centre of Early Northumbria.* London.

Houlder C.H. 1963 A Neolithic settlement on Hazard Hill, Totnes. *Proc. Devon Archaeol. Exploration Soc.* 6.21:2–31.

Houlder. C.H. 1968 The henge monuments at Llandegai. *Antiquity* 42:216–221.

Houlder C.H. 1976 Stone axes and henge monuments. In G.C. Boon and J.M. Lewis (eds) *Welsh Antiquity.* National Museum of Wales.

Kinnes I. 1978 The Neolithic pottery. In J. Hedges and D. Buckley 1978:219–308.

Kinnes I. 1979 *Round Barrows and Ring-Ditches in the British Neolithic.* British Museum Occasional Paper No. 7, London.

Kinnes I. 1984 Microliths and megaliths: monumental origins on the Atlantic façade. In G. Burenhult *The Archaeology of Carrowmore.* Theses and Papers in North-European Archaeology 14, Stockholm, pp. 367–370.

Kinnes I. and Thorpe I.J. 1986 Radiocarbon dating: use and abuse. *Antiquity* 60:221–223.

Kooi P.B. 1974 De orkaan van 13 november 1972 en het ontstaan van 'hoefijzervormige' grondsporen. *Helinium* 14:57–65.

Leeds E.T. 1927 A Neolithic site at Abingdon, Berkshire. *Antiqu. J.* 7:438–464.

Leaf C.S. 1940 Further excavations in the Bronze Age barrows at Chippenham, Cambridgeshire. *Proc. Cambs. Antiqu. Soc* 39:29–68.

Liddell D.M. 1930 Report on the excavations at Hembury Fort, Devon, 1930. *Proc. Devon Archaeol. Exploration Soc.* 12:39–63.

Liddell D.M. 1931 Report of the excavations at Hembury Fort, Devon: 2nd season, 1931. *Proc. Devon Archaeol. Exploration Soc.* 13:90–120.

Liddell D.M. 1932 Report on the excavations at Hembury Fort: 3rd season, 1932. *Proc. Devon Archaeol. Exploration Soc.* 14:162–190.

Liddell D.M. 1935 Report on the excavations at Hembury Fort: 4th and 5th seasons, 1934 and 1935. *Proc. Devon Archaeol. Exploration Soc.* 17:135–175.

Longworth I.H. 1960 The pottery. In J.G.D. Clark, E.S. Higgs and I.H. Longworth 1960:228–240.

Longworth I.H. 1961 The origins and development of the primary series in the collared urn tradition in England and Wales. *Proc. Prehist. Soc.* 27:265–306.

Louwe Kooijmans L.P. 1976 Local developments in a borderland. *Oudheid. Meded.*57:227–297.

Louwe Kooijmans L.P. 1980 De midden-neolithische vondstgroep van Het Vormer bij Vijchenen het cultuur-patroon rond de zuidelijke Noordzee circa 3000 v Chr. *Oudheidkundige Mededelingen uit het Rijksmuseum van Oudheden te Leiden* 61:113–208 (with English summary).

Lynch F.M. 1969 The contents of the excavated tombs in North Wales. In T.G.E. Powell *et al.* (eds) *Megalithic Enquiries in the West of Britain.* Liverpool, pp.149–174.

Lynch F.M. 1975 Excavations at Carreg Sampson megalithic tomb, Mathry, Pembrokeshire. *Archaeol. Camb.* 124:15–35.

Lynch F.M. 1976 Towards a chronology of megalithic tombs in Wales. In G.C. Boon and J.M. Lewis (eds) *Welsh Antiquity.* National Museum of Wales, pp.63–80.

Lynch F.M. 1984 The Neolithic pottery: discussion. In W.J. Britnell and H.N. Savory 1984:106–110.

MacInnes I.J. 1964 The Neolithic and Bronze Age pottery from Luce Sands, Wigtownshire. *Proc. Soc. Antiqu. Scotland* 97:40–81.

MacInnes I.J. 1969 A Scottish Neolithic pottery sequence. *Scottish Archaeol. Forum* 1:19–30.

MacKie E.W. 1964 New excavations on the Monamore Neolithic chambered cairn, Lamlash, Isle of Arran, in 1961. *Proc. Soc. Antiqu. Scotland* 97:1–34.

Manby T.G. 1958 A Neolithic site at Craike Hill, Garton Slack, East Riding of Yorkshire. *Antiqu. J.* 38:223–236.

Manby T.G. 1963 The excavation of the Willerby Wold long barrow, East Riding of Yorkshire. *Proc. Prehist. Soc.* 29:173–205.

Manby T.G. 1964 The pottery. In J.W. Moore, Excavations at Beacon Hill, Flamborough Head, East Yorkshire. *Yorks. Archaeol. J.* 41:191–202.

Manby T.G. 1967 *The Neolithic Cultures of the North of England,* Unpublished M.A. Thesis, University of Liverpool.

Manby T.G. 1970 Long barrows of northern England: structural and dating evidence. *Scottish Archaeol. Forum* 2:1–27.

Manby T.G. 1975 Neolithic occupation sites on the Yorkshire Wolds. *Yorks. Archaeol. J.* 47:23–59.

Manby T.G. 1976 The excavation of the Kilham long barrow, East Riding of Yorkshire. *Proc. Prehist. Soc.* 42:111–160.

Marshall D.N. 1980 Excavations at Auchategan, Glendaruel, Argyll. *Proc. Soc. Antiqu. Scotland* 109:36–74.

Masters L. 1973 The Lochhill long cairn. *Antiquity* 47:96–100.

Menghin O. 1925 *Urgeschichte der bildenden Kunst in Europa.* Vienna.

Mercer R. 1980 *Hambledon Hill: a Neolithic landscape.* Edinburgh University Press.

Mercer R. 1984 Excavations at Carn Brea, Illogan, Cornwall. *Cornish Archaeol* 20:1–204.

Miket R. 1976 The evidence for Neolithic activity in the Milfield Basin, Northumberland. In C. Burgess and R. Miket (eds) *Settlement and Economy in the Third and Second Millennia bc,* BAR Oxford.

Milne J. 1892 Traces of Early Man in Buchan. *Trans. Buchan Field Club* (1891–1892):97–108.

Mogey J.M. 1941 The 'Druid Stone', Ballintoy, County Antrim. *Ulster J. Archaeol.* 4:49–56.

Mortimer J.R. 1905 *Forty Years' Researches in the British and Saxon Burial Mounds of East Yorkshire.* London.

Newbigin A.J.W. 1937 The Neolithic of Yorkshire. *Proc. Prehist. Soc.* 3:189–216.

O'Kelly M. *et al.* 1978 The excavation of three passage graves at Newgrange. *Proc. Royal Irish Academy* 78:251–352.

Ó Nulláin S. 1972 A Neolithic house at Ballyglass near Ballycastle, County Mayo. *J. Royal Soc. Antiqu. Ireland* 102:49–57.

Ó Ríordáin, S.P. 1954 Lough Gur excavations: Neolithic and Bronze Age houses on Knockadoon. *Proc. Royal Irish Academy* 56C:297–459.

Orme B.J. 1982 The use of radiocarbon dates from the Somerset Levels. *Somerset.Levels Papers* 8:9–25.

Peacock D.P.S. 1969 Neolithic pottery production in Cornwall. *Antiquity* 43:145–149.

Pierpoint S. 1979 Three radiocarbon dates for Yorkshire prehistory. *Antiquity* 53:224–225.

Phillips C.W. 1935 The excavation of the Giant's Hills barrow, Skendelby, Lincolnshire. *Archaeologia* 85:37–106.

Piggott S. 1932 The Neolithic pottery of the British Isles. *Archaeol. J.* 88:67–158.

Piggott S. 1933 The pottery from the Lligwy burial chamber, Anglesey. *Archaeol. Camb.* 88:68–72.

Piggott S. 1934 The mutual relations of the British Neolithic ceramics. *Proc. Prehist. Soc. East Anglia* 8:373–381.

Piggott S. 1936 Handley Hill Dorset — a Neolithic bowl and the date of the entrenchment. *Proc. Prehist. Soc.* 2:229–230.

Piggott S. 1937 The long barrow in Brittany. *Antiquity* 11:441–455.

Piggott S. 1943 The pottery. In R.E.M. Wheeler 1943.

Piggott S. 1954 *The Neolithic Cultures of the British Isles.* Cambridge

Piggott S. 1955 Windmill Hill — east or west?. *Proc. Prehist. Soc.* 21:96–101.

Piggott S. and Powell T.G.E. 1949 The excavation of three Neolithic chambered tombs in Galloway, 1949. *Proc. Soc. Antiqu. Scotland* 83:101–161.

Pollard S.H.M. 1966 Neolithic and dark age settlements on High Peak, Sidmouth, Devon. *Devon Archaeol. Exploration Soc.* 6.23:35–59.

Powell T.G.E. 1973 Excavation of the chambered cairn at Dyffryn Ardudwy, Merioneth, Wales. *Archaeologia* 104:1–50.

Priddy D. (ed) 1982 Work of the Essex Council Archaeology Section, 1981. *Essex Archaeol and Hist.* 14:111–132.

Proudfoot E. 1965 Bishop's Cannings, Roughridge Hill. *Wilts. Archaeol. Magazine* 60:133.

Pryor F. 1974 *Excavation at Fengate, Peterborough, England: the first Report.* Royal Ontario Museum Archaeology Monograph 3.

Ralegh-Radford C.A. 1958 The chambered tomb at Broadsands, Paignton, *Proc. Devon Archaeol. Exploration Soc.* 5:147–166.

Reaney D. 1968 Beaker burials in south Derbyshire. *Derbyshire Archaeol. J.* 88:68–81.

Saville A. 1985 Preliminary report on the excavation of a Cotswold-Severn tomb at Hazelton, Gloucestershire. *Antiqu. J.* 64:1–9.

Schuchhardt C. 1919 *Alteuropa.* Berlin and Leipzig.

Scott J.G. 1964 The chambered cairn at Beacharra, Kintyre, Argyll, Scotland. *Proc. Prehist. Soc.* 30:134–158.

Scott J.G. 1969 The Clyde cairns of Scotland. In T.G.E. Powell *et al.* (eds) *Megalithic Enquiries in the West of Britain.* Liverpool.

Scott J.G. 1977a The pottery. In D.M. Marshall and I.D. Taylor, The excavation of the chambered tomb at Glenvoidean, Isle of Bute. *Proc. Soc. Antiqu. Scotland* 108:26–37.

Scott J.G. 1977b A note on Beacharra pottery. *Antiquity* 51:240–243.

Scott J.G. 1980 The pottery. In D.N. Marshall 1980:50–60.

Scott W.L. 1933 The chambered tomb of Pant-y-Saer, Anglesey. *Archaeol. Camb.* 88:185–228.

Selkirk A. 1972 Ascott-under-Wychwood. *Current Archaeology* 24:7–10.

Sharples N. 1982 Excavations at Ord North, Lairg, Sutherland. *Proc. Soc. Antiqu. Scotland* 111.

Sharples N. 1986a Radiocarbon dates from three chambered tombs at Loch Calder, Caithness. *Scot. Arch. Review* 4:2–10.

Sharples N. 1986b In discussion, Neolithic Studies Group, Meeting Nov. 1986.

Sheridan A. 1986 *The Role of Exchange Studies in Social Archaeology with Special Reference to the Prehistory of Ireland from the 4th to the Early 2nd Millennium bc.* Unpublished Ph.D Thesis, University of Cambridge.

Simpson D.D.A. 1963 A barrow on Seamer Moor, Yorkshire. *Archaeol. Newsletter* 7:213–214.

Smith A.G., Pilcher J.R. and Pearson G.W. 1971 New radiocarbon dates from Ireland. *Antiquity* 45:97–102.

Smith C. 1981 Trefignath burial chambers, Anglesey. *Antiquity* 55:134–136.

Smith I.F. 1956 *The Decorative Art of Neolithic Ceramics in South-Eastern England and its Relations.* Unpublished Ph.D. Thesis, Institute of Archaeology University of London.

Smith I.F. 1965 *Windmill Hill and Avebury: excavations by Alexander Keiller, 1925–1939.* Clarendon Press, Oxford.

Smith I.F. 1974a The Neolithic pottery from Fengate, 1972. In F. Pryor 1974.

Smith I.F. 1974b The Neolithic. In C. Renfrew (ed) *British Prehistory: a new outline.* Duckworth, London, pp.100–136, 280–287.

Smith I.F. 1984 The Neolithic pottery. In R. Mercer 1984:161–179.

Trent and Peak Archaeol. Trust 1985 *Lismore Fields Buxton, 1985: Summary Report.*

Vatcher F. de M. 1961 Seamer Moor, Yorkshire. *Proc. Prehist. Soc.* 27:34–35.

Vyner B.E. The excavation of a Neolithic cairn at Street House, Loftus, Cleveland. *Proc. Prehist. Soc.* 50:151–196.

Wainwright G.J. 1967 *Coygan Camp: A Prehistoric, Romano-British and Dark Age Settlement in Carmarthenshire,* Cambrian Archaeological Association Monograph.

Wainwright G.J. 1972 The excavation of a Neolithic settlement on Broome Heath, Ditchingham, Norfolk. *Proc. Prehist. Soc.* 38:1–97.

Walker I.K. 1968 Easterton of Roseisle: a forgotten site. In J.M. Coles and D.D.A. Simpson (eds) *Studies in Ancient Europe.* Leicester, pp.95–115.

Warren S.H. *et al.* 1936 Archaeology of the submerged land-surface of the Essex coast. *Proc. Prehist. Soc.* 2:178–210.

Waterman D.M. 1963 A Neolithic and dark age site at Langford Lodge, County Antrim. *Ulster J. Archaeol.* 26:43–54.

Waterman D.M. 1965 The court cairn at Annaghmare, County Armagh. *Ulster J. Archaeol.* 28:3–46.

Waterman D.M. 1978 The excavation of a court cairn at Tully, County Fermanagh. *Ulster J. Archaeol.* 41:3–12.

Watts W.A. 1960 C-14 dating and the Neolithic in Ireland. *Antiquity* 34:111–116.

Wheeler R.E.M. 1943 *Maiden Castle, Dorset.* Res. Rep. Soc. Antiqu. London No.12 London.

Whelan C.B. 1938 Studies in the significance of the Irish Stone Age: the culture sequence. *Proc. Royal Irish Academy* 44C:115–137.

Whittle A.W.R. 1977 *The Earlier Neolithic of Southern England and its Continental Background.* BAR S–35, Oxford.

Williams A. 1952 Clegyr Boia, St David's Pembrokeshire: excavations in 1943. *Archaeol. Camb.* 102:20–47.

Woodman P. 1977 Problems of identification of Mesolithic survivals in Ireland. *Irish Arch. Research Forum* 4:17–27.

Wymer J.J. 1966 Excavations of the Lambourn long barrow. *Berkshire Archaeol. J.* 62:1–16.

Young H.W. 1896 Further excavations at Easterton of Roseisle. *Reliquary Illus. Arch.* 2:39–44.

Zvelebil M. and Rowley-Conwy P. 1984 Transition to farming in northern Europe: a hunter gatherer perspective. *Norwegian Archaeol. Review* 17:104–128.

3. The Living, the Dead and the Ancestors: Neolithic and Early Bronze Age Mortuary Practices

John C. Barrett

The Archaeology of Death

If we are to make sense of the considerable variation in our Neolithic and Bronze Age mortuary data we must be clearer about the procedures used in its analysis. Renfrew has argued that archaeologists should move beyond description and reconstruction to grasp the possibility of explaining the past (Renfrew 1982 & 1984:3ff). This much may be agreed, even if we have only now begun to understand the problems of site formation, making reconstruction a more reliable task. But if we accept that the methodological procedures of reconstruction can be developed we are still faced with the question of what constitutes an explanation.

Renfrew (and others) have argued that our explanations should be concerned with classes of events or general processes, such as 'state formation' or 'the origins of agriculture' (Renfrew 1982). In other words, explanation seeks out the cross cultural process which lies behind empirical regularities. In our case it means that a cross cultural explanation should be possible for variations in mortuary practices. Only in this way, implies Renfrew, can the archaeologist avoid a type of historical particularism which has no general validity and therefore no scientific value. I wish to demonstrate something of the weakness in such an argument and show that, in the particular case of mortuary variability, no general explanation is possible. Instead explanation must take account of the specific historical conditions under which those people acted who made the histories we study. This does not lead to a dead end of historical particularism. To claim that such a thing exists misunderstands the nature of historical scholarship.

Many recent reviews of the archaeological study of mortuary practices place the publications of Saxe (1970) and Binford (1971) at the centre of the current 'conceptual framework' (Tainter 1978; Chapman and Randsborg 1981; O'Shea 1984). Certainly the 'New Archaeology' marks a dislocation in the history of mortuary studies, for it was here that mortuary variability was no longer seen as an expression of cultural belief but rather as a reflection of the organisational principles of the social system itself.

The underlying principle employed by Binford and Saxe was that the treatment of the corpse depended upon the selection and the marking of a number of the social identities which an individual had achieved in life. That selection was made by those who accepted certain social responsibilities towards the deceased. If we consider the social system as comprising a system of roles and statuses, each of which has a call upon particular obligations,

then the formal organisation of burial (described by the range of symbolism and the degree of energy input) supposedly mirrors the formal organisation of the social system. Various ethnographic tests were carried out to support the cross cultural generalisation that social complexity will be matched by mortuary complexity (Binford 1971).

If the argument is accepted a number of methodological issues still remain, and O'Shea has been concerned to follow these through in a specifically archaeological treatment of the data. They include problems of recognising the distinction between 'vertical' divisions of rank and 'horizontal' divisions of status, understanding the historical development of symbolism in a single cemetery, and a more detailed consideration of the formation processes affecting the archaeological record itself (O'Shea 1981 & 1984). But beneath these methodological issues lie more fundamental questions.

We cannot proceed by analysing the organisational form of mortuary data to reveal the form of the social system, and then use the form of the social system to explain the form of the burial data. For example, in his 'hypothesis 8' Saxe states that formal disposal areas may be maintained by particular corporate groups whose claim to the use or control of crucial but restricted resources depended upon lineal descent from the dead (Saxe 1970:119). In archaeology this idea has tended towards circularity; cemeteries are taken to indicate the existence of corporate groups, the need for corporate groups to establish control over 'critical resources' is then assumed (Chapman 1981) and the cemeteries are seen to result from the need to legitimate that claim.

If explanations involve linking general principles to particular cases it is hardly adequate simply to describe the particular in terms of the general. As Hodder has noted, the specific character of the mortuary remains, cemetery architecture and so forth cannot be dealt with in these terms (Hodder 1984:52). Archaeologists often appear trapped in describing the same types of social system by reference to different sets of archaeological material. This has become the basis of so much cross cultural generalisation and model building that the past becomes increasingly uninteresting as we move from one study to the next.

To build an alternative we must recognise that social systems are constructed out of particular social practices. These practices take place within the specific cultural and historical conditions they maintain. Archaeological evidence can tell us something about the way such practices were maintained over time, contributing towards the reproduction of one social system (Barrett 1987). Corporate groups do not *do* anything. They result from institutionalised practices by which people maintain relations of affinity, obligation and enmity, thereby controlling access to certain material and human resources. As Parker Pearson has said, "the reconstruction of social organisation through the identification of roles....can be challenged by the theoretical stance that social systems are not constituted *of* roles but *by* recurrent social practices." (1982:100).

Mortuary rituals are particular types of social practice and we must examine the way they were enacted by the living around the corpse and the grave. The dead do not participate in their own funeral, nor is the entire essence of the social system mapped out by this single practice. Instead death precipitates a requirement for the living to renegotiate certain of their own relations of affinity and obligation. This they may do with reference to the dead, ancestors and gods. The corpse, and the way it was treated, presents a powerful symbolic medium by which the transition from life to death can be represented, a process during which the living reconsider their own legitimate claims of social position and inheritance.

The Archaeology of Ritual

Cultural archaeology seems to have assumed that human action was determined by a received cultural doctrine. However humans are inventive in the formation and maintenance of particular practices. They act in, and upon, a world which is already culturally formed. Their actions are both structured by their experiences of that world and in turn those actions structure their own conditions. By such reflexive monitoring of action the fabric of a social and cultural existence is constructed, including the knowledge people have of the conditions and aims of their actions. Knowledge here is meant to include a practical day to day knowledge of 'how to go on' as well as a discursive awareness whereby the cultural conditions of the world can be brought to mind.

Different practical knowledges therefore exist, but people are able to combine those practical experiences within dominant readings of the wider, cultural regularities of their world. Bloch has recently argued that anthropological work, particularly that of V. Turner, shows that ritual often plays a central role in building these forms of shared discursive knowledge (Bloch 1985; Turner 1967). It is during rituals that fundamental cultural regularities are exposed to participants and observers, because it is during rituals that transitions across social categories are achieved. This means that the categories have to be defined, transgressed and then redefined (Turner 1969).

These ideas have two important implications for archaeology:
1: Ritual is made up of actions, not things. There are no such things as 'ritual sites' or 'ritual objects'. The places where rituals may be enacted and the artefacts used will also have been encountered in the daily routines of life (including the avoidance of sacred ground). The selections of specific times, places and artefacts for ritual dramas are the means by which people draw diverse experiences towards a dominant reading of cultural order. We have to allow for the ambiguities which run through the material world rather than attempt to recover a single meaning for some element of archaeological remains. Hodder has suggested that the megalithic monuments of western Europe "had symbolic associations and meanings and this meaningful context must be considered." He goes on to argue that formal similarities indicate that the tombs "referred symbolically to earlier and contemporary houses in central Europe" (Hodder 1984:53). But meaning is not inherent in the shape of the tomb nor in the house. It is constructed out of people's occupancy, their practical experience, of that architecture. Hodder has not demonstrated how those experiences can be retrieved archaeologically.

2: Particular types of archaeological deposit do not necessarily reflect the occurrence of ritual activity. Archaeologists regularly equate 'ritual' with deposits which they regard as 'symbolic'. But symbolism pervades all areas of life, and it is meaningless to assign ritual to cover all non-mechanical actions (Goody 1961). Daily activities may be organised with reference to ever present gods and ancestors, they may maintain ideas of cultural purity, or they may express divisions of status between the living. The organisation of sites and archaeological deposits are therefore likely to be structured according to particular cultural values without deriving from ritual practices.

Mortuary Rituals

Mortuary rituals are taken here to be those rituals which construct passages between life and death. They may include the passage of human burial, or the intervention of ancestors in the world of the living and they may draw upon ideas of death and rebirth (Bloch and Parry 1982). We must distinguish between ancestor rituals and funerary rituals because human remains may be employed in both. As Kinnes has argued human remains do not simply imply burial (Kinnes 1975:17).

1: *Ancestor rituals* establish the presence of ancestors in rites concerned with the living. Amongst the places and symbols used may be funerary architecture and the bones of the dead. Ancestor rituals may also play a part in the rites of burial.

2: *Funerary rituals* are specifically concerned with human burial. Within this context we can distinguish between inhumation, secondary burial (by which I do *not* mean the perceived order of interment in a barrow or grave) and cremation, depending upon the particular form the 'rite of passage' takes. Van Gennep (1960) recognised a threefold division in rites of passage into rites of separation, rites of liminality and rites of incorporation. The first and last are moments of cultural stability, separated by the transformation of the liminal period. Turner has developed this observation and examined the way each stage in the ritual process may be marked out by different forms of symbolism.

31

Archaeologists do not observe the entire sequence of a burial rite. In the case of inhumation the liminal period may terminate as the body is placed in the grave; the body is incorporated into death as the mourners return to the living. Symbolism associated with the liminal transformation of the body, and the segregation of the mourners, may therefore be carried over into the grave and thus preserved archaeologically. Such symbolism may include the adornment of the corpse (not to be confused with the dress of the living *contra* Pader 1982), an adornment which forms the basis for some of our 'richer' grave assemblages (Barrett 1985:104). With these ideas in mind it is obviously important to distinguish carefully between objects found within and those placed outside a coffin; for these different sets of material are likely to derive from different moments of the ritual process.

Secondary burial (Hertz 1960; Huntington & Metcalf 1979:13) involves a lengthy liminal period with the corpse being buried or stored before being recovered and reinterred at the close of the burial process. These final rites may be separated spatially from the places associated with liminality. A similar separation may be achieved by cremation. Here the rites of incorporation may commence with the lighting of the funeral pyre, only to be completed by the collection and sorting of the ashes and their final dispersal or burial. The separation of rites of incorporation from the earlier rites of liminality in both secondary burial and cremation may be great enough to ensure that the symbolism associated with liminality is discarded by the time deposits finally enter the 'archaeological record'. The methodological implication is to prevent comparisons between inhumation and cremation assemblages, for we are not comparing like with like.

These different rites also structure the topographical relationships of death in different ways. Whilst inhumation appears to fix both the place and the moment at which the transition of death is arrested for both the mourners and the corpse at the grave with its infilling, secondary burial and cremation establish a topographical separation between rites of liminality and the final rites of incorporation. The place of transition is separated from that place at which the ritual sequence as a whole is brought to a close. These differences are important for any consideration of funerary ritual which is concerned with the way the mourners use the process to construct their relation with the dead and ancestors. It is by the construction of these passages between life and death, within an architectural and topographical framework which may be constantly re-used, that certain lines of inherited authority are preserved or challenged.

Neolithic and Early Bronze Age Mortuary Practices

It has been a commonly agreed convention that the late Neolithic witnessed a change in mortuary rituals, with a shift away from 'communal burial'

towards a 'single-grave tradition'. Alongside this other trends have been identified, including the construction of round, in place of the earlier long, mounds, and the inclusion of 'grave goods' in the mortuary rituals. These changes, recognised in the nineteenth century (Thurnam 1869 & 1872), came to be taken as a distinct horizon of cultural discontinuity associated with the introduction of beakers (Abercromby 1912).

The abandonment of this apparent cultural horizon arose from the desire to break with cultural explanations, and with the empirical realisation that the sequence of material is more complex. Radiocarbon dates have lengthened the timescale of the period, loosening those cultural horizons which were simply artefacts of a short chronology (c.f. Piggott 1954, Fig. 64; Burgess 1980:37–78). At the same time round barrows are now recognisable in the Neolithic (Kinnes 1979), and the division between 'communal' and 'single grave' traditions can no longer be held as an adequate description of Neolithic and Bronze Age mortuary practices (Petersen 1972; Burgess and Shennan 1980; Thorpe 1985). As I have argued, however, little is gained if having recognised the complexity of these data, if we are forced to depict them as general patterns to facilitate their explanation. If we no longer accept descriptions and explanations in terms of cultural norms we should be equally critical of description and explanations in terms of social norms.

We must confront the full diversity of our data. This is only possible with the aid of a theoretically competent framework designed to expose the nature of specific practices. I have attempted to outline some of the general principles which guide mortuary practices. The development of these general principles along with an investigation of specific data should lead to the construction of historical syntheses.

In many parts of Britain Neolithic mortuary rituals left little or nothing in the way of archaeologically identifiable monuments or deposits. It is certainly true that a mound is not an invariable feature of mortuary activity (Kinnes 1975), and mortuary rituals clearly occurred amongst other activities on some sites (Mercer 1980). Archaeological sites were part of an architectural landscape. These landscapes were inhabited through different cycles of activity, each defined as particular temporal and geographical occurrences. Sites were the focus for some activities, guiding the way they were structured. Sites were permanent only in the physical sense of their material existence. No site was permanent in the way it was inhabited through different social practices, for practices began and ended as people passed through these landscapes.

We know little about the way the vast majority of those who died were treated during the Neolithic, but a few human remains were incorporated in some of the architectural forms which survive. The places selected for such deposits were never arbitrary, they were located in a landscape already structured by routine and ritual cycles. Through their inclusion in this timespace matrix of activity, mortuary rituals may have played a part in constructing a particular,

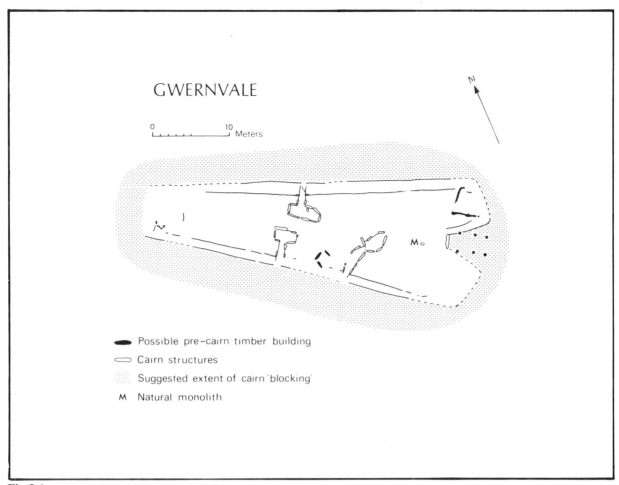

Fig.3.1: (after Britnell & Savory 1984).

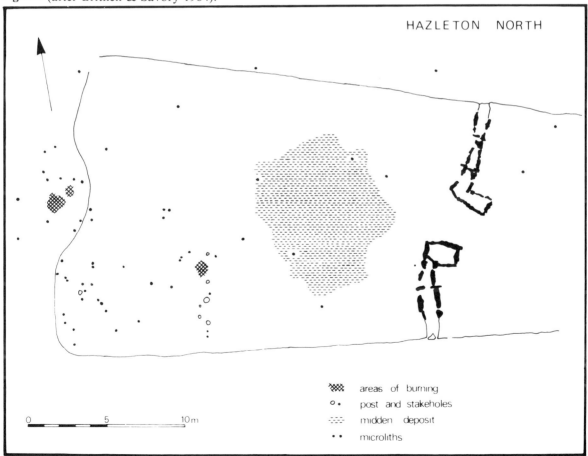

Fig.3.2: (after Saville 1984).

33

dominant meaning out of more routine practices. These mortuary rituals may have include rites of burial, but seem more often concerned with the relocation and veneration of ancestral remains. The architecture often defines an area or areas in which human remains may be located, the paths of access in and out of those areas and the focal point(s) where the entire architectural form could be considered and incorporated within particular ritual and ceremonial practices. Kinnes has demonstrated how different architectural elements may be combined to satisfy such requirements (Kinnes 1975, 1981) and Fleming has stressed the importance of considering the focal stage presented by the cairn or mound (Fleming 1972, 1973).

At Gwernvale, south Wales (Fig.3.1), on a terrace overlooking the river Usk to the south and overlooked itself on the north by a 700m rocky summit, an area of cleared ground had seen repeated visits by hunting parties moving along the upper reaches of the valley (Britnell and Savory 1984). Here on the margins of the cultivated land two, possibly three, small timber buildings were erected, not all of which were necessarily contemporary. Occupying the site of earlier middens one of these buildings was aligned upon a natural stone monolith. Whatever use was made of these buildings and the clearing itself, pottery, quernstones, flints and carbonised grain ultimately accumulated around them.

It was from these activities that the architectural elements of a chambered cairn also came to be constructed. An orthostat was erected to the west of one building, between it and the monolith. This stone preserved one focal axis of activity, and ultimately formed the eastern façade of the cairn. Cairn material was piled behind this stone and built out to form hornworks around the still standing timber building. The cairn mound ran westwards to enclose three separately constructed chambers, two of which opened towards the river on the south and one towards the valley side on the north. The cairn was surrounded by a revetment wall.

This process of integrating specific activities to produce a monumental form is similar to the sequence recently outlined for the Hazleton North long cairn (Saville 1984). Initial activity is represented by hearths, flints and midden deposits (Fig.3.2). Two orthostatic chambers were constructed independently, facing north and south and lying to the east of a midden of flint, pottery, bone, quernstone fragments and carbonised seeds. The cairn was then constructed from rubble derived from two flanking quarries. Dumps of rubble were built up and revetted by dry-stone walling. They ran west and east from the northern chamber before returning to enclose the southern chamber (Saville 1984, Fig. 3). At the western end of the cairn a broad façade was formed, at a point already marked by earlier activity. The whole cairn was again enclosed by a revetment wall.

In both these cases the cairn and chambers are the material product of a prolonged sequence of activity. As the monuments were constructed so those activities which took place around them would have accommodated their existence, perhaps becoming more formalised in their execution. Ultimately they would have made some reference to the mortuary deposits which came to be included within the cairns. The architectural form of each resulting cairn is complex; access to the various chambers is displaced one from the other, and the long axis of each cairn and the façade establishes a separate architectural focus away from the chamber entrances. The lack of any permeability (paths of access) between these various architectural elements might suggest that each was employed separately, otherwise a processional path would have been the only means by which each element could be linked during a single ritual (c.f. Hillier & Hanson 1982). In the case of Gwernvale, Britnell argues that the outer revetment wall was built across the entrances to the chambers, necessitating its dismantling to gain access (Britnell and Savory 1984:47). This alone might imply an infrequent movement into the chambers.

The use of each monument and its surrounding ground can therefore be represented in terms of different occupancies of time and space. These included the incorporation of the monument in the routine landscapes of daily activity; forecourt ceremony and ritual where the mortuary deposits lay hidden in the 'back space' of the chambers; mortuary rituals where ancestral remains were recovered or the dead were incorporated within the chamber; and perhaps processional rituals where each element of the monument was visited in turn.

An architectural practice which established these spatial distinctions of separate access around the cairn contrasts strongly with a monument such as West Kennet (Fig.3.3) where the chambers were originally accessible through the façade (Piggott 1962). We know little about the the history of the West Kennet mound, for example the status of the dry-stone walling abutting stones 7 and 36 is unknown. Beyond these stones lay a deep façade (Fig.3.3: façade 1). Although a distinction of front/back space is maintained by this façade (i.e. forecourt/chambers) it was possible, although not always necessary, for rituals and ceremonies to unite observers in the forecourt with the spaces behind by means of a procession. The redesign of this façade, beginning with the erection of stones 44 and 46, and then stones 43, 45 and 47 producing a second, massive, façade prevented further access to these chambers which had themselves been infilled and blocked (Thomas & Whittle 1986).

Many writers have divided the architectural traditions of Neolithic mortuary monuments between the stone structures of western Britain and the non-megalithic monuments of the east. The different building materials mediated between architectural intentions and the resultant form. In this process the world was crafted within the limits of its own physical conditions. Earlier writers have sometimes proposed that a single cultural rule determined the building plan achieved using different materials, or that the architectural form established in one material led to its skeuomorphic representation in another. But such attempts as Ashbee's to identify

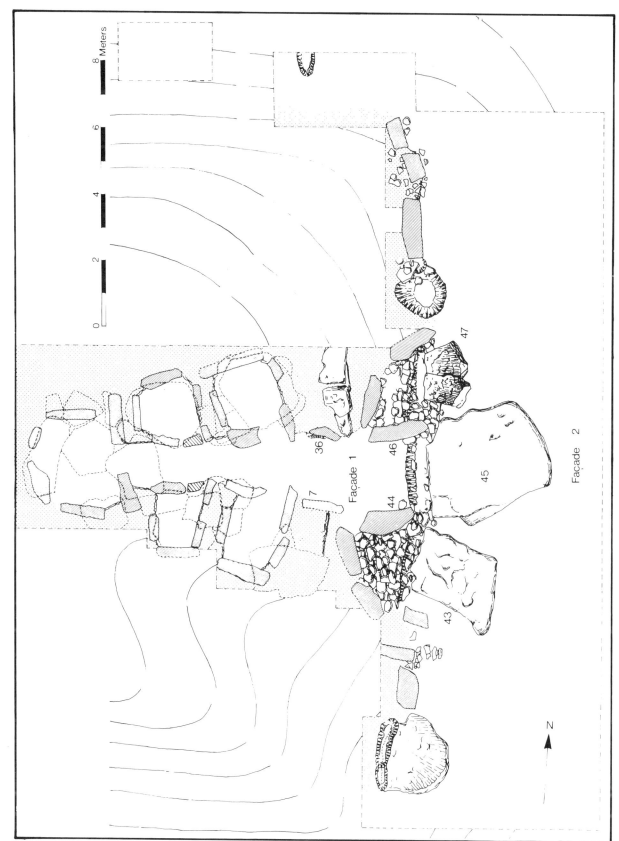

Fig.3.3: West Kennet, structures at the eastern end (after Piggott 1962).

35

the wooden counterparts of megalithic chambers misunderstands the recursive process which links knowledgeable action, its material conditions and its results (Ashbee 1970). The processes by which locations were selected, construction undertaken, and the monuments employed in routine or ritual activities, resulted from people's practical experience, evaluation and control over the conditions within which they acted. There is always an interplay between motivation, material conditions and execution.

The non-megalithic monuments known in southern and eastern Britain also display a long constructional history. Again the early phases can display a separation between forecourts and mortuary structures. At Street House, Loftus (Vyner 1984), a double row of timbers ran westwards towards a continuous timber façade. Behind this lay an embanked mortuary structure to the west of which a kerbed platform was built (Fig.3.4B). Each element would have been approached separately for no internal path linked the forecourt area to the enclosures behind the façade. At Nutbane (Morgan 1959) a more complex set of forecourt buildings was identified (c.f. Kinnes 1981, Fig. 6:7), these were ultimately separated from the mortuary structure by a single timber barrier (Fig.3.4A). This mortuary structure was itself fenced off in a late stage of its history.

A number of forecourt buildings have been recognised elsewhere (Atkinson 1965; Ashbee 1966; Manby 1976) but none presuppose direct access from such buildings to the adjoining mortuary structures. Occasionally, as in the case of Skendleby (Phillips 1936), the mortuary structure may be displaced from the façade and forecourt.

No single use or purpose can be assigned to these monuments. The inclusion of groups of human bone certainly does not make them 'burial monuments'. Burial and ancestor rites may have taken place during history of a site's use, but even the activities appear unattested at South Street and also, seemingly, at the Beckhampton Road and Windmill Hill long barrows (Ashbee, Smith & Evans 1979).

Each architectural form came into being out of the execution of a far wider range of activities and rituals, only some of which need leave a direct archaeological signature (c.f. Kinnes 1981:84). The archaeological site, with its sequence of deposits and architectural modifications, is the objective realisation of the history of these different ritual and routine practices. The evolution of each monument was not a matter of forward planning. Nor was it the laborious application of successive cultural rules resulting in a typological sequence of tomb morphologies. Instead these histories were made by the reconstitution of a seemingly timeless order in Neolithic life. People inhabited these particular foci as part of their daily and seasonal landscapes, reaffirming relations and obligations one to another. That reaffirmation may have been demanded by a death, or through the labour of harvesting, but it was possible because an accepted order between people and things could be built out of these various experiences. The discovery of such an order was

partly facilitated by the symbolic resources stored in the architecture of these monuments. As they were occupied and acted upon, so they guided those actions and their own structural modifications. As the mound came to be built up over the earlier timber buildings at Nutbane different deposits of material were placed in the different sections of the structure (Morgan 1959, Figs. 4 & 5). A similar distinction in building materials was traced in the low capping placed over the burnt mortuary structure and the platform at Street House (Vyner 1984, Fig. 10).

New obligations or challenges to a dominant authority would have required different readings of the cultural order, and these resources would have had to have been rethought and remodelled. The reforming of the West Kennet façade and the infilling of the chambers removed the space and contents of these chambers from further contemplation. This was not the abandonment of the monument but a shift in the focus of activities, ancestral remains could no longer be recovered and the dead could no longer be carried through to join them. By this act these once crucial symbolic resources were no longer available for direct intercession in the rituals played out in front of the monument, they became a hidden background of authority which would slowly have slipped from the collective awareness.

Establishing new codes of authority, capturing new obligations and challenging earlier practices, all are procedures of social reproduction and transformation. Shifts in the dominant symbolism of certain practices seem to characterise the use of the monuments we have been discussing. These changing practices effected the means by which burial and ancestor rituals were integrated within the use of the various monuments. The burial rituals appear to vary between sites, and in the history of a single site. They include inhumation, secondary burial and cremation.

Given this variation, and given the recognition that round barrows also contain multiple deposits (Petersen 1972), the nature of the distinction between the classic 'Neolithic' and 'Bronze Age' mortuary practices has become unclear. I wish now to demonstrate that certain changes do occur at the end of the third millennium bc affecting some aspects of mortuary practice. It is necessary, however, to stress that the mortuary deposits contained in all these monuments represent only a small proportion of the dead. It is a common fault of almost every approach to these data to assume that they represent the full pattern of the way the dead were treated (c.f. Fraser, Kinnes & Hedges 1982). The reason for such an assumption is never argued and it is simply not supported by the attempts to establish demographic projections on the basis of the mortuary data (Atkinson 1968, 1972).

We must begin from the perspective of landscape and architecture, and an understanding of the movement of people in time and space. I have argued that the megalithic and non-megalithic monuments of the late fourth and third millennia bc represented architectural foci in landscapes of time-

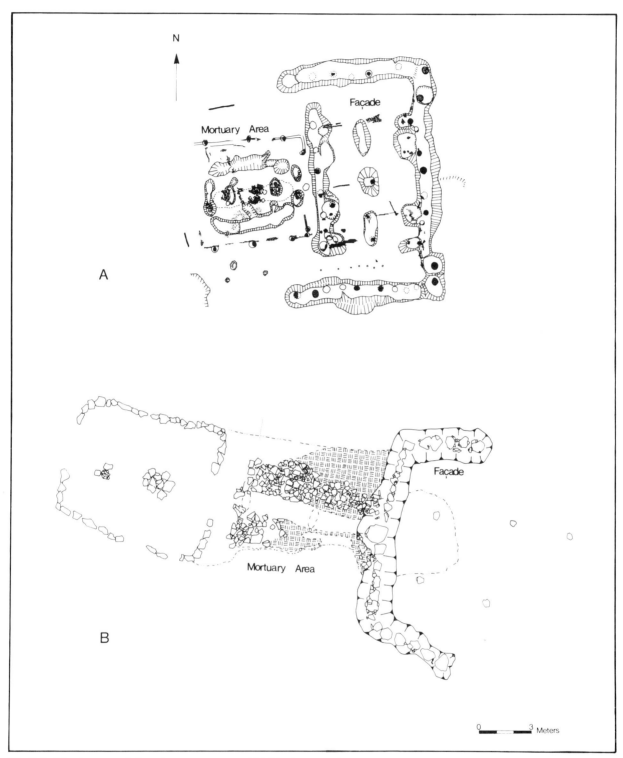

Fig.3.4: Mortuary and façade structures at (A) Nutbane and (B) Street House (after Morgan 1959 & Vyner 1984).

space. Here we find the occasional enactment of ancestor and burial rituals. By the second millennia bc new foci for such rituals emerged and the architectural framework which encompassed them was differently structured. I do not mean by this that the difference is simply a matter of form (round mounds rather than long mounds) but that the sequences of construction, paths of access, and the primacy given to certain rituals were all transformed. The occupancy of these new foci and the transformation of the ritual procedures therefore represent the emergence of new areas of social practice at the end of the third millennium bc (Braithwaite 1984).

I will explore these changes through the example of a single barrow, Amesbury G.71 (Christie 1967). This mound was part of a linear barrow cemetery and survived to a height of 2.5m. The publication presented the history of the site in terms of three phases, the sequence offered here is based upon a re-reading of that report and deals with the major constructional and burial sequence in terms of four periods. Each period contained a number of structural phases (Fig.3.5).

Period I. A ring ditch some 8m in diameter was dug, within which lay a semi-circular setting of stakes. At the centre was a grave, seemingly containing an adult inhumation. This grave was subsequently re-opened cutting a new grave to a depth of 2m. The inhumation of an adult male, possibly in a coffin, was placed on the bottom of the grave. Chalk blocks were put around the burial and the grave infilled with chalk rubble. This infilling contained the disturbed bones of the earlier inhumation. A combined sample of wood from the grave gave a radiocarbon date of 2010 ± 110bc (NPL–77).

Period II. A circle of stakes was erected around the outer lip of the earlier ring ditch and a second double stake ring of 13m diameter around this. A spread of chalk, possibly derived from the grave digging, or from a further re-excavation into the top of the grave, covered the earlier ditch and the ground surface within the outer stake circles.

Period III. When the stake circle was no longer standing a turf mound *c.* 13m in diameter was raised over the entire area. A kerb of flint nodules surrounded the turf stack and a layer of chalk, derived from an encircling ditch, was thrown up over the flints and the edge of the mound. A 2.5m wide berm separated the mound from the ditch. This mound came to be used as a platform, and a spread of chalk on the south side seems to mark one line of access onto the platform. A number of graves were dug down through this elevated surface. They include: 1) The contracted inhumation of an adult female accompanied by a perforated stone bead. 2) The contracted inhumation of a child accompanied by a wooden object lying beside the legs. Over the top of this grave, on the surface of the platform, lay a concentration of flint nodules (some struck) and a few animal bones. 3) The flexed inhumation of a child accompanied by a Food Vessel placed in front of the body and the lower part of a red deer antler. 4) The contracted inhumation of an 18 month old child lay at the base of the turf mound. No grave pit

was observed and it is possible that this burial was included in the mound construction. A large flint lay by its head and a layer of carbonised material lay in front of its head and arms. 5) The cremated remains of an adolescent and child placed beneath an inverted Enlarged Food Vessel in a shallow scoop in the turf stack. 6) The cremated remains of a young adult were placed in a shallow scoop in the top of the turf stack.

A large fire had been built towards the centre of the platform, this may have been a cremation pyre. A radiocarbon date of 1640 ± 90 bc (NPL–75) was obtained for charcoal from this area. A single post had been driven into the mound near this fire setting and an irregular ring of stakes was erected on the chalk bank around the edge of the platform. A mixture of soil and chalk was finally spread over the platform. It contained sherds of an Enlarged Food Vessel, an unburnt human bone, a scatter of cremated bone and three perforated stone beads. A small amount of flint knapping debris lay above the primary silts of the ditch in the southeast quadrant.

Period IV. A second turf stack was erected over the top of the mound, thus covering the platform. Around this a new ditch, 29m in diameter was dug, chalk from which was thrown up around the edge and onto the top of the mound. Further burials were then placed in the mound and into the silted ditch. These include: 1) A cremation beneath an inverted Collared Urn dug into the chalk capping. 2) A cremation, associated with a razor and beneath an inverted Biconical Urn, dug into the mound. 3) An adult inhumation in a shallow grave towards the top of the mound (the excavator believed this to be post-Roman). 4) The contracted inhumation of a child in the upper silting of the ditch. 5) The contracted inhumation of an adult male with trephined skull, placed in the upper silting of the ditch. The skull was surrounded by flecks of charcoal and covered by a large mound of flints. 6) The contracted inhumation of an adolescent in a grave dug into the upper silts of the ditch. This was covered by large flints with a number of struck flakes placed under the head. 7) The cremation of an adult male buried in a Bucket Urn in the ditch. 8) The cremations of an adult female and infant in a Globular Urn buried in the ditch. 9) Fragments of an adult cremation buried above (8) and probably associated with a Bucket Urn. 10) Cremated bone and ash placed in a flint-lined pit dug into the ditch. 11) The cremation of a young adult in a pit lined by flint nodules dug into the ditch. 12) The cremation of a child in a shallow pit dug into the ditch.

The burial deposits from the ditch were clustered in the southeast quadrant, and a scatter of cremated bone was also recovered from this area. Sherds of additional urns were also found in the southeast and northeast ditch quadrants. In the northeast, and over the upper silts of the ditch, lay a quantity of knapping debris.

Circular mounds, covering a variety of burial and ancestral deposits, begin to appear from the third millennium onwards (Kinnes 1979). The one feature common to all such monuments is that they have a single focal point at their centre. In Amesbury G. 71

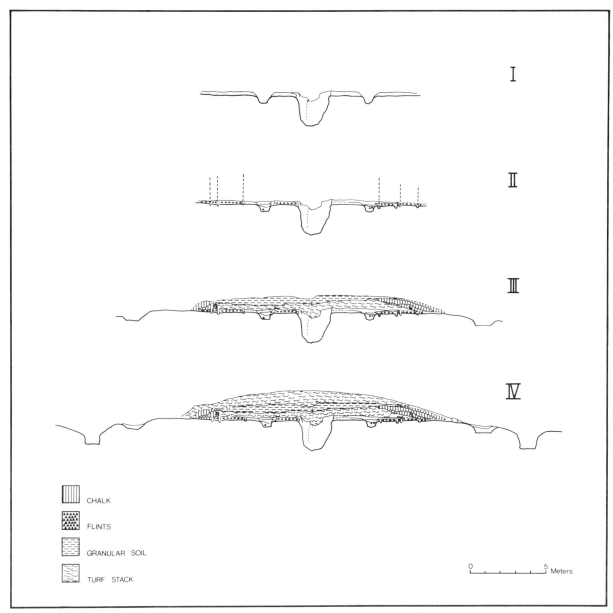

Fig.3.5: Amesbury G.71, suggested structural sequence (after Christie 1967).

the focal point is originally defined by a grave which is re-opened and a new burial inserted. In its earliest development there is little sign of a covering mound. The circular form is preserved when a mound is erected, and this mound elevates activity within the ditched area above that of the surrounding ground surface. Burials are dug into the platform and a fence erected around it. Finally the form of the mound is maintained but burial activity shifts to focus upon the periphery with a number of deposits being dug into the ditch. A high proportion of these burials are cremations.

A series of contrasts can be drawn between this architectural development and that outlined for the megalithic and non-megalithic monuments. The single focal point contrasts with the multiplicity of foci presented by the long mounds, and that focus is now placed *within* the monument. The focus, and thus the entire monumental development, is defined by burial rituals in the earliest stages of the monument's development. A recall of ancestral

deposits was still observed with the reopening of the grave but entry into the monument required re-excavation for there were no open passages and chambers. But burial now structures and dominates the organisation of the monument rather than being included within an architectural form structured around other practices. Indeed we seem to be observing a monument which is at times specifically concerned with burial, something which cannot be claimed for the Neolithic mounds. By the later phases of its history the importance of the central deposit is maintained, but now by acts of avoidance. Burials, often cremations, were placed on the periphery of the mound in the ditch. The early graves meant that the point of transition with death defined the topography of the monument, but ultimately that point of transition is shifted away to the new location of a cremation pyre. The final deposition of cremated remains is fixed at a specifically subsidiary position within the spatial hierarchy of the mound.

Conclusion

In some areas of Britain mortuary practices can be observed archaeologically to have followed particular lines of development during the Neolithic and Early Bronze Age. By the third millennium a number of buildings had been established which reserved spaces for various mortuary and ritual activities. It seems likely that a particular emphasis was placed upon ancestral rites, and that burial rites often go unattested. Because human bones may relate to both types of rite, detailed taphonomic and stratigraphic analysis is required for all bone deposits in an attempt to disentangle which processes of deposition may have been at work. If the emphasis upon ancestral rites is accepted, then this helps to explain the architectural form of many of these monuments with their chambers and passages allowing access to the mortuary remains. Such monuments therefore allowed mortuary rites to be integrated within a wider sphere of ritual and routine activities; it was not the mortuary rites alone which structured the form of the architecture.

The apparent changes which have long been observed in the mortuary practices at the end of the third millennium can still be accepted. But these are not changes in burial practice, from communal to single grave, but the appearance of burial for the first time on a large scale in the archaeological record. Now the burial rites for some people actually appear to have instigated the foundation of monuments. But these monuments, at first small mounds, sometimes with encircling ditches and fences, were solid 'sculpture' (Zevi 1957) within the landscape. Further use for burial required them to be broken open by re-excavation. As some mounds were enlarged the graves were not re-opened but burials were placed instead in the mounds above the earlier burials. Finally the place of the monument shifts within the scheme of ritual practice as an increasing emphasis is placed upon cremation and the peripheral location of burial around the edge of some mounds.

These practices maintained or developed particular lines of authority and inheritance between the living, lines of authority which could be drawn upon in other fields of social action. To develop these approaches we must develop detailed regional analyses which attempt to build syntheses out of all the available data which relate to these different fields. In this way we may learn something about the processes of social reproduction without recourse to general, and spurious, models of social totalities.

Acknowledgements

A number of people commented upon earlier work which contributed towards this paper including Richard Bradley, Ann Clark, Ian Kinnes and Nicholas Aitchison. I have also benefited from detailed discussions with Pamela Graves and Colin Richards whilst preparing this paper. Julian Thomas kindly let me read his and Alasdair Whittle's paper on West Kennet before publication. I must also thank those Glasgow students who worked with me on the 'Mortuary Practices' course. Alison McGhee prepared Fig.3.1 and Lorraine McEwan Figs.3.2–5.

References

Abercromby J. 1912 *A Study of the Bronze Age Pottery of Great Britain and Ireland and its Associated Grave Groups.* Vol. 1. Oxford.

Ashbee P. 1966 The Fussell's Lodge Long Barrow. *Archaeologia* 100:1–80.

Ashbee P. 1970 *The Earthen Long Barrow in Britain.* London.

Ashbee P., Smith I.F. & Evans J.G. 1979 Excavation of three long barrows near Avebury, Wiltshire. *Proc. Prehist. Soc.* 45:207–300.

Atkinson R.J.C. 1965 Wayland's Smithy. *Antiquity* 39:126–133.

Atkinson R.J.C. 1968 Old mortality: some aspects of burial and population in Neolithic England. In J.M. Coles & D.D.A. Simpson (eds) *Studies in Ancient Europe.* Leicester, pp.83–93.

Atkinson R.J.C. 1972 Burial and population in the British Bronze Age. In F. Lynch & C. Burgess (eds) *Prehistoric Man in Wales and the West.* Gloucester, pp. 107–116.

Barrett J.C. 1985 Hoards and related metalwork. In D.V. Clarke, T.G. Cowie & A. Foxon (eds) *Symbols of Power.* Edinburgh, pp. 95–106.

Barrett J.C. 1987 Fields of discourse: reconstituting a social archaeology. *Critique of Anthrop.* 7(3):5–16.

Binford L.R. 1971 Mortuary practices: their study and potential. In J.A. Brown (ed) *Approaches to the Social Dimensions of Mortuary Practices.* Memoir 25 Soc. American Archaeol, pp.6–29.

Bloch M. 1985 From cognition to ideology. In R. Fardon (ed) *Power and Knowledge: anthropological and sociological approaches.* Edinburgh, pp. 21–48.

Bloch M. & Parry J. 1982 (eds) *Death and the Regeneration of Life.* Cambridge.

Braithwaite M. 1984 Ritual and prestige in the prehistory of Wessex c. 2,200–1,400 BC: a new dimension to the archaeological evidence. In D. Miller & C. Tilley (eds) *Ideology, Power and Prehistory.* Cambridge, pp. 92–110.

Britnell W.J. & Savory, H.N. 1984 *Gwernvale and Penywyrlod: two Neolithic long cairns in the Black Mountains of Brecknock.* Cambrian Archaeol. Monograph 2.

Burgess C. 1980 *The Age of Stonehenge.* London.

Burgess C. & Shennan S. 1976 The Beaker phenomenon, some suggestions. In C. Burgess & R. Miket (eds) *Settlement and Economy in the Third and Second Millennia BC.* Oxford, pp. 309–327.

Chapman R. 1981 The emergence of formal disposal areas and the 'problem' of megalithic tombs in prehistoric Europe. In R. Chapman, I. Kinnes & K. Randsborg (eds) *The Archaeology of Death.* Cambridge 71–81.

Chapman R. & Randsborg K. 1981 Approaches to the archaeology of death. In R. Chapman, I. Kinnes & K. Randsborg (eds) *The Archaeology of Death.* Cambridge, pp. 1–24.

Christie P.M. 1967 A barrow-cemetery of the second millennium BC in Wiltshire, England. *Proc. Prehist. Soc.* 33:336–366.

Fleming A. 1972 Vision and design: approaches to ceremonial monument typology. *Man* (NS) 7:57–72.

Fleming A. 1973 Tombs for the living. *Man* (NS) 8:177–93.

Fraser D., Kinnes I. & Hedges J. 1982 Correspondence: the archaeology of Isbister. *Scottish Archaeol. Review* 1:144–148.

Goody J. 1961. Religion and ritual: the definitional problem. *British J. Sociol.* 12:142–164.

Hertz R. 1960.A contribution to the study of the collective representation of death. In R. Hertz, *Death and the Right Hand.* London.

Hillier W.R.G. & Hanson, J. 1982 *The Social Logic of Space.* Cambridge.

Hodder I. 1984. Burials, houses, women and men in the European Neolithic. In D. Miller & C. Tilley (eds) *Ideology, Power and Prehistory.* Cambridge, pp.51–68.

Huntington R. & Metcalf P. 1979 *Celebrations of Death.* Cambridge.

Kinnes I. 1975 Monumental function in British Neolithic burial practices. *World Archaeol.* 7:16–29.

Kinnes I. 1979 *Round Barrows and Ring-ditches in the British Neolithic.* British Museum Occas. Papers 7.

Kinnes I. 1981 Dialogues with death. In R. Chapman, I. Kinnes & K. Randsborg (eds) *The Archaeology of Death.* Cambridge, pp. 83–91.

Manby T.G. 1976 Excavation of the Kilham long barrow, East Riding of Yorkshire. *Proc. Prehist. Soc.* 42:111–159.

Mercer R. 1980 *Hambledon Hill: a Neolithic landscape.* (Edinburgh).

Morgan F. de M. 1959 The excavation of a long barrow at Nutbane, Hants. *Proc. Prehist. Soc.* 25:15–51.

O'Shea J. 1981 Social configurations and the archaeological study of mortuary practices: a case study. In R. Chapman, I. Kinnes & K. Randsborg (eds) *The Archaeology of Death.* Cambridge, pp. 39–52.

O'Shea J. 1984 *Mortuary Variability: an archaeological investigation.* London.

Pader E.-J. 1982 *Symbolism, Social Relations and the Interpretation of Mortuary Remains.* Oxford.

Parker Pearson M. 1982 Mortuary practices, society and ideology: an ethnoarchaeological study. In I. Hodder (ed) *Symbolic and Structural Archaeology.* Cambridge, pp. 99–113.

Petersen F. 1972 Traditions of multiple burial in later Neolithic and early Bronze Age England. *Archaeol. J.* 129:22–55.

Phillips C.W. 1936 The excavation of the Giant's Hill long barrow, Skendleby, Lincolnshire. *Archaeologia* 85:37–106.

Piggott S. 1954 *The Neolithic Cultures of the British Isles.* Cambridge.

Piggott S. 1962 *The West Kennet Long Barrow Excavations, 1955-56.* London.

Renfrew C. 1984 *Approaches to Social Archaeology.* Edinburgh.

Renfrew C. 1972 Explanation Revisited. In C. Renfrew, M.J. Rowlands & B.A. Segraves (eds) *Theory and Explanation in Archaeology.* London, pp. 5–23.

Saville A. 1984 Preliminary report on the excavation of a Cotswold-Severn tomb at Hazelton, Gloucestershire. *Antiqu. J.* 64: 10–24.

Saxe A.A. 1970 *Social Dimensions of Mortuary Practices.* Michigan.

Tainter J.A. 1978 Mortuary practices and the study of prehistoric social systems. *Advances in Archaeol. Method & Theory* 1:105–141.

Thomas J. & Whittle A. 1986 Anatomy of a tomb: West Kennet revisited. *Oxford J. Archaeol.* 5:129–156.

Thorpe I.J. 1985 Ritual, power and ideology: a reconstruction of earlier Neolithic rituals in Wessex. In R. Bradley & J. Gardiner (eds) *Neolithic Studies: a review of some current research.* Oxford, pp. 41–60.

Thurnam J. 1869 & 1872 On Ancient British barrows, especially those of Wiltshire and adjoining counties. *Archaeologia* 42:161–244 & 43:285–544.

Turner V. 1967 *The Forest of Symbols: Aspects of Ndembu Ritual.* London.

Turner V. 1969 *The Ritual Process: structure and anti-structure.* New York.

Van Gennep A. 1960 *The Rites of Passage.* London.

Vyner B.E. 1984 The excavation of a Neolithic cairn at Street House, Loftus, Cleveland. *Proc. Prehist. Soc.* 50:151–195.

Zevi B. 1957 *Architecture as Space.* New York.

4. Altered Images: A Re-examination of Neolithic Mortuary Practices in Orkney.

Colin C. Richards

This paper attempts a new approach to a body of data which encompasses specific areas of archaeological enquiry and controversy, namely megalithic chambered tombs and associated mortuary practices. The selected study area is Orkney, with particular reference to the centrally positioned islands of Rousay and Mainland. The aim of this exercise is to demonstrate the potential of this particular approach through its application to a body of data which is well known and extensively discussed (Henshall 1963, 1985; Renfrew 1973, 1979; Hodder 1982a; Hedges 1983, 1984; Fraser 1983; Sharples 1985).

The subject of megalithic tombs and collective burial remains prominent in archaeological studies, as does the general discussion regarding the nature and status of ritual–particularly in the context of death and burial. However, analytical conjunction between these two areas remains negligible (see, however, Parker-Pearson 1982; Shanks and Tilley 1982). The approach offered here stresses the point that contexts of ritual activities will employ highly structured spatial and material categories. Thus, the conception and use of a chambered tomb will embody the symbolic strategies which are employed within a particular ritual context. An obvious bias in recent studies of Neolithic burial in Orkney has been the emphasis placed upon monumentality, construction and design. A self created typological problem, together with a belief that mortuary practices mirror social status or/and rank, has served to encourage inappropriate research, oriented towards totalistic social analysis.

Two distinct trends are recognisable in the archaeological literature: first, regional studies which are encumbered by preformulated theoretical models imposed onto the available evidence (e.g. Renfrew 1979; Darvill 1979) and second, particularistic studies in which chambered tombs are treated as independent physical entities, seemingly maintaining a life of their own. Here examination takes place within a framework possessing no coherent theoretical structure linking the monuments to human goals and interests (e.g. Fraser 1983).

Besides this inability to provide any viable method for social analysis a common failing of these schemes is the way in which variation in the burial record is overlooked or ignored. Indeed, presupposed uniformity of purpose is essential for the type of general models suggested to account for megalithic tombs (Renfrew 1979; Hedges 1983).

We must reject assumptions that mortuary practices should be regarded as a direct index of social organisation. Instead, our concern should be with the way such occasions influence and reorder relationships between the living. This is not just an acknowledgement that ideological factors displayed through ritual practices distort reality (Parker Pearson 1982:100–1), but a complete reorientation of analytic procedure. The contexts of activities surrounding death are here seen as providing a powerful medium of social discourse. Mortuary ritual, therefore, becomes a single element of a continual process, in which all areas of human action, within a structured material world, serve to present the comprehending subject with an objective knowledge of social practices.

Since social practices constitute structured relations between individuals and groups, in the form of relations of dominance and obligation, they perpetuate institutions which are a formal manifestation of such relationships. Social practices, therefore, appear objectified to the individual, although they are continually recreated through human agency. It is in this way that an apparently objectified social world is in a continual state of flux and is manipulated to serve and sanction particular human interests.

Viewed from this perspective we can see the importance of focusing on particular contexts of human activity, using different scales of analysis which are appropriate to examining different forms of social interaction. Here then social relations determine the scales of analysis as opposed to selecting purely quantitative spatial categories (e.g. Bradley 1984:5–6). We have, therefore, the ability to examine particular spatial contexts, and their material and formal content. These contexts will embody the discursive knowledge of social practices, reproduced through the relationship between human agency, material culture and structured space. It is this intimate relationship which may be reconstructed from analysis of the archaeological record.

Temporality is integral to any social analysis, and within traditional societies time is perceived as being analogous to the natural world. Both agricultural processes and the nature of human existence dictate a cyclical notion of time governed by the repetition of annual seasons. Ritual occasions may also conform to the cyclical and repetitive nature of time through recurrent sanctioning of specific key stages, elements or events within various cycles (Bloch 1977:285–9). Such occasions provide a context within which change itself can be presented as traditional, since there is often a tendency to see the old in the new (Gurevich 1976:231). Thus at conjunctions between changing social relations and the introduction of alternative authoritative discourses we may see transformations occuring in overt ritual activities.

Such manipulation in overt ritual occasions will involve the mobilisation and juxtaposition of traditional and alternative symbols. This produces what may be termed a hierarchy of discourse. While there is an ambiguity of meaning inherent within the symbols employed, according to the social position of the observer, dominant themes of meaning will be powerfully communicated. This will be produced by the juxtaposition of material symbols within a similarly constructed space. Here then is Turner's (1967) dominant symbolism which is located within overt ritual occasions. This introduces a methodology for the archaeological analysis of symbolism, particularly within the context of overt ritual practices. This potential is enhanced where a comparison is possible with the symbols employed in everyday relationships and actions. Importantly, the factor which differentiates overt rituals from what may be termed everyday ritual activities is the ability, on the part of the observer, to assess the general themes of meaning but significantly, to be unable to challenge directly or question their presentation within the ritual process (Bloch 1985).

Fortunately, there should be little argument over recognition that mortuary practices constitute overt ritual occasions. The chambered tomb provides a context for part if not all the rites surrounding interment. By examining the historical context we may recognise the discursive strategies embodied within such purposeful depositional practices.

The active qualities of material culture, in structuring and restructuring social practices have been heavily stressed in recent years (Hodder 1982a; 1982b). Spatial concepts, however, have on the whole tended to play a subservient role in material analysis. Under these circumstances space is merely seen as providing a two dimensional paradigm or structuring medium in which materials operate. In any social context the organisation and definition of space creates and recreates knowledge of social practices. This knowledge involves rules and meanings which govern the individual's understanding of the cultural and natural worlds (Tuan 1979). Under these circumstances it seems important to examine the way in which architectural design delineates space and conveys knowledge to the observer (see Hodder 1982a:221–6). Once the active role of 'space' is appreciated, a coherent framework integrating what appears to be different aspects of archaeological context (e.g. monumentality, design, material deposits, etc), may be constituted.

The application of these ideas to the archaeological record makes severe demands upon the data, but in return it provides a coherent theoretical basis for the analysis of an extensive and varied material base. Of particular importance is the ability to fully integrate all aspects of the available evidence.

Orcadian Chambered Tombs

For analytical purposes chronological integrity and adequately recorded excavations are of obvious importance. Unfortunately, it is the lack of these qualities which generally serve to characterise chambered tombs. These problems stem from one of the defining features of chambered tombs, that of accessibility. In fact, analysis and interpretation of the internal deposits of these monuments has been largely neglected on the grounds that a lengthy period of access will permit the disturbance, destruction or removal of deposits. As a result the discussion of tomb contents became a purely descriptive exercise (Darvill 1982; Fraser 1983; Henshall 1963, Henty 1974). However, these deposits are transforms of processes which embody the history of the tombs, therefore a more positive yet critical stance is necessary. Surely, the provision of access on the part of the builders points to the importance attached to the facility of both insertion and extraction (c.f. Kinnes 1981:84).

Of the 80 recognised Orcadian chambered tombs 33 have been excavated over the last 200 years (Fig.4.1.). Out of these examples two distinctly different types of tomb have been recognised, referred to here as the tripartite/stalled cairns and the cellular type. The former falls within the Orkney-Cromarty group recognised by Henshall (1963:57-8); the latter includes Henshall's (1963:121–34) Maes Howe group and Renfrew's (1979:201–3) Quanterness/Quoyness group. The stalled type is defined by a long rectangular chamber sub-divided into spatial units by paired orthostats projecting internally at right angles from the outer wall. The cellular type is characterised by a long passage leading to a central chamber from which radiate a number of discrete side chambers. A reconsideration of these types as strict groups will be undertaken below. Further typological distinctions resulting from cluster analysis (Fraser 1983:125–38) have received comment elsewhere (Sharples 1985).

The chronology of these tombs is far from sound, although the bi/tripartite form of stalled cairn would appear to be the earliest type being similar to certain mainland examples which, on the basis of radiocarbon dates, can be placed early in the third millennium (Sharples 1986:4). The larger stalled cairns are clearly an elaboration of these earlier forms, and therefore can be placed at a slightly later date. Only the cellular type can be placed with reasonable certainty in the later part of the third millennium (Renfrew 1979). The relatively later position of the cellular type is demonstrated at Howe of Howe, Mainland, where a Maes Howe type tomb structurally overlies a stalled cairn (Carter et al.. 1984; B. Smith and S. Haigh pers. comm.). The ceramic evidence from the excavated sites tends to support this general sequence with the potentially early uncarinated types, heavy rimmed and lugged, predominating in the tripartite tombs. The well fired carinated forms of classic Unstan Ware feature strongly in the extended stalled cairns, while Grooved Ware is the sole ceramic represented in the cellular type.

We can posit, therefore, a very general chronological ordering of tomb types but this cannot be seen as an evolutionary sequence. In fact even if the initial construction of the different tomb types maintains a chronological distinction, the radiocarbon dates obtained for three stalled cairns on Rousay (Renfrew 1979:206) demonstrate a continued use concurrent with the cellular form of tomb. It would appear that only under exceptional circumstances (e.g. Howe of Howe) was it deemed nece-

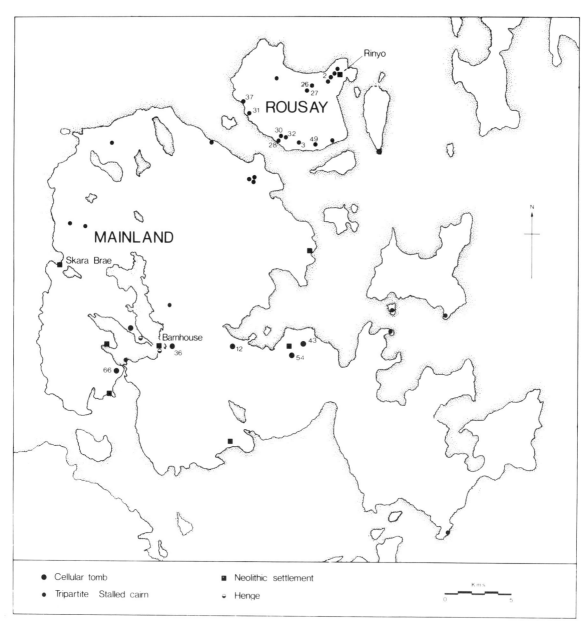

Fig.4.1. Map of the central Orkney islands showing the Neolithic sites mentioned in the text. Tomb numbers correspond to Henshall's catalogue.
2. Bigland Round. 3. Blackhammer. 12. Cuween Hill. 26. Kierfea Hill. 27. Knowe of Craie. 28. Knowe of Lairo. 30. Knowe of Ramsey. 31 Knowe of Rowiegar. 32. Knowe of Yarso. 36. Maes Howe. 37. Midhowe. 43. Quanterness. 49. Taversoe Tuick. 54. Wideford Hill. 66. Howe of Howe.

Material Analysis

ssary to supercede one form by another.

It will be noted that little reference has been made to support this chronological scheme with the currently available radiocarbon dates. The reason for this lies in the uncertain relationship between tomb construction and use of skeletal material. Strong reservations are held about the viability of using human bone to date all the deposits within a particular context and even less the tomb itself. As will be argued below, the apparent discrepancy and incoherence of the radiocarbon dates relates to the removal and redeposition of bones, both within and between sites.

Taking an overall view of the Orcadian burial record at our disposal, of the 33 excavated sites only 27 have been recorded in a manner which facilitates further analysis. Human remains have been found at 21 of these sites. Unfortunately, the quality of excavation reports is extremely variable and a large amount of skeletal material has been lost. In some cases however, where explicit information is missing, it is still possible to produce a confident estimate of the number of individuals buried (Fig.4.2). The significant aspect of this evidence is the obvious variability in the numbers of individuals deposited in different tombs. This is most strikingly illustrated by

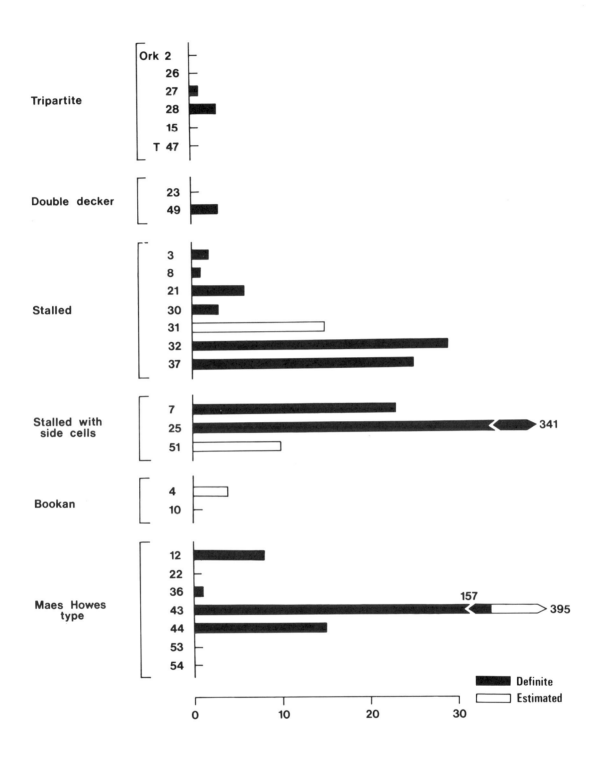

Fig.4.2. Minimum numbers of individuals from excavated Orcadian tombs; the tomb numbers correspond to Henshall's catalogue. Note the very high numbers at Quanterness (Ork 43) and Isbister (Ork 25).

the extraordinary difference in numbers noted at Quanterness and Isbister as compared with the other tombs, a fact absolutely unconnected with different conditions of survival.

A general examination of the condition and arrangement of the skeletal deposits from excavated tombs (Fig.4.3) reveals strong evidence of a burial tradition involving the inhumation of complete bodies (Henshall 1963:93). Almost half the sites (Fig.4.3) include both articulated and disarticulated skeletal remains. Logically the presence of articulation demonstrates that bodies were deposited in complete form; thus, the noticed disarticulation may well be due to the selective removal, addition and/or rearrangement of human bones subsequent to interment. This conflicts with the suggestion of Chesterman (1979, 1983), uncritically adopted by others (Renfrew 1979; Hedges 1983; Fraser 1983), that the predominant form of mortuary practices involved external excarnation and that this was consistently employed throughout the Neolithic period.

Tripartite/Stalled Tombs

A clear example of the occurrences outlined above comes from Midhowe, Rousay (Callander and Grant 1934). Here 9 individuals out of 25 represented were crouched or 'sitting' articulated inhumations. These were positioned on stone shelves situated along the right hand side of the chamber (Fig.4.4). Earlier deposits of the same nature had been pushed to the back of the shelves in order to create room for the new residents of the tomb.

During this process the remains had become disarticulated and in certain cases the bones were heaped up with the skull placed on the top. These remains are incomplete, however, with particular bones missing, a trend noted consistently in all the Orcadian chambered tombs.

Apart from the virtual absence of human remains in the tripartite tombs (Fig.4.2), when we take a closer look at the burials in two other large stalled cairns on southern Rousay an interesting pattern emerges. At Blackhammer (Callander and Grant 1937) (Fig.4.5), two burials were recorded: one in the western end compartment, the other in the entrance passage. In examining the extent of the skeletal remains (Fig.4.6) we find that neither individual is fully represented. Again at Knowe of Ramsay (Callander and Grant 1936) (Fig.4.7) where three burials were discovered, the skeletal remains are incomplete. Any interpretation involving the selective deposition of human skeletal parts must also acknowledge the biases which will be introduced through post-depositional decay. Nevertheless, a pattern exists in the human remains which defies solely taphonomic explanation. The burial deposits within Knowe of Yarso (Callander and Grant 1935), a smaller stalled cairn situated on high ground to the south of Rousay, again reveal a disproportion in human body parts. In this example there is a marked bias towards skulls. This differentiation is apparent not only in presence/absence, but also in spatial distribution (Fig.4.8). The importance attached to the innermost compartment of stalled cairns will be discussed later but the predominance of skulls must surely relate to the discrepancy noted in skeletal

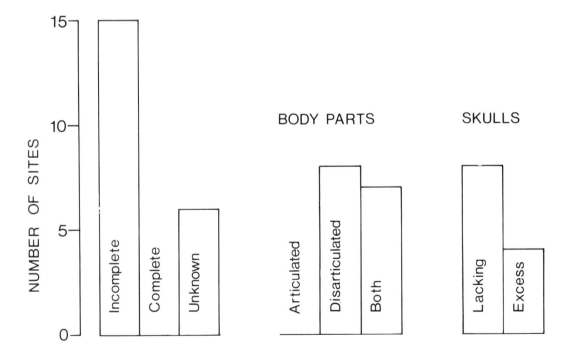

Fig.4.3. Chart showing the articulation/disarticulation of body parts recorded in Orcadian tombs. Also the disproportion of body parts noted within particular tombs.

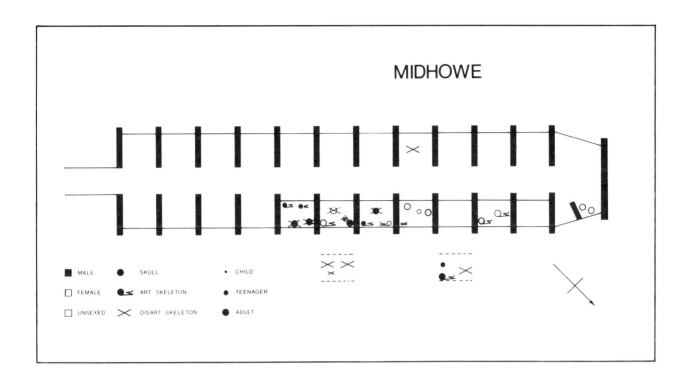

Fig.4.4. Schematic representation of Midhowe, Rousay, (Ork 37) showing the differential nature of human skeletal material.

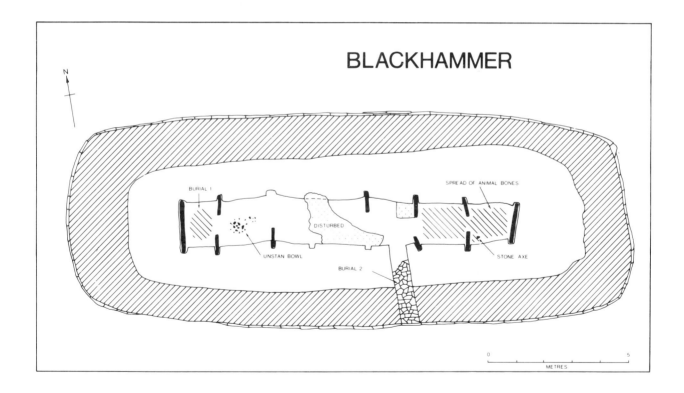

Fig.4.5. Blackhammer, Rousay, (Ork 3) showing the distribution of material within the tomb. Note the manner in which the deposits are arranged within a similarly structured spatial arrangement.

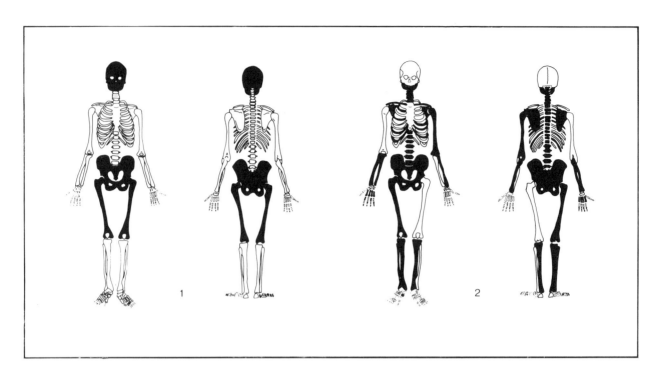

Fig.4.6. Diagram of skeletal material represented in Blackhammer burials 1 and 2. See Fig.4.5 for location.

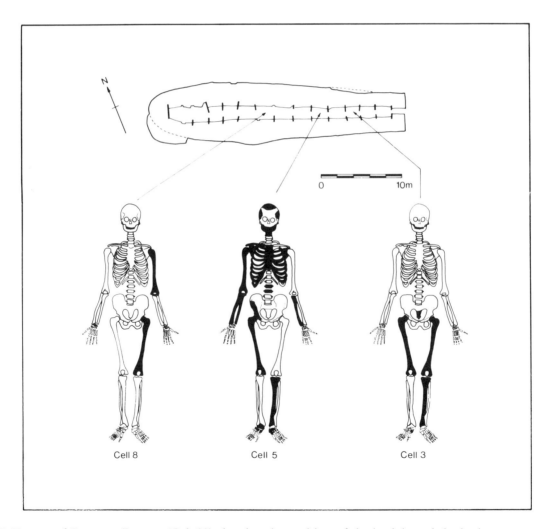

Fig.4.7. Knowe of Ramsay, Rousay (Ork 30) showing the position of the burials and the body parts represented for each individual.

48

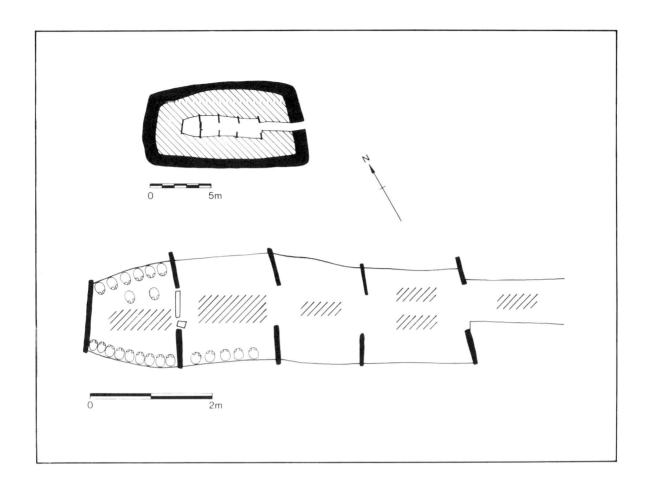

Fig.4.8. Knowe of Yarso, Rousay, (Ork 32) showing the position of the human skeletal material within the tomb. Skulls surround the inner compartments, placed in a position in which they are 'looking' into the central area of the tomb. In the inner compartments the shaded area represents a mixed amount of bones, mainly longbones. The more discrete shaded areas in the passage and first and second compartments are incomplete skeletal deposits representing single individuals.

remains for other Orkney stalled cairns. A more detailed examination of the deposits in Knowe of Yarso reveals a complete absence of mandibles from the tomb; furthermore, the skulls were variable in condition and preservation (Callander and Grant 1935:333–9), one notable example having undergone burning. Clearly the skulls originated from different mortuary contexts, being later redeposited together at Knowe of Yarso.

Taken together, the evidence indicates a complex sequence of events occurring within the context of the tripartite/stalled cairns over an indeterminate period of time. Following Henshall (1963:93), we can suggest that inhumation, often in a crouched position, was the initial method of burial, this practice being exemplified at Midhowe. The radiocarbon dates obtained for several of the Rousay stalled cairns (Renfrew 1979:72), albeit from unstratified contexts, demonstrate periods of activity in the later part of the third millennium rendering them contemporary with the use of the cellular types. These activities apparently incorporated the movement of deposits within and between tombs as well as to other external contexts.

In rejecting the widely held belief that excarnation was an integral part of mortuary practice in Orkney, it is no longer justifiable to invoke chance loss during the excarnation process to account for the partial nature of human remains within the tombs. Instead it is suggested that at certain times after initial deposition within the tomb, the bones of the deceased were disturbed, involving the rearrangement and removal/deposition of selected body parts.

The human bones would appear to have been primarily transported to other tombs and redeposited; however, this may be only one aspect of ancestral veneration and manipulation in the early-mid third millennium. A hint of the complex role of ancestors and their physical representation is to be found at the settlement of Knap of Howar, Papa Westray (Ritchie 1983, 1985; Traill and Kirkness 1937). Here a fragment of human skull was located in the 'domestic' deposits within the house structure (RCAMS 1946:183). Further indication of ancestral rituals external to the chambered tombs comes from an isolated deposit within the Knoll of Skulzie, Westray (RCAMS 1946:360) comprising a large number of human skulls associated with two polished stone axes. At this point it is worth clarifying the two main forms of ritual activities which will involve the rearrangement of deposits within the chambered tomb. First, there is the initial interment sequence, which occurs after the death of an individual deemed appropriate for burial within the tomb. This event will almost certainly involve some form of rite of passage to sanction the transformation from life to death. Second are the rituals which occur in external contexts but require the participation of ancestral spirits. The latter may involve the withdrawal of particular ancestral emblems, either skulls or other significant skeletal parts (Kinnes 1975:17). We can be fairly certain that both forms of activity occured within chambered tombs. Returning to specific Orcadian contexts, the contents of stalled cairns reveal a complex sequence of events which includes the transportation of ancestral remains between tombs, suggesting the importance attached to specific ancestors and their physical and metaphysical accessibility. Under these circumstances the incorporation and presence of ancestral bones within new contexts of deposition may have been an essential part of the ritual process. Here it is worth recalling that the two skulls situated within the deepest compartment at Midhowe were so fragmented and decayed that no age or sex determination was possible (Callander and Grant 1934:334).

It is now possible to account for the variability noted in burial deposits within tripartite and stalled tombs, yet allowing for the movement of bones between contexts we must still account for the apparent lack of burials generally and for the large number of missing body parts.

Cellular Tomb Types

In contrast to Rousay, the cellular type of passage grave features strongly on Mainland and while numerous examples of tripartite/stalled tombs are known these remain generally unexamined. As with the tripartite/stalled cairns, variability exists in the skeletal deposits from the excavated examples of the cellular type. The tomb of Quanterness (Renfrew 1979), however, displays a marked contrast in the nature of its deposits.

Excavated in 1972–4, the sequence of deposition at Quanterness may be reconstructed in a more detailed manner. The primary burials comprised three single cists which were dug into the floor of the central chamber (Fig.4.9a). Of these, two were excavated and found to have contained initially two crouched inhumations, one of which was male aged between 30–40 years. This deposit produced a mean radiocarbon date of 2315 bc (2410 ± 50bc, SRR–754; 2350 ± 60bc, Pta–1626; 2220 ± 75bc, Q–1479). At a later time, after the body had decomposed, the burial of the adult male was disturbed and bone fragments of a female teenager and child were inserted. The cist was then sealed with stone slabs.

Directly above the cist lay a thick stratum of disarticulated human bone, layers 3–4, representing the partial remains of at least 150 individuals (Fig.4.9b). As the tomb was not completely ex-

cavated, a hypothetical figure of 394 was offered as a reasonable estimation of the total number of individuals present (Renfrew 1979:165). Attention should be drawn to several important features of this deposit.

First, Chesterman found the bone to be in extremely varied condition: "the condition of the material is amazingly variable from a few vertebrae and small bones in mint condition through to others so weathered and broken as to be almost indistinguishable" (1979:97). Second, there were relatively few skulls present. Third, the deposit showed no sign of stratigraphic integrity. Instead, the bone was jumbled and parts of the same body were widely separated both horizontally and vertically within the layer, though the Grooved Ware pottery and other finds showed a less widespread distribution. Finally, parts of the same skeleton were generally found in the same compartment, although always incomplete (Renfrew 1979:157). Two radiocarbon dates were obtained from this layer: 2590 ± 110 bc (Q–1363) and 2160 ± 100 bc (Q–1451).

The final phase of activity at Quanterness is the insertion of a crouched burial within Pit C which cuts through the disarticulated bone. Importantly, although this deposit was disturbed, a certain amount of articulation was noted during excavation (Renfrew 1979:60). This demonstrates that the lower disarticulated layer was not a result of later ransacking but a genuine product of Neolithic activity. Radiocarbon dates of 1920 ± 55bc (SRR–755), 1955 ± 70 (Q–1480)and 2180 ± 60bc (Pta–1606) were obtained for this burial.

It is obvious that the deposits at Quanterness represent a complex sequence of events involving contrasting methods of mortuary practices and interment. Renfrew (1979:158–9) suggests that the human remains may have been deposited "already in some disorder", explaining this in terms of excarnation (1979:166–8). It is suggested here that Renfrew was correct in his assertion that human remains were deposited at Quanterness in some disorder, but wrong in contending that this was the result of excarnation. What we may be seeing at Quanterness is the deliberate deposition of human bones from other mortuary contexts within a single tomb. This occurrence not only accounts for the variable nature of the skeletal material at Quanterness but also for the extremely high numbers of individuals apparently interred within a single tomb, a phenomenon which is atypical (see Fig.4.2). The ancestral remains of widespread groups were removed from localised tombs, including tripartite/stalled cairns, and then broken, burnt and deposited within Quanterness. This effectively removed both the identity of individual ancestors and their localised sphere of influence. The ancestors become a single undifferentiated body which, importantly, is no longer accessible to everyone. Indeed, the actual positioning of human remains within a single monument stresses the physical and metaphysical monopolisation of the dead by particular elements of the living.

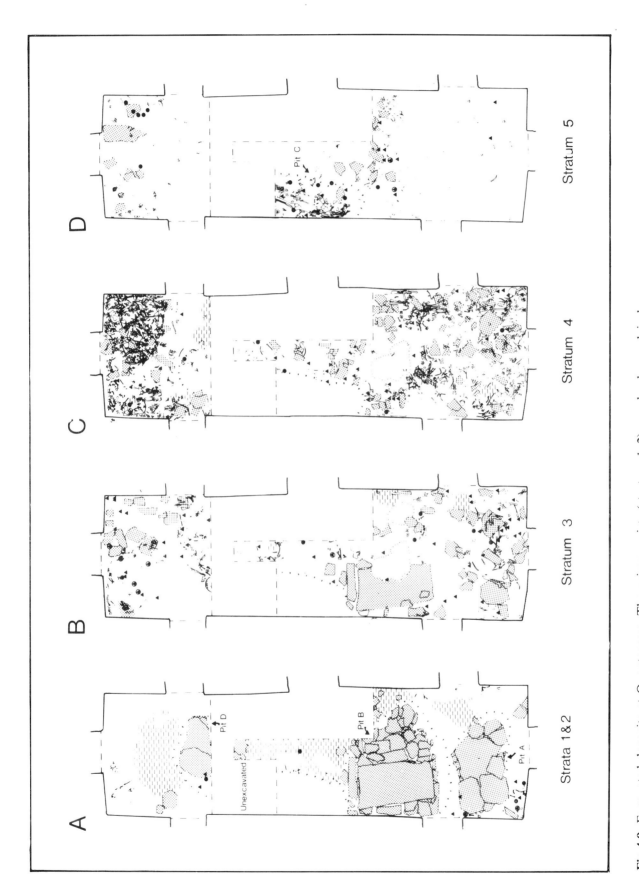

Fig.4.9. Excavated deposits at Quanterness. The primary cists (stratum 1–2) are clearly overlain by the disarticulated skeletal material (stratum 3–4). The remains of an articulated burial are represented in the overlying deposit (stratum 5). After Renfrew 1979. *Reproduced by kind permission of the Society of Antiquaries of London.*

51

The Use of Space within the Tombs

Others (Fraser 1983; Chippindale 1985) have recognised the potential of examining the spatial arrangements of Orcadian tombs but their analyses have failed to consider three important issues. First, defined space is multidimensional, though the tendency amongst archaeologists is to categorise it two dimensionally. Second, an apparently objective approach is applied in which it is implicitly assumed that a plan of the tomb incorporates a single reality, open to measurement and thus classification. Third, as discussed earlier, the definition and enclosure of space employs categories which have meaning within the particular historical context (see Hodder 1982a). Thus spatial arrangement represents an active discursive medium necessarily embodying time and human action.

In construction the tripartite/stalled cairns employ similar and particularistic spatial characteristics. A comparatively short passage leads directly into a long rectangular chamber, itself subdivided into linear segments by paired upright stone slabs, projecting at right angles from the side walls. The passage amplifies the linear aspect of the chamber being sited centrally on the long axis (tombs which have side entrances e.g. Blackhammer, Isbister and Unstan, employ a completely different spatial arrangement).

In examining the difference in height between the passage and chamber within the tripartite/stalled cairns we find little variation (Fig.4.11). This lack of differentiation serves to de-emphasise any distinction between passage and chamber but assists in promoting the tomb as a lineal projection. The whole tomb is constructed from an external point of view, allowing an external audience visual access to the interior of the tomb and the actions which occur within. Under these circumstances the area directly outside the entrance passage becomes a focal point (Fig.4.10) from which a single line of progression from the outside world, through lineal defined sub units, leads to a single goal: the deepest compartment. The hornworks, which define an area or forecourt around the entrance to long stalled cairns in both Caithness (Henshall 1963:74–83) and examples in Orkney, serve to increase the already existing emphasis on the forecourt, enhancing the importance of the external area. Stalled tombs, therefore, employ an unrestricted spatial configuration; the focal point is outside and the graduating space of the interior is quite visible. This spatial uniformity in a mortuary context will automatically involve a ranking order of ritual space.

In these terms the inner compartment takes on a more significant role, being the inner point to which every action has to relate. The inner area is structurally distinct at many of the stalled tombs. Stone shelves feature in only three of the tripartite tombs: Sandyhill Smithy (Calder 1937:115–54); Big-

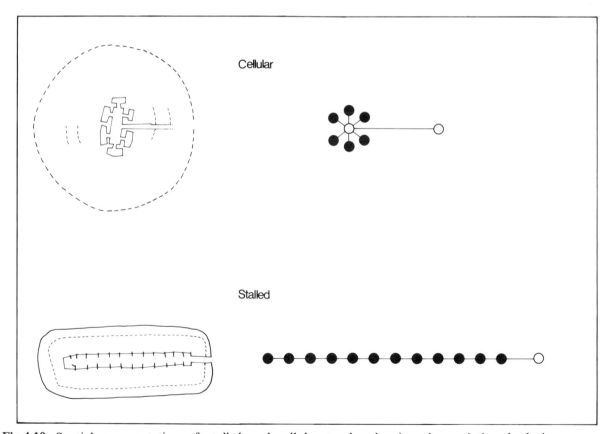

Fig.4.10. Spatial representation of stalled and cellular tombs showing the variation both in accessability and lines of visibility, note that in the cellular tomb only the central chamber is discernable from the exterior and the choice of chamber is only realised *after* reaching the central area.

52

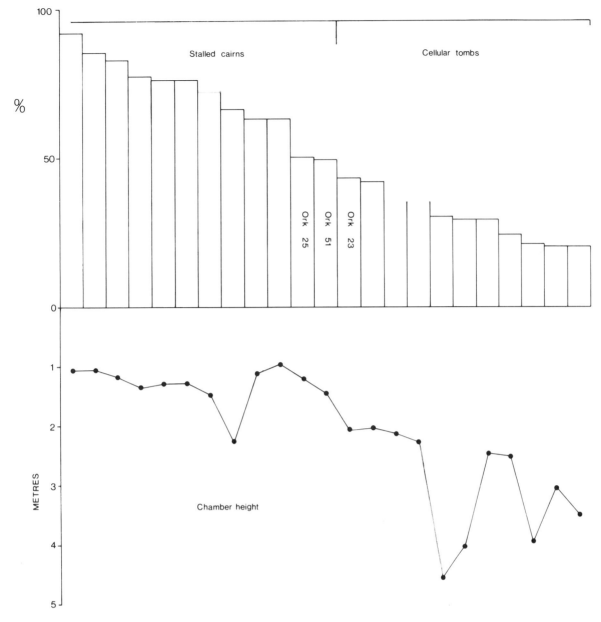

Fig.4.11. Variation in height between the passage and chamber in the different types of Orcadian tomb. Above the axis the passage height is shown as a proportion of the chamber height. Below the axis the chamber heights are shown graphically in real values. Falling within the cellular group are both Isbister (Ork 25) and Unstan (Ork 51) which both have a cellular arrangement of space, as does the lower chamber at Huntersquoy, Eday (Ork 23). The increase in chamber height, within the cellular tombs, is accompanied by a decrease in overall passage height.

land Round (Henshall 1963: 183–4); and Knowe of Craie (Henshall 1963:208). In each case it is exclusive to the inner compartment. Similarly, Knowe of Yarso has a scarcement to hold a shelf and a stone sill delineating the inner area; the latter feature is paralleled at Holm of Papa Westray North (Ritchie 1983). Midhowe has a paved inner compartment, while at Point of Cott (John Barber, pers. comm.) and Calf of Eday Long (Calder 1937:115–29) cists or stone boxes occupy the same area.

The material deposits are also structured in a manner which emphasises the deepest compartment. At Knowe of Yarso the inner compartment was subdivided; in the outer section five skulls were positioned against the wall; in the inner section some

seventeen skulls were placed, mainly in juxtaposition, around the outer walling, cranium upwards, facing the centre of the chamber (Callander and Grant 1935:332–3). At Midhowe, as already mentioned, two single skulls were located in the inner chamber in a decayed condition. The single skull located at Knowe of Craie, Rousay, being the only skeletal material from this or any other tripartite cairn, was located in the innermost chamber (RCAMS 1946:206). At Calf of Eday Long (Calder 1937:115–29) the only human skeletal material, representing a single burial, was located in the innermost chamber below a shelf upon which two polished stone axes were placed. The innermost chamber at Holm of Papa Westray North, apart from having deliberate burial deposits, has a small corbelled cell in the end wall in which were deposited human and animal skulls together with deer tines (Ritchie 1983).

It is clear from this evidence that the inner chamber maintains a special role which is manifest in the order of space. Another aspect of this type of tomb design relates to social participation within the context of ritual activities. From the spatial configuration it is clear that events taking place within the tomb would have been clearly discernible from the forecourt area. The inclusion of a short entrance with a comparatively high roof effectively minimises the physical boundary between life and death and more importantly the perception of proximity and involvement between the living and the ancestors.

The appearance of passage graves within Orkney may well relate to wider influences, though here they are manipulated to serve particular political interests. The Maes Howe/Quanterness-Quoyness cellular tombs employ a completely different conception of space to that seen in the tripartite/stalled cairns, with the emphasis being placed on an internalised spatial configuration. In direct contrast to the stalled cairns, the design of the cellular type removes the public focal point from an area outside the entrance to a private central area situated at the heart of the tomb. This effectively removes the activities, the visual knowledge of the chamber form and the material deposits away from the public domain. To support this proposition one need only examine the way in which height is used to emphasise particular areas (Obata 1962). Within the cellular tomb the passage height is decreased while the height of the central chamber is dramatically increased (Fig.4.11). This serves to accentuate the importance of the central chamber relative to the passage. Within this spatial arrangement there is no particular chamber or compartment which is identifiable as an end point or goal. Instead, the central chamber becomes the focus of the monument, significantly concealed within the tomb. From the central area radiate a number of smaller chambers; each cell is a discrete entity and to move from one to another always involves returning to the central chamber. Here then we are dealing with the conglomeration of discrete units or chambers linked to the central area, as opposed to a single linear chamber. It is suggested that this particular use of space symbolises the amalgamation of disparate units in relation to the centre.

Importantly, the chambers are deep within the tomb; the long passage effectively removes the contents and any activities from the outside world. In this case depth of space is employed in a restrictive manner. Access to both the actions that occur within the tomb and the burials themselves is severely curtailed, as will be the knowledge which accompanies such ritual occasions. It is clear that we are dealing with spatial categories consciously exploited to serve particular social ends; the discursive elements employed within this ritual context are a symbolic transformation of the nature of particular social relationships.

Discussion

This study has selected a particular area of human activity which shows an alteration in social practices. It has been argued that this disjunction involves a diachronic element. Although the stalled cairns definitely precede the cellular type, they also overlap each other in use for several centuries in the later part of the third millennium. In only two cases do cellular tombs supercede stalled cairns; the first at Howe of Howe, Mainland, where a cellular tomb is constructed over a stalled cairn; and the second example, Knowe of Lairo, Rousay (Grant and Wilson 1943), where a long mound with a tripartite chamber is structurally altered into a cellular type.

The variation in the construction of space and material deposits within the chambered tombs cannot be understood in typological or evolutionary terms; in reality what is occuring is the conscious manipulation and alteration of an area of social discourse, utilizing perhaps the most powerful medium available in Neolithic society.

We must break with established orthodoxy and examine variation between contexts in terms of the construction of space and material content, by understanding that these cultural entities represent the means by which social practices were constituted and reproduced.

In past studies of chambered tombs a critical stance has been sadly lacking. It is assumed almost universally (see, however, Kinnes 1975, 1981) that chambered tombs represent collective/communal burial, indeed the two are taken as synonymous. It is suggested here that this is a false assumption, ungrounded in archaeological data. Rather than lumping all chambered tombs together, whether or not variation has been noted, we should look to the differences in an attempt to understand why they occur.

Initially, it is important to examine the context of the tombs in space and time. Immediately a contrast is apparent between the stalled and cellular types. The stalled variety in tripartite form constitute a widespread component of Henshall's Orkney-Cromarty group (1963:45–61) which maintains a distribution over large areas of northeast Scotland. In contrast the cellular type, though conforming to a passage grave tradition, takes on a unique and quite distinctive form in Orkney. While our understanding of the relationships behind such distributions is only beginning to be re-evaluated (c.f. Buteaux 1985; Bradley and Chapman 1986), it is apparent that two entirely different processes are in operation.

Hodder (1982a, 1984) has related both the stalled and cellular tomb types to the domestic house structures at Knap of Howar and Skara Brae, respectively. This study was concerned with general trends and thus overlooks the variation which exists in this material. The earlier tripartite cairns conform both in spatial layout and construction technique with the early house identified at Knap of Howar (Ritchie 1983, 1985). In this respect the stalled cairns are simply houses for the dead/ancestors, relating almost certainly to discrete family units. The significance of employing conceptions of deep linear space remains problematic in the absence of a basic understanding of how such categories operated in the domestic sphere. That this conception of space is a fundamental property consistently employed in the stalled cairns is amply demonstrated in the extension of the tripartite into the longer chamber form. Whereas originally the inner compartment of the former had stone shelves, presumably for burial, the latter form of tomb transfers this facility to the side of the chamber, with shelves being situated along the main axis between the stalls. Even so, the innermost compartment remains distinctive in both construction and material deposits.

The similarity between the cellular tombs and the 'village' sites of Skara Brae and Barnhouse, Mainland, and Rinyo, Rousay, is of a completely different nature. While the underlying structuring principles of both types of site must involve some form of transformation, there are more crucial aspects of changing social relations coming into operation involving new forms of discursive knowledge. It is not coincidental that both the cellular tombs and the village settlements appear to come into existence at the same time. They are both manifestations of changing social practices.

This analysis, however, is restricted to the tombs and to understanding their role in the renegotiation of social relations. To achieve this we must re-examine the cellular tombs. The primary feature in the design of Quanterness is the cellular arrangement of the chambers, for while remaining evenly balanced discrete units they are unified through the central chamber. At the same time the construction of three dimensional space serves to remove the focal point, with regard to an audience, from the outside (a feature of the stalled cairns which tend to emphasise the forecourt area) to the centre of the tomb. It is reasonable to suggest that knowledge of particular elements of ritual activity is being restricted and that significant parts of the ritual process are available to the majority outside the tomb in sound only (Pam Graves pers. comm.).

The primary deposits at Quanterness consist of three burials, one of which was an adult male; the secondary deposit by contrast, was a mass of disarticulated skeletal material, broken and burnt and, importantly, derived from different contexts. Here again amalgamation is being physically expressed through another symbolic medium; within the tomb spatial categories and skeletal material are juxtaposed to create a consistent symbolic expression. This overall theme of unification, as suggested earlier, incorporates other levels of meaning within a hierarchy of discourse. The destruction of individual ancestors and their spheres of influence effectively creates a unified ancestral body, which by its deposition within the tomb removes it from the public domain. No longer are ancestors identifiable or accessible, but are instead monopolised by a small element of the living; this is the underlying logic of the cellular tomb.

The cellular tombs, particularly Quanterness, are not collective/communal burial monuments in the normative sense, but constitute powerful, perhaps, short-lived political expressions mediated through ancestor rituals. Whilst drawing on traditionally potent forms of discourse, they introduce an alternative discursive knowledge of social practices. Thus discontinuity is sanctioned through continuity, with political expression dominating ideological representations.

The 'real' burial deposits at Quanterness are the cist burials, as from *c.* 2300 bc there is strong evidence to suggest that individual inhumation becomes the dominant mode of burial. Within a single tomb, therefore, the past and present merge.

By varying our scales of analysis we can identify the way human relationships are renegotiated at particular times through the use of traditional practices manipulated within a ritual context. By understanding the role of ritual in reproducing social practices we can begin to make clear statements regarding the variation in the Orcadian burial record and how this may be interpreted.

We can also discuss the significance of tombs which previously appeared problematic, such as the 'double decker' tombs. Here two completely different conceptions of space are amalgamated in a single monument. One chamber is constructed above another and both have opposed entrances. Such juxtaposition is surely more significant than to merely establish the contemporaneity of two different typological classes of monument (Sharples 1985:65). Similarly it should be apparent that we can now effectively deal with monuments which were typologically problematic e.g. Blackhammer (Callander and Grant 1937), Isbister (Hedges 1983), and Unstan (Clouston 1885), which employ a side entrance. In these examples which have stalled construction, categories of choice and lateral balance are being substituted for depth of space and it is not coincidental that Isbister and Unstan have a cellular arrangement and that the polarised material deposits at Blackhammer emphasise the dualistic quality of culture:nature (Fig. 4.5). The search for precursors or hybrids become irrelevant within the framework offered here.

Finally it is suggested that by understanding the structured role of space and material culture in reproducing and manipulating social practices we can start to use fully the diversity of the archaeological record as opposed to its suppression through the imposition of preformulated models.

Acknowledgements

I would like to thank John Barrett, Simon Buteaux, Ian Kinnes, David Sanderson, Niall Sharples and Nick Thorpe with whom I have had countless discussions over the ideas expressed above. Further encouragement has come from Colin Renfrew who is now collaborating on a C14 project which will undoubtedly provide a clearer picture of the Orcadian tomb chronology. Richard Bradley commented on an earlier version of this paper and John Barber and Anna Ritchie kindly provided unpublished information. Also to be thanked are my colleagues in Glasgow, particularly discussion with

Alan Leslie whose efforts have hopefully made this paper intelligible. Finally, I would especially like to thank Miranda Schofield who produced most of the illustrations and provided continual support throughout my research.

References.

Bloch M. 1977 The past and the present in the present. *Man* 12:278–92.

Bloch M. 1985 From cognition to ideology. In R. Fardon (ed) *Power and Knowledge*. Scottish Academic Press. Edinburgh, pp. 2–48.

Bradley R. 1984 Regional systems in Neolithic Britain. In R. Bradley and J. Gardiner (eds) *Neolithic Studies: a review of some current research* BAR 113, Oxford, pp. 5–14.

Bradley R. and Chapman R.W. 1986 The nature and development of long distance relations in later Neolithic Britain and Ireland. In C. Renfrew and J. Cherry (eds) *Peer Polity Interaction*. Cambridge, pp. 127–136.

Buteaux S. 1985 *Diffusion, Radiocarbon and the Megaliths*. Paper given at the Theoretical Archaeology Group Conference, Glasgow 1985

Calder C.S.T. 1937 A Neolithic double-chambered cairn of the stalled type and later structures on the Calf of Eday, Orkney. *Proc. Soc. Antiqu. Scot.* 71:115–54.

Callander J.G. and Grant W.G. 1934 A long stalled chambered cairn or mausoleum near Midhowe, Rousay, Orkney. *Proc. Soc. Antiqu. Scot.* 68:320–35.

Callander J.G. and Grant W.G 1935 A long stalled cairn, the Knowe of Yarso, in Rousay, Orkney. *Proc. Soc. Antiqu. Scot.* 69:325–51.

Callander J.G. and Grant W.G. 1936 A stalled chambered cairn, the Knowe of Ramsey, at Hullion, Rousay, Orkney. *Proc. Soc. Antiqu. Scot.* 70:407–19.

Callender J.G. and Grant W.G.1937 Long stalled cairn at Blackhammer Rousay, Orkney. *Proc. Soc. Antiqu. Scot. 70:* 297–308.

Carter S.P., Haigh D., Neil N.R.J. and Smith B. 1984 Interim report on the structures at Howe, Stromness, Orkney. *Glas. Arch. Journ.* 11:61–73.

Chesterman J.T. 1979 Investigation of the human bones from Quanterness. In C. Renfrew *Investigations in Orkney*. Rep. Res. Comm. Soc. Antiqu. London, 38 pp. 97–111.

Chesterman J.T. 1983 The human skeletal remains. In J.W.Hedges *Isbister: A chambered tomb in Orkney*, Brit. Arch. Rep 115, Oxford, pp. 73–132.

Chippindale C. 1985 *A shape grammar treatment of megalithic Orkney*, paper given at The Theoretical Archaeology Group Conference, Glasgow 1985.

Clouston R.S. 1885 Notice of the excavation of a chambered cairn of the Stone Age, in the Loch of Stennis, Orkney. *Proc. Soc. Antiqu. Scot.* 19:341–51.

Darvill T.C. 1979 Court cairns, passage graves and social change in Ireland. *Man* 14:311–27.

Darvill T.C. 1982 *The Megalithic tombs of the Cotswold Severn Region*. Vorda, Highworth.

Fraser D. 1983 *Land and Society in Neolithic Orkney*. BAR 117, Oxford.

Grant W.G. and Wilson D. 1943 The Knowe of Lairo, Rousay Orkney. *Proc. Soc. Antiqu. Scot.* 77:17–26.

Gurevich A.J. 1976 Time as a problem of cultural history. In *Cultures and Time*. Unesco Press, Paris.

Hedges J.W. 1983 *Isbister: a chambered tomb in Orkney*. BAR 115, Oxford.

Hedges J.W. 1984 *Tomb of the Eagles*. John Murray, London.

Henshall A.S. 1963 *The Chambered Tombs of Scotland*. Edinburgh University Press.

Henshall A.S. 1985 The chambered cairns. In C.Renfrew (ed) *The Prehistory of Orkney*. Edinburgh University Press, pp. 83–117.

Herity M. 1974 *Irish Passage Graves*. Irish University Press, Dublin.

Hodder I. 1982a *Symbols in Action: ethnoarchaeological studies of material culture*. Cambridge University Press.

Hodder I. (ed) 1982b *Symbolic and structural archaeology*. Cambridge University Press.

Hodder I. 1984 Burials, houses, women and men in the European Neolithic. In D. Miller and C. Tilley (eds) *Ideology, Power and Prehistory*. Cambridge University Press, pp. 51–68.

Kinnes I. 1975 Monumental function in British Neolithic burial practices. *World Archaeology* 7:16–29.

Kinnes I. 1981 Dialogues with death. In R.W. Chapman, I. Kinnes and K. Randsborg (eds) *The Archaeology of Death*. Cambridge University Press, pp. 83–91.

Obata G. 1962 Mind, body and stimuli. *Journal of the American Institute of Architects* 38.

Parker Pearson M. 1982 Mortuary practices, society and ideology: an ethnoarcheological study. In I. Hodder (ed), *Symbolic and Structural Archaeology*. Cambridge University Press, pp. 99–113.

RCAMS 1946 *Twelfth Report with an Inventory of the Ancient Monuments of Orkney and Shetland*. Vol.2, Edinburgh.

Renfrew C. 1973 *Before Civilization: the radiocarbon revolution and prehistoric Europe*. Jonathan Cape, London.

Renfrew C. 1979 *Investigations in Orkney*. Rep. Res. Comm. Soc. Antiqu. London, 38.

Ritchie A. 1983 Excavation of a Neolithic farmstead at Knap of Howar, Papa Westray, Orkney. *Proc. Soc. Antiqu. Scot.* 107:40–121.

Ritchie A. 1985 The first settlers. In C. Renfrew (ed) *The Prehistory of Orkney*. Edinburgh University Press, pp. 36–53.

Sharples N. 1985 Individual and Community: the changing role of megaliths in the Orcadian Neolithic. *Proc. Prehist. Soc.* 51:59–74.

Sharples N. 1986 Radiocarbon dates from three chambered tombs at Loch Calder, Caithness. *Scottish Archaeol. Rev.* 4:2–10.

Traill W. and Kirkness W. 1937 Howar, a prehistoric structure on Papa Westray, Orkney. *Proc. Soc. Antiqu. Scot.* 71:309–21.

Tuan Y. 1979 *Space and Place: the perspective of experience*. Edward Arnold, London.

Turner V. 1967 *The Forest of Symbols*. Cornell University Press, New York.

5. Isbister, Quanterness and the Point of Cott: The Formulation and Testing of Some Middle Range Theories.

John Barber

"...the archaeologist must have a strong body of theory — middle range theory — which guides him in making statements about dynamics from observed statics. In short we must have a strong and well founded understanding of the formation processes of the archaeological record."

(Binford and Bertram 1977:77)

The chambered tomb at the Point of Cott, Westray, Orkney, was excavated by the author in 1984/5. The theories which formed the basis of the research design for the excavation were drawn largely from the two most recent publications of excavations in Orkney: Quanterness (Renfrew 1979), and Isbister (Hedges 1981). The present paper describes the middle range theories relating to chamber deposits based on the interpretations offered for Quanterness and Isbister, and describes in outline the results of the Point of Cott excavations and their bearing on these theories.

Human Bone Deposition

To "...specify the relationship between the organization of a living society and its practices for the disposal of the dead." (O'Shea 1981:40)

It is a truism that pattern identification is a basic feature of the New Archaeology. "...human behavior left a fossilized record in the form of spatial patterns of variation and co-variation of artefacts and features on archaeological sites." (Chapman and Randsborg 1981:10–11) Surprisingly perhaps, the spatial distribution of human bone in Isbister and Quanterness has not formed a significant part in their contribution to the interpretation of funerary ritual. The presence of bones of sea eagles at Isbister suggested to Hedges that the funerary rite involved a strong totemic element (Hedges 1983:270). However the inadequacy of its excavation and its recording (it was excavated by the local landowner), severely restricted the range of contextual evidence available to the report's compilers (Hedges 1983:1; but see also Chesterman, in Hedges 1983:75). At Quanterness, the random distribution of the bone throughout the chamber deposits defied pattern identification. Thus the interpretation of the funerary rite at both sites has been based on information intrinsic to the bone assemblages, animal and human.

At both sites the apparently complete disarticulation of the human skeletal material has been adduced as proof of the practice of excarnation, while the absence of gnaw marks on the bones suggested, variously, that the bodies were exposed on platforms (Hedges 1983:269), or that they were buried in shallow sandy graves (Chesterman, in Hedges 1983:127). At any rate the prevailing view on the Neolithic funerary rite of Orkney is that it consisted of excarnation, followed by the deposition of some of the bones in the megalithic tomb. At Isbister, there is the further suggestion that the primary deposition within the tomb consists of the emplacement of groups of bones from the skeleton, followed, perhaps after a reasonable interval, by their separation into skull and other bones which are then redeposited separately into 'ossuary' side-chambers.

The operational hypothesis for the funerary rite in the light of the Isbister and Quanterness publications seemed to be one of progressive loss of 'self', as the deceased was first excarnated; then incomplete, and apparently random selections of bone were interred in individual groups; and finally the surviving remains were stripped of their individuality and stored in the communal ossuary, at Isbister in the side chambers, at Quanterness in the chamber deposit.

Animal Bone

"Beside human bone found in the chambers, the inclusion of animal bone is a widespread practice in Scottish tombs." (Henshall 1985:106).

Quanterness and Isbister both contained bones of cattle, dog, otter, pig, rabbit, red-deer and sheep/goat (all sheep where identifiable), while Isbister also contained bones of seal, and Quanterness bones of cat, fox and horse. Some 17 taxa of fish were discovered at Isbister, though 60% of the fish bone was unidentifiable. The identified species were mainly small types, most less than 100g, and none apparently heavier than 0.5kg. At Quanterness there were only 9 identified taxa and these included some larger specimens, some between 1kg and 1.5kg. At Quanterness some 41 species of bird were identified, while, at Isbister 21 species, with 88% of the bird bone representing the white tailed or sea eagle. The remains of some 207 Orkney voles, together with those of 9 wood mice were retrieved from Quanterness and these numbers prompted their analyst to interpret them as the product of owl pellets. Although neither owl remains nor intact owl pellets were retrieved from the site, it is not possible to suggest any other mechanism for the introduction of these bones.

While it is clear that some of these species were introduced in recent times (viz. cat, domestic fowl and rabbit), and that others (including possibly the fox) are not native to Orkney, and that others again (like the voles) may have arrived in the tombs by natural agencies, it is argued that the bulk of the assemblages represent the remains either of funerary offerings (Hedges 1983:269), or of funerary feasting (Renfrew 1979:168).

It would appear then that the operational hypothesis for the utilization of animals, including birds and fish, in the funerary rites at these tombs involves their identification as foodstuffs, either for ritual consumption or for ritual deposition at some stage in the funerary process.

Point of Cott: A Summary

Like most megalithic tomb chambers, that at the Point of Cott was erected by corbelling. Corbelling is the technique which sets each course of stone oversailing that on which it lies, progressively narrowing the space to be roofed, until it may be closed with a slab, or slabs (Angell and Barber, forthcoming). Stability in a corbelled structure requires that the weight of the oversailing mass be balanced by the weight of the mass of the material 'in the tail', i.e in the wall or cairn being built (Fig.5.1). Thus, corbelled structures must be erected as complete walls or cairns, unlike a true arch, which can be erected free-standing, with the rest of the wall being built up around it later. The Point of Cott chamber was erected as part of a rectangular 'construction-cairn', slightly splayed at the higher, front end (south end). It was boat-shaped in cross section and reduced markedly in height from the front to the rear. The construction-cairn contained a four compartmented stalled chamber, and occupied about half of the surviving length of the trapezoidal, horned cairn.

The trapezoidal plan and the hornworks were achieved by enclosing the construction cairn in a series of onion-skin walls (Fig.5.2). Some large and irregular slabs and boulders had been dumped between these walls, in places, and lay on the Neolithic old ground surface, but the greater part of the inter-wall space was void. North of the construction-cairn, the body of the trapezoidal cairn was built by first erecting a series of stone 'boxes'. These were partly megalithic and partly of drystone walling and were loosely infilled with soil and irregular slabs and boulders. Like the inter-wall spaces, the bulk of the spaces in these boxes was void. The wall lines of the finished cairn ran outside and over these boxes, and they would not have been visible in the finished monument.

The chamber, as noted above, consisted of four compartments, separated by jamb stones, and with a pair of cist-like structures in the innermost, fourth, compartment (Fig.5.2). The roof and upper part of the chamber had collapsed in at least two phases, and human and animal bone was found throughout

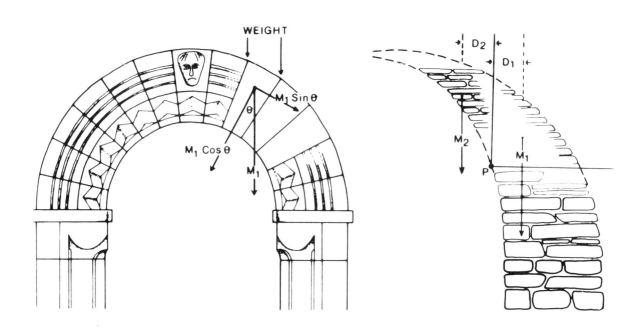

Fig.5.1. Comparison of structural forces in an arch and corbelled vault. The weight resting on an arch (left), can be resolved into two forces. One is dispersed along the curve of the arch, while the second, directed radially inwards, is counteracted by the wedge-shaped voussoir's inability to slip inwards (i.e. it is again converted into compressive forces within the arch). The mass of a corbelled structure (right), if it is to be stable, must be so disposed that, for any point P on its inner surface, the moment of the overhanging mass (D2xM2) must be equal to or less than the moment of the mass in the tail (D1xM1). Thus, to construct a corbelled chamber, the mass in the tail must be emplaced as the structure rises. Hence constructional-cairns, or 'chamber-cairns', are a structural necessity.

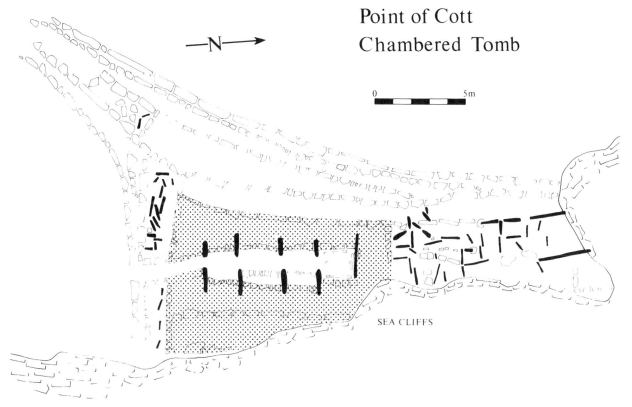

Point of Cott
Chambered Tomb

0   5m

SEA CLIFFS

Fig.5.2. Point of Cott. Plan of the chambered cairn at the level of the lowest course of stones in the cairn-walls. Earthfast orthostats, in solid black, include the jamb stones which segment the chamber, the 'constructional-boxes' at the north end, and a scatter of stones to the south of the construction-cairn (shaded).

this collapse, albeit concentrated in the lower levels. The human bone may have lain in aumbries in the upper part of the chamber walls, similar to those found in the lower levels of the east wall of compartment 3. However the possibility that wooden tomb furniture was used is suggested by the remains of such structures, also found in compartment 3, where it had been replaced by a stone built bench containing the aumbries mentioned above.

The chamber, both floor deposits and collapse, contained animal and human bone, while pottery and whale tooth beads were retrieved from the chamber floor. The human remains represented at least 13 individuals: 5 adults, 2 teenagers and 6 infants. The animal bones represented sheep, dog, otter, cattle and deer, together with rodent bones present in relatively large numbers and bird bones, including talons of a large bird of prey. Numerous localized nodular masses of macerated fish bone were also noted. Of the larger mammals only sheep bone were noted in the floor deposits, apart from some otter bones in compartment 1. The dog bones were concentrated on the top of the first phase collapse material within the chamber, together with bones of sheep.

The matrix of the chamber floor deposit consisted of a dark brown clay loam, with many embedded spalls of shattered stone. It was clearly rich in soil organic matter. The bone and other finds were scattered through this deposit, apparently randomly, and individual bones penetrated the full depth of the deposit which was nowhere greater than 15cm.

The entire cairn was removed at Point of Cott, leaving only the lowest course of every wall *in situ*. During the removal, it was noted at the north end that birds had nested on, and in, the 'boxes' deep within the cairn; that otters had penetrated between the onion-skin walls; and that rabbits were still in residence in the old otter holts. Some of this activity is ancient, and we have noted otter bones sealed by ancient structural-settlement and collapse within the cairn. Some of it is clearly modern, and the grass of the birds nests was still relatively fresh. Details of the animal bones presented here are drawn from the report prepared by Mr E. Halpin, which will be published in full with the site report.

At the south end of the cairn otters had penetrated along the full length of the innermost void, between the first onion-skin wall and the outside of the construction cairn. Their recent presence there may be deduced from the rusted boat nail and the rubber docking-ring (used on lambs) found within the holt and lying directly on the Neolithic old ground surface. A family of otters now occupies the burn near the site, and may well be those responsible for these most recent introductions. Compartment 4 and the rear of the construction-cairn had been breached by the sea and have suffered considerable storm damage, being now very ruinous. Compartment 4 contained some 36 talons of a large bird of prey, as well as many other bird bones.

The passage, giving entry to the chamber, had been blocked incompletely in antiquity. Large numbers of dog bones and the bones of young sheep and cattle were recovered from the blocking material. The surface of the cairn yielded one almost complete cat skeleton, and the broken foot of a cow, trapped between two walls. Burials of deer, horse and sheep in the forecourt had been inserted, in living memory.

First Principles

Archaeological deposits are usually distinguished from 'natural' or geological deposits by their inclusion of some anthropogenic component. This component can itself be natural or man-made, and its inclusion can have been intentional or accidental. The interpretation of archaeological deposits, in terms of the human activities which they, in whole or part, represent can only be soundly based if it considers the 'natural' component and the depositional history of the deposits matrix, as well as the nature and significance of the anthropogenic contribution. In obedience to Occam's principle, the null hypothesis to be employed when distinguishing between a deposit's matrix and its anthropogenic component must be that any element whose inclusion in the deposit can be explained in terms of normal, natural depositional mechanics must be considered part of the matrix, rather than of the anthropogenic component. The corollary is also true, that what cannot be explained by reference to normal, natural agencies, must be anthropogenic.

Chamber Deposits

Chamber deposits, like all other archaeological deposits, consist of three elements: the soil matrix; the natural, non-soil element; and the anthropogenic component. The soil matrix may be viewed as two separate, but related elements, the mineral element and the soil organic matter. The source of the latter at Point of Cott is of some interest. It cannot have been derived from the Neolithic old ground surface. Excavation has revealed that the upcast from the jamb stones which segment the chamber, lies in the chamber area, directly on undisturbed boulder clay. Thus the Neolithic A- and B-horizon material had been removed from the area of the chamber during its construction. There is no obvious natural depositional mechanism which could explain the introduction of the soil organic matter to the chamber deposit and it must either form part of the natural, but non-soil element, or part of the anthropogenic component, or perhaps part of both.

The mineral element does not seem to present major difficulties, at least on the macroscopic scale, but work is required to characterise and 'source' this element of the deposit before we can accept that it is entirely natural, or rather, that it owes nothing to human intervention. Perhaps the author may be forgiven a brief aside at this point to lament the weakness of existing analytical techniques for the similar characterization of the organic matter within soils. Early indications suggest that soil organic chemistry offers great hope for the unambiguous detection of human activity, by the analysis of decay products, preserved in the soil organic matter (Anderson and Hepburn 1985:157–161).

The natural, non-soil element of the deposit at Point of Cott is mainly represented by animal bones, birds' nests, otter holts, rabbit burrows, etc. The rodent bones at Point of Cott are probably best interpreted as the remains of owl pellets, or the regurgitations of other birds of prey, as they were interpreted at Quanterness (Corbet 1979:135). The nodular masses of fish bone are interpreted as otter spraints, both on the basis of their form and their association with the otter remains. The presence of the holts shows that the otters were resident in the cairn, and thus their remains form part of the natural non-soil element of the chamber deposit. The bones of the large bird(s) of prey were deposited late in the cairn's history and probably represent a resident population. These, in turn, may explain the presence of some larger fish bones, and the latter, on the null hypothesis, must therefore be considered part of the natural element as well. The bones of sheep, especially those of lambs and young sheep are commonly found within chambered tombs in Scotland. MacCormack has noted the natural tendency of such creatures to seek out sheltered areas when ill (1984:109) and Boyd et al. (1964) have observed that c. 70% of the dead sheep found on St Kilda lay within deserted buildings. These comments have induced MacCormack (1984) to suggest that the sheep remains from the tomb at Pierowall Quarry, Westray, may not be ritual deposits, as their excavator has argued (Sharples 1984:113). This would account for the absence of butchery marks of any type from the bone assemblages of Quanterness, Isbister, and Point of Cott.

In general it would seen that the greater part, if not the entire animal bone assemblage from Point of Cott, including bird, fish and rodent bones, must be attributed to the natural non-soil element of the deposit, on the null hypothesis, i.e in the absence of positive evidence for their deposition by man. If this be the case, the source of some of the soil organic matter is indicated, in that the organic parts of owl, or other pellets, and of the bodies of the birds, rodents and other animals, together with the organic parts of their faeces must all have contributed to the soil organic matter of the chamber and other deposits. It is, however, possible, indeed probable, that some part of the soil organic matter is anthropogenic.

At present, before the completion of the post excavation analyses, the only unambiguously anthropogenic contributions seem to be human bone, pottery and whale-tooth beads and, of these, only the human bone will be considered further here.

The information intrinsic to the bone assemblage has been studied by Ms F. De J. Lee and her report, upon which this author has drawn heavily, will be published with the report in due course. Here it will suffice to consider only the depositional history of the assemblage, in the light of the operational hypothesis outlined above. The evidence adduced for excarnation seems to subsist in the disarticulation and partial representation of individual skeletons.

The partial survival of remains is attributed, in general, to selection, but if this be so, the selection seems remarkably arbitrary. It is at least equally probable that the surviving assemblages are representative of survivable conditions, rather than of deliberate selection. Chesterman has commented on the "...amazing *variability in the condition of the bones...*" (1979:101, his emphasis) and it seems probable that they represent a spectrum of decay and destruction ranging from perfectly preserved bones to unrecognizable fragments. It is to be regretted that we do not have a suitable technique for the identification and quantification, even in orders of magnitude, of the decay products of bone in chamber deposits. Standard analysis reveals extraordinarily high concentrations of phosphate in the chamber soils of Point of Cott, and while these may confidently be interpreted as derived from bone decay, it is not possible to suggest the amount of bone involved.

Since the evidence shows that we are dealing with assemblages which have undergone decay, and which perhaps continue to undergo decay up to the time of excavation, and, further, that extensive if unquantifiable decay is evidenced in the chemical composition of the chamber deposit matrix, it seems unsafe to base any conclusion on the absence of bone from the assemblages in chambered tombs. In this instance, the absence of evidence is, demonstrably, not evidence of absence. It may be helpful to add here that the partial or differential loss of bone as a result of differences in microenvironment, even in small or restricted archaeological deposits, is by no means uncommon. The loss of the bones of the feet and lower legs in a short cist excavated by Gordon Barclay at Strathallen provide a striking example of this phenomenon (1983:136, Plate 10).

At Quanterness some five skeletons, and the partial articulation of other body parts were noted, and this suggests that disarticulation was not a universal element of the burial rite. The quality of excavation at Isbister does not allow of any sound interpretation of the state of the bones, although the grouping of disarticulated remains was noted. At Point of Cott, approximately 70% of the bone was contained in compartment 3, which contained the most complete, while still disarticulated, skeletons. Of particular interest were two fragments of frontal bone, exhibiting *cribra orbitalia*, one from compartment 3, the other from the body of the construction-cairn east of the chamber. The nature of the lesions and the general character of the bone suggest quite strongly that these fragments are from the same individual, but do not 'prove' this. In interpreting the taphonomy of these bones the nature of the chamber floor deposit must again be considered. It is an anthropic soil, devoid of stratigraphic implication. The deposit is completely mixed, and the bones are distributed throughout its depth, with, in some cases, individual bones extending through the full depth. This can only have been achieved if the deposit underwent large scale turbation after the deposition of the human bone. This need not have been rapid, nor yet of a single phase, but it certainly took place. The occurrence of the frontal fragment outside the chamber need not be interpreted as indicative of some ritual foundation offering since it is quite possible that it was removed thence by the same agencies of disturbance as were responsible for the turbation of the chamber deposit.

The deposit within the Quanterness chamber is also anthropic and the fact that the radiocarbon dates do not reflect the stratigraphic order of the site's 'strata' is only to be expected. At this site also the inclusion of modern material especially in the animal bone assemblages suggests that the process(es?) of incorporation and turbation may continue to the present.

One result of this turbation has been the destructuring of the patterns of archaeological information contained within the deposit. It is possible, at Point of Cott for example, that the remains in compartment 1 represent a single individual interred as a complete cadaver. Those in compartment 3 may have been gathered thence once defleshed, perhaps still grouped together as individuals, while the curious cist-like structures in compartment 4 may have served as the site's ossuary-chambers. Destructuring of the pattern within the chamber and destruction of the material in compartment 4, together with the loss of material from unsuitable micro-environments throughout the deposit, added to the intrusion and a range of birds and animals, all contribute to the final form of the chamber deposit. This represents our present view of the formation of the chamber floor deposit at Point of Cott.

The seductive fruitlessness of reinterpreting old excavations is best borne out by the success with which it is done by supporters of opposing viewpoints. However, it is seductive and this author succumbs at least to the extent of pointing out that the apparent differences in the mortuary practices evidenced in the Orcadian tombs may represent nothing more than different stages in the progression from deposition to the formation of floor deposits. Crouched inhumations and grouped bones are evidenced at Midhowe, where little in the way of chamber floor deposits was noted. Henshall notes that crouched inhumations were also noted at Korkquoy and in the lower chamber at Taversoe Tuick (Henshall 1985:102). At Knowe of Yarso, only the later stages of the proposed rite seems evidenced in that grouped bones were observed, while an ossuary deposit had been formed in the end chamber. Henshall (*ibid*) comments on the division into skulls and other bones evidenced in this ossuary deposit, which corresponds with the Isbister evidence. This separation may owe as much to the difficulty of storing spherical and prismatic (in essence) forms together as to ritual considerations, especially since it comes only after the loss of individuality, implicit in ossuary storage, had occurred.

In conclusion, it is argued that the existing hypotheses for the involvement of animal remains in the funerary rites of chambered tombs may be irrelevant, or can be so considered until unequivocal evidence for their association with the funerary function of the tombs has been recovered. The hypothesis that excarnation was the principal funerary rite is not well founded and is not borne out, either at the Point of Cott, nor at those other sites for which adequate records exist. An alternative hypothesis has been offered, based on the observations made at Point of Cott and this, it is hoped, may be tested by future excavations. It is well recognised that archaeological monuments of all types undergo post-depositional changes (Atkinson 1957; Reynolds and Barber 1984; Rees 1986). Renfrew has explored the processes involved for Quanterness (1979, Ch. X and Fig.40) in some detail. However one is left with the feeling that we have all underestimated the extent and degree of changes involved. It is hoped that by more rigorous examination of the deposits with which we deal, especially with the non-anthropogenic elements, that we may begin to acquire that strong body of middle-range theory for which Binford and Bertram have so rightly called.

Note in Press:

In the interval between completion of this paper and its publication a sample of fox bone from "one of the chambers" at Quanterness has been radiocarbon dated to 30 ± 80 bc (OxA-1117; Hedges *et al* 1987:300). Armour-Chelu notes that the fox bone was, "as suspected", intrusive (*ibid*). This view is a little difficult to reconcile with Clutton-Brock's suggestion that the fox bones may have been deliberately included by Neolithic man (Renfrew 1979:118). The implications of this Iron Age date are of some significance when the distribution of fox bone in the tomb deposits is considered. Fox bone was retrieved from every area of the main chamber, the entrance and side chamber D. Fox bones were found in a total of ten contexts (2, 3, 4, 50, 55, 56, 57, 103, 152 and 154), spread over five 'strata' (3, 4, 5a, 5b, and 6) attributed to periods ranging from the Neolithic to the recent (Renfrew 1979, 117).

If we make the reasonable assumption that all of the fox bone is approximately contemporaneous it must be accepted that the entire chamber deposit was substantially disturbed during, or after, the Iron Age. This adds emphasis to the suggestion made above that the Quanterness chamber floor deposit is, like that of the Point of Cott, an anthropic soil with processes of incorporation and turbation continuing long past the currency of the tomb's usage.

References

Anderson H. and Hepburn A. 1985 Biochemical and other soil analyses. In Barber 1985.

Angell I.O. and Barber J. (forthcoming) Corbelling.

Atkinson R.J.C. 1957 Worms and weathering. *Antiquity* 31:219–33.

Barber J. 1985 The pit alignment at Eskbank Nurseries. *Proc. Prehist. Soc.* 51:149–166.

Barclay G.B. 1983 Sites of the third millennium BC to the first millennium AD at North Mains, Strathallen, Perthshire. *Proc. Soc. Antiqu. Scot.* 113:122–281.

Binford L.R. and Bertram J.B. 1977 Bone frequencies and attritional processes. In L.R. Binford (ed) *For Theory Building in Archaeology*. London.

Chapman R. and Randsborg K. 1981 Approaches to the archaeology of death. In Chapman *et al.* (eds) 1981.

Chapman R., Kinnes I. and Randsborg K. 1981 (eds) *The Archaeology of Death*. Cambridge University Press.

Chesterman J.T. 1979 Investigation of the human bones from Quanterness. In Renfrew 1979:97–111.

Chesterman J.T. 1983 The human skeletal remains. In Hedges 1983:73–132.

Corbet G.B. 1979 Report on rodent remains. In Renfrew (ed) 1979:135–7.

Hedges J. 1983 *Isbister: a chambered tomb in Orkney*. BAR 115.

Hedges R.E.M., Housley R.A., Law I.A., Percy C. and Gowlett J.A.J. 1987 radiocarbon dates from the Oxford AMS system. Archaeometry Datelist 6. *Archaeometry* 29:289–306.

Henshall A.S. 1985 The chambered cairns. In Renfrew (ed) 1985.

MacCormick F. 1984 Large mammal bone. In Sharples 1984:108 112.

O'Shea J. 1981 Social configurations and the archaeological study of mortuary practices: a case study. In Chapman *et al.* (eds) 1981.

Rees H. 1986 Dreams and nightmares of a pottery analyst...the worms. *The Field Archaeologist* 5:64–5.

Renfrew C. 1979 *Investigations in Orkney*. London.

Renfrew C. (ed) 1985 *The Prehistory of Orkney BC4000–1000AD*. Edinburgh University Press.

Reynolds N. & Barber J. 1984 Analytical Excavations. *Antiquity* 58:95–102.

Sharples N.M. 1984 Excavations at Pierowall Quarry, Westray, Orkney. *Proc. Soc. Antiqu. Scot.* 114:72–125.

6. Earlier Neolithic Organised Landscapes and Ceremonial in Lowland Britain

Francis Pryor

Introduction

Archaeologists tend to ask more general questions of their data the older they (the archaeologists and the data) become. As far as the data are concerned, this must merely reflect on their quality, quantity and availability; if Neolithic scholars had inscriptions and kilns to work with I am sure they would be arguing *minutiae* with the best of their colleagues. There is, however, a danger in a too ready acceptance of this state of affairs; in the case of Neolithic studies, for example, it has become increasingly acceptable to base general explanations on poor, or non-existent data, secure in the knowledge that proof or disproof will be hard to find in the field. Detailed regional research does offer one way out of this dilemma, but it is not an easy path to follow; earlier Neolithic data will always prove elusive and the search protracted and time-consuming.

The database of the British Neolithic is small and the tendency is still to paint on a broad canvas (e.g. Whittle 1977, 1985). I do, however, detect signs of change; our general model of the British Neolithic, such as it is, is not appropriate to an explanation of the data that is now being produced by intensive regional research in Britain (much of which is still in the process of analysis and publication). We require new frameworks for study if the gap between synthesis and fieldwork is not to broaden any further.

This paper is an attempt to draw wider conclusions from observations made during some fifteen years of intensive study of ancient sites and landscapes in the Peterborough area. We begin (part I) with a description of a recently discovered early Neolithic organised landscape at Fengate; Part II considers some of the methodological and interpretational implications of the discovery. Finally, in part III, we question some widely held assumptions about the nature and origins of the British lowland Neolithic and its surviving field monuments.

I. An Earlier Neolithic Organised Landscape

It might well be thought that Fengate has by now been studied-to-death (Pryor 1974, 1978, 1980, 1984), and that nothing significantly new remains to be discovered. However, this is not the case. I was asked to write-up an excavation that took place three years before the main Fengate Project and in the process happened upon a new and unexpected orientation of sites and features that bore no relation to the well-known ditched fields and enclosures of the second millennium bc Fen-edge (Pryor 1980). The first part of this paper is extracted from the forthcoming detailed report on the earlier excavations (Pryor, forthcoming).

The site in question is known as Fengate Site II, following the Royal Commission inventory of sites and monuments in the Peterborough area (RCHM 1969, Fig. 1). The threat to the site was imminent and delay could not be brooked, and it is very much to the excavator's (C.M. Mahany) credit that it has proved possible subsequently to offer a number of reinterpretations, suggested by discoveries made during the subsequent, and much larger, Fengate project.

Fengate Site II consisted of a rectilinear ditched enclosure, and other features, aligned northwest/southeast and centred on OSGR TL 213993. Figure 6.1 shows the site (D) in relation to the principal relevant sites or features of the later Fengate Project. The site has already been discussed, in interim form, by its excavator (Mahany 1969), and has subsequently been destroyed by factory development; it was excavated in a series of trenches, the locations of which are shown in Fig.6.2.

The enclosure ditch (Fig.6.2) measured 50×30 metres and was, on average three metres wide; the depth varied somewhat, but 70 centimetres was typical. It is hard to be certain, but the evidence for recutting is not convincing; the ditch had a regular, even, profile, with no obvious steps in its sides and the bottom was not ridged. There is some evidence (in the ditch sections only) that the ditch was accompanied by an internal bank.

A *terminus ante quem* for the enclosure ditch is provided by two hearths which had been cut into the uppermost (tertiary) ditch filling (Mahany 1969). One of the hearths contained weathered sherds, most probably of plain Beaker Ware. The uppermost, tertiary, layer of ditch produced a relatively fresh sherd of late Beaker (Clarke S2; Lanting and van der Waals, Step 6). It is, of course, extremely difficult to estimate how long a given feature took to fill-in, but the Etton causewayed enclosure ditch — a feature of broadly comparable size and cut into similar loose gravel — was producing Beaker material from its tertiary levels. Its primary levels produced middle Neolithic pottery. The flint assemblage from the Site 11 enclosure ditch, although small, is of earlier Neolithic character, and includes a number of diagnostic items; taken as a whole, the flints from the Fengate enclosure ditch would not be out of place at the Etton causewayed enclosure (R. Middleton, pers.comm.), or the Fengate earlier Neolithic house (Pryor 1974).

The artefactual evidence suggests an early date for the enclosure and its alignment tends to support this.

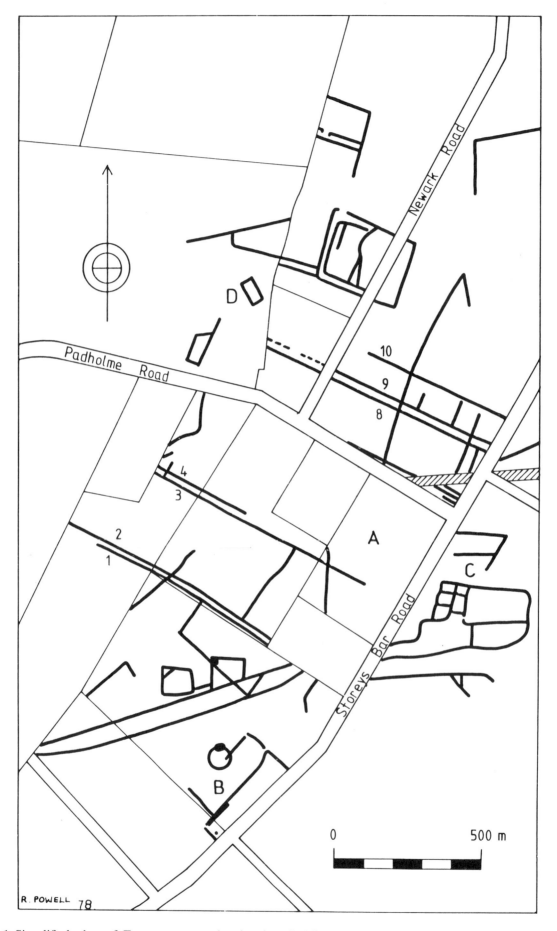

Fig.6.1 Simplified plan of Fengate cropmarks showing (1–10) second millennium bc ditches, and location of Neolithic house (A), Storey's Bar Road Grooved Ware settlement (B), Neolithic multiple burial (C) and Site 11 (D).

64

It is aligned northwest/southeast and clearly does not respect the orientation of the main second millennium bc ditched fields and enclosures (Fig.6.3, orientations A and B). This apparently 'skew' layout is, however, entirely consistent with that of the Padholme Road house (Fig.6.3). It would also seem that the two structures are approximately aligned on each other; this could of course be coincidental, but it is nonetheless most striking. The Padholme Road house is dated by a radiocarbon sample taken from a corner post: 2445±50 bc (GaK-4197). This date would accord well with the available evidence for Site 11.

The re-examination of Site 11 has shown that the enclosure was probably *not* a settlement feature. The hearths, interior features and the 'bridge' (Mahany 1969) can be demonstrated to post-date it, and most probably belong with the second millennium bc ditched fields and droves which (we now know) surround the site. There is some evidence to suggest that the features of the enclosure's interior may be compared quite closely with the Newark Road settlement nearby (Pryor, forthcoming & 1980, Figs.34-6 etc.). In short, the enclosure ditch is chronologically far removed from the features it encloses (yet another reason why one should look outside enclosure ditches, ring-ditches and the like). Finally, the severely rectangular layout of the ditch, and its regular profile, indicates that it was laid out in a single operation, and was not maintained open by recutting; Ian Kinnes (in Pryor, forthcoming)

suggests that the site probably served a funerary role.

We have seen that Site 11 and the Padholme Road house shared a common orientation and alignment and it is quite probable that the two may have been associated. Let us now examine other features of probable earlier Neolithic date at Fengate.

The Neolithic multiple burial on Cat's Water, where one of the individuals had been killed by a leaf arrow (Pryor 1976, 1985:19-27), also included disarticulated bones. Admittedly the dating evidence is slight, but if excarnation took place locally, then the enclosure would (as Dr. Kinnes has pointed out) provide a suitable place for so doing. In this regard it is interesting to recall that the oval barrow/enclosure at Maxey may also have been used for the storing or exposure of bones or bodies (Pryor and French 1985:233-4).

We have already mentioned the three best-known sites or features of the earlier Neolithic period at Fengate: the Site 11 enclosure, the Padholme Road house and the Cat's Water multiple burial. It should be recalled, however, that the Vicarage Farm subsite, to the northwest, included two parallel ditches which passed through an area of dense Iron Age occupation, but which produced very few finds (including a flake from a Group VI polished stone axe) (Pryor 1985, Fig.5, features 14 and 17). It is quite possible that these features which are orientated northeast/southwest, precisely the same as the Site 11 enclosure, are also of earlier Neolithic

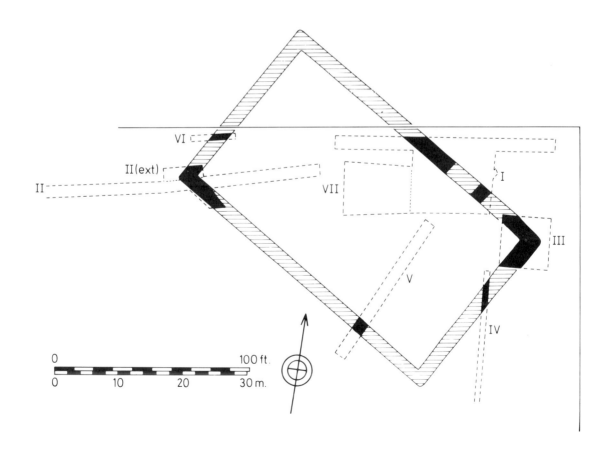

Fig.6.2 Fengate, Site 11, plan of the enclosure ditch.

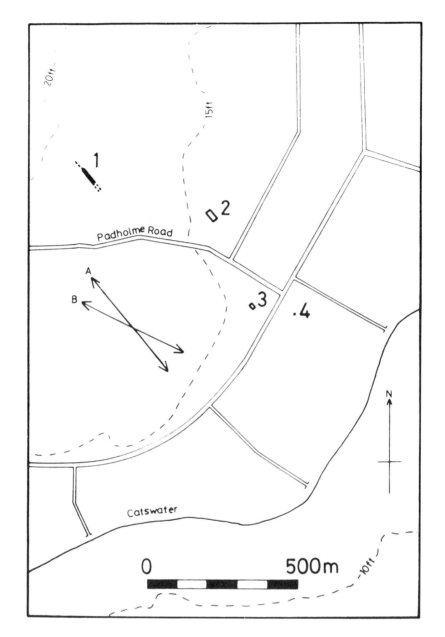

Fig.6.3 Map showing location and orientation of probable earlier Neolithic monuments, 1, Vicarage Farm linear ditches; 2, Site 11; 3, Padholme Road sub-site house; 4, Cat's Water sub-site multiple burial. The two principal prehistoric landscape orientations are shown by the crossed arrows (A: earlier Neolithic orientation; B: second millennium bc orientation).

date; it should be noted, however, that they do not share the alignment; if extended to the southeast the Vicarage Farm ditches would pass some 250 metres to the south of Site 11 — a spacing very approximately similar to the main elements of the later, second millennium bc, system of ditched droveways. Their orientation is, however, significantly different from that of the second millennium bc system.

A guessed estimate would suggest that the Fengate Project excavated perhaps 5%, by area, of the surviving archaeology of the Fengate Fen-edge. That small sample revealed three, and possibly four features of earlier Neolithic date, of which three (the present site, the house and the Vicarage Farm ditches) were substantial. It is hard to imagine this kind of site density in a forested setting. Recent

work at Etton and Maxey has demonstrated that the lower Welland valley landscape was substantially deforested by the middle Neolithic (Pryor and French 1985; Pryor, French and Taylor 1985), and there now seems to be no good reason to suppose that this did not also apply further south, in the lower Nene Valley. Studies of the buried soils of the Orton Meadows barrows, in the Nene floodplain immediately upstream of Peterborough, should prove particularly instructive in this regard (Pryor and French 1985:234 — with refs.).

If the cumulative evidence from Fengate suggests a largely cleared landscape, the common northwest/southeast orientation of the earlier Neolithic sites and features surely also suggests that the landscape was organised. The division of the land-

66

scape may have been by ditches (as at Vicarage Farm), but hedges, or other less archaeologically-visible means might also have been employed.

Finally, if our ideas on the earlier Neolithic landscape of Fengate are at all correct, it is tempting to wonder why the alignment was altered in the late third millennium, when the main, second millennium bc system was being laid-out. There may well have been a hiatus between the two episodes of land-use, but this cannot be established definitively as yet. It is perhaps worth noting that the later Neolithic does see widespread retrenchment (and forest regeneration) in parts of Britain where suitable regional studies have taken place (summarised by Bradley 1978a, 1978b:106); it is just possible that the changed landscape orientation at Fengate is a result of this process; the initial northwest/southeast landscape was laid out without regard to the Fen, the edge of which would have been significantly further east at this time (i.e. just prior to the main episodes of Fen Clay deposition). There then follows the period of retrenchment, which coincides with the deposition of Fen Clay and a general rise in ground water levels. Some local evidence for this retrenchment is provided by Godwin and Vishnu-Mittre (1975, Fig.11, 586–7): the two most pronounced peaks of clearance and agricultural activity, prior to the large scale clearances of the later Bronze and Iron Age are in the earlier Neolithic (where more indicators other than elm alone are selected) and the early/middle Bronze Age. By the onset of the second millennium, the Fen-edge is significantly closer to Fengate and the landscape is newly laid-out in the now familiar pattern, that takes into account different categories of land-use potential: from very wet to flood-free (Pryor 1980:182ff). It must be admitted that the evidence for the earlier Neolithic landscape orientation is slight, but it is, nonetheless there, and cannot be ignored. It is, moreover, most probable that we will never find earlier Neolithic landscapes preserved in the lowland zone in large, easily recognisable, patterns. Ours is indeed one of Bradley's (1978b) *Antique Fragments*, but it includes all the elements one would expect of a landscape: settlement, ceremony and land division; these elements are spread across the modern landscape, covering an area of at least 850 by 350 metres; as fragments go, it is quite substantial — and very antique.

II. Earlier Neolithic Organised Landscapes: Origins and Implications

We have seen that the suggested earlier Neolithic organised landscape at Fengate seems to pay little respect to the dominating features of the present landscape, namely, the Fen. Its layout, to modern eyes at least, seems therefore haphazard at best. The latter part of the following discussion will attempt to see to what extent we can extend this principle of apparent haphazardness to other landscapes in the region. First, however, we must consider the context of the whole: the characteristically British features of the British Neolithic landscape.

Livestock and the Emergence of Neolithic Culture in Fourth Millennium Lowland Britain

Our appreciation of the origins of our landscape is still partial; recently, it is true, we have learned much about the later Neolithic landscape and the monuments that populated it, and we also know a certain amount about the later Mesolithic; but it is the intervening period (very broadly speaking the fourth millennium bc and slightly earlier) that still proves elusive. On present evidence the earlier Fengate landscape would belong to the latter part of this period, although its origins remain obscure.

The demise of the 'invasion hypothesis' in British archaeology has enabled archaeologists to think anew about the problems of origins. By and large their conclusions have tended to stress compromise: new ideas, social organisations, technologies, etc. become modified to suit local requirements. The mechanisms or constraints necessary to achieve these ends — be they invasions, climatic changes, population growth/contraction etc. — are seen in context, perhaps as being of marginal relevance; at all events, such speculations no longer litter the pages of the archaeological literature. However, for reasons I do not fully understand, the British Neolithic is still strangely 'invasive': we speculate (e.g. Whittle 1977) as to which continental pottery style matches our earliest plain bowls, and necessarily imply that the best match marks the source of our Neolithic culture (I use the word advisedly). The main shortcoming of this approach is that it ignores the fourth millennium and the important role Mesolithic communities must have played in the development of (their) Neolithic culture. Surely our native population played a greater part in the formation of Neolithic culture than the mere influence of Neolithic 'B' (or the Secondary Neolithic) flint industries, as was once widely believed? In part III we will discuss this matter further.

The origins of the British Neolithic have now been freed from the abrupt synchroneity always inherent in the concept of the elm decline (Girling and Greig 1985). We may accordingly take a longer term, more gradual, view of our Neolithic. Inevitably such a view requires that we consider the major part played by Mesolithic communities in the origins of the archaeologically visible Neolithic, primarily of the third and second millennia bc; these origins, however, lie in the fourth millennium bc for which direct archaeological evidence is still slight. Accordingly, the early Fengate organised landscape has a significance that is more than local or regional. Accordingly, too, we must make every effort to find archaeological evidence, especially for fourth millennium land-management practices, elsewhere in Britain, no matter how slight, or how tentative.

By and large the continental picture seems far more straightforward and one may reasonably wonder why we may not suggest something similar for Britain: Childe's Danubian I, our Bandkeramik-using cultures/groups/families/communities expand/travel/populate across loess plains and up fertile river valleys, where they meet no existing Mesolithic groups with which they might fight/interact/stimulate or diffuse. It seems to the present author far too simple to be credible; much has been written, but relatively little has been intensively surveyed or excavated, especially in the valley bottoms, where the sites of the apparently non-existent Mesolithic groups doubtless lie hidden beneath deposits of alluvium or colluvium. Where work has taken place in an intensive, thoroughgoing, regional context (e.g. Louwe Kooijmans 1974), the true complexities of the situation become readily apparent.

If we cannot draw on the 'classic' continental model to explain the nature of our earliest Neolithic landscape, may we not examine work in similar topographic areas where at least some *new* data have been gathered? The similarities originally pointed out by Louwe Kooijmans (1976) between pottery and water-side settlement locations of our earlier Neolithic (eastern style Plain Bowl tradition) and the middle Neolithic Hazendonk-2 groups of the Netherlands have already been extensively reviewed and further discussion would be superfluous (Pryor 1984:246ff). It does, however, come as a slight surprise to learn that these groups might have occupied an organised landscape; but the evidence, as presented here, is hard to disregard out of hand. Perhaps a change of terminology might help; the majority of British Neolithic groups that Professor Louwe Kooijmans cites as contemporary with the middle Neolithic communities of the Netherlands are indeed closely comparable in all significant respects with their middle Neolithic counterparts elsewhere along the Continental fringes of the North Sea basin. It must surely make sense to adapt our terminology accordingly. The British earlier Neolithic *sensu stricto*, like its counterparts around the North Sea (Swifterbant, Hazendonk-1 etc.) lies in the fourth millennium bc.

Landscapes that are very broadly comparable with those of eastern England may be found in Denmark. Madsen and Jensen (1982), writing on the early Neolithic of that country, suggest a model of early land-use that utilises natural and artificial clearings in the dense lime forest, especially in or around damp places where "the highest natural feeding potential for animals could be found". They discuss the types of animal that were kept and conclude that pigs and cattle were of importance. Their conclusions are of particular relevance to the present discussion:

> It should seriously be considered whether this type of land use was a much more prominent and important part of the early farming economy than was grain growing on a slash and burn basis. Despite their small numbers, scrapers also seem to indicate a much higher index of hide working than is the case later on in the Middle Neolithic. Whatever it may be worth statistically, this can be taken as a point in favour of a relatively high dependence on animals.
>
> (Madsen and Jensen 1982:82–3).

It would clearly be most foolish to transpose this model *holus bolus* to Britain, but it is entirely appropriate to a coastal climate; there are, moreover, reasons to suppose that it might well apply to the Fen-edge, where damp places abounded and where seasonal flooding would have confined the growing of cereals to land not subject to regular inundation in springtime. A more mobile population in the Neolithic of fourth millennium bc Britain might help to account for the scarcity of finds of that period, even in areas such as the Peterborough Fen-edge (or south Lincolnshire Fen-edge — Peter Chowne, pers.comm.) where archaeological survey has been intensive. In these areas, winter protein could have been provided by fish, eels and wildfowl, rather than by grain. Such a pattern of life is not far removed from that of the true hunter-gatherer; indeed one might suggest that it has more in common with the Mesolithic than with the Neolithic of the 'classic' Linearbandkeramik regions. It seems entirely reasonable to assume that the folk who might have lived in this fashion in Britain were ultimately of Mesolithic origin. It is unfortunate that this pattern of life, by its very impermanence, leaves so slight an archaeological trace. In Denmark Madsen and Jensen appreciated that these areas of good natural grazing could soon become objects of competition and suggested that Trichterbecherkeramik graves could have been symbolic markers to rights of land. Here we are suggesting that the British landscape was more formally parcelled-up.

There is, of course, nothing new in the idea that a formal landscape of fields, or rather paddocks, may be required in situations where grazing land is under a degree of pressure. The 'degree' of pressure may be very slight indeed and will reflect social custom and practice as much as 'absolute' pressure on grazing; in the modern British highland zone grazing on hillsides and valley bottoms is parcelled-up, whereas that above the tree line, or on higher moors or fells is often open and used in common. As a rule archaeologists tend to disregard the former types of grazing when considering pasture as a whole. Land divisions of this type might account, for example, for the development and use of the second millennium bc enclosures at Fengate. The contemporary and closely similar ditched droves and fields/paddocks of Mucking are probably another example of the phenomenon (Jones 1976). Some social implications of such land management practices have been convincingly discussed by Andrew Fleming (1985).

In short, it simply is not necessary — indeed it may be actively misleading — to posit widespread cereal agriculture in order to account for the existence of a field or enclosure system. The probable role of agriculture, or more properly perhaps, of cereal horticulture, will be considered further in Part III.

We have emphasised the central role of livestock to the Neolithic of Britain in the fourth millennium bc (and subsequently), and we have suggested that the changes involved in the emergence of an archaeologically recognisable Neolithic culture took place very gradually. We have also implied (although proof positive will be hard to come by) that native, essentially Mesolithic, groups played an important part in the process. Towards the end of the fourth millennium the changes in the landscape wrought by these socio-economic developments become archaeologically visible. We will now return to the Peterborough area in search of further evidence of this elusive period.

Further Evidence for Early Neolithic Land-use in the Peterborough Region — and its Implications

Some ten miles north of Peterborough the plain that fringes the Fen merges imperceptibly with the first terrace gravel soils of the lower Welland valley. Here there is now good evidence, outlined in Part I above, to suggest that large tracts of the low-lying landscape were cleared of forest by the end of the fourth millennium bc, or very shortly thereafter. In a recent paper (Pryor, French and Taylor press 1985) it was suggested that the Etton causewayed enclosure was itself (at least in part, if not in whole) a 'field' in which cereals were grown; another recent paper (Pryor 1988) has suggested that the causewayed enclosure might be seen symbolically to represent the wider landscape in miniature. This hypothesis has been given added support by the discovery in 1985 of a single, cursus-like ditch (of early second millennium bc date) which traversed the enclosure interior diagonally, just as the main Maxey cursus traverses and divides Maxey island nearby. The causewayed enclosure, it should be recalled, sits on a low knoll of gravel — in effect a small 'island' within a pronounced meander of a relict course of the larger Welland system.

The orientation of the main Maxey cursus seems wholly illogical, given the layout of the modern landscape, as it manifestly fails to respect the lie of the land or the presence of the surrounding Fen/floodplain. By the way of contrast one should compare the layout of the near by Billingborough Bronze and Iron Age Fen-edge landscape (Chowne 1980, Fig.2), where land divisions run, conventionally, at right-angles to the Fen-edge. Could the Maxey cursus, like the Fengate earlier Neolithic landscape discussed in Part I, owe its orientation to an earlier landscape, in which Maxey had still to achieve (probably in the Iron Age) its later 'island' status? During the mid- and later Neolithic it is probable that the rising land of Maxey would have been seasonally flooded to north and south only, i.e. along the axis of streams forming part of the braided Welland system. In the fourth millennium bc it would have been drier still; as time progressed, so flooding became worse and waterlogging more permanent. Being so large a monument it is hard to conceive that the Maxey cursus would have completely ignored the arrangement of its contemporary landscape and surroundings. If that was indeed the case, then we now have at least a suggestion of the organisation of the broader landscape in which the causewayed enclosure sat. The cursus is shallow and would make little sense in a wooded environment; it is over two kilometres long, and by implication must have run across many hundreds of hectares of open

country; certainly this would agree with the picture revealed by pollen analysis at the Etton causewayed enclosure, a site hard by the cursus (Scaife in Pryor, French and Taylor 1985). There is also clear stratigraphic evidence that shows the cursus alignment was used for several centuries (Pryor and French 1985; Pryor, French and Taylor 1985). During that time earlier lengths of the ditch *must* have filled-in completely (Pryor and French 1985:232), yet their alignment was generally accurately resumed during later episodes of ditch-digging. It is of course possible that the traditional course of the monument was marked by some permanent surface marker, but there is no evidence for this whatsoever; it is surely more straightforward to suggest that the cursus followed the alignment of the landscape, where the orientation of every hedge, drove, coppice stand and garden plot would have directed and emphasised its course.

Explanations of this sort are required if one is satisfactorily to account for large-scale forest clearance at so early a period. It is hard to imagine that prime land was simply left open, unmarked and unorganised for any- or every- one to make us of. In the lowland zone where the absence of stone does not allow the construction of archaeologically visible land divisions we must use these shreds of evidence, whilst freely acknowledging their tenuous nature.

If large tracts of the earlier Neolithic landscape in the area under review was organised, then to what extent does this imply permanence — either of settlement or of year-round land-use? So far the evidence suggests that the situation was probably complex and that different patterns of settlement and land-use might have existed side-by-side *within the same landscape.* Our current model for Etton suggests that the site was occupied in the drier months of the year, roughly speaking from late spring/early summer until autumn. Many of the enclosure ditch's so-called 'placed' deposits contain sloe stones or hazel nuts, which are also found in associated (and contemporary) middle Neolithic cremations on the interior. It is possible that these deposits were placed in position shortly before the site's seasonal abandonment. There is now no evidence that the interior of the enclosure was occupied by large numbers of people for extended periods of time, and some four acres have so far (by mid-May 1986), been cleared. We might suppose, therefore, that following the sowing of the spring cereals (Pryor, French and Taylor 1985), a proportion — and perhaps the greater part — of the population left the enclosure, together with the herds they tended, which then grazed the pastures round about. This grazing probably took place, as we have seen, within an organised landscape.

The autumn then saw the return of the livestock and their herdsmen to the causewayed enclosure, doubtless to help gather the harvest and afterwards to celebrate the fact. The cremations were probably of bodies, parts of bodies (skulls?) or other representations of people who had died earlier that year, whether resident within the enclosure or with the livestock outside; it would thus be unwise to estimate the enclosure's *resident* population from the number of cremations found there. Given this explanation, it is not hard to see why the causewayed enclosure was a place of special significance to the community.

The Place of Monuments within an Ancient Developing Landscape

We have seen that the Etton causewayed enclosure was constructed in a cleared landscape, and most probably in the earlier part of the third millennium bc. We may thus see it — and other monuments like it — as the first archaeologically apparent physical manifestation of symbol and ceremony within a landscape that was already perhaps a millennium old; the same applies to long barrows, monuments such as Fengate Site 11, cursuses and, of course, henges. It is not the purpose of this paper to discuss funerary monuments as such, but it is nonetheless worth noting that the interior of the Etton causewayed enclosure has produced, as we have mentioned previously, some 15 excavated cremations that are undoubtedly contemporary with the first use of the monument; some 50 additional probable cremations have recently been exposed, but still await excavation. The Etton cremations processed to date resemble rakings from a pyre and incorporate much flint debris (conjoining flakes have been found in separate cremation pits), burnt and unburnt human and animal bone. Quite frequently the quantities of burnt bone are slight. These small pit cremations bear a striking resemblance to the two circles of pits excavated by Simpson within the interior of the Maxey henge complex (Simpson, in Pryor and French 1985:245–64); similar features are of course known from a number of British lowland henge monuments.

Like the Etton causewayed enclosure, the main Maxey henge complex was also the scene of short episodes of activity; we cannot prove that these took place in the autumn, but they may well represent a more formalised expression of earlier practices. I do not wish to over-stress the morphological and other similarities between some henge/hengiform monuments and causewayed enclosures — both are frequently more or less circular — but the layout of, for example, the smaller Maxey henge (Site 69) ditches is markedly 'interrupted' (Simpson 1981). Although much further afield, it is perhaps worth recalling the accumulations of 'debris' (including antler picks) in the ditch butt-end at Marden; this deposit may not necessarily represent casual loss — as was indeed hinted by the excavator (Wainwright 1969:155, caption). Whether significant or not, the Marden deposit is highly reminiscent of Etton. In short it is suggested that henge monuments of lowland Britain (and I omit here the major monuments of the Wessex chalk) may reflect earlier causewayed enclosure practices in certain important respects; generally speaking the former are a more formal, specialised expression of the latter in which settlement, whether permanent or episodic, plays a very reduced role.

Finally, we have suggested above that animal husbandry played an important part in the development of the earlier Neolithic landscape, at least in our area, and probably elsewhere in lowland Britain. We are not suggesting that *all* causewayed enclosures were used to separate the growing of grain from a landscape in which grazing predominated and where the pattern of life was essentially mobile; but an association of the two can be argued. For the purpose of the present discussion I suggest that the lowland causewayed enclosures can be seen as the physical, and doubtless symbolic, manifestation of a different, and largely new, pattern of land-use within an existing and *long-established* landscape with a mobile population heavily reliant on the exploitation of livestock. The causewayed enclosure ditches make little sense in a wooded, undeveloped landscape, where the enclosure (as has often been pointed out) is the edge of the surrounding forest itself. Similarly, cursus are essentially monuments of the open countryside, and their close resemblance to ditched droveways might well betray their actual ancestry prior to their formal, archaeologically-visible manifestation. Again, the explanation of the origin and role of these peculiarly British monuments must lie in a close examination of their regional, landscape, contexts, as by and large, with the notable exception of Springfield (Hedges and Buckley 1981), excavation has been signally unenlightening. I will return to the relationship of cursus and henge monuments, and what they might represent, towards the conclusion of this paper. It is now necessary to return to our principal theme.

III. The Origins and Nature of the British Lowland Neolithic Landscape

Britain is an island with an Oceanic climate not always well-suited to the growing of modern cereal varieties, let alone emmer, einkorn, or spelt. British archaeologists, however, have played a distinguished and prominent part in monitoring the spread of cereal cultivation across Europe (e.g. Childe 1957; Clarke 1965; Murray 1970); similarly their studies of the origins of ancient *agriculture* are well known (e.g. Higgs 1972; Hutchinson *et al.* 1976; Renfrew 1973). There can be no doubt, as anyone who attended a British university in the 1960s and 1970s could attest, that these ideas have played an important part in the way we think about the origins of farming in these islands. It is hardly surprising that we tend to view our own Neolithic through at best central European, and at worst Near Eastern spectacles. At all events we often adopt (in climatic terms) a continental perspective. Is this, however, appropriate? Is it not equally probable that livestock was *far* more important than is generally realised? Unfortunately it is hard to compare the relative importance of these two strands of the ancient economy from our excavated data; in nearly all cases the quantitative or relational comparison of carbonised cereal and animal bone debris is meaningless; the data are often gathered in non-comparable fashions and have pre-depositional (culture/ systemic, call it what you will) and taphonomic histories that may differ widely. Indeed for the purposes of that particular comparison, it is perhaps best to proceed on a simple presence/absence basis. The matter is further complicated by the fact that few specialists feel confident to attempt both types of study (and the taphonomic problems of such a comparison are horrendous). Accordingly, and far too often, the presence of the all-but-ubiquitous charred cereal grains on most British prehistoric sites is taken to indicate that fields of waving corn grew nearby. This, surely, should be *demonstrated,* not assumed. After all fields can just as well be used for livestock, and droveways of one sort or another are an integral part of British ancient fields, be they 'Celtic', Fengate/Billingborough style, 'banjo' enclosures, reaves, or whatever.

Our view of our own Neolithic is necessarily conditioned by our view of the subject as a whole. In Britain at least we have seen a resurgence of what would once have been called Armchair Archaeology where, as I mentioned above, explanations are not always matched against new evidence from the field. In part this doubtless reflects British archaeology's straitened financial circumstances, but the reliance on literature alone has tended to fossilise an already outmoded data-base where the original data retrieval methods and research objectives were simply not appropriate to the questions now being asked to them. If the interpretational usefulness of our Neolithic data-base is flawed, we follow our traditional imperial inclinations and looked abroad. We seek 'continental parallels' to give our work respectability, yet at the same time we fail to observe our own landscape with any sympathy or precision. Too often our modern lowland landscape, which is largely shaped by the requirements of the Common Agricultural Policy, serves as the inspirational background to our interpretive models. Certainly there are notable exceptions (the Somerset Levels Project, Dartmoor Reaves, etc.), but by and large British Neolithic Explanations say more about archaeology in Britain than they do about British archaeology.

Our archaeological explanations may owe much to History, but they are also indebted to historians; if indeed there ever was a type of infield/outfield system in British prehistory, may it not have been quite different from the well-known Medieval model? Cereals and vegetable crops could have been grown in small plots or gardens in and around the settlement area, with the livestock in the surrounding fields. Such an arrangement might help account for the presence of grain processing debris and the dense spread of pottery in the close vicinity of many British prehistoric and 'native' Roman settlement sites. Recent work at an Iron Age and Romano-British site at Maxey, for example, has suggested that the land immediately adjacent to the farmstead was manured — and that this may have been the area where crops were grown; doubtless livestock was kept in the surrounding land outside the settlement's immediate vicinity (Pryor and French 1985). Clearly one should not extrapolate from the Iron Age to the Neolithic without a word of caution, but it is hard to imagine that the Neolithic situation saw an *increased* intensification of cereal agriculture. British Neolithic site reports frequently mention

fields of cereals, yet I cannot recall a single *excavated* example of the phenomenon in the literature. Much reliance is placed on pollen analysis, especially on the supposed 'weeds of agriculture'. However, a field grubbed up by pigs (a more probable contender as agent of large-scale land-clearance than ring-bark or slash-and-burn) or over-grazed by other livestock will rapidly be colonised by a closely similar flora. Pollen can help monitor land clearance, it is true, but greater precision of interpretation requires a reliable, excavated, archaeological context as well. The same contextual caveats apply to palynology as to radiocarbon. The few examples of ard-marks below barrows could just as well result from plot horticulture in the immediate vicinity of settlement. Indeed, given the enormous number of excavated barrows, is it not extraordinary that so few have produced clear evidence for ploughing? Viewed as simple exercises in farm or land management, the vast majority of British ancient fields betray the unmistakable signs of livestock. Incidentally, lynchets need not necessarily indicate plough agriculture, as strip lynchets clearly demonstrate. In short, the role of cereals (and the timing and manner of their introduction) in the British Neolithic requires urgent investigation.

If cereal farming did indeed take longer to become firmly established in Britain than on the continent, it is probable that the majority of the population also took longer to adopt permanent, fixed, year-round settlement. This might help to account for the otherwise extraordinary dearth of *long-lived* late Neolithic/Bronze Age settlement sites, which by comparison are so frequently found on the continent. On the rare occasions when settlement sites of this age are found they are often single period and show little signs of maintenance or re-occupation — and this despite the fact that such sites are often located within ancient and long-lived, organised landscapes. Permanent land division should not be equated with permanent settlement; we too often bracket 'settlement and land-use' together. The two are far from synonymous.

We have argued that livestock played a far larger role in the British Neolithic than is generally appreciated. We have also argued that the presence of livestock does not imply an open un-organised "outfield" style of landscape. Grazing requires management, like any other aspect of farming. If (some) causewayed enclosures can indeed be associated with the large-scale growing of cereals, then they might also have seen fixed settlement, at least while the crops were growing and ripening. Given these arguments, it is possible to imagine a population out of harmony with itself; put simply, a (slow growing) minority of cereal-growing, or more probably of mixed farmers, living alongside a majority community of transhumant, or less rigidly fixed, pastoral farmers. The slow change from the former to the latter may well have been accompanied by tensions; certainly the different requirements of cereal farmers and pastoralists are often at odds with one another. Could these tensions, or simple expressions of identity, find manifestation in henges and cursuses — ceremonial monuments that must surely have origins in the earlier Neolithic social and physical landscape? At all events these uniquely British monuments require explanations that take the peculiarities of our Atlantic islands into account.

Conclusion

I have suggested that livestock played a far more important role in the earliest stages of the British Neolithic than has been generally appreciated and that it was the native Mesolithic communities who were the herdsmen involved. The keeping of animals, at first within natural clearings, eventually led to the creation of open landscapes which, in certain cases, were organised along agreed orientations. This hypothesis would imply that the earliest Neolithic of Britain had far more in common with, for example, the Mesolithic/Neolithic transition of northern Europe. An essential corollary of this suggestion is that important elements of native Mesolithic social structure and ideology formed an integral part of our full Neolithic. If the third millennium bc sees a widespread change towards a more settled way of life — as the simple quantity of archaeological evidence implies — then it is not unreasonable to assume that the change gave rise to certain social tensions which find archaeological expression in the widespread, but uniquely British field monuments of the later Neolithic. Whether or not the monuments themselves can be traced back to the fourth millennium bc seems to me irrelevant — the ideas, traditions and societies in which they were rooted were already ancient (and indigenous).

References

Bradley R.J. 1978a Colonisation and land use in the Late Neolithic and Early Bronze Age. In S. Limbrey and J.G. Evans (eds) *The Effect of Man on the Landscape: the lowland zone*. CBA Res. Rep. 21:95–102.

Bradley R.J. 1978b *The Prehistoric Settlement of Britain* London.

Childe V.G. 1957 *The Dawn of European Civilization*. 6th ed. London.

Chowne P. 1980 Bronze age settlement in south Lincolnshire. In J. Barrett and R.J. Bradley (eds), *Settlement and Society in the British Later Bronze Age* Vol. ii. BAR 83:295–306.

Clark J.G.D. 1965 Radiocarbon dating and the expansion of farming culture from the Near East over Europe. *Proc. Prehist. Soc.* 21:58–73.

Evans C. 1988 Excavation at Haddenham, Cambs.: a 'planned' enclosure and its regional affinities. In C.B. Burgess (ed) *Enclosures and Defences in the Neolithic of Western Europe*. BAR Oxford.

Fleming A. 1985 Land, tenure, productivity and field systems. In G. Barker and C. Gamble (eds) *Beyond Domestication in Prehistoric Europe*. London, pp. 129–146.

Girling M.A. and Greig J. 1985 A first record for *Scolytus scolytus...* and the implications for Neolithic elm disease. *J. Archaeol. Sci.* 12:347–352.

Godwin H. and Vishnu-Mittre 1975 Studies of the post-glacial history of British vegetation XVI. Flandrian deposits of the fenland margin at Holme Fen and Whittlesey Mere, Hunts. *Phil. Trans. Roy. Soc. London,* ser. B, 270:561–604.

Hedges J.D. and Buckley D.G. 1981 *Springfield cursus and the cursus problem*. Essex County Council Occ. Paper No.1. Chelmsford.

Higgs E.S. (ed) 1972 *Papers in Economic Prehistory*. Cambridge.

Hutchinson J., Clark J.G.D., Jope E.M. and Riley R. 1976 *The Early History of Agriculture*. London.

Jones M.U. 1976 The Mucking excavations. *Panorama*, J. of Thurrock Local History Society (Essex) 20:34–43.

Louwe Kooijmans L.P. 1974 *The Rhine/Meuse Delta*. Leiden.

Louwe Kooijmans L.P. 1976 Local development in a borderland. *Oudehiedkundige Mededelingen uit het Rijksmuseum van Oudheded te Leiden* 57:227–297.

Mahany C. 1969 Fengate. *Curr. Archaeol.* 17:156–7.

Murray J. 1970 *The First European Agriculture*. Edinburgh.

Pryor F.M.M. 1974 *Excavation at Fengate, Peterborough, England: the first report*. Royal Ontario Museum Archaeology Monograph 3, Toronto.

Pryor F.M.M. 1976 A Neolithic multiple burial from Fengate. *Antiquity* 50:232–3.

Pryor F.M.M. 1978 *Excavation at Fengate, Peterborough, England: the second report*. Royal Ontario Museum Archaeology Monograph 5, Toronto.

Pryor F.M.M. 1980 *Excavation at Fengate, Peterborough, England: the third report*. Northampton Archaeol. Soc. Monograph 1/Royal Ontario Museum Archaeology Monograph 6, Toronto and Northampton.

Pryor F.M.M. 1984 *Excavation at Fengate, Peterborough, England: the fourth report*. Northampton Archaeol. Monograph 2/Royal Ontario Museum Archaeology Monograph 7, Toronto and Northampton.

Pryor F.M.M. 1988 Etton, near Maxey, Cambridgeshire: a causeclosure on the Fen-edge. In C.B. Burgess (ed) *Enclosure and Defences in the Neolithic of Western Europe*. BAR Oxford.

Pryor F.M.M. forthcoming Excavations at Site 11, Fengate, 1969. In W.G. Simpson, D.A. Gurney and F.M.M. Pryor *Excavations in Peterborough and the Lower Welland Valley 1961–1969*. Fenland Project Monograph, East Anglian Archaeology.

Pryor F.M.M. and French C.A.I. 1985 *Archaeology and Environment in the Lower Welland Valley*. 2 vols, East Anglian Archaeol. 27.

Pryor F.M.M., French C.A.I. and Taylor M. 1985 An Interim Report on Excavations at Etton, Maxey, Cambridgeshire (1982–84). *Antiqu. J.* 65:275–311.

Pryor F.M.M. and Kinnes I.A. 1982 A waterlogged causewayed enclosure in the Cambridgeshire Fens. *Antiqu. J.* 56:124–26.

RCHM 1960 *A Matter of Time: an archaeological survey* H.M.S.O. London.

Renfrew J.M. 1973 *Palaeoethnobotany*. Columbia.

Wainwright G.J. 1969 Marden. *Curr. Archaeol.* 17:152–155.

Whittle A.W.R. 1977 *The Earlier Neolithic of Southern England and its Continental Background* BAR S-35, Oxford.

Whittle A.W.R. 1985 *Neolithic Europe: a survey*. Cambridge.

7. The Landscape Setting of Causewayed Camps: Recent Work on the Maiden Castle Enclosure

J.G. Evans, A.J. Rouse, N.M. Sharples

Introduction

In recent years there has been considerable interest in the causewayed camps of southern Britain. Several recent excavations have now been published, sites such as Briar Hill (Bamford 1985), Orsett (Hedges and Buckley 1978) and Offham (Drewett 1977), providing a reliable sample of high quality information from different regions. Approaches to the landscape setting of the camps have seen subtle changes. Earlier emphasis on the morphology and distribution of monuments within Britain and Europe (Whittle 1977; Palmer 1976) has been replaced by more recent interest with the local position of the enclosures (Barker and Webley 1978; Smith 1984), with emphasis on the relationship with other monuments and the environment of the surrounding land. It is the latter approach which is the main aim of this paper. We hope to demonstrate the subtlety of land use through the Neolithic and to establish that the local environment was being deliberately manipulated by human communities. The work has considerable implications in analysing the many interpretations of these monuments (Drewett 1977).

The focus of this paper is the enclosure at Maiden Castle (Wheeler 1943). Recent work on the site and its surrounding landscape has the potential to alter radically our perception of the role of the enclosure since the environmental evidence is exceptionally well preserved. The juxtaposition of a causewayed camp, bank barrow and early Iron Age hillfort has resulted in the preservation of land surfaces and ditch fills of several periods. In most contexts the soil conditions are such that molluscs are well preserved, and these provide the basic evidence for the environment of the hilltop described in this paper.

The enclosure at Maiden Castle is a slightly atypical example for a southern British chalkland causewayed camp (Palmer 1976). It consists of two closely set ditches *c.* 14m apart enclosing an area of *c.* 20 acres. The early Iron Age bank is built over the inner ditch of the enclosure, and the ditch fill and the surrounding area have been sealed since this period. There is no significant bank. A large part of the interior was examined by Wheeler and, though much of this was sealed under the bank barrow, very little was found. Features consisted of several shallow pits and a grave containing two children. Many of the features were thought to be associated with the construction of the bank barrow but there is no evidence for this. The occurrence of several burials in the primary fill of the enclosure ditches suggests that the burials from the interior might also be contemporary with the use of the enclosure.

The enclosure appears to have been abandoned for a short period before the bank barrow was constructed. The bank barrow is 546m long and 18.3m wide. It is an unrevetted mound lying between two parallel ditches. The mound is hardly visible today, but surface examination and excavation have shown that its position was subject to detailed consideration. The most striking feature in plan is that the mound changes its alignment around the centre of the fort. There are three sections, each with a different alignment. This is best interpreted as a long barrow adjacent to the enclosure which was extended when the enclosure went out of use (Bradley 1984).

Final evidence for early prehistoric occupation consists of domestic debris in a cultivation horizon at the top of the ditches of all the early prehistoric monuments. There is no evidence for the locus of this occupation and it is not associated with any structures.

The 1985 Excavation: Molluscan Sample Contexts

The 1985 excavation comprised three trenches in the centre of the fort (Fig.7.1; Sharples 1986). These allowed the examination of the following prehistoric features: the inner ditch of the early Neolithic enclosure (two sections); the northern ditch of the bank barrow (two sections); the northern half of the bank barrow mound; a badly truncated segment of the outer ditch of the enclosure; and a small bank associated with the inner ditch of the enclosure.

A total of eight mollusc columns was taken through these features using techniques described in Evans (1972). In general, sampling was done at 10cm intervals, the rubbly nature of the deposits (Fig.7.4 and 7.5) precluding anything closer. In the turf-lines, where one could have sampled more finely, the very low numbers of shells made this invalid. For the purpose of this paper, three columns have been fully analysed.

MC XIII: west section through the inner ditch of the enclosure in trench I, where the ditch is sealed by the bank barrow (Fig.7.2).

MC IV: east section through the northern ditch of the bank barrow in trench I, where it was sealed by the Iron Age rampart (not illustrated, but the equivalent section on the west side is shown in Fig.7.2).

MC III: north section through the inner ditch of the enclosure in trench II. The ditch is sealed by the Iron

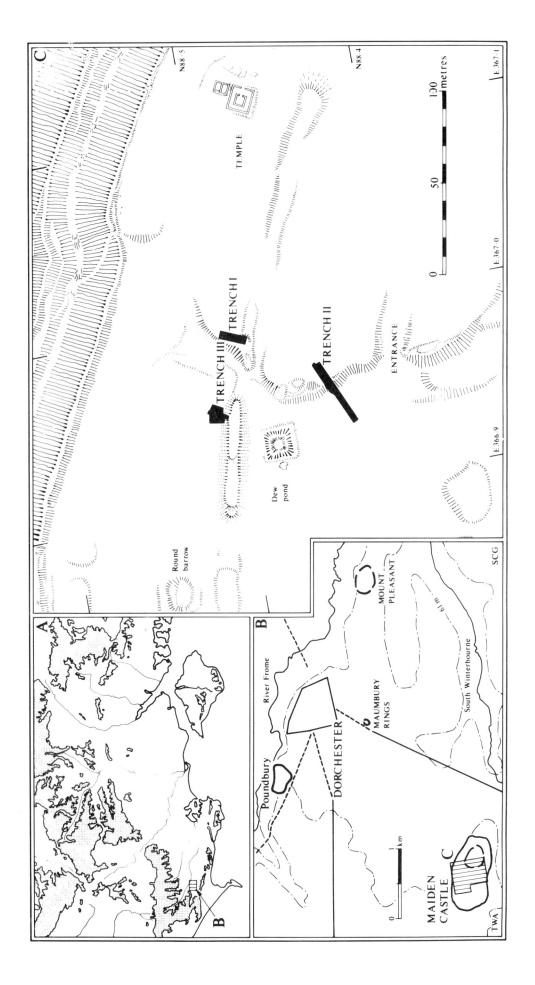

Fig.7.1 Location of the 1985 excavations at Maiden Castle. Reproduced by permission of the Dorset Natural History and Archaeological Society and the Royal Commission on Ancient and Historical Monuments (England).

74

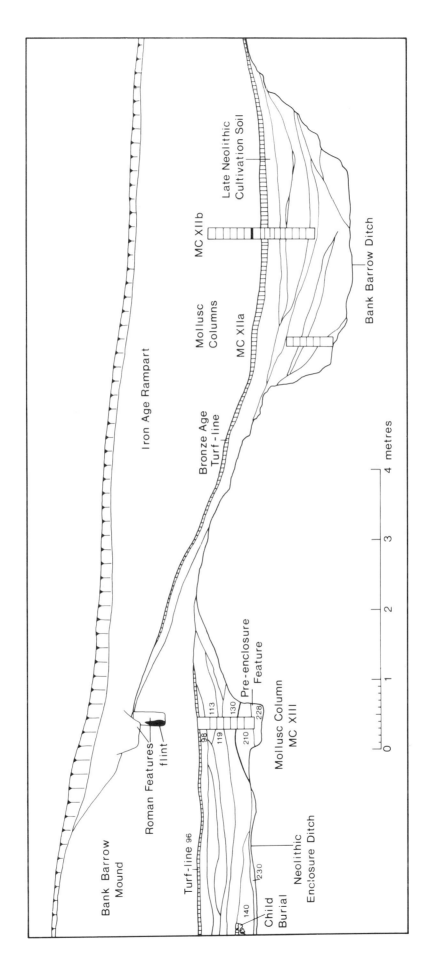

Fig.7.2 Trench I, west section, showing the main stratigraphic divisions and the infill layers of the inner enclosure ditch and the northern bank barrow ditch. The molluscan columns taken from this section are marked. MC XIII is discussed in the text, but MC XII has yet to be analysed. MC IV was taken from the section facing MC XII.

Bank Barrow Mound

Iron Age Rampart

Roman Features flint

Turf-line 96

Bronze Age Turf-line

Mollusc Columns

MC XIIa

MC XIIb

Late Neolithic Cultivation Soil

Bank Barrow Ditch

Pre-enclosure Feature

98

119

113

130

210

228

230

140

Child Burial

Neolithic Enclosure Ditch

Mollusc Column MC XIII

0   1   2   3   4 metres

Age rampart, but contains a late Neolithic occupation (Fig.7.3).

Other samples came from treeholes at the base of the buried soil under the bank associated with the enclosure ditch (MC VIIa and b, MC VIb) (Fig.7.3).

The earliest evidence comes from the bottom of MC XIII where the enclosure ditch cuts an earlier feature (contexts 228 and 210), and from the treeholes (MC VIIa and b, MC VIb).

The pre-enclosure feature was largely removed by later activity but what survived suggests that it was a relatively open feature which filled up slowly. Evidence for human activity in the infilling was virtually absent.

Archaeological evidence suggests that the bank associated with the enclosure ditch was not a primary feature. It is best interpreted as redeposited ditch fills from the cleaning of the ditches. The underlying soil, however, is not seriously disturbed so it does provide an indication of the pre-enclosure environment. The absence of a marked worm-sorted horizon and the presence of treeholes in the underlying subsoil suggest woodland.

Evidence for the environment during the use of the enclosure is preserved in the enclosure ditch fill (MC XIII and MC III). The fill of the enclosure ditch can be divided into four main units. On the base of the ditch there is a series of thin silt layers (context 230), above which are several thick layers of chalk rubble (140). These two primary fills represent the initial rapid weathering of the ditch sides. Finds were infrequent, but in the rubble there was a large quantity of charcoal from an *in situ* fire and, at the top of the layer, a child burial. The primary fill was sealed by a series of silty clay loams which varied only slightly and were intermixed with several contexts rich in artefacts and charcoal (between 130 and 98). The final layer in trench I was a thin stone-free turfline (96) which directly underlay the bank barrow.

The bank barrow ditch in trench I had a homogeneous fill (MC IV). Although thirteen separate layers were identified, they were only differentiated by subtle changes of colour, texture and rubble content. At the south edge, where the ditch cut the earlier enclosure ditch, the rich midden fill of the latter had almost immediately begun to erode into the bank barrow ditch. The stratigraphy was clearer in trench III, where it was split into primary rubble and clay layers, a secondary rubble-free silt, humic and chalk-free upper fills and, last, a thick turf-line. The upper fill in both trenches was dated by small fragments of Beaker, and probably resulted from settlement and cultivation.

In summary, MC XIII provides an environmental sequence through the early Neolithic until the construction of the bank barrow; MC IV continues the sequence from this point up to the abandonment of the hilltop in the early Bronze Age; and MC III provides a continuous sequence for the entire period.

The Molluscan Assemblages

Ideally, in presenting the results of analysis, diagrams of both percentages and numbers of shells per unit weight should be used, although considerations of space usually preclude this. Percentage diagrams are the most convenient (Evans 1972), not least because they are of manageable size. Plots of numbers per unit weight may demonstrate more realistically changes in abundance (Thomas 1985) but they may also be illustrating changes that are caused by taphonomic processes. The main problem is that the situation is not constant. Different processes may operate variously, alone or in conjunction, and at different levels, and it is therefore difficult to adopt a common policy in any one sequence.

A similar problem arises with the "intermediate species". It has been suggested (Thomas 1985) that, after a consideration of the main trends indicated by the "woodland" and "open-country" species, some of the intermediate species be reassigned to one of these groups. But in any one sequence, one or more of the intermediate species may behave variously, going with the woodland species at one level and the open-country species at another.

In plotting the results we have used numbers of shells per kilogram for MC XIII since total numbers are sometimes low, and percentages for MC IV where the large numbers of some species would have made plots per kilogram unwieldy. Summary diagrams of the percentages of the main ecological groups show broad trends through the sequences. Two indexes of diversity, the Shannon index (H') and the Brillouin index (H), have been calculated (using natural logarithms) as described by Pielou (1975). H' incorporates numbers of species and the distribution of numbers of shells amongst the various species — the evenness of the assemblage. H, in addition, takes account of total numbers (see also Evans and Smith 1983).

Other refinements (Thomas 1985) such as the separation of immature and adult shells, the separation of weathered and fresh shells, metrical studies and the use of statistical methods such as association analysis have not been applied systematically, although we have noted especially weathered shells. All these ideas have been applied previously, but in practice the data often precludes little more than the basic treatment. Essentially, we see a detailed understanding of the site and its contexts, meticulous sampling, and the changes of species abundance in long and continuous sequences as being the most important aims at present. Methodological and statistical refinements must go along with the collection of good data, and, in the case of the latter, molluscan analysis is still in its infancy.

MC VIb, MC VIIa and b, MC XIII (Fig.7.4)

The earliest assemblages are from treeholes at the base of the buried soil below the enclosure bank (MC VIb, MC VIIa and b). They indicate woodland. *Vertigo pusilla* is important, being the only occurrence of this species on the site. Open-country species are present in very low numbers, but it is very likely that the relevant shells are contaminants from the backfill of Wheeler's excavation.

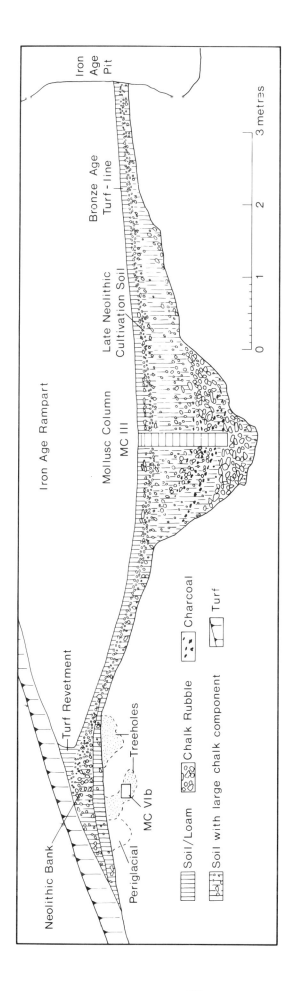

Fig.7.3 Trench II, north section, showing the early prehistoric contexts. The different contexts are shown schematically to give an impression of the nature of the buried soils and the infilling of the inner enclosure ditch. The position of molluscan columns MC III and MC VIb are indicated. MC VIIa and b were taken from a similar context to MC VIb on the other side of the trench.

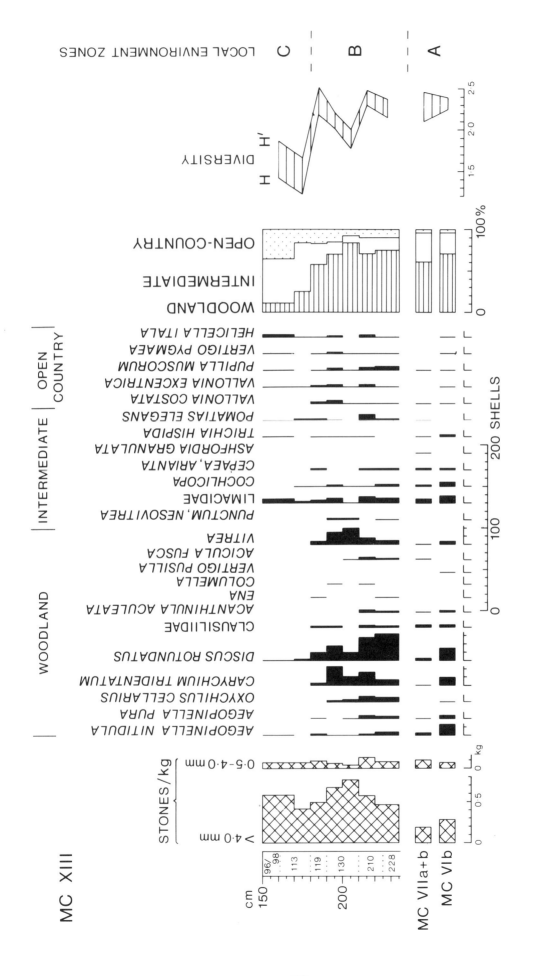

Fig.7.4 Molluscan histogram, MC VIb and MC VIIa and b from treeholes beneath the enclosure bank, and MC XIII from the pre-enclosure feature (210 and 228) and the enclosure ditch (130 to 96). Numbers in the stratigraphical column are archaeological contexts.

The buried soil itself was virtually devoid of shells.

Woodland assemblages occur in the pre-enclosure feature (MC XIII, contexts 210 and 228) and in the lower part of the enclosure ditch fill (119 and 130). Open-country species are present, but the general environment was woodland. In combination with the assemblages from the treeholes, the presence of a distinct group of three species — *Vertigo pusilla, Columella* sp. and *Acicula fusca* — which are characteristic of undisturbed woodland and which are absent from later levels indicates that the primary woodland was of a different character from that which regenerated in the later Neolithic. The diversity of these assemblages is generally high.

In the upper part of the sequence (MC XIII, 96/98 and 113), shells become sparse. The reduction of woodland species and the persistence (and relative increase) of open-country species along with a fall in diversity indicates a trend to open country. Woodland clearance was taking place on a larger scale than previously.

MC IV (Fig.7.5)

At the very base of the sequence (140–160 cm) there is a significant, if low, abundance of open-country species. This is a direct continuation of the open-country assemblage at the top of MC XIII.

The main part of the sequence is woodland, and two main assemblages occur. In the lower (90–140 cm), shell numbers are high, *Carychium* is extremely common, and the assemblage is characterised by *Ashfordia granulata* and the absence of *Pomatias elegans*. There is a reduction in the amount of chalk rubble towards the top of this section. In the upper assemblage (30–90 cm), shell numbers are lower, the abundance of *Carychium* is lower, and *Pomatias elegans* becomes characteristic; *Ashfordia* dies out. There is an increase in the amount of chalk rubble coming into the ditch at the base of this section. These differences reflect different amounts of disturbance and moisture, with the lower part reflecting damper and less disturbed conditions than the upper.

Between 5 and 30cm, open-country species and *Pomatias elegans* increase and there is a reduction in the woodland element. Diversity, which up to this point has been above 2.0, falls. This assemblage corresponds to a layer interpreted as a cultivation soil of Beaker age.

The assemblage from the Bronze Age turf-line (0–5cm) is sparse, and little significance can be placed on the percentages or diversity values. This is where a histogram of shell numbers would bring out the changes more clearly. Partial decalcification of the soil before burial is indicated.

MC III

This sequence repeats those already described from the base of the enclosure ditch to the Bronze Age turf-line, and is not discussed in detail or illustrated. Woodland occurred in the early stages of

infilling, and clearance took place at some time prior to the construction of the bank barrow. The two episodes of secondary woodland characterised by first *Ashfordia* and then *Pomatias* can be recognised. Further clearance ensued at a level coincident with the Beaker cultivation soil. The Bronze Age turf-line is totally decalcified.

The Environmental Sequence

The sequence is divided chronologically into seven "local environment zones", lettered A to G, based on the molluscan assemblages and the stratigraphy (Fig.7.6). These refer to the environment at the site scale. We cannot necessarily extrapolate from them to the region as a whole, while at the other extreme, local episodes relating to processes going on only within the ditches — e.g. the deliberate backfilling of the enclosure ditch — are not separately zoned.

Zone A. Primary woodland. Treeholes beneath the enclosure bank (MC VIb, MC VIIa and b).

Zone B. Woodland with open-country influence, probably a woodland clearing. Pre-enclosure feature (MC XIII 210–235cm) and lower part of enclosure ditch (MC XIII 180–210cm).

Zone C. Open country. An extension of zone B, lasting from shortly prior to the construction of the bank barrow to shortly after this event. Upper part of enclosure ditch (MC XIII 150–180cm) and lowest part of bank barrow ditch (MC IV 140–160cm).

Zone D. Secondary woodland, relatively damp and undisturbed. Bank barrow ditch (MC IV 90–140cm).

Zone E. Secondary woodland, relatively dry with localised disturbance, but no clearance. Bank barrow ditch (MC IV 30–90cm).

Zone F. Woodland clearance and cultivation. Bank barrow ditch, Beaker cultivation horizon (MC IV 5–30cm).

Zone G. Grassland, probably species poor. Partial decalcification of the soil prior to burial beneath the early Iron Age bank. Bank barrow ditch, Bronze Age turf-line (MC IV 0–5cm).

The sequence has implications at various spatial scales — feature, site and region. Thus we are interested in the environments and functions of specific types of Neolithic monument, especially the enclosures and bank barrows. More widely, we are interested in the history of the Maiden Castle hilltop as a whole and its surrounding valleys. And on a regional and countrywide scale the Maiden Castle sequence can be compared with that in other areas of the chalklands of southern England.

At Maiden Castle, the natural vegetation of the mid-Postglacial was woodland. There was small-scale clearance in the Neolithic associated with the building of the enclosure, and in this respect the situation was similar to that in north Wiltshire (Evans 1972; Dimbleby and Evans 1974) and the South Downs (Thomas 1982) for this class of monument. On the other hand, the bank barrow too was built in a landscape that had only minimally been cleared of woodland, and this is unusual (Evans 1972; Ashbee *et al.* 1979). For the later Neolithic, woodland regeneration has been recorded

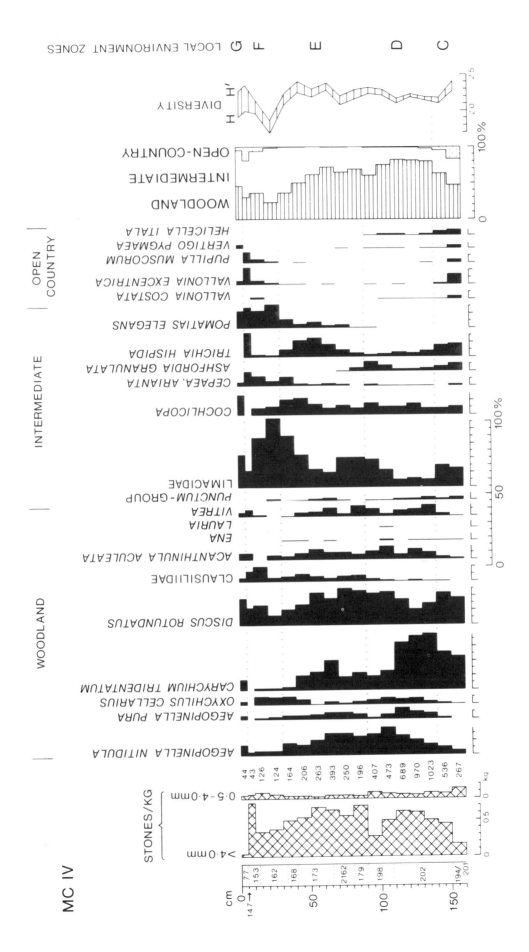

Fig.7.5 Molluscan histogram MC IV from the north ditch of the bank barrow. Numbers in the stratigraphical column are archaeological contexts.

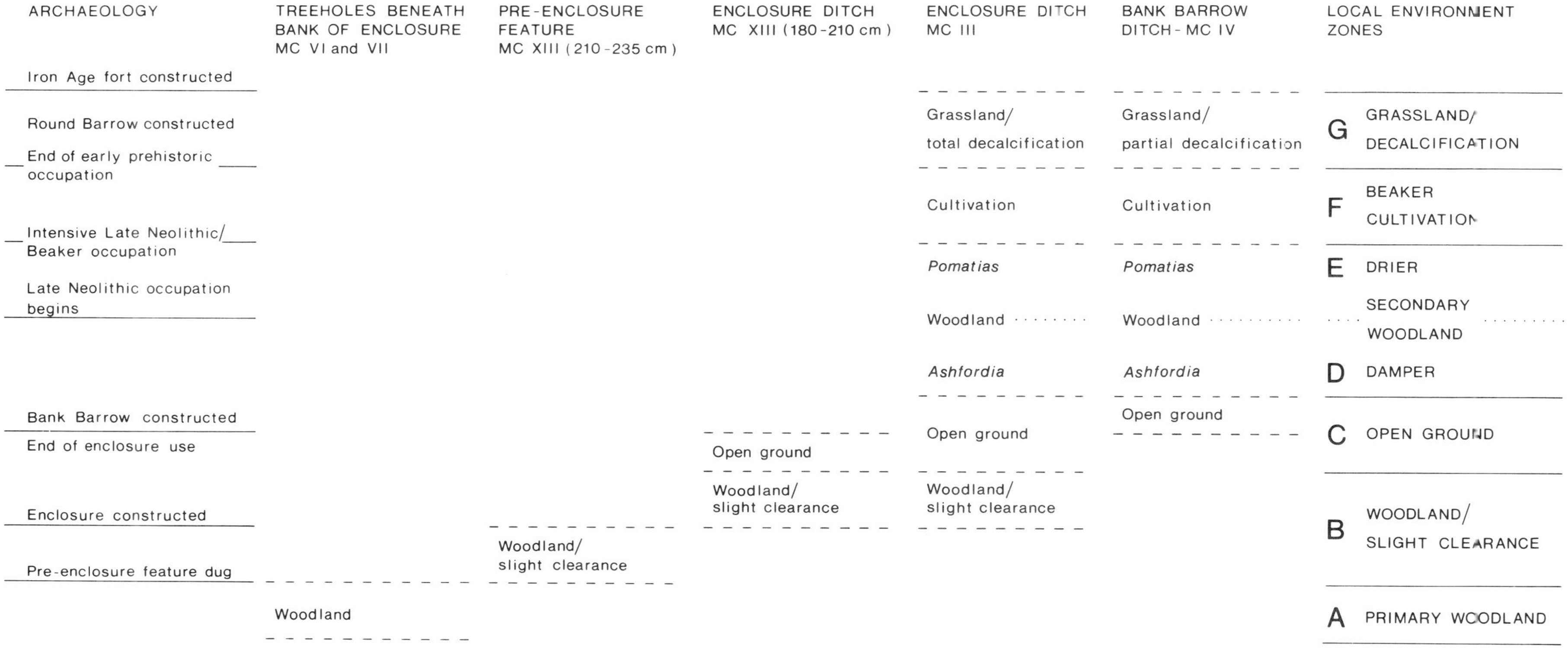

ARCHAEOLOGY	TREEHOLES BENEATH BANK OF ENCLOSURE MC VI and VII	PRE-ENCLOSURE FEATURE MC XIII (210–235 cm)	ENCLOSURE DITCH MC XIII (180–210 cm)	ENCLOSURE DITCH MC III	BANK BARROW DITCH – MC IV	LOCAL ENVIRONMENT ZONES	
Iron Age fort constructed							
Round Barrow constructed					Grassland/ partial decalcification	G	GRASSLAND/ DECALCIFICATION
End of early prehistoric occupation				Grassland/ total decalcification			
Intensive Late Neolithic/ Beaker occupation				Cultivation	Cultivation	F	BEAKER CULTIVATION
Late Neolithic occupation begins				*Pomatias*	*Pomatias*	E	DRIER .... SECONDARY WOODLAND
				Woodland	Woodland		
				Ashfordia	*Ashfordia*	D	DAMPER
Bank Barrow constructed			Open ground	Open ground	Open ground	C	OPEN GROUND
End of enclosure use			Woodland/ slight clearance	Woodland/ slight clearance		B	WOODLAND/ SLIGHT CLEARANCE
Enclosure constructed		Woodland/ slight clearance					
Pre-enclosure feature dug							
	Woodland					A	PRIMARY WOODLAND

Fig.7.6 The earlier prehistoric environmental and archaeological sequence at Maiden Castle as represented in different contexts.

81

from a number of sites, so the Maiden Castle episode was probably part of a widespread event, even though the significance of its division into two zones is unclear and probably local. Likewise, clearance and cultivation in Beaker times is attested elsewhere (Ashbee *et al.* 1979; Evans and Smith 1983; Evans and Simpson 1986). On the other hand, soil decalcification on the Chalk in the Bronze Age is not something that has been widely reported. It is, however, a feature of the Giants' Hills 2, Skendleby, sequence (Evans and Simpson 1986), and is hinted at in the South Street sequence (Ashbee *et al.* 1979). Open country, and especially grassland, was typical of the Bronze Age.

There are differences between the Maiden Castle sequence and that at Mount Pleasant (Wainwright 1979). At Mount Pleasant, clearance and the establishment of grassland had been achieved by at least the later Neolithic, *c.* 2100bc. Woodland regenerated over part of the site, perhaps just in the large enclosure ditch, between *c.* 1800 and 1500bc. This was destroyed at *c.* 1500bc to be succeeded by a long period of grassland through the Bronze and Iron Ages until the site was ploughed in Roman times. There was no Beaker cultivation, although substantial Beaker reorganisation took place around 1700bc. A thick deposit of wind-blown material accumulated in the southwest entrance of the main enclosure ditch during the later prehistoric period but was absent from some other parts of the site. The Bronze Age/Iron Age soil showed no signs of decalcification, but there was incipient decalcification in some levels of the wind-blown deposit.

Archaeological Implications

The results are of crucial importance to the interpretation of early Neolithic enclosures. This is the most detailed evidence that the enclosures were not "central places" as suggested by Barker and Webley (1978) but relatively isolated monuments sited away from agricultural land. What we know of the landscape around Maiden Castle provides further details. The site is situated on an isolated spur of the South Dorset Ridgeway. Immediately to the south is the narrow, steep-sided valley of the South Winterbourne. To the north is a wide open plain separating Maiden Castle from the Frome valley. Within the landscape are several early Neolithic long barrows. Their distribution concentrates in three clusters on the Ridgeway around the bank barrows of Broadmayne, Long Bredy and, to a lesser extent, Maiden Castle. It is likely, however, that this distribution is seriously distorted by differential preservation. Recent excavations in and around Dorchester have uncovered several early prehistoric monuments, the upstanding parts of which were completely destroyed during the prehistoric period. This involved the destruction of the stone circle and palisade at Mount Pleasant (Wainwright 1979), and recent excavations at Allington Avenue by the Trust for Wessex Archaeology (Davies *et al.* 1986) revealed a long barrow which had had its mound removed by the Iron Age. This suggests a former

concentration of monuments around the River Frome as impressive as that still surviving on the Ridgeway.

Fieldwork provides a more direct picture of Neolithic settlement patterns. Information from excavations, survey, and fieldwalking for the South Dorset Ridgeway study area (Woodward, in prep.) and from the landscape survey around Maiden Castle (Woodward, pers. comm.) suggest that there were two distinct zones in the early Neolithic, the Ridgeway and its surrounding valleys, including the South Winterbourne, and the River Frome. Maiden Castle lies on the margins of the Ridgeway, and there is a marked absence of settlement debris in the plain to the north. The marginal location for the enclosure is paralleled at other sites, most noticeably Windmill Hill (Smith 1984), and argues against them having an important agricultural function as has been suggested for Hambledon Hill (Mercer 1980). It seems more likely that these monuments had a symbolic/religious function in early Neolithic society.

Radiocarbon dates for causewayed camps have consistently placed the construction of these monuments in the first half of the third millennium bc (with the one exception of the enclosure at Hembury in Devon). Thus it seems that the enclosures were constructed well after the appearance of settled agricultural communities. The date range for long barrows is wider and suggests the Neolithic communities were capable of monument construction a long time before the appearance of the enclosures. The early date for Hembury does not contradict this statement as the pattern of dates suggests an earlier beginning for settlement in the southwest (Palmer 1976). An explanation for this pattern is that the enclosures appeared only after a sufficient number of agricultural communities had become established in any region. Unlike long barrows, enclosures are concerned with the relationships between groups at the community level. They are a deliberate attempt to impose a structure on inter- and intra-group relationships.

If the enclosure played such a role then it might be expected that the sites would be centrally situated within the community. However, such a position would have disadvantages due to the nature of the activities taking place there. Family and individual allegiance to the community would have required regular affirmation, by rituals, at important life-cycle events such as birth and death. These rituals would most likely occur at the enclosures. Evidence for such a use is impossible to discover but we do know that enclosures were closely involved in the burial activities of the Neolithic community (Thorpe 1984; Sharples 1986). Such rituals are of considerable importance to the community but are often conceived to be extremely dangerous. Consequently it would be appropriate for the centres to be situated outside the main settlement zone on the boundary of the community territory.

Several more specific roles arise from the function and position of the enclosures, as they provide a basis not just for the organisation of internal community relationships but also the relationships between communities. The primary role of inter-group contact would be to exchange important resources, i.e. crops, raw materials, craft produce and people. The peripheral position of these enclosures would be ideal for this role, as outsiders could be kept isolated and conflicts arising from contact could be contained away from the productive base. There is good evidence for the importance of these enclosures in exchange networks. At Windmill Hill there is a very high local concentration of imported axes and numerous sources for the ceramics (Howard 1981). At Maiden Castle, Cornish axes are present in large numbers and gabbroic wares are common. Perhaps the most important exchange process involved the local production of flint, and it seems likely that the enclosure was a very important part of an exchange network based on the good quality flint sources on the Ridgeway (Care 1982).

During the Neolithic, warfare becomes increasingly attested. This is dramatically shown by Crickley Hill and Hambledon Hill (Mercer 1980) where the enclosures were defended by massive ramparts and subjected to violent attack. Associated with the attacks were leaf-shaped arrowheads, and the distinctive design of these can be interpreted as an attempt to produce an efficient arrowhead for killing people. There are large numbers of these arrowheads from Maiden Castle but only two examples have been found in the survey of the surrounding landscape and these in the zone immediately around the site (Woodward pers. comm.). The sequence at Hambledon Hill and Crickley Hill suggests that the massive defences are a later addition, indicating that conflict was escalating during the early Neolithic. This would suggest that population had continued to grow and that communities were expanding and coming into conflict with each other over critical resources. At Maiden Castle there are no elaborate defences; instead the enclosure was abandoned and the hilltop was cleared. Then the bank barrow was constructed. This monument may represent the growing need for symbolic boundaries in the increasingly crowded landscape of south Dorset. Ultimately the pressures of inter-communal rivalry were too great a strain on the social and economic structure of early Neolithic society and there was a dramatic collapse from which late Neolithic society emerges with a completely different social structure and economic base.

The interpretation of the role of the early Neolithic enclosures has two distinct levels. On a general level the enclosure is a monument designed to bind the dispersed farmsteads of the agricultural community together and to formalise relations between different groups. At this level the interpretation should be applicable to most of the enclosures in southern Britain. At a separate level an attempt has been made to interpret specific activities taking place at some enclosures. At this level the interpretation is much more regionally specific to the enclosures on the chalklands of Wessex. The important ritual significance of the monument could be interpreted in a variety of ways in the different social and environmental regions to the east and north. Restrictions could easily be placed on what may or

may not have taken place within the confines of the enclosure.

Acknowledgements

We thank P.J. Woodward, M. Parker Pearson and P. Bellamy for assistance and information during the writing of this paper. The Maiden Castle Committee has given valuable encouragement, and we acknowledge too the work of the team of excavators during the summer of 1985 in exposing the sections. The work, including the Research Assistantship of Miss A.J. Rouse, is being financed by the Historic Buildings and Monuments Commission for England.

References

Ashbee P., Smith I.F. and Evans, J.G. 1979 Excavation of three long barrows near Avebury, Wiltshire. *Proc. Prehist. Soc.* 45:207–300.

Bamford H. 1985 *Briar Hill: excavation 1974–1978*. Northampton Development Corporation, Archaeological Monograph No. 3.

Barker G. and Webley D. 1978 Causewayed camps and early Neolithic economies in central southern England. *Proc. Prehist. Soc.* 44:161–186.

Bradley R. 1984 The bank barrows and related monuments of Dorset in the light of recent fieldwork. *Proc. Dorset Nat. Hist. Arch. Soc.* 105:15–20.

Care V. 1982 The collection and distribution of lithic materials during the Mesolithic and Neolithic periods in southern England. *Oxford J. Archaeol.* 1:269–285.

Davies S.M., Stacey L.C. and Woodward P.J. 1986 Excavations at Allington Avenue, Fordington, Dorchester, 1984–85: interim report. *Proc. Dorset. Nat. Hist. Arch. Soc.* 107:101–110.

Dimbleby G.W. and Evans J.G. 1974 Pollen and land-snail analysis of calcareous soils. *J. Arch. Sci.* 1:117–133.

Drewett P. 1977 The excavation of a Neolithic causewayed enclosure on Offham Hill, East Sussex, 1976. *Proc. Prehist. Soc.* 43:201–241.

Evans J.G. 1972. *Land Snails in Archaeology*. London: Seminar Press.

Evans J.G. and Simpson D.D.A. 1986 Radiocarbon dates for the Giants' Hills 2 Long Barrow, Skendleby, Lincolnshire. In J.A.J. Gowlett and R.E.M. Hedges (eds), *Archaeological Results from Accelerator Dating*. Oxford University Committee for Archaeology Monograph Series, Oxford.

Evans J.G. and Smith I.F. 1983 Excavations at Cherhill, north Wiltshire, 1967. *Proc. Prehist. Soc.* 49:43–117.

Hedges J. and Buckley D. 1978 Excavations at a Neolithic causewayed enclosure, Orsett, Essex, 1975. *Proc. Prehist. Soc.* 44:219–308.

Howard H. 1981 In the wake of distribution: towards an integrated approach to ceramic studies in prehistoric Britain. In H. Howard and E.L. Morris (eds). *Production and Distribution: a ceramic viewpoint*. BAR S-120, Oxford, pp. 1–30.

Mercer R. 1980 *Hambledon Hill: a Neolithic landscape*. Edinburgh University Press.

Pielou E.C. 1975 *Ecological Diversity*. London: John Wiley.

Palmer R. 1976 Interrupted ditch enclosures in Britain: the use of aerial photography for comparative studies. *Proc. Prehist. Soc.* 42:161–186.

Sharples N.M. 1986 Maiden Castle 1985: an interim report. *Proc. Dorset Nat. Hist. Arch. Soc.* 107:111–120.

Smith R.W. 1984 The ecology of Neolithic farming systems as exemplified by the Avebury region of Wiltshire. *Proc. Prehist. Soc.* 50:99–120.

Thomas K.D. 1982 Neolithic enclosures and woodland habitats on the South Downs in Sussex, England. In M. Bell and S. Limbrey (eds). *Archaeological Aspects of Woodland Ecology*. BAR S-146:147–170.

Thomas K.D. 1985 Land snail analysis in archaeology: theory and practice. In N.R.J. Fieller, D.D. Gilbertson and N.G.A. Ralph (eds). *Palaeobiological Investigations: research design, methods and data analysis.* BAR S-266:131–156.

Thorpe I.J. 1984 Ritual, power and ideology: a reconstruction of earlier Neolithic rituals in Wessex. In R. Bradley and J. Gardiner (eds). *Neolithic Studies: a review of some current research.* BAR 133:41–60.

Wainwright G.J. 1979 *Mount Pleasant, Dorset: excavations 1970–71.* Rep. Res. Comm. Soc. Antiqu. No. 37, London.

Wheeler R.E.M. 1943 *Maiden Castle, Dorset.* Rep. Res. Comm. Soc. Antiqu. No. 12, Oxford.

Whittle A. 1977 Earlier Neolithic enclosures in northwest Europe. *Proc. Prehist. Soc.* 43:329–348.

Woodward P.J. 1983 South Dorset Ridgeway: the presentation and management of the pre-Iron Age archaeological landscape. *Proc. Dorset Nat. Hist. Arch. Soc.* 105:141.

Woodward P.J. (in prep.) The South Dorset Ridgeway survey and excavation 1977–83. The pre-Iron Age landscapes.

8. Acts of Enclosure: A Consideration of Concentrically-Organised Causewayed Enclosures.

Christopher Evans

Considerable research and certainly much speculation has been expended on the monumental constructions of the middle and later Neolithic in Britain. Limited attention, however, has been given to the fact that one of the main distinguishing traits of so many of the enclosures of the third millennium bc is a concentric spatial organisation. This paper will concern itself with the implications of this spatial pattern and will consider the interpretation of concentrically-planned causewayed enclosures, whose specific spatial properties have only seriously been considered in the interpretations of these enclosures as cattle kraals (Case 1956:43; Catherall 1976:2). This paper will not presume to offer a definite interpretation of these complex sites, but rather will emphasise the extent to which concentricity is an extraordinary spatial configuration which has major ramifications relating to the character and construction of these enclosures.

As a consequence of this discussion the procedures of enclosure planning and the status of prehistoric design/architecture will be considered. In this context, furthermore, the recently published Briar Hill enclosure will be discussed at some length and an alternative phasing sequence will be proposed for this site. It is not the intention to restrict the scope of this study solely to a 'logic of monuments', but rather to attempt to consider the phenomenon of early enclosure in the broader context of the development of landscape in southern Britain during the Neolithic.

Monuments as Projects

"Works are not finished, they are abandoned" (Valery)

Until recently there has been a tendency to consider causewayed enclosures as some manner of undifferentiated radial form, whose multiple causeways were equally open to the seasonal influx of Neolithic communities as if on the spokes of a great wheel. In fact, the plan or 'design' of these ambiguous enclosures (Evans 1988a) has been treated rather like the patterns of 'random walks' insomuch as there have been few serious attempts made to understand the variations in their ditch circuits and the relative phasing of their construction and re-cutting. In this regard Bradley has recently cautioned that by the physical scale and endurance of 'monuments' there is an inclination to 'assume' their surviving form as given and to ignore the sequence of their construction and re-definition (Bradley 1984:62).

In the phasing of monuments there is, furthermore, an inherent tendency to assume a sequent-

ial magnitude of construction which progresses rationally from smallest to greatest. This latter point is particularly relevant when studying the plans of concentric ring enclosures in which there is a natural temptation to assume a ripple-like expansion of concentric forms (cf. Palmer 1976, Fig.5) and a direct correspondence between an increasing enclosure and community size through time (i.e. Case 1982:2ff, Fig.1). However the reduced area of the secondary middle Neolithic (MN 1b) causewayed enclosure which overlies the much more extensive Fuchsberg-phase enclosure system excavated at Sarup, Fyn, Denmark (Anderson 1980:98ff. Fig.6, 21), demonstrates that we must guard against the presumption of a rational or sequential expansion of enclosure forms.

The relative phasing of concentrically-planned enclosures is notoriously difficult. For example, Smith, in her analysis of Windmill Hill, could not establish any sequence of construction for its three ditch-rings, though from the distribution of pottery sherds from single vessels it could be demonstrated that some segments of all the three circuits were open at the same time (Smith 1965:4, 14). Of course the major problems in the phasing of concentric causewayed enclosures relates to the coarseness of radiocarbon dating and the fact that complex sequences of ditch re-cutting such as are apparent at Hambledon Hill (Mercer 1980:27ff) and other enclosures, make the distinction and dating of in-phase primary deposits very difficult to determine. It is, therefore, largely through the relative coherence of construction (i.e. ditch size, shape) and the integrity of individual ditch circuits that we can phase the rings of most concentrically-planned enclosures.

In this context the excavators of the Briar Hill enclosure (Bamford 1985) are certainly to be applauded for their attempts to come to terms with its apparently complex sequence of pit/ditch recuttings. There are, however, basic problems in their analysis of its plan and its phasing, and this is all the more unfortunate as the Briar Hill enclosure is one of the few sites definitely known to have a spatial overlapping between its concentric ditch circuits. For by the very 'eccentricity' of its three ditch circuits, this enclosure can inform us as to the character and procedure of concentric construction.

While it is admitted by its excavator that the innermost enclosure at Briar Hill (referred to as 'the spiral arm') may have been a simpler primary enclosure (Bamford 1985:39), this interpretation is dismissed on the grounds of the apparent 'site-wide' pattern of re-cutting and due to the 'geometric analysis' and cohesion of its overall plan:

"The complete plan of the excavated features shows the length of the ditch which defines the inner enclosure to be integral with the main inner ditch circuit in that the two form a single continuous spiral. Geometric analysis of the plan demonstrates, furthermore, that it had an internal coherence which is consistent with it having been planned and constructed at one time" (Bamford 1985:39).

A statement of this kind is simply wrong in terms of methodology — the landscape is always integral or coherent within a range of relevant possibilities. It is the variation within this range which establishes relative cultural/stratigraphic sequence, and 'cohesion' is a matter of the scale of analysis.

A consideration of the inner ditch at Briar Hill indicates that it has an independent integrity apart from the two outermost rings which it can be argued have a mutual cohesion (Fig.8.1). Whereas the plan of the inner ditch circuit defines it as a discrete entity which has been recut along its eastern side and from which the circuit of the two outer rings has been deflected. Furthermore, the mean relative size of the inner ring's pits/ditches stands in marked contrast to that of the two outer ditch circuits, and the minte scale of its construction could also suggest that it is out of phase with the outer rings (Bamford 1985, Fig. 19, Table 1).

The excavators of this important site have failed to see their forest due to relative complexity of their re-cut trees. While the phasing of any site can prove to be a matter of endless dispute what is truly questionable concerning the Briar Hill report is its reliance upon Chapman's geometric analysis of its 'design' (Bamford 1985:57, Appendix 3). For Chapman accredits principles of formal geometry to its Neolithic engineers, such as bisecting lines of symmetry based on Pythagorean triangles founded on the presumption that all three ditch circuits are contemporary in their layout. While these design techniques are apparently simple to put into practice they beg the question as to whether they are in any way appropriate to the study of these enclosures, and do we really intend to take causewayed enclosures down the thorny path of Thom's megalithic mathematics?

I do not intend to question the basic mathematics of Chapman's analysis except to note that one of the main problems with approaches such as this lies in its emphasis on plan as opposed to appearance. For convincing mathematical polygons can be constructed for any shape, and the temptation to impose geometric order on the bewildering array of sub-circular plans which causewayed enclosures display is great. Nevertheless, we must try to differentiate between what are no more than our abstract exercises on paper and what would have been appreciable spatial forms.

In recent years the accuracy of proposed Neolithic measurement systems (megalithic yard) has been severely criticised and doubts have even been expressed concerning the numerical competence of the builders of stone circles (Burl 1976:29). Barnatt and Moir (1984), in a recent analysis of stone circles, convincingly demonstrate that many megalithic circles may have been laid-out by eye and that apparently ovoid forms in plan would have probably

been as close to circular as to give the impression of a circle on the ground. This is not to say that the construction of a true circle was beyond their skills, but their builders were un-interested in peg and string, and mathematical precision:

"In many cultures it is sufficient that an object or building looks satisfying, high accuracy being irrelevant to the constructor's aims." (Barnatt and Moir 1984:204).

While Chapman is justified in using mathematics to describe the apparent eccentricities in the plans of causewayed enclosures, this does not imply their Neolithic builders applied formal geometric design. For a descriptive technique does not necessarily constitute an explanation and in this regard the purposes behind this proposed design sophistication is not questioned and certainly its validity is not self-apparent: "Even if nature does work mathematically, this does not imply that man the artificer also does" (Hiller et al., 1978:343). While any two-dimensional representation or appreciation of three-dimensional form entails a formal or abstract methodology (reduction, perspective or geometry), at issue here is to what extent the values/entities we measure are imposed upon a construct as opposed to being reflective or 'sympathetic' of its constituent parts and structure (Evans, 1988a). In this regard the manner in which we analyse spatial form is not unrelated to what we envisage were the procedures of its original construction. In effect, that which we measure is assumed to have been appreciable in the past and it is this relationship which determines whether an analytical procedure is 'appropriate' to its subject.

This is not to say that causewayed enclosures are not determined or planned constructions — and it was Smith who recognised that by their uncomfortable topographic situation a number of these enclosures can be seen to have an orientation which she referred to as their 'aspect' (Smith 1971:92), and more recently a façade-principle has been recognised in the spatial organisation of some enclosures (Evans 1988b). Yet, to what extent is this evidence of formal design?

It is this status of 'design' which we must determine and it must be questioned to what extent we envisage it as a specialist activity undertaken by proto-engineers and architects, and we employ such terms as 'megalithic architecture' without fully considering what are the social consequences of this implied specialisation[1]. Such a formal definition of design would restrict its application to only a limited number of prehistoric structures (monuments) and dismiss a range of vernacular constructs to some manner of unconscious 'beehive-like' behaviour lacking in design qualities per se. It is, however, possible to consider 'design' in a broader context so that it entails the range of choice processes by which humans change their physical environment. Rapoport (1976) sees this choice process, whether expressed in tribal camps or modern cities, as a matching or emulation between the built environment and an ideal conceptual scheme. Among relative 'simple' (preliterate) societies this social and spatial matching is more integrated because of the degree to which "a

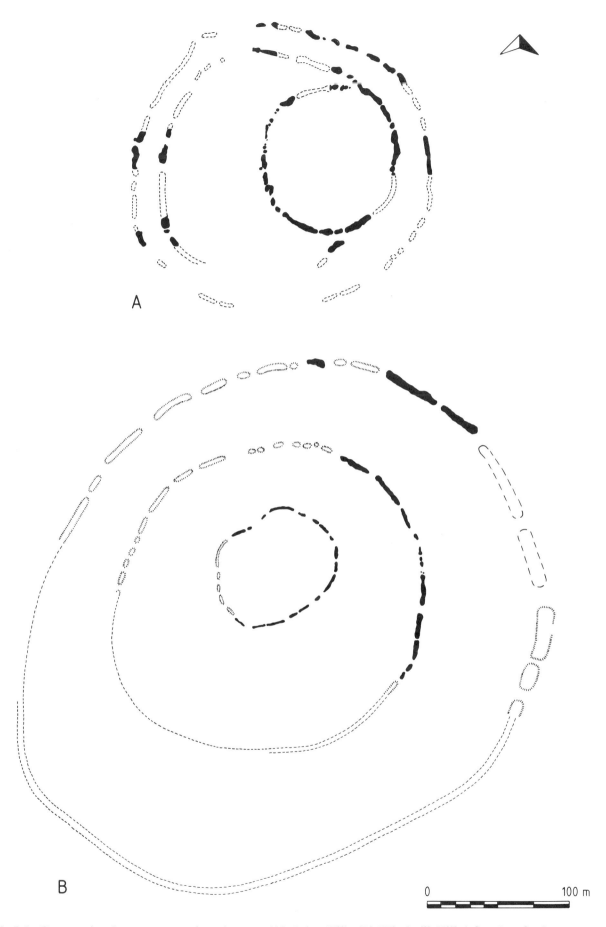

A

B

0   100 m

Fig.8.1. Concentric plan causewayed enclosures (A) Briar Hill; (B) Windmill Hill (after Bamford 1985; Smith 1965).

87

core set of beliefs" is shared by society at large (Rapoport 1976:20ff.). Some prehistoric structures would of course have demanded greater formal design principles, but it is unlikely that their construction was undertaken as an exercise in architectural or spatial appreciation, but rather they physically manifested more complex or rarified symbolic concepts. Though the very fact that these social or symbolic structures were given such concrete or monumental expression could reflect that the simplicity or homogeneity of contemporary society was itself fragmenting.

Renfrew, similarly, has defined 'design' as 'the implementation of deliberate intention' and 'planning' as 'deliberate action carried out to a preconceived design'(Renfrew 1982:21ff.). The determining criteria here lies in the emphasis on 'deliberate' so as to distinguish the work of humans as opposed to the behaviour of animals and insects, and the patterns of natural order. Such definitions would, of course, be equally applicable to, and would not differentiate between the decorative schemes upon a pot and the 'architecture' of Stonehenge. For in trying to envisage the process of enclosure planning and organisation it is essential to remember that they were large communal constructs and that they cannot be approached as if they were no more than a monumental form of vernacular construction. A communal enclosure could, for example, have been originally modelled on an ideal house-form, the organisation of which may ultimately have related to the body or a cosmology, but the resulting enclosure is not just an exaggerated house. The construction of large enclosures required the channelling of extensive resources and the control of a greater number of potential variables. These would have been open to range of contemporary interpretations which would have varied by social position and which would have changed through time. We should not, therefore, expect that any simplistic structural 'key' or answer will be found that will suddenly elucidate the 'meaning' of these complex sites. In this manner the archaeological ambiguity of causewayed enclosures and our failure to categorise them satisfactorily by discrete site function may reflect a 'truth' insomuch as their contemporary role may have been multiple and socially negotiable (Evans 1988a).

It can be questioned whether such concepts as vernacular practice and monumental architecture are appropriate in prehistory. There is, nevertheless, an essential difference between constructions whose aggregate form represents the reproduction of a given unit, such as a house or chamber in villages and tombs, and what were non-aggregated constructs[2]. This distinction is not just a matter of scale but also of approach and the various conceptual structures by which constructs/forms were cognitively organised and abstractly planned. This does not imply, however, that one should over-emphasise the role of 'architectural' (non-vernacular) invention. For insomuch as causewayed enclosures constitute a class or type, they resonate through the repetition of their construction. This, therefore, demonstrates a transmitted knowledge of form, and it is the repetition of form that provides the context

of individual variation. The supposition of the linguistic communication of form, moreover, asserts the social context of design and determines it as a structured or 'coded' activity.

In this context, therefore, it may be more appropriate to consider prehistoric constructs as *projects* rather than in the criteria of formal architecture /geometries. By this it is meant that to a greater or lesser extent they were resolved (conceived) only through their construction and that given spatial qualities may have only been 'emergent' in the sequence of their construction (Evans 1988b). Given the fact, furthermore, that some of these constructs physically endured and hosted various social activities over considerable spans of time and consequently were re-defined and modified, means that they cannot be treated as if they were static and pristine products. The final form of these enclosures cannot be assumed in their origins, their construction ultimately was accumulative and resolved only through sequence.

Certainly by the end of the Neolithic we can discuss mathematical design techniques, but we do a disservice to the question at hand if we take such a concept as design for granted. For while by the end of the third millennium bc a number of basic concepts such as 'monument', 'enclosure' and 'design', can be said to have been established in that they are archaeologically evident (and the monumental extravagance of the later Neolithic in Britain is without parallel on the continent — Evans, in prep.), but they cannot be assumed to exist formally in the earlier Neolithic. For these concepts are not necessary attributes of Neolithic societies but rather they emerge as given settled communities develop and the relationship of culture and nature is redefined. We are not dealing with absolutes here, but we must question to what degree we are witnessing formal design in the constructs of the earlier Neolithic and to what extent we are dealing with spatial orders which manifest social activity and cultural responses in the development of landscape.

Construction and Performance

To consider the spatial order of causewayed enclosures we must begin by looking at their most apparent spatial unit — the pitted or segmented ditch. For the lobate causewayed ditch is composed of interrupted strings of intercutting pits. This 'quarrying technique' has implications for the participation of labour as it would have lent itself to small gangs working in relative isolation. This implies that a maximal labour force could have been employed along a ditch circuit with only a minimal level of team co-ordination, and given these conditions divergence from 'design' (circuit regularity) would not be unexpected.

It has been suggested by Bradley and Startin (1981) that the technique of pit-digging may have been appropriate to a segmentary society insomuch as the participation of diverse social groups would have been evident and made manifest in the appearance of the standing enclosure. This inferential interpretation is to some extent supported by the bayed or segmented construction of long barrows. Conversely, the continuous trench-digging technique, which was employed for example in the henge enclosure of the later third and early second millennium bc, would have entailed a greater unification of the work force and would thus be appropriate to a more highly stratified society, as is suggested by contemporary burial evidence (Bradley and Startin 1981:293; Bradley 1982).

The pitted construction technique of causewayed enclosures, however, has clearly more than just functional implications. For often *in situ* deposits are found along their ditches and intentional deposits of apparently symbolic intent are not uncommon in their butt-ends. In this manner the interrupted ditch pattern can imply multiplication of ditch terminals. This spatial fragmentation has a temporal counterpart in the lengthy and complex sequences of ditch circuit recuttings found at a number of enclosures (Smith 1971:98). Sites such as Briar Hill and Hambledon Hill display a tradition of patterned pit-digging (Bamford 1985; Mercer 1980) and the implications of this long-term activity are far reaching. For while the primary cutting of these ditches can be largely interpreted as providing quarrying materials for the construction of often archaeologically ephemeral ditch-side banks, the secondary quarrying potential of a pit or ditch partially backfilled with weathered slips and cultural debris is obviously less than that of its original excavation. These often 'irrational' patterns of circuit re-cutting in which non-entrance causeways were maintained and apparently respected (in other words their secondary quarrying potential ignored) certainly does not reflect a strictly functional logic in practice. Rather these highly structured operations suggest the maintenance of the ditch segments for their own sake, and could relate to a tradition of social identification made manifest in the physical appearance of an enclosure. Mercer, in fact, has suggested that the recutting of ditch segments by possible family or clan gangs could have been maintained by oral traditions (Mercer 1980:36). The segmented ditch therefore, expresses what could be considered a basic contradiction or underlying structure of these enclosures, for on one hand they display an apparent spatial diversity or fragmentation, yet at the same time a number of enclosures reflect a strong temporal coherence.

We must however be wary of assigning *de facto* functional meaning to the frequency of interruptions in ditch circuits. While, of course, it is conceivable that during the 'lifetime' of causewayed enclosures the concept of 'enclosure' may have altered and that some enclosures may have taken on a more specific functional role (funerary, defensive or settlement) and that this development may be reflected in the maintenance and variance of ditch construction (Mercer 1980:45ff; Bradley and Holgate 1984:116). Yet there is a risk of being too mechanical in the functional assessment of ditch character based on a premise of the evolution of its form, as if somehow the destiny of 'enclosure' necessarily lay in continuous ditch construction. For the maintenance of

the pitted ditch form in some causewayed enclosures chronologically overlaps with the construction of some early cursus monuments and completely (or nearly so) ditched long barrows and ring-ditches (Kinnes 1979; Bradley and Holgate 1984). This demonstrates that the pitted ditch was maintained for given reasons and not due to a conceptual inability to construct a continuous ditch circuit.

As has been mentioned a great part of our misunderstanding of causewayed enclosures relates to the conceptualisation of ceremonial and communal enclosures based on their 'monumentality' as closed and stable constructs, rather than the social context of their execution. Pryor has recently stated that the sequential and relatively piecemeal construction of the Maxey cursus could be seen as "episodic sites of significant alignment" (Pryor and French 1985:301). This interpretation of a cursus as, in effect, an on-going event rather than a finished construct might reflect similar social processes in action as those which lay behind the sequential ditch recuttings of causewayed enclosures.

There is a risk of over-emphasising the monumentality of causewayed enclosures, for certainly most are not nearly so impressive as earthworks as they are in two-dimensional plan. While their limited survival is partially due to later plough-damage and clearly varies according to the differential rates of erosion of their up-cast sub-soils, nevertheless their diminutive form also reflects upon the concept and maintenance of enclosures at this time. For as Smith has noted in a number of enclosures there is definite evidence that banks had been intentionally levelled in the backfilling of adjacent ditch segments (Smith 1971:96ff), and elsewhere the necessary existence of ditch-side banks has been questioned (Evans 1988b). In this regard the structured or possibly 'ceremonial' element of causewayed enclosures resides in their frequency of re-cutting and associated depositional patterns, rather than in the sheer monumentality of their construction. This phenomenon can be witnessed in the complex series of cropmarks recorded at Fornham All Saints Suffolk. There a multi-aligned cursus overlies two apparently overlapping multivallate causewayed enclosures which lack any spatial integration (St. Joseph 1964). This remarkable sequence of enclosures while suggestive of a lasting significance of locality, graphically demonstrates the relatively ephemeral character of some enclosures and emphasizes the act of enclosure as an event or activity rather than as a stable or lasting construct. Causewayed enclosures can, therefore, be interpreted as being monumental only in so long as they were maintained, and the social context of their execution may have been as important a factor in their construction as the resulting physical earthwork. In the same manner that the maintenance of ditches and repetition of patterned deposition within them represents the temporal re-investment of the enclosure form, so too can a concentric enclosure organisation be interpreted as a re-definition of social space and a replication of an original ditch circuit.

Both Wilson (1975) and Palmer (1976) have proposed classification schemes for causewayed or interrupted enclosures based essentially on the number of ditch-circuits. Both have stressed an essential regional variation in the spacing of ditch-rings — with single circuits and widely-spaced concentric rings of *c.* 25–50m across being predominantly located in the south; and complex closely-spaced concentric plans having double and triple outer ditch circuits *c.* of 9–18m across, distributed largely in the midlands and the east. While more recent discoveries have shown that this regional distinction is not so rigid as originally thought (Evans 1988b) this classification by ditch distance does seem to be valid. The narrow gap of 10–15m between the outer ditches at Briar Hill and Orsett, for example, clearly restricts any functional activities between these rings, especially if we have to account for an up-cast bank between them (Hedges and Buckley 1978, Fig.21). This is in marked contrast to more southerly sites such as Robin Hood's Ball, Whitehawk and Windmill Hill, the latter of which has a distance of 50–90m between its middle and outer ditch circuits, and it would be surprising if an area this size was not utilised in some manner. Furthermore in some sites, such as Abingdon and Hambledon Hill there is certainly evidence to show that there were discrete functional differences between the enclosed rings, with a greater frequency of human skeletal material found in the inner enclosures, and differentiated patterns of recutting in their ditch circuits (Bradley and Holgate 1984). In the excavations at both Briar Hill and Orsett, and at a number of other enclosures, a far greater quantity of artefacts was recovered from their inner ditch circuits (Bamford 1985:60, Fig. 3.4; Hedges and Buckley, 1978:248), and it is interesting that the inner enclosures of these two sites are so generally similar, covering an area some 0.71 and 0.79 hectares respectively. This size roughly compares both with the inner ring at Windmill Hill (0.50 hectares) and with the Stepleton enclosure in the Hambledon outworks, which Mercer has suggested might represent a basic Neolithic settlement unit of *c.* 1 hectare (Mercer 1980:61). We should, however, bear in mind that the evidence for permanent settlement in most causewayed enclosures is certainly not conclusive and that the interiors of many of these enclosures are relatively barren.

It is relevant in this regard that the plan of Briar Hill would suggest the inner ditch to be an earlier construction than its double outer-circuit. The radiocarbon dates from Orsett could also suggest a similar relation between its inner and outer ditch circuits, though these dates could prove to be rather late given the dating of the palisade and its spatial integration with the outer ditch system (Hedges and Buckley 1978, Appendix 2, Fig.3). Certainly, in these two enclosures there is a mutual correspondence between the ditches of the outer circuits which is not shared with the innermost — and in both cases this would suggest the multiple outer ring to be somewhat later constructions.

In this context it is instructive to compare the plans of the Windmill Hill and Briar Hill enclosures (Figs. 8.1 and 8.2). Though at Windmill Hill there is certainly evidence to suggest localised re-cutting (Smith 1965, Fig. 6,7), the spatial structure of this enclosure remains relatively coherent when compared to that of Briar Hill which is largely 'buried' within its intense sequence of ditch re-cutting. The innermost circuits of these two enclosures are nevertheless in some respects remarkably similar. Smith postulated that the situation of an extended

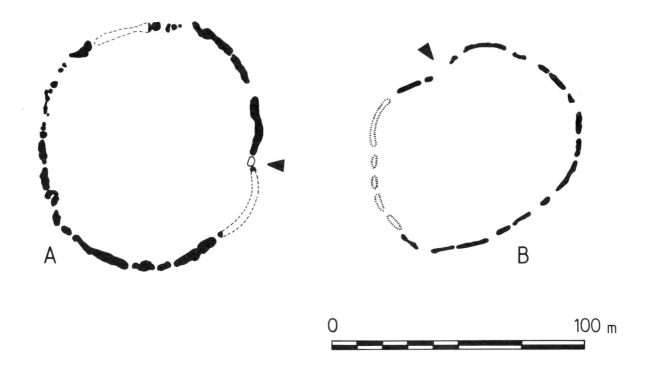

Fig.8.2. Innermost ditch circuits (A) Briar Hill; (B) Windmill Hill. Arrows indicate location of proposed main entrances in 'front' façade/aspect.

causeway between the inner ditches XVI and VII at Windmill Hill, and the relative concentration of pottery in the latter ditch, could indicate the location of an entranceway on the northwestern side (Smith 1965:5). Moreover, it has elsewhere been argued that the inturning of ditches XVII/VII and XVI/XV which flank this gap could relate to the construction of a façade of hornwork 'front' (Evans 1988b). While the eastern side of the innermost enclosure at Briar Hill has been extensively re-cut in the course of constructing the middle ditch (which is evident in the greater length of ditch segments on this side when compared to its western perimeter), a similar hornwork-like ditch arrangement may still be apparent in its eastern perimeter. Furthermore, if pit 14 and possibly 23 are generally phased as secondary features (in other words contemporary with the construction of the two outer ditches; c.f. Bamford 1985, Figs. 62–64), then this ditch configuration could also indicate the location of a major primary entranceway. What is particularly interesting in this regard is that in the proposed secondary encirclement of this enclosure this primary eastern orientation may have been reversed, for as its excavator notes (Bamford 1985:7, Fig. 20) major entrances were then situated on its western side as can be extrapolated from the location of extended causeways and out-turned ditch terminals.

It is relevant to this discussion to mention that the complex, multivallate eastern enclosures, such as Briar Hill and Orsett, have been referred to as an insular or 'English' development of causewayed enclosure form (Whittle 1977a:336ff.; Hedges and Buckley 1978:250). If, however, we are able to disentangle the sequence of sites like Briar Hill, then it is obvious that in their individual single and double-ditch system phases they are very similar to continental enclosures and those distributed elsewhere in southern Britain (i.e. Orsett/Briar Hill = Bochum — Harpen (Whittle 1977a, Fig. 5) & Sarup (Andersen 1980)). What might if anything distinguish a British enclosure 'style' is a relative continuity of enclosure location and a tradition of ditch maintenance which ultimately results in complex concentrically-organised enclosures.

The above proposals should not be understood as any manner of ideal 'growth model' for causewayed enclosures (i.e. 1 + 2 rings, etc.). For example at Windmill Hill there was also an extended causeway in the middle ditch line which directly corresponded with the postulated entrance in the innermost circuit (Smith 1965). This could conversely demonstrate a closer spatial and possibly temporal integration between its two inner ditches in contrast to the more massively proportioned outermost circuit (2 + 1 ring?). What is proposed is simply that given the demands of labour on communities which the construction of these enclosures would have entailed, it would be surprising if their construction was not sequential. Their episodic/periodic construction and maintenance may in fact have been integral both to their ultimate 'design' and spatial structure, and could well have interrelated with the social and agrarian/pastoral cycle. This therefore implies that enclosure size and complexity may not necessarily

have been in direct proportion to a parent community, but could as much reflect the character and longevity of its (site) sequence.

To acknowledge that concentric causewayed enclosures may have been phased and sequential constructs has repercussions relating to the determination and appreciation of their spatial organisation. While the discrete area enclosed by concentric rings was obviously relevant to their 'holding' capacity and the investment of labour required for the construction of its circumference, it can be questioned whether area as such was an appreciable concept. Rather, spatial scale may have been determined by an assessment of manageable space based on ring distance in a visual perspective framed by receding banks and ditches as one progressed through the enclosure. Relative spatial scale may, therefore, have ultimately been established by the innermost ring. In this regard it may be relevant that the off-set distance of the outer ditch system at Briar Hill along its secondary western orientation roughly equates with the diameter of its innermost (primary) ditch circuit. Similarly, though the ditch circuits at Windmill Hill vary considerably, the distance between the three rings along the northwestern entrance orientation is approximately 50m, which is generally comparable to the diameter of the inner enclosure on this axis. Certainly the overall irregularity between ditch circuits in these enclosures would indicate that they were not always simply constructed by off-setting a given distance from an established unit-core and yet their local regularities of layout would suggest that some other planning principle was involved. This is not to argue for systems of absolute measurement, but simply that a sense of spatial scale within an enclosure may have its foundation in its primary phase and which in the case of concentric configurations may often equate with its innermost ring(s).

It can, furthermore, be questioned, whether the 'uncomfortable contour situation' of a number of the more elevated enclosures could actually relate to the appearance of concentricity upon approach. For to off-set topographically a concentric construct allows for its visual appreciation and its spatial structure to be 'read'. If, however, this was the case, then while concentric encirclement might still have been sequential, it nevertheless implies that a concentric organisation was intended from the outset of enclosure construction and was related to its topographic situation.

Enclosure as Classification

"The world is based on the limit. Heaven and earth are separated by the limit. The eyes have an enclosure. The mouth has a limit. Everything has a limit" (An 'old Kabyle' quoted in Bourdieu 1979:124).

Though they are simple to execute, there is an essential flaw in undifferentiated circular forms insomuch as it is only their circumference and centre which are focally defined with the rest of their enclosed space being essentially neutral (Fleming

1972:59). While in theory this drawback can be compensated for by the distortion of the circumference so as to define more than a single point (Fleming 1972, Fig.1), this lack of spatial definition is nevertheless an underlying fault in the planning of large (communal) circular enclosures. For, if restricted to the basic components of circumference and ctre, their interiors have as inherent lack of articulation and as a result the periphery can become so vast as to be unmanageable and the central focus too small to be proportionally useful. The concentric division of a circle remedies this dilemma and yet at the same time it does not undermine the integrity of the circular form. For concentric spatial organisation, as opposed to a radial sub-division, retains the basic distinction between centre and circumference but the centre can be expanded to become a focal ground at the expense of the peripheral space, and thereby establishing a manageable ratio between periphery and core.

One must, of course, be aware of the underlying theatrical or ceremonial logic behind this argument insomuch as it analyses space as an interaction between performer and audience (initiated and non-initiated). We cannot, however, ignore the fact that concentricity also lends itself to fortification in terms of succeeding lines of defence. Yet while some causewayed enclosures show evidence of fortification (Crickley, Stepleton enclosure; see Mercer 1981:187ff.) a defensive capacity is certainly not an attribute common to all such enclosures.

What distinguishes concentric form, whether its rings are of a sequential or contemporary construction, is tat its organisation is determined by a single core. Whether its rings expand or sub-divide an original circle is irrelevant to the fact that it redefines space without creating secondary foci. It is thereby an extremely formal, if unsophisticated, spatial construct. Certainly, encirclement requires an extraordinary investment of labour, for the proportions of outer secondary enclosed zones can often never be fully appreciated because their extent is masked by and is dependent upon an inner core. For example, the outermost ditch circuit at Windmill Hill, which is some 1100m in length, encloses a discrete area of only some 5.3 hectares if the area defined by the middle and innermost ditches is deducted from the total area enclosed (8.5 ha, after Smith 1965:4). A similar size area, however, could have been independently enclosed by the construction of a single (non concentric) circle whose circumference was only 3/4 of that length (c. 800m). It is obvious, therefore, that the rationale of concentric enclosure does not relate to utilitarian principles of labour efficiency.

Concentricity can be interpreted as a coherent or integral expansion of a 'closed-system' (circle) as opposed to an 'open-system' (linear or grid pattern) the basic organisation of which is related to modular expansion. It is therefore evident that a concentric organisation of space is very much a determined action, which structures space so that none of its components has an independent integrity apart from its innermost ring. It is for this reason that concentric forms readily lend themselves to a ranked

ordered structure, and are so often used to depict cosmologies and theoretical constructs — ranging from Dante's *Commedia* to Site Catchment Analysis. For concentricity expresses a hierarchical relationship between its spatially successive zones (Allen 1985:25ff, Fig.1); it can be ranked according to access or distance between its periphery and core or 'deepest space', and it is because concentric forms define space by depth or sequence that they are often associated with the sacred (Hillier *et al.* 1978:363, Fig.19).

It is through the ordering of the world and its physical manifestation that cultures make the continuum of time and space meaningful (Leach 1976:33ff; Rapoport 1976:23). In this capacity enclosure or the demarcation of the landscape can be interpreted as having three basic attributes: it circumscribes that which is enclosed and demarcates that which is outside, and between the two it creates a boundary which can be simultaneously a physical or cognitive barrier and a transitional zone; and boundaries, as has often been stated, can have sacred connotations through their association with taboo and passage (Leach 1976, Fig.4). This latter point is extremely important for our concept of enclosure for is essentially based on the principles of containment and exclusion, yet the relatively open and fragmented spatial character of causewayed enclosures could suggest that the act of 'crossing' was of significance.

It is, therefore, possible that concentrically-organised causewayed enclosures could represent the intentional multiplication of boundaries. While undoubtedly such boundaries fulfilled various functional roles, they could also have manifested social segmentation and cultural structures, which could have been expressed and maintained in the temporal succession of ring construction — who or what lies inner, whether human (the living or dead divided by descent, gender or age) or animal (as totem, herds or flesh), as opposed to that which have access only to the periphery. Yet here we can also recognise what can be considered as a contradiction in concentric forms. For while they may be formally organised according to the spatial juxtaposition of hierarchical opposites, at the same time by providing multiple paths of access or the means of contextual crossing they can also be interpreted as an integrating structure which allows for the interpenetration and cultural articulation of oppositional forces or principles.

This line of argument is relevant for how we attempt to understand these enclosures. For we keep hoping that the character of these enclosures will eventually be revealed though the sum of their parts and that contextually these enclosed sites will be explained if only we can find contemporary unenclosed occupation sites. But so far, with few exceptions, the flint scatters and pit clusters which have been excavated have not really been very illuminating. The sheer scale and character of causewayed enclosures does not, furthermore, represent an 'organic' or cell-like aggregation of minor units, instead they are large, formally organised constructs. Given their status as a primary enclosure form this is quite remarkable, and it is possible that it may have been a cultural or linguistic concept which provided the 'template' or metaphor of their organisation. This does not imply that there is a direct one-to-one relationship between spatial and social structure (Hillier *et al.* 1978; Leach 1978), nor should spatial patterns and principles be assumed to have a given universal significance. We must, nevertheless, recognise that we are considering an initial act of landscape enclosure and that it is reasonable to presume that its layout must have derived from some source. In this context, therefore, the formal spatial organisation of concentric causewayed enclosures could ultimately have related to a cultural framework which encompassed and structured the concept of enclosure, rather than formal principles of design.

We should certainly not underestimate the profound 'world-view' consequences of what it is to physically enclose and systematically scar nature for the first time. It may, in fact, be in a context of spiritual (nature) appeasement that 'symbolic packages' were intentionally deposited in causewayed ditches such as are found at the Etton enclosure (Pryor 1983). It is, however, important to recognise that while causewayed enclosures are a primary form of large-scale landscape enclosure, in Britain they are not a product of the primary Neolithic but rather of middle or fully developed Neolithic societies. While there are obvious early/middle Neolithic continental sources for this particular enclosure form (Whittle 1977a), it is nevertheless feasible to speculate to what extent concentricity is a basic response to or model of the act of Neolithic colonisation of the landscape. For pollen analysis suggests that at least for the early Neolithic we must consider limited cultivation and settlement occuring within localised forest clearances. In this environmental situation and given the frequency of approximately circular camp/settlement configurations (Flannery 1972; Whitelaw 1983), we can envisage a central core of occupation ringed by cleared waste ground and minor cultivation plots, which would itself have been surrounded by forest utilised as woodland pasture (Fowler 1981:16; cf.Fowler 1983, Fig. 42). Effectively, though not formally enclosed, this could create a concentric spatial model with settlement or 'culture' at its core and nature at is extremities, and in this manner concentricity may be a phenomenon integral to settled communities in a forest environment (Levi-Strauss 1979:132ff, Figs. 7, 8, 11).

Of course a spatial metaphor of this type would not be wholly exclusive to the Neolithic and one could expect that hunter-gathering societies occasionally assembled under similar circumstances. How they would have differed would be in terms of the definition between a zoned (Jarman *et al.* 1972:26ff) and a domesticated nature, the latter of which would have created a 'buffer' of transitional boundary between the wild (nature) and the settled (culture). What might, however, have been common to their environmental experience is a focal definition of space and territory.

Yet, any major act of construction/enclosure represents a reworking or modification of the 'natural world' and its cultural order. Insofar as its materials are derived from the visible world (stones, trees, turf and sub-soil) the action of human construction is a reworking of a 'natural' or pre-agrarian order and a juxtaposition of any classification system or cosmology which structured it. This is a question of scale as opposed to absolutes (the monumental as opposed to the incidental), but it must be envisaged that this human re-deposition of the visible world would eventually supercede a strictly 'natural' or unconsciously sympathetic environmental relationship. For by the same process by which 'Man creates himself through labour' so too do societies objectify themselves through their acts in nature. The physical 'trace' or inscriptions of societies in landscape (i.e. earthworks) can thereby act as a projected 'skeleton' which externalizes social structure, whereas previous to this phenomenon of landscape delineation this 'code' was carried within its corporate membership — 'in the very flesh of each generation' (Wilden 1972:395ff; Vestergaard 1983). It is because of the lasting character of landscape constructs (barrows, communal enclosures, linear systems, etc.) that they can potentially express and generate a temporal segmentation insomuch as they register that which is past. Formal enclosure and monumental construction essentially enshrines an action and thereby landscape lasts as a social framework and medium. In other words it is the very endurance of constructions that can potentially distance the code of society from its membership by the demonstration of temporal depth or plurality and can therefore influence social development insofar as tradition structures social behaviour and can be manipulated (Giddens 1979; Hobsbawn 1983). In this regard it maybe relevant that concentric patterns are so frequent in the organisation of later Neolithic stone circles and henge enclosures, sites whose discrete ritual character and formal design qualities are relatively self-apparent (Evans, in prep.). We can question whether the 'principle of concentricity' had by that time become something of a rarified concept directly associated with the ceremonial in contrast to its earlier role as a socially integrating structure in causewayed enclosures. This apparent rarification of a spatial/social structure could represent the employment or manipulation of an earlier and more fundamental concept so as to create a cultural focus in a relatively fragmented social landscape (Bradley 1982).

If we are to strive towards any conclusion we must examine the relationship between the act of enclosure and the creation/generation of 'land'. It is widely accepted that the advent of agriculture would have resulted in a fundamental change in the relationship between humans and land/culture and nature. The development of agriculture marks a major shift in society's relationship to nature insomuch as an agrarian basis of subsistence transforms nature in contrast to previous modes of its immediate exploitation (Godelier 1977). Meillassoux has emphasised the social differences between hunter-gathers whose subsistence production is immediate, in contrast to agriculturalists whose long-term investment in subsistence requires the reproduction of the social group and its ancestral rights to land (Meillassoux 1972). While this change in the basis of subsistence may have had a profound social impact, it is unlikely that culture would have undergone an immediate 'sea-change' or revolution and rather its consequences should be understood as more gradual process of definition in relationship to landscape/nature.

At issue here is not whether or when nature or landscape is socially defined (Evans 1985), but rather the processes involved when humans begin to systematically manage and control (domesticate) land. At which point does 'landscape' become differentiated from 'wildscape' (cf. Fowler 1981) and when does nature become a socially defined category in a 'man-managed' landscape (Olwig 1984). The implications of this subsistence change are fundamental in terms of the relationship between culture and nature, for if the pre-agrarian world was animated by the spiritual, where then does the 'spiritual world' reside after the domestication of nature, and what are the processes by which societies fuse themselves with locality to the point that 'land owns people' (Coppet 1985)? From a theoretical perspective it is convenient to see this transition from Mesolithic to Neolithic as occuring quite rapidly. But if the relative archaeological invisibility of much of the fourth millennium bc in British prehistory reflects its island status and only limited Neolithic inroads in contrast to the relatively instantaneous Linearbandkeramik 'wave' phenomenon on the continent, does this 'retarded' neolithicisation result in a more gradual process of cultural definition in the relationship of society to land?

In this regard it is relevant that the construction of causewayed enclosures by middle Neolithic cultures in western Europe has been associated with Sherratt's 'secondary products revolution' (Sherratt 1981; Mercer 1981:195ff.). Sherratt's model has received severe criticism (Chapman 1982) and some of its arguments, such as its emphasis on mobile pastoralism, are clearly not applicable to western Europe. Yet while recognising its limitations as a general theory, it does nevertheless offer at least as an interim measure an avenue by which to approach the archaeological invisibility of fourth millennium bc Britain. For it is in the later or developed phase of the Neolithic that the advent of plough cultivation, milk exploitation and modes of pastoral production, permitted the expansion of population into relatively marginal lands which resulted in the infilling of the later fourth millennium bc landscape (Whittle 1977b). It is argued that this secondary Neolithic is distinguished by greater flexibility and intensity of new land-use systems which would have had marked social consequences such as craft specialisation and more widespread trade interaction. It is furthermore thought that these developments in production and land-use could have generated new male-dominated social structures with a greater emphasis on marriage as an agency relating to the transmission and control of land (Sherratt 1981).

While we may not be able to readily categorise the status of causewayed enclosures (Evans 1988a), it is precisely the above-mentioned processes that we can see at 'play' within them: a changing relationship to land as is represented in the very act of enclosure itself and their relatively marginal locations and long-term maintenance; an emphasis on the control of animals as can be extrapolated from the physical organisation of the enclosures (concentric ditch circuits, fenced paddocks, etc.) and the sheer number and frequency of domesticates in faunal assemblages. At the same time the very quantity of artefactual material recovered from causewayed enclosure ditches would certainly point to large-scale social interaction and the range of material would suggest a participation in trade networks (Smith 1971:102; Bradley 1984a:25ff.). Against this background we must set a major 'ritual' component (human skeletal remains, *in situ* 'symbolic' assemblages) which is both the most widely (mis-)interpreted and yet one of the most consistent attributes of these enclosures as a type or class. Herein lies 'the rub', for it is our inability to integrate ritual with subsistence and symbol with function which generates our failure to come to terms with these complex enclosures. Yet it is this ritual component, or the evidence of cultural structures, which provides a framework for and which meshes these various processes, by which means culture associates itself with domesticated land and animals, and thereby defines itself in relationship to 'nature', and which articulates both the patterns of land-holding and social structure through the agency of ancestors and the interplay between the living and the dead, the wild and the domesticated.

Given the current state of research the construction of long barrows and causewayed enclosures not so much emerges from out of the earlier fourth millennium bc, as suddenly arrives to mark a distinct horizon in the archaeological record. This phenomenon we can either interpret as representing the impact of very close contacts between British and western continental middle Neolithic cultures, or alternatively as representative of the coming together and the cultural articulation of a number of developed (secondary) Neolithic processes at *c.* 3000 bc (3200–2700 bc) after a long phase of 'silent' gestation in the fourth millennium bc. Taking either approach what is important is not so much that causewayed enclosures demonstrate a number of successful subsistence processes in action, but rather they result from these processes interacting within complex social and cultural structures.

Notes

1) One of the basic problems in approaching the question of prehistoric 'design mathematics' is that as an issue it is either dismissed or over-exaggerated with the result that we create a British school of prehistoric Pythagoreans whose abstract practices can only be explained by recourse to astronomer-priests (Thom 1967:3; MacKie 1977). If, however, we consider the development of measurement sy-

stems as relating to the 'mapping of the world' (Renfrew 1982:18) by the description of space and form, then its practice is not divorced from cognitive systems of cultural order and is not necessarily dependent upon universal values/procedures (formal geometry).

Similarly, in recent archaeological literature there has been much discussion as to whether what has been proposed as 'megalithic science' is really just ritual and symbolism (Burl 1980; Thorpe 1983). It is, however, necessary to recognise that the foundations of this debate (and its frequent absurdity) rests upon the formal definition of scientific knowledge made by its extreme advocates. Yet, if classification is understood as 'the science of the concrete' (Levi-Strauss 1966) then much of the distinction between these two approaches becomes, if not reconciled, then at least irrelevant. For each are 'distinct modes of scientific thought' and which, while not necessarily ancestral in their relationship, are equally sophisticated and articulated systems directed toward the acquisition and ordering of worldly knowledge (Levi-Strauss 1966:13ff).

2) A similar situation exists concerning the interpretation of earlier Neolithic mortuary enclosures (megalithic and non-megalithic). Piggott, in his analysis of the West Kennet long barrow, argued that there was evidence of regular mathematical planning involving units of measurement (Piggott 1962:15). This has yet to be convincingly demonstrated and rather Ashbee's proposal of a proportional regularity (Ashbee 1966:36–37) and Kinnes' modular combinations (Kinnes 1975:19ff., Fig. 7) would seem more appropriate avenues of analysis.

The distinction here relates to a level of abstract procedure and the formality of planning, for proportional regularity can be achieved by gauged (relative) measurement. Similarly, a system of modular components suggests a degree of spatial description/control related to vernacular practice insomuch as a chamber can be considered as a modification of house or room form, and it has frequently been argued that Neolithic mortuary structures related to contemporary house forms (e.g. Kinnes 1981:85; Hodder 1984:54ff.).

Acknowledgements

A draft of this paper was presented in the 'Social Construction of Space' session at the TAG conference held in Glasgow, 1985, and I would like to thank its organiser, M. Nieke. This paper has specifically benefited from discussion with and the astute criticism of M.L. Stig Sørensen and J. Barrett. I would also like to acknowledge a productive discourse with R. Boast, C. Chippindale, A. Herne, I. Hodder, and I. Kinnes, without necessarily implicating any of the above with the paper's present state.

References

Allen N.J. 1985 Hierarchical organisation. In R.H. Barnes, D. de Coppet and R.J. Parkin (eds) *Context and Levels*. Oxford, pp. 21–32.

Andersen N.H. 1980 Sarup: befaestede neolitiske anlaeg og deres baggrund. *Kuml* 63–103.

Ashbee P. 1966 The Fussell's Lodge long barrow excavations 1957. *Archaeologia* 100:1–80.

Atkinson R.J.C., Piggott C.M. and Sandars N.K. 1951 *Excavations at Dorchester, Oxon*. Oxford.

Avery M. 1982 The neolithic causewayed enclosure, Abingdon. In H.J. Case and A.W.R. Whittle (eds) *Settlement patterns in the Oxford region: excavations at the Abingdon causewayed enclosure and other sites*. Oxford, CBA Research Report 44:10–50.

Bamford H. 1985 *Briar Hill*. Northampton Archaeological Monograph No. 3.

Barnatt J. and Moir G. 1984 Stone circles and megalithic mathematics. *Proc. Prehist. Soc.* 50:197–216.

Bourdieu P. 1979 *Outline of a Theory of Practice*. Cambridge.

Bradley R. 1982 Position and possession: assemblage variation in the British Neolithic. *Oxford J. Archaeol.* 1–1:27–38.

Bradley R. 1984a *The Social Foundations of Prehistoric Britain*. London.

Bradley R. 1984b Studying monuments. In R. Bradley and J. Gardiner (eds) *Neolithic studies: a review of some current research*. Oxford, BAR 133:61–66.

Bradley R. *et al.* 1984c The neolithic sequence in Cranborne Chase. In R. Bradley and J. Gardiner (eds) *Neolithic Studies: a review of some current research*. Oxford, BAR 133:87–105.

Bradley R. and Hodder I. 1979 British prehistory: an integrated view. *Man* 14:93–104.

Bradley R. and Holgate R. 1984 The neolithic sequence in the upper Thames Valley. In R. Bradley and J. Gardiner (eds) *Neolithic studies: a review of some current research*. Oxford, BAR 133:107–134.

Burl A. 1976 Intimations of numeracy in the neolithic and bronze age societies of the British Isles (*c.* 3200–1200 B.C.). *Archaeol. J.* 133:9–32.

Burl A. 1980 Science or symbolism: problems of archaeoastronomy. *Antiquity* 54:191–200.

Case H.J. 1956 The neolithic causewayed camp at Abingdon, Berks. *Antiqu. J.* 36:11–30.

Case H.J. 1982 Settlement patterns in the Oxford region: an outline. In H.J. Case and A.W.R. Whittle (eds) *Settlement patterns in the Oxford region: excavations at the Abingdon causewayed enclosure and other sites*. Oxford, CBA Research Report 44:1–9.

Catherall P.D. 1976 Henge Monuments: monument or myth? In C. Burgess and R. Miket (eds) *Settlement and Economy in the Third and Second Millennia B.C.* Oxford, BAR 33:1–9.

Chapman J.C. 1982 The 'Secondary Products Revolution' and the limitations of the Neolithic. *Bull. Inst. Archaeo. London.* 19:107–122.

Cohen A.P. 1985 *The Symbolic Construction of Community*. London.

Coppet D. de. 1985 Land owns people. In R.H. Barnes, D. de Coppet and R.J. Parkin (eds) *Context and Levels*. Oxford, pp. 78–90.

Evans C. 1985 Tradition and the cultural landscape: an archaeology of place. *Archaeological Review from Cambridge*. 4-1:80–94.

Evans C. 1986 A 'Matrix' Technique for the analysis of causewayed enclosures. *Oxford J. Archaeol. 5:273-7*

Evans C. 1988a Monuments and analogy: the interpretation of causewayed enclosures. In C. Burgess and P. Topping (eds) *Enclosures and Defences in the Neolithic of Western Europe*. Oxford, BAR

Evans C. 1988b Excavations at Haddenham, Cambs: a 'planned' enclosure and its regional affinities. In C. Burgess and P. Topping (eds) *Enclosures and Defences in the Neolithic of Western Europe*. Oxford, BAR.

Evans C. (in preparation) Design as strategy: enclosure, community and landscape in the third millennium b.c.

Flannery K.V. 1972 The origins of the village as a settlement type in Mesoamerica and the Near East: a comparative study. In P. Ucko, R. Tringham and G.W. Dimbleby (eds) *Man, Settlement and Urbanism.* London, pp. 23–53.

Fleming A. 1972 Vision and design: approaches to ceremonial monument typology. *Man* 7: 57–73.

Fowler P. 1981 Wildscape to landscape: 'enclosure' in prehistoric Britain. In R. Mercer (ed) *Farming practices in British Prehistory.* Edinburgh, pp. 9–54.

Fowler P.J. 1983 *The Farming of Prehistoric Britain.* Cambridge.

Giddens A. 1979 *Central Problems in Social Theory.* London.

Godelier M. 1977 Economy and religion: an evolutionary optical illusion. In J. Friedman and M. Rowlands (ed) *The Evolution of Social Systems.* London, pp. 3–11.

Hedges J. and Buckley D. 1978 Excavations at a neolithic causewayed enclosure, Orsett, Essex, 1975. *Proc. Prehist. Soc.* 44:219–308.

Hillier B., Leaman A., Stansall P., Bedford M. 1978 Space syntax. In D. Green, C. Haselgrove and M. Spriggs (eds) *Social Organisation and Settlement.* Oxford, BAR S-47:343–381.

Hillier B. and Hanson J. 1985 *The Social Logic of Space.* Cambridge.

Hobsbawn E. 1983 Introduction: inventing traditions. In E. Hobsbawn and T. Ranger (eds) *The Invention of Tradition.* Cambridge, pp. 1–14.

Hodder I. 1984 Burials, houses, women and men in the European Neolithic. In D. Miller, C. Tilley (eds) *Ideology, Power and Prehistory.* Cambridge, pp. 51–68.

Jarman M.R., Bailey G.N. & Jarman H.N. 1982 *Early European Agriculture.* Cambridge.

Kinnes I. 1975 Monumental function in British neolithic burial practices. *World Archaeology* 7-1:16–29.

Kinnes I. 1979 *Round barrows and ring-ditches in the British Neolithic.* British Museum Occasional Paper No. 7.

Kinnes I. 1981 Dialogues with death. In R. Chapman, I. Kinnes and K. Randsborg (eds) *The Archaeology of Death.* Cambridge, pp. 83–91.

Leach E. 1976 *Culture and Communication.* Cambridge.

Leach E. 1978 Does space syntax really "constitute the social"? In D. Green, C. Haselgrove and M. Spriggs (eds) *Social Organisation and Settlement.* Oxford, BAR S-47:385–401.

Levi-Strauss C. 1966 *The Savage Mind.* London.

Levi-Strauss C. 1979 Do dual organisations exist? *Structural Anthropology* Harmondsworth, pp.132–163.

MacKie E.L. 1977 *Science and Society in Prehistoric Britain.* London.

Meillassoux C. 1972 From reproduction to production. *Economy and Society.* 1-1:93–105.

Mercer R. 1980 *Hambledon Hill: A Neolithic Landscape.* Edinburgh.

Mercer R. 1981 Excavations at Carn Brae, Illogan, Cornwall, 1970–73:a Neolithic fortified complex of the third millenium bc. *Cornish Archaeology.* 9:17–46

Olwig K. 1984 *Nature's Ideological Landscape.* Research Series in Geography 5. London.

Palmer R. 1976 Interrupted ditch enclosures in Britain: the use of aerial photography for comparative studies. *Proc. Prehist. Soc.* 42:161–186.

Piggott S. 1962 *The West Kennet Long Barrow.* London.

Pryor F. 1983 Questions, not answers: an interim report on excavations at Etton, near Maxey, Peterborough, 1982. *Northamptonshire Archaeology* 18:3–6.

Pryor F. and French C. 1985 *Archaeology and Environment in the Lower Welland Valley.* East Anglian Archaeology, Report No. 27.

Rapoport A. 1976 Socio-cultural aspects of man-environment studies. In A. Rapoport (ed) *The Mutual Interaction of People and their Built Environment.* Hague, pp. 7–36.

Renfrew C. 1982 *Towards an Archaeology of Mind.* Cambridge.

Sherratt A.G. 1981 Plough and pastoralism: aspects of the secondary products revolution. In I. Hodder, G. Isaac and N. Hammond (eds). *Pattern of the past.* Cambridge, pp. 261–305.

Smith I.F. 1965 *Windmill Hill and Avebury.* Oxford.

Smith I.F. 1971 Causewayed Enclosures. In D.D.A. Simpson (ed) *Economy and Settlement in Neolithic and Early Bronze Age Britain and Europe.* Leicester, pp. 89–112.

Startin B. and Bradley R. 1981 Some notes on work organisation and society in prehistoric Wessex. In C.L.N. Ruggles and A.W.R. Whittle (eds) *Astronomy and Society in Britain during the Period 4000–1500 BC.* Oxford, BAR 88:275–288.

St. Joseph J.K. 1964 Air Reconnaissance: recent results, 2. *Antiquity* 38:290–291.

Thom A. 1967 *Megalithic Sites in Britain.* Oxford.

Thorpe I.J. 1983 Prehistoric British Astronomy — towards a social context. *Scottish Archaeological Review.* 2-1:2–10.

Vestergaard T.A. 1983 On kinship theory, clocks, and steam-engines: The problem of complex structures. In J. Oosten and A. Ruijter (eds) *The Future of Structuralism.* Göttingen.

Whitelaw T. 1983 People and space in hunter-gather camps: a generalising approach in ethnoarchaeology. *Archaeological Review from Cambridge* 2-2:48–66.

Whittle A. 1977a Earlier neolithic enclosures in northwest Europe. *Proc. Prehist. Soc.* 43:329–348.

Whittle A. 1977b *The Earlier Neolithic of southern England and its Continental Background.* Oxford, BAR S-35.

Wilden A. 1972 *Systems and Structure in Communication.* London.

Wilson D.R. 1975 'Causewayed camps' and 'interrupted ditch systems'. *Antiquity* 49:178–186.

9. Environmental Change and Land-Use History in a Wiltshire River Valley in the Last 14000 Years

J.G. Evans, S. Limbrey, I. Máté and R.J. Mount

In this paper we present a preliminary account of work in hand on the archaeology and environment of the Winterbourne and upper reaches of the Kennet river valley floor in north Wiltshire. The area extends from just below the Neolithic enclosure of Windmill Hill to the meadows at West Overton, a stretch of valley of about seven kilometres. We are studying the development of the valley floor from the late-glacial period to the present day — a period of about 14000 years. Here we discuss mainly those changes which took place from around the later Mesolithic period on into the Middle Ages.

By comparison with the situation on slopes and hilltops there has been a distinct paucity of archaeological work on chalkland river valley floors. Chalkland areas were clearly important, especially during later prehistory, and it would seem sensible to investigate the valley floors. Likewise there has been a lack of environmental work in the chalkland river valleys. Most work on the Chalk has been in the context of terrestrial deposits and soils — the thin chalk soils of the slopes and hilltops, archaeological sediments such as ditch fills, and colluvial deposits in dry valleys. A small amount of work has been done on the archaeology and environment of tufa deposits (Evans and Smith 1983; Preece 1980), but this is the nearest to true alluvial deposits that such work has come. Again, therefore, as with the archaeology, there is a need to work in the river valley floors.

The reasons for this lack of research into what is clearly an important zone, both archaeologically and environmentally, is that the archaeology is buried although not always very deeply, and there has been little commercial exploitation of the valley sediments which would expose it. The most suitable methods of environmental investigation — molluscan analysis and soil and sediment studies — have not been pursued by the innovative and imaginative techniques employed by Quaternary scientists in their search for long records of biological and environmental change in other contexts. This is especially true of the last 14000 years, the late-glacial and post-glacial periods. Though valley floors are occupied in part by active channels, abandoned channels and transient deposits, whose extent is variable in time and place, there have almost certainly been periods when considerable areas were ideally suited to occupation, and it is unlikely that sediments containing evidence for such occupation would not be preserved. It is, however, difficult to locate and investigate good sites hidden in valley floors.

The point about good sites is important. We are not solely concerned with establishing sequences of environmental history, however complete and well-dated. We are interested in the interaction of past human communities and their environment, and for any investigation to be successful, all aspects, including conventional archaeology and economic data must be available. River valleys would seem to be especially promising for such work because not only are they likely to preserve long sequences of deposits and buried land surfaces with occupation traces, but they offer the chance of studying the reactions of human communities to the very processes responsible for laying down the sediments and forming the soils.

The objectives of the present study are to investigate the potential of chalkland river valley floors for preserving traces of prehistoric occupation in buried land surfaces, and to obtain environmental and economic evidence for any such occupation, along with the establishment of a chronology. In its broadest objective thus stated, the work was inspired by the investigations of G. Schwantes and A. Rust in the nineteen-twenties and thirties into the late-glacial settlement of the Hamburg area of north Germany (Rust 1937). By excavating deep trenches in tunnel valley deposits adjacent to areas rich in surface scatters of upper Palaeolithic flints these workers showed that similar artefact assemblages were to be found stratified in the valley deposits along with organic material suitable for reconstructing the lifestyle and environment of the Upper Palaeolithic communities. We felt that chalkland river valleys in areas suitably rich in surface remains of the Neolithic and Bronze Age periods might similarly reward investigation.

In addition to the above considerations, the selection of the chalklands was dictated by the interest of J.G.E. in molluscan analysis, especially of later prehistory, while the selection of a river valley was dictated by the investigations of S.L. into palaeohydrology and the use of soil and sediment analytical techniques, especially the application of thin section studies. Both molluscan analysis and the use of thin sections have reached a stage in their development when they can be applied without too much concern over technical problems.

On the chalklands of southern Britain, molluscan analysis has proved an excellent technique in the investigation of ancient environments, and since the earliest work of A.S. Kennard in the 19th century it has been applied to hundreds of archaeological sites. Various approaches have been adopted. Some workers have investigated dry-valley floor deposits (e.g. Kerney et al. 1964; Evans 1966; Bell 1983) and we now have a clear picture of the late-glacial and post-glacial history of these features. Several molluscan biozones have been established for this period (Kerney 1977; Kerney et al. 1980) and deposits may be broadly dated by their molluscan assemblages. Specific interest in archaeological sites has allowed various of the environmental changes associated with human activities to be detailed, especially those connected with forest clearance and agriculture (Evans 1972; Ashbee et al. 1979). Refinements in techniques of sampling, presentation of the results and interpretation have been proposed by several workers (e.g. Cameron 1978; Thomas 1985).

Soil analytical techniques have been developed to the point where they are now routinely used in many archaeological laboratories. Micro-morphological studies were pioneered by Kubiëna (1953) and first applied in an archaeological context by Cornwall (1953, 1958). Recently, the use of large thin sections, prepared by special equipment, has become routine in many soil science laboratories, but as yet no archaeological department has suitable facilities. Micromorphological study of soil provides information on processes involving mobility of colloidal materials and organo-metallic complexes, formation and modification of soil structure, and the incorporation of organic matter and of such extraneous particles as charcoal. Evidence for soil creep and colluviation, gleying, the formation of argillic and podzolic horizons, the effects of cultivation, fire and human occupation can be detected. Sequences can be determined, so that the succession of natural pedogenic processes and those induced by human activity can be established. In alluvial deposits, evidence of pedogenic processes in the source soils can be distinguished from post-depositional soil formation, and a sequence of effects of changing groundwater levels in the deposit can be established.

Research Design

In initiating our research, the first decision was whether to study several different types of valley site over a wide area of southern England or to confine our investigations to a smaller area in a single topographic location. We adopted the latter procedure for three reasons: financial constraints; a greater chance of locating archaeological horizons; and the fact that other similar work is going on in a variety of situations. We can quote here the work of Martin Bell (pers. comm.) in the valley of the River Iwerne at the foot of Hambledon Hill, Dorset; of Mark Robinson and George Lambrick (1984) in the Upper Thames, where sedimentological and pedological studies by S. Robinson and S.L. are also being carried out; of Sue Lobb (pers. comm.) at Anslow's Cottages, Burghfield, in the lower reaches of the Kennet near Reading; of Roy Entwistle (pers. comm.) in the Wiltshire Avon; and of Diane Williams in the Department of Archaeology, U.C.C., in the river valleys around Danebury, Hampshire. In all these investigations the intimate link between the archaeology and environmental evidence which we are pursuing is also fundamental to the research.

We selected the valley of the Winterbourne and upper Kennet for two reasons. First, molluscan analysis from Mesolithic, Neolithic and Bronze Age sites in the area had been carried on for several years and several good sequences were available (Evans

1972; Ashbee et al. 1979; Evans and Smith 1983; Evans et al. 1985). Second, the area is archaeologically rich, if somewhat atypical, and therefore the chances of locating cultural material seemed better than average.

The research took place in the following stages:
(a) *Auger survey.* In 1983, using a 10cm-diameter posthole auger the sequence of sediments and soils was established. Samples were taken for molluscan and sediment analysis and were studied by Mary Evans in the Department of Archaeology, University College, Cardiff for her undergraduate thesis. The limitations of this approach were that the auger would not penetrate thick flint horizons, thin but significant layers were missed, and sampling could be done at only coarse intervals.
(b) *Small-scale excavation.* In July 1984, several 1.5m-square pits were excavated in three locations in the valley floor, namely in the area immediately to the west of the Avebury henge, in the fields below the West Kennet long barrow, and in the water-meadows to the north of West Overton church. This work was funded by U.C.C. and carried out by students from the Department of Archaeology under the direction of J.G.E.
(c) *Research programme.* The work in 1983 and 1984 demonstrated the presence of two buried land surfaces, one of which contained Mesolithic and Neolithic occupation debris, and a sequence of deposits spanning the period from the late-glacial to the present. A research programme was established of which there were two main aspects. First, financial support was obtained from the British Academy, the Society of Antiquaries of London, the Wiltshire Archaeological and Natural History Society and University College Cardiff for a large scale excavation into the deposits at Avebury and West Overton where the best sequences occurred. This took place over six weeks in July and August 1985. Second, two Research Assistantships were granted by the Science and Engineering Research Council for three years from July 1985, one based in Birmingham to work on the soils and sediments (Ian Máté), the other based in Cardiff to work on the Mollusca (Rosina Mount). A Leverhulme Scholarship was awarded to J.G.E. for a Research Assistant (Annie Milles) to work in Cardiff on the exceptional series of early post-glacial tufaceous deposits discovered at West Overton. Further support from the SERC was obtained for the study of cereal remains (Jane Fitt, working under the supervision of Gordon Hillman at the Institute of Archaeology, London University), for accelerator mass-spectrometer dates to be done in the Research Laboratory for Archaeology and the History of Art, Oxford University, and for thermoluminescence dating of burnt flint, also to be done at Oxford. Work on prehistoric flint and pottery, animal bone, medieval pottery, other artefacts and biological material is being carried on in Cardiff and Birmingham.

After a short field season in 1986, it is planned to complete the work and have the final report ready for publication by June 1988.

The main areas of research and techniques being employed are as follows:

(a) Field and laboratory studies of soils and sediments. The establishment of a litho-/pedostratigraphy.

(b) Analysis of biological material and the establishment of a biostratigraphy. The main groups are Mollusca, Ostracoda, vertebrates and charred plant remains.

(c) Analysis of economic data, mainly bone and charred cereal remains.

(d) Study of artefactual material, mainly pottery and stone, with smaller amounts of bone and metal artefacts, and some structural features.

(e) Radiocarbon, both conventional and accelerator, and thermoluminescence dating.

(f) Survey of soils in the river catchment. This will be used to reconstruct the pattern of soils based on chalk, loess and clay-with-flints, the erosion of which provided the source of the alluvial deposits. This reflects land-use in the catchment.

Results

Since the work is at an early stage we are presenting some preliminary results in a semi-interpretative way rather than trying to anticipate the eventual establishment of a definitive scheme of litho-pedostratigraphy, biostratigraphy, archaeology and dating. The results from several pits and excavations, both in 1984 and 1985, are used to give an overall view. Two sequences have been established, one at Avebury, the other at West Overton. Here we concentrate on the former.

Avebury

The basic stratigraphy and molluscan sequence was obtained from Pit 6 (Figs. 9.1 and 9.2), excavated at a point 35m north of the bridge where the A361 crosses the Winterbourne (NGR: SU 09906958). The profile was as follows:

Depth below
surface (cm)

0–18/20	Topsoil. Stone-free clay loam.
18/20–75/80	Stone-free clay loam, with abundant granules of arionid slugs.
75/80–105	Stony humic clay loam. Medieval ploughsoil.
105–110	Humic silty clay loam with occasional chalk and flint fragments. Medieval soil.
110–162	Clean, coarse silt, rich in shell. 'West Overton Formation'.
162–175	Humic silty clay loam with large amounts of chalk fragments and a line of flints at 167–169cm. 'Avebury soil'.
175–195	Silty clay loam with large amounts of chalk fragments.
195 +	Variable small chalk and flint gravel.

Using this profile and the molluscan sequence from it, together with the evidence of archaeological trenches excavated in 1985 in a shallower part of the valley floor 300m to the north, we have established a number of 'local environment zones'. These are defined by a combination of evidence — soils, sediments, biological material and archaeology. Since this is a preliminary statement we have not numbered or lettered the zones. In chronological order from earliest to latest they are as follows:

Gelifluxion and meltwater runoff. Equivalent to 195 + cm in Pit 6. Ill-sorted coarse flint and chalk material, formed mainly by gelifluxion and meltwater processes in conditions of extreme cold. Biological material absent.

Open marsh with temporary pools. Not present in Pit 6. Marl. Molluscan assemblage of restricted type, indicative of open, marshy ground and temporary standing water. Cold climate. Probably late-glacial.

Woodland. 180–195cm in Pit 6. Ill-sorted fine chalky material infilling localised hollows, probably tree-holes. High diversity molluscan assemblage, rich in species, indicative of closed woodland. *Discus rotundatus* and *Pomatias elegans* indicate a mid-postglacial age.

Paludification. 175–180cm in Pit 6. Fine chalky material. Molluscan assemblage essentially woodland, but with two species characteristic of marshes — *Zonitoides nitidus* and *Carychium minimum*. Slight drop in diversity. The ground surface was probably becoming waterlogged — a process known as paludification — and this may have been a response to the very earliest effects of human interference with the vegetation, although a climatic influence cannot be ruled out at this stage.

Grassland. 162–175cm in Pit 6. Palaeosol and prehistoric occupation. Variously calcareous/non-calcareous, chalky/flinty silty clay loam with a stone-free horizon (sometimes two) possibly caused by earthworm sorting. Molluscan assemblage indicates dry grassland, especially in the presence of *Helicella itala*. Diversity, after an initial rise, falls sharply. Artefacts include late Mesolithic flints (rod microliths and waste), Windmill Hill pottery, and a range of earlier and later Neolithic flintwork, including a leaf-shaped arrowhead. Cereal grains and other charred plant remains are abundant but some of this material may be intrusive from overlying Medieval layers. Samples are being radiocarbon dated at Oxford. Burnt flints are being dated by thermoluminescence, also at Oxford. This horizon has provisionally been named the 'Avebury soil'.

Flooding and alluviation. 110–162cm in Pit 6. Coarse silt or silt loam, probably alluvial. A low diversity molluscan assemblage indicates open marshland becoming increasingly wet and subject to flooding. This deposit is provisionally termed the 'West Overton Formation' since it is almost certainly equivalent to much better developed deposits in the West Overton area.

Medieval settlement/arable/grassland. 75/80–110cm in Pit 6. Dark, humic silty clay loam with abundant chalk and flint. Molluscan assemblages indicate impoverished grassland and arable environments. Diversity is extremely low. A lower horizon in which

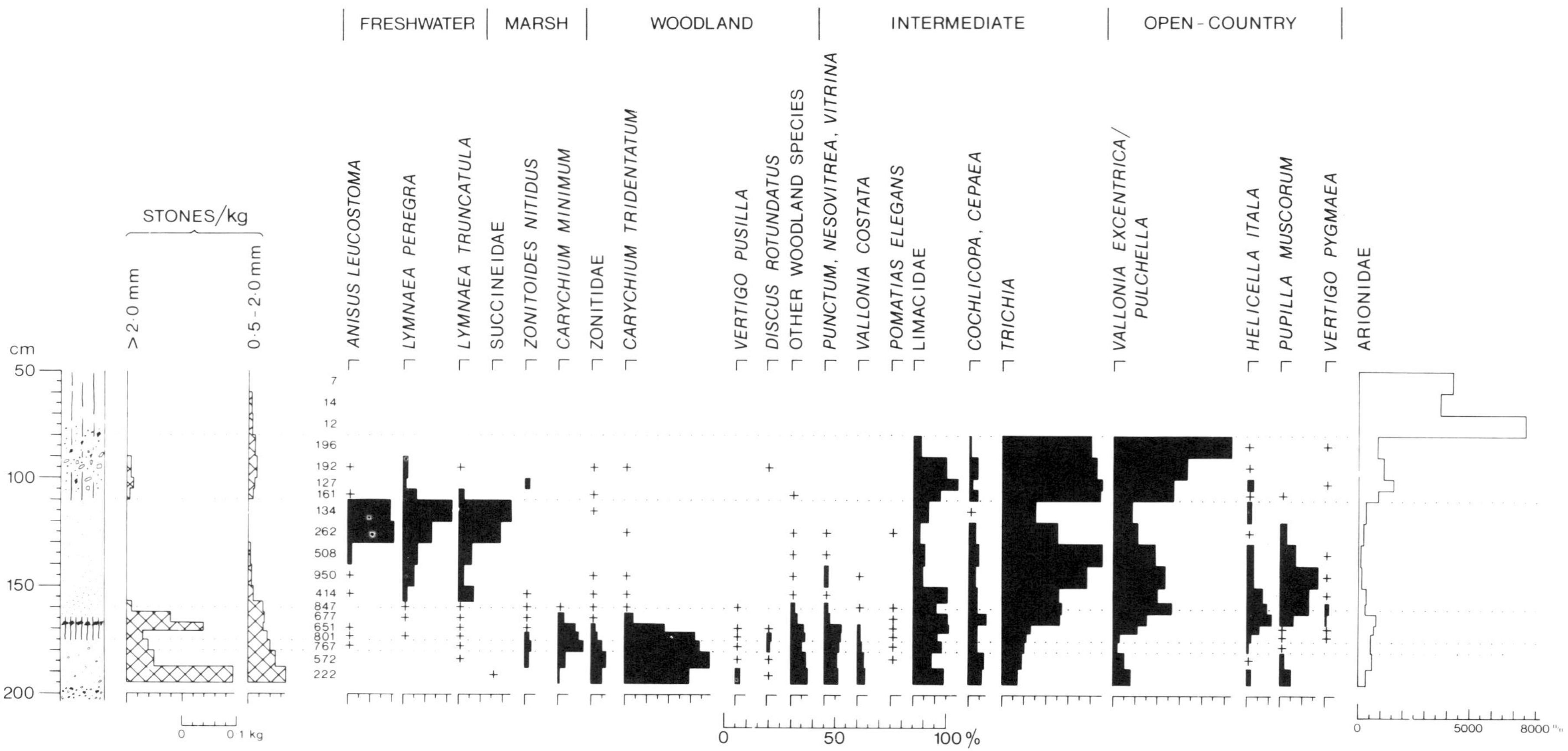

Fig. 9.1. Avebury, Pit 6, molluscan diagram. Arionidae granules in 0.125kg, plotted as a percentage over and above the other molluscan totals.

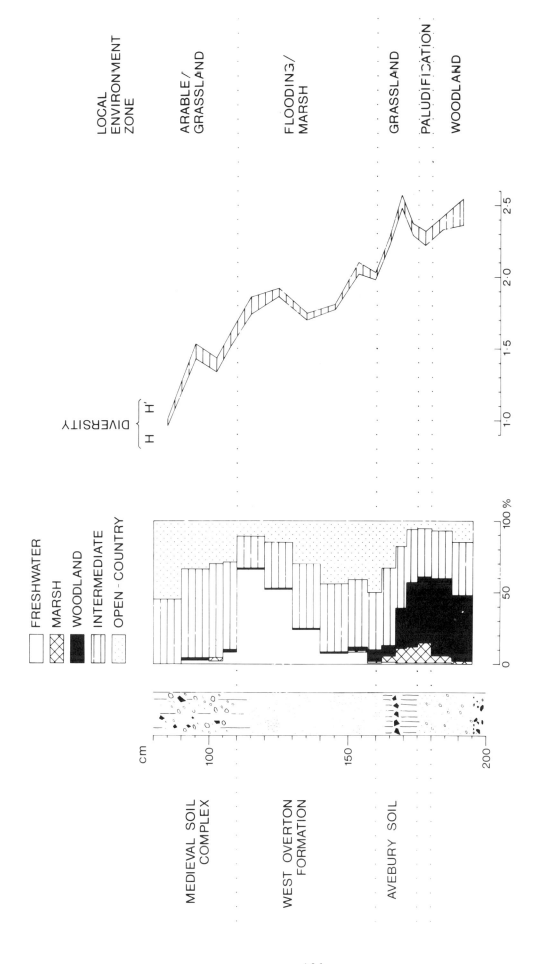

Fig. 9.2. Avebury, Pit 6, main molluscan groups and diversity indexes; (see Evans and Smith 1983 for the latter).

there are various features such as ditches, pits, bedding trenches with much wood charcoal, cereal grain and animal bone (but little pottery) is succeeded by an upper horizon lacking features and with a uniform and abundant distribution of pottery. The former represents settlement, the latter is probably a ploughsoil. A date in the 12th/13th centuries AD is indicated for both horizons.

Flooding and alluviation. 18/20–75/80cm in Pit 6. Clay and silty clay loam. Molluscan assemblage made up largely of the internal granules of arionid slugs. Probably a marsh/alluvial deposit formed by seasonal flooding of meadowland. Post-Medieval pottery.

Pasture, with slight flooding and alluviation. 0–18/20cm in Pit 6. Clay and silty clay loam. Mollusca sparse. This is the present-day soil. It is associated with various channels, although these do not indicate a properly organised water-meadow system.

West Overton

It will be appreciated from the above account of the Winterbourne valley floor at Avebury that deposits of earlier post-glacial age (say prior to *c.* 6000 bc) are absent. At West Overton we have located deposits of just this age. They occur immediately to the east of North Farm, towards the back edge of the floodplain, where they occupy a shallow channel (NGR: SU 13506855). The deposits are essentially tufaceous gravels with horizons of finer material, and they overlie a late-glacial marl. There is a long and detailed sequence of change in the molluscan and ostracod assemblages. In outline, an early post-glacial freshwater environment — possibly a slow-moving stream — is succeeded by a heavily wooded swamp. Mammalian remains include wild boar and aurochs. There are a very few artefacts of Mesolithic type. These deposits are provisionally named the 'North Farm Formation'.

A palaeosol, later truncated, formed on these deposits. It is probably equivalent to the Avebury Soil.

Overlying the palaeosol were thick deposits of alluvial silt with occasional thin layers of gravel. These deposits are probably equivalent to the silts already described from Avebury and are provisionally named the 'West Overton Formation'. Close to the base of these deposits were several structures made up of large sarsen stones, including two alignments, possibly field boundaries similar to those occurring as surface features on the plateau of the Marlborough Downs to the north.

At the back of the floodplain, the silts of the West Overton Formation interdigitate with and are overlain by colluvium which spreads from the valley side and wedges out onto the floodplain.

Discussion and General Conclusions

The main result arising from this work is that in the two areas of the valley floor investigated in detail at Avebury and West Overton, there is a sequence of stratified deposits spanning the period from the late-glacial to the present. Land surfaces are present and these contain cultural and economic material. At least two clear archaeological horizons have been located. A variety of biological data has been obtained and we are beginning to build up a really detailed sequence of environmental change for the area. Ultimately it will be possible to date this sequence.

In terms of the local environmental sequence it has been shown that during the later Mesolithic and throughout the Neolithic periods the valley floor was dry ground, subject to neither flooding nor alluviation. A palaeosol, probably equivalent to the Avebury Soil, has been located in many of the auger holes and practically all the excavations. Although this is a localised study, at least here ideas about uninhabitable swamps at that time must be abandoned. This is an important result, with fundamental implications for settlement studies.

At Avebury, it has been demonstrated that woodland clearance took place prior to alluviation and in a context associated with later Mesolithic and Neolithic artefacts. Paludification was an early episode in this process and we tentatively ascribe these changes to the activities of human communities. Similar clearance of woodland in the Neolithic took place at sites on either side of the floodplain at Avebury (Evans 1972; Evans *et al.* 1985) and South Street (Ashbee *et al.* 1979).

Flooding and alluviation occurred at some time between the later Neolithic and Medieval periods, possibly during the later Iron Age as suggested by archaeological evidence from West Overton. It is not yet clear how or why these deposits formed but their formation must have resulted in periods when the potential of the floodplain for grazing, cultivation and settlement was subject to very considerable changes. The land from which the deposits were derived suffered truncation of soils, of which part at least was formed on material having a high loess content, resulting in changes of soil depth, moisture retention and potential fertility over wide areas of the catchment. Again the archaeological implications could be fundamental.

Acknowledgements

In addition to the organisations and individuals mentioned in the text, the following have given valuable assistance with the project. Robin Butler (of Manor Farm, Avebury Trusloe), David Hues (of West Kennet), R.J. Hues (of Pellins, Chirton), Robin and Gill Swanton (of North Farm, West Overton), and the Salisbury Diocesan Board of Finance kindly allowed the excavations to take place on their land. The Swantons gave freely of their hospitality throughout the project, and both they and Robin Butler assisted materially with tool storage, finds sheds and water supplies. The Historic Buildings and Monuments Commission and the Trust for Wessex Archaeology lent equipment. The work on the ostrocods is being done by Judith Atkinson under the supervision of Eric Robinson, and the work on the animal bone is being supervised by Barbara Noddle. Martin Aitken, Joan Huxtable and John Gowlett visited the excavations in connection with the radiocarbon and thermoluminescence dating. To all we are extremely grateful.

References

Ashbee P., Smith I.F. and Evans J.G.1979 Excavation of three long barrows near Avebury, Wiltshire. *Proc. Prehist. Soc.* 45:207–300.

Bell M. 1983 Valley sediments as evidence of prehistoric land-use on the South Downs. *Proc. Prehist. Soc.* 49:119–150.

Cameron R.A.D. 1978 Interpreting buried land-snail assemblages from archaeological sites — problems and progress. In D.R. Brothwell, K.D. Thomas and J. Clutton-Brock (eds). *Research Problems in Zooarchaeology.* London: Institute of Archaeology, Occ. pub. no. 3:19–23.

Cornwall I.W. 1953 Soil science and archaeology with illustrations from some British Bronze Age monuments. *Proc. Prehist. Soc.* 19:129–147.

Cornwall I.W. 1958 *Soils for the Archaeologist.* London: Phoenix House.

Evans J.G. 1966 Late-glacial and post-glacial subaerial deposits at Pitstone, Buckinghamshire. *Proc. Geol. Ass. London* 77, 347–364.

Evans J.G. 1972 *Land Snails in Archaeology.* London: Seminar Press.

Evans J.G., Pitts M.W. and Williams D. 1985 An excavation at Avebury, Wiltshire, 1982. *Proc. Prehist. Soc.* 51:305–310.

Evans J.G. and Smith I.F. 1983 Excavations at Cherhill, north Wiltshire, 1967. *Proc. Prehist. Soc.* 49:43–117.

Kerney M.P. 1977 A proposed zonation scheme for late-glacial and post-glacial deposits using land Mollusca. *J. Archaeol Science* 4:387–390.

Kerney M.P., Brown E.H., and Chandler T.J. 1964 The late-glacial and post-glacial history of the chalk escarpment near Brook, Kent. *Phil. Trans. R. Soc.* (B) 248:135–204.

Kerney M.P., Preece R.C. and Turner C. 1980 Molluscan and plant biostratigraphy of some Late Devensian and Flandrian deposits in Kent. *Phil. Trans. R. Soc.* (B) 291:1–43.

Kubiëna W.L. 1953 *The Soils of Europe.* London: Thomas Murby.

Preece R.C. 1980 The biostratigraphy and dating of the tufa deposit at the Mesolithic site at Blashenwell, Dorset, England. *J. Archaeol. Science* 7:345–362.

Robinson M.A. and Lambrick G.H. 1984 Holocene alluviation and hydrology in the upper Thames basin. *Nature* 308:809–814.

Rust A. 1937 *Das altsteinzeitliche Rentierjägerlager Meiendorf.* Neumünster.

Thomas K.D. 1985 Land snail analysis in archaeology: theory and practice. In N.R.J. Fieller, D.D. Gilbertson and N.G.A. Ralph (eds). *Palaeobiological Investigations: research design, methods and data analysis.* BAR S-266:131–156.

10. A Review of Neolithic Domestic Activity in Southern Britain

Robin Holgate

The excavation of Neolithic monuments in Britain has produced a variety of carefully contrived deposits of ceremonial or funerary character, but evidence for domestic activity has hitherto remained elusive. As Dennell (1983:182) comments, we "seem to be in an odd position of knowing more about the environment in which the dead were buried than about what the living did when not constructing enclosures, barrows, henges and trackways". The search for the missing settlement evidence is a major research priority in British prehistory (Groube and Bowden 1982:31) and the subject of this paper.

Less than ten Neolithic domestic structures are known from the highland zone in areas that have not been subjected to intensive mechanized ploughing. These consist of rectangular timber-built houses with internal hearths (Piggott 1954:32–5; McInnes 1971; Smith 1974:104; Whittle 1977:46–8; Megaw and Simpson 1979:85–6). The best known examples are the 6.5 by 6m structures at Ballynagilly, Tyrone, made of vertically set oak planks set in bedding trenches with two internal hearths (ApSimon 1976:19–20; two carbon-14 dates of 3280±125 bc (UB–199) and 3215±50 bc (UB–201) have been obtained from charcoal from parts of the structural timbers); and the 8 by 5m house at Haldon Hill, Devon, represented by post-holes and wall footings of stone with a hearth inside one of the corners (Willock 1936).

Timber structures have been found in the lowland zone, either in areas that have not been ploughed e.g. Crickley Hill, Gloucestershire (Dixon 1981:145) or preserved under chambered cairns and long barrows e.g. Hazleton, Gloucestershire (Saville 1984:19). It is clear that some of these structures are mortuary houses, as they contain human burials e.g. Nutbane, Hampshire (Morgan 1959:20–2); indeed the only complete structures not to be found under or within a Neolithic monument, namely Fengate, Cambridgeshire (Pryor 1974, 1978:7–10) could be interpreted as a 'cult house' (c.f. Kjaerum 1967), on account of the absence of an internal hearth and the high quality pottery and jet bead found at the site. Houses found with domestic debris underneath chambered cairns elsewhere in Britain, whose alignment and position are not respected by the construction of the burial chamber, can be interpreted as domestic structures e.g. Ballyglass, Mayo (Ó Nualláin 1972, *passim*). Apart from structural remains, domestic sites have also been inferred from the discovery of pits, either found individually (Field *et al.* 1964) or in clusters e.g. Hurst Fen, Suffolk (Clark *et al.* 1960). In one or two cases, shallow post-holes e.g. at Eaton Heath, Norfolk (Wainwright 1973:6) and gullies e.g. at Bishopstone, East Sussex (Bell 1977:7–44) have survived in addition to pits. The selective deposition of certain pottery vessels and flint artefacts within some of these pits suggests that not all isolated Neolithic pits should automatically be interpreted as resulting from domestic activity e.g. Remenham, Berkshire (Holgate and Start, 1985).

The Effect of Post-Depositional Processes in the Neolithic Landscape

Present knowledge of Neolithic domestic sites both in Britain and on the continent would suggest that these consisted of one or more timber houses and other structures with shallow foundations and internal hearths, surrounded by pits, working areas and middens. Post-depositional processes have a considerable effect on the distribution, preservation and visibility of archaeological remains (Foley 1981:166). Ploughing, solution, hillwash and soil creep are probably the main agents of denudation that have eroded upper slopes and led to the accumulation of colluvium on lower slopes and in dry valley bottoms in the lowland zone. Atkinson (1957:229) has suggested that solution of chalk bedrocks has lowered the surface of the ground by as much as 0.5m in the last 4000 years, while Mercer (1980:23) has estimated that modern ploughing, hillslope erosion and solution has resulted in the loss of 0.3–0.4m from the original Neolithic land surface at the main causewayed enclosure at Hambledon Hill, Dorset. A further attempt at quantifying the degree of erosion on upper slopes has been made by Bell (1983) in the course of analysing colluvial deposits in dry valleys on the South Downs in Sussex and east Hampshire. By dividing the cross-sectional area of colluvium by the length of the contributing slope, he produced figures between 0.025 and 0.18m for the depth of eroded soil on upper valley slopes since the Neolithic period (Bell 1983:147). As these figures ignore the loss of material by solution and the movement of sediment down the valley axis, they could underestimate the degree of soil depletion. However, soil pits dug in valley bottoms elsewhere in southern Britain, e.g. in the Lambourn valley, Berkshire and around Stonehenge, Wiltshire, have yielded insignificant deposits of colluvium (Bell 1983), thus indicating that not all chalk areas have suffered the same intensity of erosion as the South Downs.

Erosion has been severe in other landscape regions off the Chalk in southern Britain. The old land surface preserved under the Neolithic enclosure bank at Broome Heath, Norfolk, situated on a river terrace overlaid by glacial sands and gravels, was 0.4m higher than the present ground surface (Wainwright 1972:3–5). Despite this, a number of shallow post-holes was identified within the confines of the enclosure (*ibid.*). In the Weald, substantial volumes of sediments occur in some of the river valleys draining this area of clay and sandstone lithography e.g. the rivers Ouse and Cuckmere in East Sussex (Scaife and Burrin 1983; 1985). Although the dating evidence for the accumulation of these alluvial deposits is, at present, based solely on pollen data, it is suggested that alluviation had begun by the Boreal period and was particularly extensive in the Neolithic and Bronze Age when human activity led to valley side soil erosion (Scaife and Burrin 1985:32–3). In the upper Thames valley, the start of the alluviation has been dated to the Iron Age by investigating the stratigraphic association of archaeological material and floodplain deposits (Robinson and Lambrick 1984:813). These examples illustrate that soil erosion has taken place not only on calcareous bedrocks but also on adjacent plateaux and clay vales, which inevitably has resulted in the severe truncation of domestic sites and the transfiguration of monuments of Neolithic date. A corollary to this is that Neolithic remains on lower slopes and in valley bottoms can be buried under colluvium and alluvium and thus protected from erosion e.g. the earlier Neolithic site at the Devil's Kneadingtrough near Brook, Kent (Kerney et al. 1964; Burleigh and Kerney 1982).

Paradoxically, while ploughing can destroy Neolithic sites by truncating upstanding remains, the original ground surface and subsoil features, it can also enhance the visibility of these sites by bringing a number of the artefacts from the disturbed contexts to the surface of the ploughsoil. In cases of drastic hillslope erosion these artefacts can travel downslope; certainly artefacts are encountered in colluvial deposits (Bell 1983, passim). However, the majority of artefacts found in these deposits in valley bottoms and in positive lynchet accumulations on slopes consist of small, abraded fragments of pottery, most of which probably result from Iron Age and later manuring practices (Clarke 1982:17–18; Mercer quoted in Crowther et al. 1985:65–7). Recent fieldwork at the Neolithic flint-mining sites at Harrow Hill, Long Down and Church Hill, Findon in West Sussex shows that even on west-, south-, and east-facing slopes of gradients up to 1:6 there has been limited lateral and downhill displacement of flintwork associated with working floors at these sites, despite annual ploughing in recent years (Holgate, in prep. a). Furthermore, sample excavations at the extensive later Neolithic domestic site at Bullock Down, East Sussex, which is situated on a 1:20 slope and has been ploughed intermittently since the Napoleonic War, produced 'Peterborough ware' sherds on the surface of the clay-with-flints under the modern ploughsoil (Drewett 1982:49; Holgate forthcoming a). Microwear analysis of the flint implements from both the surface of the clay-with-flints and the modern ploughsoil revealed relatively few traces of post-depositional surface modification, indicating that these artefacts have not moved far from where they were deposited in the Neolithic (Grace, in Holgate, forthcoming). It is suggested, therefore, that as with the load of a river, it is largely the smaller and lighter artefacts that move downslope with ploughing, soil creep and hillwash. Except in cases of significant hillslope erosion most artefacts that have been disturbed by ploughing oscillate in the ploughsoil in the vicinity of their place of deposition (Haselgrove 1985:8).

Recovering the Remains of Neolithic Domestic Activity

A substantial number of Neolithic monuments and domestic sites in southern Britain have been truncated by ploughing, solution and hillslope erosion. In the case of ditched monuments, these can be discovered and mapped by aerial photography. As domestic sites leave shallow subsoil remains, it is only in exceptional cases that they can be detected using this method. The discovery of most domestic structures has been purely accidental; for example at Balbridie, Angus the Neolithic structure which showed as marks in a parched grass field was excavated because it was initially interpreted as a Dark Age building (Reynolds 1980:55), and the house at Ballyglass, Mayo came to light while excavating a court cairn (Ó Nualláin 1972:49). Most other subsoil remains have emerged during the excavation of sites dating to other periods, often under rescue conditions, e.g. Bishopstone, East Sussex (Bell 1977).

The best survey method for locating and recording the distribution of Neolithic domestic activity is surface artefact collection in areas under cultivation (Holgate, 1985:51). As Neolithic pottery was poorly fired, it disintegrates rapidly on exposure to weathering agencies. Thus stone artefacts, comprising mostly humanly-struck flints, are usually the only domestic component of this date to survive in the ploughsoil. Substantial flint collections were amassed by amateur archaeologists at the end of the 19th and start of the 20th centuries e.g. by members of the Prehistoric Society of East Anglia who "were animated by a shared passion for flint implements"; excursions to the Breckland were organised, where "members would be ... let loose to collect surface flints and guided to Icklingham Hall, there to gloat over the largest private collection of flints (that belonging to Dr. Sturge) in the country" (Clarke 1985:2). A significant number of collections of this nature reside in museums throughout Britain and, in conjunction with the artefacts retrieved by controlled surveys carried out in recent years, form a considerable body of data which can be combined with the results of aerial photography and rescue excavation to map Neolithic settlement patterns (e.g. Holgate, 1986).

The Recognition of Domestic Assemblages

A number of ethnoarchaeological studies have been made of how contemporary stone-using societies use and dispose of artefacts (e.g. Binford 1978; Gould 1980); these provide an insight in to Neolithic site formation processes. Most studies are concerned with hunter-gathering societies, but there are some which relate to farming societies. Gould studied a group of Australian Aborigines and found that over 99% of the total stone materials they used were to be found in task-specific localities that were ephemeral and widely dispersed over the landscape. However, while less than 1% of the total stone materials occured on a habitation base camp, the widest range of artefact types within the total stone assemblage was used and disposed of in this context (1980:132). Hitchcock's study (1980:302) of the Botswana Bushmen showed that as a group became more sedentary, both a greater range of activities and an increase in specialized implement types were in evidence at domestic sites. The domestic sites of farming societies are likely to display a similar variety of specialized implement types; and the more sedentary the group, the greater the quantity of total stone material to be found at domestic sites.

Except in the case of a catastrophe, few serviceable objects are left behind when a domestic site is abandoned (Hodder 1982:56); only the rubbish remains. Murray (1980) reached two main conclusions in her general survey of rubbish disposal. First, that for sites permanently occupied for more than one season, the rubbish resulting from performing various tasks was not left at the place where these tasks were carried out. Second, on sites occupied for less than one season, rubbish was left where it fell. Thus while discrete activity areas could be discerned on hunter-gatherer or short-stay task-specific sites, they could not be detected on sedentary sites where houses and working areas were kept clean and rubbish was dumped elsewhere. The domestic sites of small-scale farming societies frequently consist of living, working and storage areas interspersed between or surrounded by middens or pits (often dug initially for other purposes, e.g. storage) which were used for rubbish disposal (e.g. the Fulani, West Africa: David 1971:113; the Lozi, Central Africa: Hodder 1982:121; in the Maya Highlands: Hayden and Cannon 1983, *passim;* Ethiopian skin dressers: Gallagher 1977:413; Clark and Kurashina 1981:316–17). Some sorting of where specific materials are to be deposited can take place and special effort is usually made to dispose of sharp materials, e.g. glass, obsidian and flint, on middens or in pits where people and animals are unlikely to walk around and cut themselves. This is an important point because it has been argued elsewhere using archaeological data from Neolithic sites in the northwestern part of the Cambridgeshire Peat Fens that flint debris can undergo specialized disposal "and may occur *in situ* as primary refuse on or off-site", whereas pottery and other materials can be redeposited off-site as secondary refuse (Crowther *et al.* 1985:65). These examples come from a range of social contexts; it could be argued that it is impossible to seek general rules regarding the manufacture, use and disposal of stone implements and that these concerns are governed by social context (c.f. Hodder 1982:215–16). However, Gallagher's study of Ethiopian skin dressers suggest that stone technology is related to subsistence practices and not ethnic group identity.

The domestic sites of small-scale farming societies are likely to be recognizable from concentrations of discarded stone implements and debitage from middens and rubbish pits. However, it is difficult to locate specific living and working areas from surface artefact spreads alone, as the surface artefact distribution usually bears little correspondence to the underlying subsoil features relating to houses or working areas e.g. Hatchery West, Illinois (Binford *et. al.* 1970: 70–1). These sites, though, are characterized by the presence of considerable quantities of flintwork, including a high proportion and variety of implements. Despite the fact that the daily work schedule often involves working away from the settlement, for example in fields or at various other task-specific sites, the flint assemblages from domestic sites can be differentiated from those associated with other sites, as domestic sites are places where a range of activities is performed, involving the manufacture, use and disposal of a variety of different implements. This is supported by a study of the flint assemblages from excavated Neolithic sites in southern Britain (Holgate, in prep. b): domestic sites e.g. Halden Hill, Devon (Willcock 1936), and Bishopstone, East Sussex (Bell 1977), produce a high percentage of implements to debitage and a variety of different types of implement, while flint mines e.g. the Sussex flint-mining sites (Holgate, in prep. a), barrows e.g. Fussell's Lodge, Hampshire (Ashbee 1966) and Alfriston, East Sussex (Drewett 1975) and cursus monuments e.g. the Stonehenge Greater Cursus, Wiltshire (Saville 1980:17), all yield a low percentage of implements to debitage and a limited range of different implement types. In theory, a diffuse scatter of humanly-struck flints would be expected in areas exploited by past stone-using societies with clusters of flints in localities where repeated acts of deposition took place. These clusters represent domestic sites, quarries and other task-specific sites which, in certain cases, contain distinctive flint assemblages. It should thus be possible to locate domestic and other task-specific sites of Neolithic date by plotting the surface distribution of flintwork in areas presently under cultivation.

Recently, the implementation of controlled surface artefact collection surveys has taken on a greater prominence in archaeological fieldwork (Haselgrove 1985:7). The results of these surveys show that there is an almost continuous low density scatter of flintwork over much of southern Britain, which varies in character and intensity according to the nature of past land use and the availability of flint resources. Discrete high density flint scatters occur in a number of places; these often include a range of different types of implement e.g. scrapers, knives, microdenticulates, piercers, arrowheads, fabricators, notched flakes, rods, ovates and ground flint axe fragments. The percentage of implements to debitage and the presence of certain types of implement and products of debitage in some of these high density scatters implies that they represent sites of domestic or industrial activity (Holgate 1985:53–6; Richards 1984:178). It is possible, therefore, to isolate domestic flint assemblages from the material produced by surface collection survey.

The Dating of Flint Assemblages

Changes in subsistence, work schedule and the use of objects as symbols of prestige and status from the Mesolithic to the Bronze Age have led to corresponding changes in the quality of flint selected for working, the technique used to work flint and the types and forms of implements that were produced. A study of flint assemblages from independently-dated closed contexts shows that there are changes in flint technology and typology in the post-glacial period (Holgate, in prep. b.). In the Mesolithic, good quality flint was flaked with hard and soft hammers to produce blades and bladelets which could be used to make end scrapers, burins, microliths and various other implements. During the earlier Neolithic (*c.* 3200 — *c.* 2600 bc) emphasis was was placed on producing blades using similar techniques to those used in the Mesolithic although there are certain differences in the way cores were worked (Holgate and Start 1985). Leaf-shaped arrowheads replaced microliths as projectile points and a variety of scrapers, piercers, knives, ovates and sickles were manufactured. In the later Neolithic (*c.* 2600 — *c.* 2000 bc), flint technology changed dramatically with flakes being removed from flint nodules of varying quality using hard hammers. Transverse arrowheads replaced leaf-shaped arrowheads and a limited range of implement types and forms were made. This simple method of working flint, though, does not reflect a decline in the presence of skilled flint workers, as some of the transverse arrowheads and knives were executed with a high degree of care and precision. Clearly, factors other than raw material availability and personal ability influenced the choice of techniques for working flint in the later Neolithic. There are thus changes in the choice of raw material, the techniques used to work flint and the types and forms of implements that were produced during the Mesolithic and Neolithic which enable flint assemblages to be dated.

Two Case Studies: The Upper Thames Basin and the Kennet Catchment

Although a number of detailed surveys have recently been carried out in parts of southern Britain e.g. the Stonehenge Environs Project (Richards 1984), the region as a whole has not been covered systematically; some areas have yet to be surveyed e.g. much of the lower Thames basin, while others have received haphazard treatment e.g. the Weald. The best approach to studying Neolithic settlement patterns is to take case study areas covering a variety of landscapes where comprehensive programmes of aerial photography, excavation, environmental sampling and surface collection survey have taken place. The sequence of Neolithic settlement in two areas will be summarized here: the catchment areas of the upper Thames and the Kennet rivers.

The Upper Thames Basin, Fig. 10.1

The upper Thames catchment includes the Oolitic Limestone plateau of the Cotswolds to the north, extensive gravel terraces running parallel with the Thames and the Corallian Limestone ridge and clay vales to the south and southeast. Archaeological reconnaissance has been patchy, but there are several localities which have received careful attention. A number of chambered cairns were constructed on the Cotswolds in the earlier Neolithic, while causewayed enclosures were positioned mostly around the edge of the Cotswolds, either on the crest of the scarp slope e.g. Crickley Hill, Gloucestershire (Dixon 1981), or on the Thames gravel terraces e.g. Abingdon, Oxfordshire (Avery 1982). In the later Neolithic, the use of these monuments ceased and a series of new monuments was built almost exclusively on the gravel terraces. These included long barrows e.g. Barrow Hills, Oxfordshire (Bradley and Holgate 1984:116), round barrows (ring-ditches) e.g. Linch Hill Corner, Oxfordshire (Grimes 1960:154–64), cursus monuments e.g. Drayton, Oxfordshire (Bradley and Holgate 1984:121), and henges e.g. Dorchester on Thames, Oxfordshire (Atkinson *et. al.* 1951). Environmental analysis of the land surfaces preserved beneath several Neolithic monuments and pollen analysis of peaty areas show that mixed deciduous woodland covered much of the region by the end of the Mesolithic. Lime was probably the dominant tree species on the limestone soils, with oak and alder dominant in river valleys (Robinson and Wilson, forthcoming). During the earlier Neolithic there were numerous small clearings in the woodland canopy; by the end of the Neolithic, parts of the upper Thames basin were still wooded, though there were also extensive areas that had been cleared.

Later Mesolithic sites were located at the forest margin either on the terrace edge adjacent to the Thames or on upper slopes overlooking valleys. In four cases excavation or total surface collection over two or more seasons have taken place: the two terrace edge sites, Corporation Farm and Thrupp site B, both near Abingdon in Oxfordshire, proved to be extensive with a range of flint implements represented, while the other two on upper slopes, Chilswell and Hurst Hill, Cumnor, again both in Oxfordshire, were small sites with microliths forming virtually the only implements recovered (Holgate 1986). The last two were probably task-specific sites occupied seasonally, but whether or not the upper Thames catchment was exploited by a single band or was part of a much larger territory associated with one or more social groups is at present unclear.

In the earlier Neolithic, domestic sites were established in new locations on the Cotswold uplands, while the gravel terraces and Cotswold scarp were virtually devoid of sites other than causewayed enclosures. It is clear that this pattern is unrelated to areas of intensive fieldwork or spreads of alluvial or colluvial deposits as the Thames gravels, which are free of these deposits, have been searched for traces of earlier Neolithic domestic

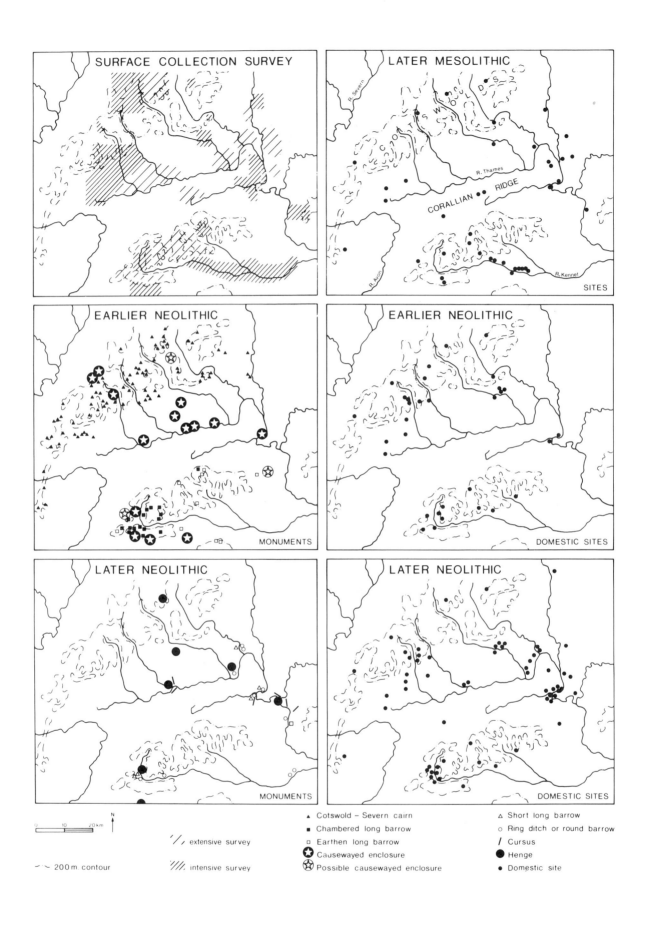

Fig. 10.1. Later Mesolithic and Neolithic settlement patterns in the upper Thames and Kennet catchments.

108

activity. Concerning the domestic sites themselves, surviving remains of domestic activity have been uncovered beneath the cairns of certain Cotswold tombs e.g. Hazleton, Gloucestershire (Saville 1984;19). These remains, along with the small totals of flints that occur in earlier Neolithic domestic assemblages, suggest that certain domestic sites were small in size and short-lived. However, the archaeological visibility of these sites on the Cotswolds could be affected by the subsequent reuse of pieces of flint worked in the earlier Neolithic e.g. cores, during the later Neolithic.

In the later Neolithic, much of the Cotswolds continued to be occupied, while new sites became established in areas where domestic activity appears to have been absent in the earlier Neolithic, as exemplified by the spread of settlement onto the gravel terraces. This phase of expansion was accompanied by the construction of monuments e.g. barrows and cursus monuments in precisely those areas that were newly settled. Surface collection survey shows that the flints recovered from individual domestic sites were spread over much larger areas than their earlier Neolithic counterparts. Furthermore, flint is worked in an extremely uneconomic fashion during the later Neolithic. This change in the working of flint could have resulted from a change in work schedule, perhaps associated with the adoption of a different farming strategy. If most daily activities were undertaken close to home, there would no longer be the need to make durable implements to carry around for use where required; implements could be manufactured quickly as and when particular activities were being performed. At Corporation Farm near Abingdon, Oxfordshire a later Bronze Age farmstead was apparently built within an existing field system (Barrett and Bradley 1980:257); ploughmarks and animal bones from two Beaker pits at the Hamel, Oxford indicate arable farming and livestock production on the floodplain and lower gravel terraces alongside the Thames at that time (Palmer 1980:12–34). The discovery of cereal remains and cattle, sheep and pig bones in Grooved Ware pits at Barton Court Farm, Abingdon, Oxfordshire (Miles 1986) and other sites on the Thames gravels, together with the flint evidence, suggest that the permanently-occupied farmsteads engaged in an infield-outfield farming strategy that are evident in the Bronze Age could have developed in the later Neolithic. A similar pattern can be observed at the Fen edge east of Peterborough, Cambridgeshire, as exemplified by the Storey's Bar Road Grooved Ware site (Pryor 1978).

The Kennet Catchment, Fig. 10.1

The River Kennet flows between two blocks of chalk downland. Surface collection surveys and excavations have taken place on the Downs and in the Kennet valley itself. Earthen long barrows or terminally-chambered long barrows were built on the Downs in the earlier Neolithic, and causewayed enclosures e.g. Windmill Hill and Knap Hill, Wiltshire (Smith 1965; Connah 1965), were positioned either on the scarp edges or in valleys defining the outer limits of the Downs. In the later Neolithic, the two long barrows at Beckhampton Road and South Street, both in Wiltshire (Ashbee *et al.* 1979) and also Silbury Hill, Wiltshire (Atkinson 1969), and the Avebury henge monument, Wiltshire (Gray 1935), were constructed on lower valley slopes near the head of the Kennet. Analysis of the land snails from the buried land surfaces below these monuments produced evidence for a similar sequence of environmental change during the Neolithic as in the upper Thames basin. The land surfaces below barrows, Silbury Hill and the Avebury henge monument indicate areas of woodland clearance followed by both arable and pastoral farming during the Neolithic, but the two causewayed enclosures, Windmill Hill and Knap Hill, were both constructed in wooded environments (Evans 1971; 1972). Further east, an elm decline clearance was recorded in the pollen sequence at Snelsmoor Common near Newbury, Berkshire, but woodland regeneration is recorded soon afterwards and subsequent disturbance to the forest cover was minimal until the early Iron Age (Waton 1982:83).

Later Mesolithic sites occur either on the edge of the terrace overlooking the Kennet floodplain, or on clay-with-flints deposits capping the tops of the Downs. All these sites have yielded large quantities of flintwork. From the Atlantic period onwards, the water table in the Kennet valley rose and peat deposits started to accumulate on the floodplain (Churchill 1962:367). In the later Mesolithic, sites were located in the upper Kennet valley (Froom 1972), and the earlier Mesolithic sites situated in the lower reaches of the Kennet valley e.g. Thatcham, Berkshire (Wymer 1962), were abandoned. At the beginning of the earlier Neolithic, the terrace edge sites were abandoned and domestic sites, along with long barrows became established on the Downs. Some of these sites, located at the interface between the clay-with-flints deposits and the Upper Chalk, have produced extremely large quantities of flintwork and could be interpreted as both domestic and flint procurement sites, possibly supplying flint nodules to Neolithic communities in the Cotswolds (cf. Saville 1982). Although there are no known domestic sites from within the Kennet valley at this time (Froom, pers. comm.), a number of flint and other stone axes were deposited in the floodplain peats near Newbury, Berkshire; in one instance, two flint axes (one of which was either a roughout or a preform) were found with a dump of animal bones (Palmer 1875:124). It is likely that these axes were placed as votive offerings in the Kennet peats; a similar practice is recorded at the Sweet Track in the Somerset Levels (Coles and Orme 1976:65).

During the later Neolithic, most of of the known domestic sites on the Downs continued to be occupied and a number of new sites were located on the lower valley slopes at the headwaters of the Kennet. As in the upper Thames basin these sites covered a greater area than earlier Neolithic domestic sites.

Discussion

Information on the form of domestic sites and the composition of local residential units during the Neolithic in southern Britain is presently lacking; an account of intra-site organization and farming practice must await the discovery and excavation of well-preserved domestic sites. However, an analysis of domestic flint assemblages and their relationship to the contemporary environment and other sites, e.g. ritual monuments, can throw light on regional patterns of settlement.

The sequence of settlement in the upper Thames and Kennet catchments is remarkably similar. The uplands were exploited in the later Mesolithic, but the main concentration of hunter-gatherer populations would appear to have been in the river valleys. At the start of the Neolithic, domestic activity shifted on to the uplands and coincided with a phase of tomb construction in these areas. Causewayed enclosures were usually sited around the periphery of settled areas. In the later Neolithic, domestic activity spread onto the lower valley slopes and terraces, and was associated with a new phase of monument building. Further developments were initiated during the later Neolithic: the area occupied by domestic sites increased; there was a marked change in flintworking techniques with, on the one hand, simple method of flaking flint and on the other, the skilled production of elaborate items e.g. transverse arrowheads and ground-edged implements; and the predominant burial rite associated with barrows switched from communal burial to the inhumation of individual adults with grave goods e.g. Linch Hill Corner, Oxfordshire (Grimes 1960:154–64). Comparable developments took place in other parts of southern Britain. In Sussex, for example, domestic activity in the earlier Neolithic was concentrated on the South Downs, with enclosures and long barrows positioned on the edge of the Downs. During the later Neolithic, flint scatters on the Downs increased in both number and size, and domestic activity also expanded into the Weald (Gardiner 1984:*passim*). A limited number of new monuments were constructed on the Downs in the later Neolithic e.g. the Alfriston oval barrow (Drewett 1975), but no monuments of Neolithic date are known from the Weald. Not all regions, however, experienced the same sequence of Neolithic settlement. In East Anglia, the scale and frequency of monuments is small compared with regions south of the Thames, a feature which cannot be related to scarcity of settlement (Cleal 1984:135); the sporadic nature of past surface collection surveys, though, poses difficulties when attempting to reconstruct settlement patterns in this area.

By the start of the third millennium bc, there are a number of social groups occupying discrete blocks of land in southern Britain, in some cases delineated by the construction of monuments. These regional groups expanded into unoccupied areas in the mid-third millennium bc, but still retained their regional identity by the use of monuments and the control of the production and deposition of certain artefact types. The origin of these developments has been explained by the arrival of pioneer farmers from the continent in the fourth millennium bc; the emergence of a settled landscape ritual monuments is characterized as a phase of 'stable adjustment' (Case 1969). However, there is no archaeological evidence for a phase of pioneer farming in Britain, and Dennell (1983) has recently argued against Case's scheme. Farming practice on the continent at this time was beyond the experimental stage and, whether introduced by Neolithic colonists or the indigenous Mesolithic population, was undoubtedly imported as a comprehensive package (Dennell 1983:174–6). Furthermore, there is no obvious source for these pioneering farmers. The Bandkeramik colonization of the hitherto sporadically settled loess-based soils in the major continental river valleys is an isolated example of pioneer farming on a large scale; after 4000 bc the loess areas witnessed a phase of settlement contraction e.g. as seen in the Aldenhovener Platte, Germany (Lüning 1982a; 1982b). Towards the end of the fourth millennium bc, farming societies became established on the north European plain, but by this stage the sequence of monument buildings, ceramic production and stone implement manufacture in northwest Europe runs as a parallel development to the British Neolithic sequence. In Scandinavia, it has been suggested that farming was adopted by the indigenous hunter-gatherer societies to ensure the availability of edible resources throughout the year in response to a sudden decline in marine resources (Zvelebil and Rowley-Conwy 1984). It is therefore pertinent to consider the Mesolithic contribution to the introduction of farming to Britain.

In the later Mesolithic, hunter-gatherer populations were prevalent in coastal and riverine settings, although certain upland areas were exploited as well e.g. clay-with-flints deposits on the Downs (Jacobi 1978:76–7). In the case study areas discussed in this paper, most of the riverine areas which experienced intensive activity during this period were abandoned and earlier Neolithic activity was focussed on the fertile, often loess-based upland soils at about the same time as the elm decline phenomenon. Despite this shift in the pattern of settlement, the same sources and quality of flint continued to be exploited using similar flintworking techniques. It could be argued that immigrant farmers only colonised the coastal zone, which has since disappeared through marine transgression, and that further inland the adoption of agriculture and Neolithic material culture was a native response to contact with these early pioneers. However, there is still the problem of tracing the antecedents of the British ceramic and stone artefact styles. In the ceramic repertoire, comparisons have been made between Grimston Ware and Hazendonk Ware from the Rhine estuary in the Netherlands (Louwe Koojimans, pers. comm.), but there are no convincing parallels for leaf-shaped arrowheads; the Michelsberg arrowheads from the lower Rhine basin championed by Piggott (1955) were shaped using soft hammers, and thus bear little resemblance to the British arrowheads, which were finished by pressure-flaking. In fact the methods of working flint in southern Britain during the earlier Neolithic cannot, at present, be matched with contemporary flint industries on the continent, although future work in northwest France could alter this picture. It is possible, then, that the initiative for the introduction of farming and the establishment of farming societies in Britain was taken by the indigenous hunter-gatherer societies. Subsequent developments could thus have been insular and conditioned by the securing of dominant social relations and access to land, and the conflicts that can arise over maintenance, inheritance and transfer of those rights.

Conclusion

In Scandinavia, the model that has been proposed for the indigenous development of agriculture in the late fourth — early third millennia bc is founded on a study of material recovered from a wealth of excavated domestic sites available for study (Zvelebil and Rowley-Conwy 1984; Larsson 1985). In southern Britain, the erosion of the Neolithic coastline and the effect of deep ploughing have destroyed a significant amount of archaeological evidence for the Mesolithic/Neolithic transition. There are, however, other avenues for research. Stratified sites undoubtedly survive in certain localities, e.g. the Cambridgeshire Fens and the Lyddon Marshes, Kent, although here the depth of peat and alluvial deposits overlying the buried Neolithic land surface limits survey work (Crowther et al. 1985:69). Systematic collection surveys of cultivated land can record the extent and nature of Mesolithic and Neolithic settlement, in the form of surface flint distributions. An analysis of flint assemblages, both from excavated sites and the surface of the plough-soil, produces information on subsistence practices and the nature of domestic sites, providing a careful assessment is made of the filtering action of site formation, post-depositional and recovery processes on the sample of flintwork available for study. This paper has emphasized the value of field survey and the study of flintwork in reconstructing Neolithic settlement patterns. Fieldwork to locate well-preserved sites in low-lying areas and record the regional extent of settlement should clarify and expand the view of Neolithic domestic activity presented here.

Acknowledgement

I am grateful to Dr. Ian Kinnes for reading and commenting on a draft of this paper.

References

ApSimon A.M. 1976 Ballynagilly and the beginning and end of the Irish Neolithic. In S.J. De Laet (ed) *Acculturation and Continuity in Atlantic Europe*. Diss. Archaeol. Gandenses 21, Bruges, pp. 15–30.

Ashbee P. 1966 The Fussell's Lodge long barrow excavations 1957. *Archaeologia* 100:1–80.

Ashbee P., Smith I.F. and Evans J.G. 1979 Excavations of three long barrows near Avebury, Wiltshire. *Proc. Prehist. Soc.* 45:207–300.

Atkinson R.J.C. 1957 Worms and weathering. *Antiquity* 31:219–33.

Atkinson R.J.C. 1969 The date of Silbury Hill. *Antiquity* 43:216.

Atkinson R.J.C., Piggott C.M. and Sanders, N.K. 1951 *Excavations at Dorchester, Oxon*. Oxford: Ashmolean Museum.

Avery M. 1982 The Neolithic causewayed enclosure, Abingdon. In H.J. Case and A.W.R. Whittle (eds) *Settlement patterns in the Oxford region: excavations at the Abdingdon causewayed enclosure and other sites*. CBA Res. Rep. 44:10–50.

Barrett J. and Bradley R. 1980 The Later Bronze Age in the Thames Valley. In Barrett J. and Bradley R. (eds) *Settlement and Society in the British Later Bronze Age*. Oxford: BAR BS83:247–69.

Bell M. 1977 Excavations at Bishopstone. *Sussex Archaeol. Coll.* 115: *passim*.

Bell M. 1983 Valley Sediments as evidence of prehistoric land-use on the South Downs. *Proc. Prehist. Soc.* 49:119–50.

Binford L.R. 1978 *Nunamiut Ethnoarchaeology*. New York: Academic Press.

Binford L.R., Binford S.R., Whallon R. and Hardin M.A. 1970 *Archaeology at Hatchery West*. Memoirs of the Society for American Archaeology 24.

Bradley R. and Holgate R. 1984 The Neolithic sequence in the Upper Thames Valley. In R. Bradley and J. Gardiner (eds) *Neolithic Studies: a review of some current research*. Oxford: BAR S-133:107–34.

Burleigh R. and Kerney M.P. 1982 Some chronological implications of a fossil molluscan assemblage from a Neolithic site at Brook, Kent, England. *J. Archaeol. Sci.* 9:29–38.

Case H. 1969 Neolithic explanations. *Antiquity* 43:176–86.

Churchill D.M. 1962 The stratigraphy of the Mesolithic sites III and V at Thatcham, Berkshire, England. *Proc. Prehist. Soc.* 28:362–70.

Clark J.G.D. 1985 The Prehistoric Society: from East Anglia to the World. *Proc. Prehist. Soc.* 51:1–13.

Clark J.G.D., Higgs E.S. and Longworth I.H. 1960 Excavations at the Neolithic site at Hurst Fen, Mildenhall, Suffolk, 1954, 1957 and 1959. *Proc. Prehist. Soc.* 26:202–45.

Clark J.D. and Kurashina H. 1981 A study of the work of a modern tanner in Ethiopia and its relevance for archaeological interpretation. In R.A. Gould and M.B. Schiffer (eds) *Modern Material Culture: The Archaeology of Us*. New York: Academic Press. pp. 303–21.

Clarke A.F. 1982 An excavation of a lynchet southwest of the Heathy Brow Iron Age settlement. In P. Drewett (ed) *The Archaeology of Bullock Down, Eastbourne, East Sussex: the development of a landscape*. Sussex Archaeological Society Monograph 1:17–21.

Cleal R. 1984 The Later Neolithic in eastern England. In R. Bradley and J. Gardiner (eds) *Neolithic Studies: a review of some current research*. Oxford: BAR BS133:135–58.

Coles J.M. and Orme B.J. 1976 The Sweet Track, Railway Site. *Somerset Levels Papers* 2:34–65.

Connah G. 1965 Excavations at Knap Hill, Alton Priors, 1961. *Wiltshire Archaeol. Nat. Hist. Mag.* 60:1–23.

Crowther D., French C. and Pryor F. 1985 Approaching the Fens the Flexible Way. In C. Haselgrove, M. Millett and I. Smith (eds) *Archaeology from the Ploughsoil: studies in the collection and interpretation of field survey data*. University of Sheffield. pp. 59–76.

David N. 1971 The Fulani compound and the archaeologist. *World Archaeology* 3:111–31.

Dennell R. 1983 *European Economic Prehistory: a new approach*. New York: Academic Press.

Dixon P. 1981 Crickley Hill. *Curr. Archaeol.* 76:145–7.

Drewett P. 1975 The excavation of an oval burial mound of the third millennium bc at Alfriston, East Sussex, 1974. *Proc. Prehist. Soc.* 41:119–52.

Drewett P. 1982 The Neolithic settlement of Bullock Down 4000-2500 B.C. In P. Drewett (ed) *The Archaeology of Bullock Down, Eastbourne, East Sussex: the development of a landscape*. Sussex Archaeological Society Monograph 1:45–57.

Evans J.G. 1971 Habitat change on the calcareous soils of Britain: the impact of Neolithic man. In D.D.A. Simpson (ed) *Economy and Settlement in Neolithic and Early Bronze Age Britain and Europe*. Leicester: University Press. pp. 27–73.

Evans J.G. 1972 *Land Snails in Archaeology: with special reference to the British Isles*. London: Seminar Press.

Field N.H., Matthews C.L. and Smith I.F. 1964 New Neolithic sites in Dorset and Bedfordshire, with a note on the distribution of Neolithic storage-pits in Britain. *Proc. Prehist. Soc.* 30:352–81.

Foley R. 1981 Off-site archaeology: an alternative approach for the short-sited. In I. Hodder, G. Isaac and N. Hammond (eds) *Pattern of the Past, Studies in Honour of David Clarke*. Cambridge: University Press. pp. 157–83.

Froom F.R. 1972 Some Mesolithic sites in southwest Berkshire. *Berkshire Archaeol. J.* 66:11–22.

Gallager J.P. 1977 Contemporary stone tools in Ethiopia: implications for archaeology. *Journal of Field Archaeology* 4:407–14.

Gardiner J.P. 1984 Lithic distributions and Neolithic settlement patterns in central southern England. In R. Bradley and J. Gardiner (eds) *Neolithic Studies: a review of some current research*. Oxford: BAR BS133:15–40.

Gould R.A. 1980 *Living Archaeology*. Cambridge: University Press.

Gray H. St. G. 1935 The Avebury Excavations, 1908–1922. *Archaeologia* 84:99–162.

Grimes W.F. 1960 *Excavations on Defence Sites 1939–45*. London: H.M.S.O.

Groube L.M. and Bowden M.C.B. 1982 *The Archaeology of Rural Dorset: Past Present and Future*. Dorset Natur. Hist. and Archaeol. Soc. Monograph 4.

Haselgrove C. 1985 Inference from ploughsoil artefact samples. In C. Haselgrove, M. Millet and I. Smith (eds) *Archaeology from the Ploughsoil: studies in the collection and interpretation of field survey data*. University of Sheffield. pp. 7–29.

Hayden B. and Cannon A. 1983 Where the garbage goes: refuse disposal in the Maya Highlands. *Journal of Anthropological Archaeology* 2:117–63.

Hitchcock R.K. 1980 The enthnoarchaeology of sedentism: a Kalahari case. In R.E. Leakey and B.A. Ogot (eds) *Proceedings of the 8th Panafrican Congress of Prehistory and Quarternary Studies Nairobi, 5 to 10 September 1977*. Nairobi: The International Louis Leakey Memorial Institute for African Prehistory. pp. 300–3.

Hodder I. 1982 *The Present Past: an introduction to anthropology for archaeologists*. London: Batsford.

Holgate R. 1985 Identifying Neolithic settlements in Britain: the role of field survey in the interpretation of lithic scatters. In C. Haselgrove, M. Millett and I. Smith (eds) *Archaeology from the Ploughsoil: studies in the collection and interpretation of field survey data*. University of Sheffield. pp. 51–7.

Holgate R. 1986 Mesolithic, Neolithic and earlier Bronze Age settlement patterns southwest of Oxford. *Oxoniensia*. 51:1–14.

Holgate R. forthcoming Excavations at later Neolithic settlement on Bullock Down, Eastbourne, East Sussex. *Sussex Archaeol. Collect.*

Holgate R. in prep. a The Neolithic flint mines in Sussex.

Holgate R. in prep. b Settlement, economy and society in the Thames basin in the 4th and 3rd millennia bc. D. Phil. thesis.

Holgate R. and Start D. forthcoming A Neolithic pit at Remenham, near Henley-on-Thames, Berkshire. *Berkshire Archaeol. J.*

Jacobi R.M. 1978 Population and landscape in Mesolithic lowland Britain. In S. Limbrey and J.G. Evans (eds) *The effect of Man on the Landscape: the Lowland Zone*. CBA Res. Rep. 21:75–85.

Kerney M.P., Brown E.H. and Chandler T.J. 1964 The late-glacial and postglacial history of the chalk escarpment near Brook, Kent. *Phil. Trans. Roy. Soc. London B* 248:135–204.

Kjaerum P., 1967 The chronology of the passage graves in Jutland. *Palaeohistoria* 12:323–34.

Larsson M. 1985 *The early Neolithic Funnel-Beaker Culture in southwest Scania, Sweden: social and economic change 3000–2500 B.C.* Oxford: BAR S-264.

Lüning J. 1982a Siedlung und Siedlungslandschaft in bandkeramischer und Rössener Zeit. *Offa* 39:9–33.

Lüning J. 1982b Research into the Bandkeramik settlement of the Aldenhovener Platte in the Rhineland. *Analecta Praehistorica Leidensia* 15:45–61.

McInnes I.J. 1971 Settlements in later Neolithic Britain. In D.D.A.Simpson (ed) *Economy and settlement in Neolithic and Early Bronze Age Britain and Europe*. Leicester: University Press. pp. 113–30.

Megaw J.V.S. and Simpson D.D.A. 1979 *Introduction to British Prehistory*. Leicester: University Press.

Mercer R.J. 1980 *Hambledon Hill: a Neolithic landscape*. Edinburgh: University Press.

Miles D. 1986 *Archaeology at Barton Court Farm, Abingdon*. London CBA Res Rep. 50.

Morgan F. de M., 1959 The excavation of a long barrow at Nutbane, Hants. *Proc. Prehist. Soc.* 25:15–51.

Murray P. 1980 Discard location: the ethnographic data. *American Antiquity* 45:490–502.

Ó Nualláin, S. 1972 A Neolithic house at Ballyglass, Co. Mayo. *J. Roy. Soc. Antiqu. Ireland*. 102:49–57.

Palmer N. 1980 A beaker burial and medieval tenements in the Hamel, Oxford. *Oxoniensia* 45:124–225.

Palmer S. 1875 On the antiquities found in the peat of Newbury. *Trans. Newbury Dist. Fld. Club* 2:123–34.

Piggott S. 1954 *Neolithic Cultures of the British Isles*. Cambridge: University Press.

Piggott S. 1955 Windmill Hill — east or west? *Proc. Prehist. Soc.* 21:96–101.

Pryor F.M.M. 1974 *Excavation at Fengate, Peterborough, England: the first report*. Toronto: Royal Ontario Museum Archaeological Monograph 3.

Pryor F.M.M. 1978 *Excavation at Fengate, Peterborough, England: the second report*. Toronto: Royal Ontario Museum Archaeological Monograph 5.

Reynolds N. 1980 Dark age timber halls and the background to excavations at Balbridie. In *Settlements in Scotland 1000 BC–AD 1000*. Scottish Archaeological Forum 10: 41–69.

Richards J. 1984 The development of the Neolithic landscape in the environs of Stonehenge. In R. Bradley and J. Gardiner (eds) *Neolithic Studies: a review of some current research*. Oxford: BAR S-133:177–87.

Robinson M.A. and Lambrick G.H. 1984 Holocene alluviation and hydrology in the upper Thames basin. *Nature* 308:809–14.

Robinson M. and Wilson R. forthcoming A survey of environmental archaeology in the South Midlands. In H.C.M. Keeley (ed) *Environmental Archaeology: a regional review, Volume 2*. London: H.B.M.C.

Saville A. 1980 Five Flint assemblages from excavated sites in Wiltshire. *Wiltshire Archaeol. Natur. Hist. Mag.* 72/73:1–27.

Saville A. 1982 Carrying cores to Gloucestershire: some thoughts on lithic resource exploitation. *Lithics* 3:25–8.

Saville A. 1984 Preliminary report on the excavation of a Cotswold-Severn Tomb at Hazleton, Gloucestershire. *Antiqu. J.* 64:10–24.

Scaife R.G. and Burrin P.J. 1983 Floodplain development in and the vegetational history of the Sussex High Weald and some archaeological implications. *Sussex Archaeol. Collect.* 121:1–10.

Scaife R.G. and Burrin P.J. 1985 The environmental impact of prehistoric man as recorded in the Upper Cuckmere Valley at Stream Farm, Chiddingly. *Sussex Archaeol. Collect.* 123:27–34.

Smith I.F. 1965 *Windmill Hill and Avebury*. Oxford: Clarendon Press.

Smith I.F. 1974 The Neolithic. In C. Renfrew (ed) *Britain Prehistory: a new outline*. London: Duckworth. pp.100–36.

Wainwright G.J. 1972 The excavation of a Neolithic settlement on Broome Heath, Ditchingham, Norfolk, England. *Proc. Prehist. Soc.* 38:1–97.

Wainwright G.J. 1973 The excavation of prehistoric and Romano-British settlements at Eaton Heath, Norwich. *Archaeol. J.* 130:1–43.

Waton P.V. 1982 Man's impact on the chalklands: some new pollen evidence. In M. Bell and S. Limbrey (eds) *Archaeological Aspects of Woodland Ecology*. Oxford. BAR S-146:75–91.

Whittle A.W.R. 1977 *The Earlier Neolithic of Southern England and its Continental Background*. Oxford: BAR S-35.

Willock E.H. 1936 A Neolithic Site on Haldon. *Proc. Devon Archaeol. Explor. Soc.* 2:244–63.

Wymer J. 1962 Excavations at the Maglemosian sites at Thatcham, Berkshire, England. *Proc. Prehist. Soc.* 28:329–61.

Zvelebil M. and Rowley-Conwy, P. 1984 Transition to Farming in Northern Europe: a hunter-gatherer perspective. *Norwegian Archaeological Review* 17:104–28.

11. Runnymede Refuse Tip: A Consideration of Midden Deposits and their Formation.

S.P. Needham and M.L.S. Sørensen

Introduction

The late Bronze Age settlement at Runnymede Bridge, Egham, entered the archaeological literature as a site with well preserved structures and a wealth of finds (Longley 1980; Needham and Longley 1980). The foundations of a waterfront palisade revetment along the northern edge of the site were striking, as were the quantity of bronze objects, the evidence for metalworking and for potentially wide trade links. On this basis a general impression has developed of a central place representing a focal point in a hierarchically structured settlement system (e.g. Bradley 1984:123f.). There is, however, another aspect to the site, founded on the physical structuring of the artefactual remains, which has great potential for understanding daily life and the domestic activities of the period. It is this aspect which has emerged as a primary objective of a new research programme of excavation undertaken by the British Museum. In this paper we shall demonstrate the promise of this approach.

This concern with 'daily-life', although apparently the study of minutiae, is necessary for the reconstruction of a regional settlement pattern and the role of the site within it. But in order to find the correct perspective on this issue we must first face up to a more central set of problems: why does so much settlement refuse survive at Runnymede; what dictates its composition; and what were the formation processes at work? If we cannot form justified opinions on these issues, we cannot make comparisons with other 'rich' sites, such as Potterne (Gingell and Lawson 1985), nor can we validate contrasts with many truncated sites on chalk or gravel. Essentially we need to assess the extent to which discrepancies in quantity and character of material are merely distortions, the products of differential survival, or the characteristics of a truly different category of site. In the former case the uniqueness of a site such as Runnymede lies only in the survival of the archaeological record, in the latter it is embedded in an appropriate cultural history.

At present Runnymede seems unique in two ways: firstly, its siting on the floodplain of a major river and, secondly, the sheer scale of activity attested by vast quantities of refuse, spread over a large area. This spread may be conveniently described as a midden and this introduces questions about the physical and social circumstances under which middens are allowed to accumulate on a settled site, as well as the uses to which midden material might be put. On the question of location, time may tell whether other substantial settlements of the early first millennium bc lie on floodplains (e.g. Wallingford in the upper Thames: Thomas *et al.* 1986). The

quantity of refuse itself on 'midden sites', after account is taken of differential survival, may indicate nothing more than larger scale activity, and not necessarily a site of different status.

In order to compensate for the various transformations of an archaeological assemblage we need to develop ways of identifying the processes behind deposition, not just composition, density and distribution of artefacts. At a site specific level this means a detailed analysis to isolate and characterise different episodes within a given sequence. In this way one would hope to identify the actual practices generating the debris being studied. If we can make a case for abnormal practices when compared with most contemporary settlements, then this might be the best evidence of special status (not necessarily high status). The behaviour responsible for our material is therefore more important than either the quantity of refuse or the quality of material in use on the site.

In pursuit of some of these objectives Area 16 East at Runnymede, which proved to be extremely productive in the *in situ* finds, was selected for detailed artefact analysis. This area does, however, need to be seen with respect to the whole site and to some overall problems which we will consider first.

General Problems at Runnymede

Intermittent rescue excavations on the site in 1976, 1978, and 1980 have been followed by a new research campaign in 1984, 1985, and 1986. Over this period it has been possible to explore widespread parts of the known site (Fig.11.1). Furthermore, the timescale involved has allowed the assimilation of results and the formulation of new strategies. Nevertheless, certain problems have yet to be solved, in particular the relationship between cut features and the occupation deposits, or midden, which in aggregate form a thick dark layer across the site. Consistently the features only become visible when dark occupation earth gives way to paler and sterile underlying silt. Thus apparently none of the features is cut from a level above the base of the occupation deposits. In reality we doubt this would be true generally across the site. The similarity of most feature fills to the dark occupation soil would easily render invisible the uppermost parts of those features, especially if post-depositional natural agencies at work in the organic rich layers had partially homogenised the soil. Accepting such possibilities does not, however, help us out of the basic predicament of identifying relationships in a specific

113

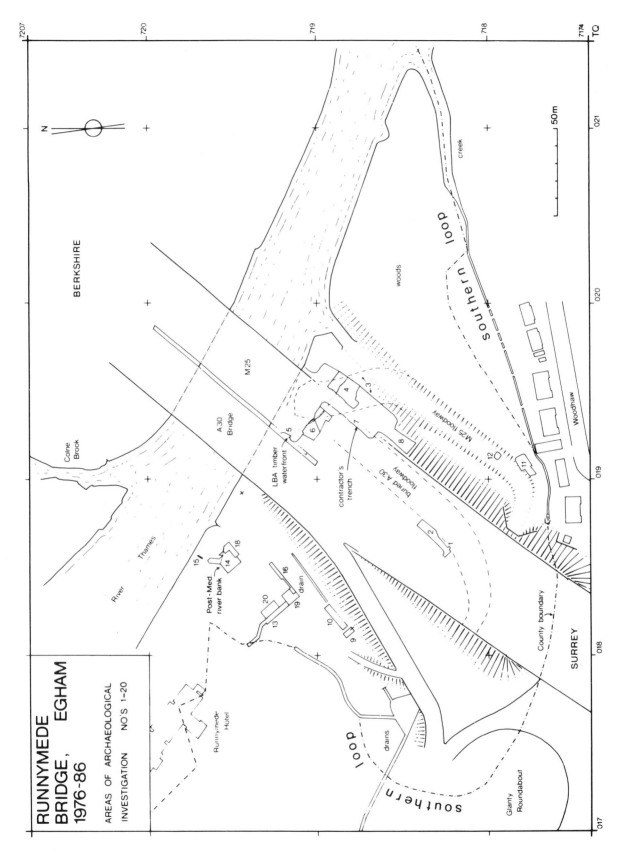

Fig.11.1 Plan of the site showing areas of excavation and salvage. Those opened during the research project are numbered 13–20.

locality. This is a critical problem since the accumulation of refuse in relation to standing structures ought to be a vital element of our enquiry. For instance, in our key area (16 East) it is difficult to conceive of much of the midden accumulating until after the plot had ceased to be used for possible dwelling purposes. Hopes for circumventing this problem depend on two things: firstly, the detailed planning of every spit excavated through the occupation deposits in order to correlate finds distributions with features vertically below. Inference in this respect will, however, be limited by the surface area excavated, which was restricted in the rescue phase. Secondly, therefore we aim in the current project to consolidate larger area plans than hitherto possible. It is hoped that this procedure will allow us to correlate structural entities with differences in artefact type, densities and conditions as well as soil types.

There are two other points to make about the 'structural' aspect of the occupation. The cut features, although numerous in every area excavated and possibly similarly dense over a total of two to three hectares, so far show remarkably little evidence of replacement. One exception is the peripheral palisade in Area 6, for the evidence now suggests that the outer pile row succeeded the inner row (*pace* Needham and Longley 1980:399). However, in the interior of the site there is a lack of structural replacement on the same plan, even though the occupation is thought to be of 200–300 years duration. It is unlikely that one set of buildings would have lasted out the whole occupation and therefore we may have to contemplate shifts in their location. Other positive features would be expected to occur on an organised and permanent domestic site, notably longstanding road- or path-ways, dwelling floors and hearths, virtually none of which have yet been recognised at Runnymede. Surfaces of dense burnt flint concentrations and localised 'floors' of pottery are often encountered, but no trodden floors, compacted and cleared of all but trampled artefacts have been found. Domestic oven bases have, however, survived in Area 10.

The late Bronze Age deposits appear throughout the site as a thick rather homogenous layer with a rich inclusion of cultural materials. Observation during excavation and the recorded stratigraphy have only established a limited number of features within this deposit. The apparent simplicity of the observed stratigraphy does not therefore permit ready reconstruction of the various phases of activity involved in the formation of the deposits. It is thus difficult to reach any clear conclusions about the nature and formation of the site; in general it has only been possible to establish a crude division of the late Bronze Age deposits into two zones:

1) The *upper zone* has a soil matrix not dissimilar from the overlying clean alluvium, although it tends to be slightly greyer due to charcoal and humic content. It is primarily distinguished from the silt above by its fairly dense artefact inclusion. The artefacts are characterised by small-medium size, a fair degree of abrasion and surface deterioration and a slight bleaching of the bone, while there are no *in situ* groups.

2) The *lower zone* is present in all but the shallowest of late Bronze Age levels. The matrix is decidedly darker than above this zone, and sometimes rather black, and the levels are rich in phosphates. The artefacts in this zone are again numerous but they are less fragmented and often show little abrasion. More strikingly, the lower zone can contain a variety of *in situ* material: pot groups (often with joining sherds), small dumps of burnt flint, articulated bone groups (including whole skeletons), clustered bone debris from butchery, feasting or manufacturing activities, fired clay (daub) lumps, and structure bases (e.g. ovens), all of which have clearly seen little or no disturbance since deposition.

Apart from the localised horizons produced by these *in situ* groups clear stratigraphic breaks within either zone are rare. Occasionally a discernible change in soil type or colour is encountered, but otherwise changes are slight and lack clear boundaries. This problem, and the general high yield of finds, can give the superficial impression of homogeneity. We aim to dispel this notion. The research project, with its in-built sieve-check controls on artefact recovery, is allowing us to show that, despite a lack of soil variation, a meaningful stratigraphic sequence is retained in the changing character of the finds.

A stratigraphic division based primarily on finds characterisation poses methodological problems for excavation procedures. Sometimes certain distinctive aspects of the finds stand out during excavation; for example some horizons at Runnymede have been noted to have a high density of burnt flint, or to be comparatively charcoal rich and artefact poor, or to have disproportionately large quantities of bone. Yet, these tangible elements are only a part of the sequence, and rather more information may be locked away in less immediately accessible attributes, such as sherd size distributions, sherd fabric assemblages, the attrition of bone, or the relative frequency of dog-gnawing. We are left with an unavoidable incompatibility between the perception of a stratigraphy as dug and a resolved stratigraphy reached through post excavation analysis. The excavated stratigraphy has to be an accommodating blend of arbitrary spits, perhaps at times with *in situ* groups as localised boundary markers, and detectable layers defined by conspicuous finds character or soil change. These coarse attributes provide a guide line which may not have the resolution to determine the optimal spit thickness (not to mention spatial variability) required for maximising the information returned subsequently from the broader spectrum of attributes. This in itself is a strong argument for a cautious excavation policy and the general removal of a thin spit at a time. This policy has been refined progressively at Runnymede as the questions being asked of the site have changed in emphasis.

It follows that it is necessary to employ a refined recording standard in order that various small yet discrete activities can be detected. The recording of these 'episodes' is a prerequisite to a proper understanding of sites with little-altered deposits. This involves the recording of the tens of thousands of bulk finds to individual metre squares as well as the planning of each spit at 1:20, but also extends to the more detailed planning and unique contexting of each find within an *in situ* group.

As a theoretical exercise in coming to grips with the occupation deposits at Runnymede it is necessary to consider a range of mechanisms which might have contributed to their formation. These comprise natural and anthropogenic forms of soil build up, as well as special circumstances affecting deposition and subsequent disturbance. Mechanisms thought to be particularly appropriate to the Runnymede context are summarised in Table 11.1. The hypotheses are by no means exclusive of one another and real difficulties of application follow if two or more mechanisms interact.

Based on observation and analysis to date, a provisional interpretation of the formation process can be made. The *upper zone* has a consistent character across the site, it lacks any internal stratigraphy other than a steady gradation in finds density and matrix colour, and also lacks *in situ* groups. The implication is that it has suffered substantial alteration by natural agencies. Detailed analysis gives the impression that the effect (which gets progressively weaker with depth) is superimposed upon a more complex stratification as established by finds characterisation; at the top it obliterates that stratification, whereas lower it diffuses it and finally gives way to an unequivocal *lower zone*, where a refined stratigraphy is maintained. The upper zone will therefore impinge variably on the original stratigraphy depending on topography and the vagaries of erosion.

Four natural agencies of alteration might be operating; discriminating between them will be a matter for future detailed analysis:
1) Flood-reworking is obviously a strong candidate on a flood-plain site; it would lead to the disintegration and washing out of charcoal, phosphates and humic matter; the resettling of artefacts differentially according to density and the differential erosion of their raw materials.
2) Thermal extremes, sun-baking and frost, could lead to cracking of the clay-loam and consequent degradation of charcoal and artefacts according to material; charcoal might also be leached downwards. It is possible that on occasion fossil cracks would record such events.
3) Roots would cause localised mixing and disruption, hopefully identifiable in terms of anomalous sub-surface features; some linear features at Runnymede might be interpreted this way.
4) Worm-sorting is likely to be of minimal significance at Runnymede. The effect would be to mix, conflate and re-orientate artefacts, as well as generally moving them downwards, rather than to fragment and degrade them.

The lower zone inevitably poses more complicated questions. The wealth of intact groups, the reflection by the finds of a fine internal stratigraphy and the general lack of artefact abrasion suggest that natural post-depositional factors have had little effect. Similarly churning under foot during occupation (not to be confused with trampling) was probably

limited. However, these generalities do not explain the variability present within any given level. In particular we have to consider the possibility that some of the better preserved artefact groups were originally buried in features which are archaeologically invisible. It is not easy to distinguish these from 'heaps' or 'spreads' of material which somehow escaped disturbance. In either case it is vital to compare these groups with the 'background' artefact characterisation for the surrounding soil at the same level. The background could easily relate to a different set of activities, yet its evidence is overshadowed by the visually more impressive remains from later insertions or pre-existing heaps. Nevertheless, some *in situ* groups remain most readily understood as part of the level at which they occur and these reinforce the concept of a broad sequential accumulation of the lower zone in a given area.

With these points in mind the general sequence may be considered in terms of a continuation of earlier alluvial deposition. The silts underlying the late Bronze Age horizon probably represent a floodplain build-up over a considerable period of time. It is assumed that this was a steady process involving small depositional increments. Given this trajectory the depth of the occupation deposit may *in general* be proportional to the duration of occupation; in this simple model flood-plain aggradation continues unchecked, but silting buries a mass of cultural detritus during perhaps two or more centuries of occupation.

Ideally we would hope for a rather more refined picture of the interaction between alluviation and occupation processes. Again, at a simple level it may be observed that no clean alluvial bands have been encountered stratified within the Bronze Age occupation deposits. Thus there is no clear stratigraphic evidence for either notable incursions of silt during occupation, nor for any prolonged hiatus in the occupation. This does not necessarily mean, however, that we can discount either possibility. In particular a hypothesis of comparatively steady alluviation in the absence of other special circumstances does not readily explain the good condition of most of the lower zone artefacts. At present three alternative explanations are favoured:
1) That alluviation was 'steady' and that widespread protection of the refuse deposits resulted from a raised platform and/or the demarcation of compounds which were virtually unused in daily life.
2) That on occasion the deposits were swamped by larger loads of silt sufficient to bury freshly dumped pot and bone. In this case we have to invoke the 'dirtying' of clean silt sandwiched between culturally rich layers by subsequent transformations (human and natural).
3) That at any given time certain areas were designated as middens and saw comparatively rapid accumulation through the dumping of rubbish as well as possibly the addition of clean soil. Either mechanism would seal and protect underlying artefactual material and account for good preservation.

Each of these explanations has its own implications for chronological relationships within the deposits, and they may also bear on our understanding of the nature of the site, its organisation and development. While the first explanation might entail a reasonably constant and gradual accumulation of soil and refuse over a long period of time, the temporal sequence in the second would be erratic in relation to the vertical stratigraphy. On the other hand, if the third explanation was dominant, accumulation might not merely be erratic, but any given local sequence might represent only a small portion, or portions, of the whole duration of occupation.

We are left to ascertain from future analysis the extent to which refuse in different areas suffered human or animal trampling (apparently little), or dog and pig disturbance. Again we are thrown back to the issues of the nature of the settlement and the extent of refuse management, issues which in detail await the compilation of a broader plan of structures and deposits as well as specific forms of artefact and soil analysis.

Intrasite Variability and the 'Midden' at Runnymede

Area 16 East, see Fig.11.1, was chosen as a test case for developing and employing various analytical techniques which might be relevant for understanding the nature of the site, and the mechanisms involved in its formation. An analysis of on-site variability, aimed at distinguishing pre- and post-depositional disturbances from the characteristics of the deposit itself, has been carried out for the pottery assemblage from this area. Various types of detailed investigation were found to be necessary in order to identify the mechanisms responsible for the development of the deposit and thus to break the apparent homogeneity suggested by each of the two zones.

Such extensive analyses of on-site variability are as yet infrequent. Moreover, they have been carried out on different types of materials, exemplified by the studies of flint knapping, or in very different contexts, such as the Mesoamerican studies (see for example the discussions in Hietala 1984). Still, various studies have had some relevance to our set of problems, either due to a comparable material or a similar or complementary set of problems. These works include publications on Potterne (Gingell and Lawson 1983, 1985), works on on-site variability by Bradley and Fulford (1980) and by Halstead *et al.* (1982) and the work on the Haddenham middle Iron Age enclosure (Evans 1986). These studies are all aimed at relating a range of variables to a definite set of activities and structures. While this is an objective for Runnymede as well, we must at this interim stage confine ourselves to the discussion of refuse accumulation in the absence of knowledge of the structural layout. The studies mentioned are to some extent a source of inspiration, but we also found that we were on our own, when attempting to build a meaningful framework for the interpretation of our particular type of deposit. We have therefore found it useful to describe in some detail the work we have carried out, the assumptions which had to be

considered and the ways in which the variables within the material could be interpreted. A fuller account of the various types of analysis carried out, discussion of the results, and an evaluation of the demands of such intensive analysis will be produced in due course (Sørensen, forthcoming); the present account must therefore be understood as preliminary.

Area 16 East: A Case Study

Area 16 was originally laid out in 1985 to clarify the relationship between the deposits in Area 13 and 14 (excavated from 1984) with particular reference to stratigraphic and spatial patterns, the underlying alluvial silt, and the Neolithic occupation on the site. It became clear during excavation, however, that Area 16 had importance in its own right. The eastern end of the trench proved to be particularly rich in *in situ* groups in the forms of pot-scatters, concentrations of differentially sized burnt flint (3 size stages), and burnt clay/daub, while the overall density of finds was very high. The trench therefore provided an appropriate area for an initial and experimental post-excavation investigation since we had the various characteristics of the 'midden-deposit' represented within a limited area.

Excavation in Area 16 became focussed on the eastern end, where just $13m^2$ produced a total of 72kg of pottery, 19kg of burnt clay, 299kg of burnt flint, 8kg of struck flint, 24kg of bones, and 18 pot-groups (including two small whole pots) in a 30–50cm thick late Bronze Age deposit. Internal structures in the nature of concentrations of various materials were recorded, and a patch of yellowish sandy clay was separated out from the rest of the soil matrix. No cut features were recognised until the base of the deposit was reached. Subsequent analysis has shown no obvious correlations between the concentrations of materials at different levels. There is, however, a general tendency of an increase eastwards in the quantity of finds (particularly obvious for bones). Based on observations during excavation it was suspected that the nature of the ceramic assemblage changed vertically, that the pot-groups were found in certain levels and in clusters which possibly sealed high concentrations of bones, and furthermore that concentrations of burnt flint and bones to some extent corresponded. It has not as yet been possible to correlate all such predictions with systematic analysis; but the pottery, including the *in situ* pot-groups, has been examined.

The pot sherds from Area 16 East were analysed on the broad assumptions that:
1) many characteristics of an object (e.g. its size or abrasion) depend on what happened to it prior to deposition, on the manner in which it was deposited, and on the various post-depositional influences it was subjected to;
2) specific types of activities (sweeping, trampling) will often leave traces on an object which are particular to that activity; and
3) certain materials may be used in activities which are particular to them, i.e. clay used as daub.

Table 11.1 Possible mechanisms involved in the formation and alteration of occupation levels at Runneymede

	Formation process/explanation for occupation soil	Destructive Agencies			Prediction and problems
		Trampling	Frost & Weathering disturbance	Dog/rodent/pig	
1)	Steady alluviation at slow rate	Reasonably constant throughout occupation			Expect similar worn artifact condition throughout sequence.
2)	Rapid, sporadic alluviation		Intermittent		In situ dumps of limited duration at discrete horizons, and possibly spatially contained.
3)	Midden-formed soil: organic matter, deliberate soil sprinkle and further inorganic rubbish itself	Sporadic: at non-midden stages		Variable according to rate of dumping or none if kept out	Presume shifting 'midden' area during occupation (otherwise would find two distinct types of deposit in discrete areas). Survival of actual middens dependent on later history of use. Implies non-synchronous in situ sequences.
4)	Regular churning under soggy conditions		Variable		Some 'negative' build-up, i.e. mixing in underlying deposits. Blurring or eradication of temporal sequences and original stratigraphies. Tendency to homogeneity in artefact distributions. Limited opportunities for in situ groups: at the end of occupation (locally) or when area 'protected'.
5)	In situ groups in shallow dug features which are archaeologically invisible		Minimal after burial		Character of feature contents, if not matrix, may stand out from background in level cut. Feature may be implied by positioning of finds.

6)	Raised structural platform or protective enclosures (of any extent)	None	Slightly reduced	Unaffected	Contrast between platform areas and ground level access routes/working areas—in artifact conditions. Destructive extent dependent on rate of soil accretion.
7)	Intermittent occupation (whole site)	Final deposits untrampled, unless not sealed before return. ?Trampled by grazing animals instead	——— Possibly oscillating in vertical succession. ——— ?Change	Repeated scavenging after each abandonment	Only clearly seen if abandonment phases long enough for silt in-oad or worm up-cast *and* restricted churning. Otherwise could be very blurred
8)	Within-site abandonment: out-of-use areas (not even rubbish dumping)	Significantly reduced	Unchanged	Continues, may reduce	Agents continue to act until soil accretion buries surface
9)	Livestock compound	Likely considerable	Increased exposure to the elements	Still some	Accentuated effects to deeper than usual levels

It was therefore assumed that size/weight and abrasion could be considered meaningful variables illuminating certain aspects of the formation/depositional processes, and furthermore that the use of pottery in many ways would be distinct in comparison to, for example, burnt flint or burnt clay, since pots are used in particular contexts and their sherds usually constitute secondary refuse.

All the sherds from Area 16 East, more than 9,000, have been considered with respect to weight, size and abrasion, and the material from three $1m^2$-columns, 2721 sherds, have furthermore been described with respect to fabric and typology (this study will not be considered here). All of the 18 pot-groups from this area have been studied separately with respect to all of these variables, and with regard to re-fit patterns.

Analysis of Pot-Groups

The *in situ* groups are materials which have been deposited together and which have generally not been further moved since their deposition. They can be interpreted as reflecting a particular event and they provide essential evidence about the formation of the deposits and about post-depositional disturbances. The analysis of the pot-groups resulted in a new level of information and supplemented the patterns extracted from other variables.

The analysis of the pot-groups was primarily aimed at reconstructing the ways in which groups of sherds had been deposited in the layers and the extent to which they had subsequently been disturbed. The pot-groups were recorded at 1:5 and each sherd was separately numbered. During post-excavation analysis the single sherds were laid out according to their original spatial configuration, and it was then possible during re-fitting to attempt three-dimensional reconstructions of the manner in which the pot fragment had broken up. These exercises made it apparent that additional information could be extracted about the characteristics of the surface on which the groups had been deposited — such as whether it was sloping or soft, — in other words how a pot is broken both reflects the manner of its deposition and the nature of the surface it rests upon, see for example Fig.11.2. The pot-groups were also checked for joining sherds from the whole sherd assemblage from the lower zone in Area 16 East (context 829–894), and the result was plotted onto a schematic section, but will not be further discussed here.

Each pot-group deserves to be described in some detail since they all reflect a particular event within the formation of the deposit, but until a fuller account can be published we must satisfy ourselves with a brief summary of the overall pattern. The majority of pot-groups were found within 3 layers/spits (context 834/836/849) with a few located in lower contexts, see Fig.11.3 for a schematic section. Two different types of activities seem to be represented throughout these spits and a third is represented at the very base of the late Bronze Age deposit. The first type of activity consists of substantial parts of a single vessel (up to half a vessel) deposited either on its own or simultaneously with a few single sherds from other vessels. The second type is represented by dumps of big sherd fragments from numerous pots including several unattached fragments from the same pots. The patterns of refitting sherds to the pot-groups suggest strongly that whole pots were not generally deposited in the *in situ* rich spits. Instead whole pots, potentially representing a third type of activity, are confined to the lowest levels of Area 16 East. Here we found two small whole pots and a dense cluster of materials including further substantial portions of other vessels. It is noteworthy, in this context, that earlier excavations of the river channel (Needham and Longley 1980) recovered several reconstructable fine ware vessels. The pot representation therefore suggests a potential difference in the activities behind the deposition of material in the various areas of the site and at different levels.

Within the pot-groups the individual sherds are generally positioned in close proximity to each other (<0.03m), and joining sherds were at times found immediately adjacent to each other. Joining sherds have at times been extracted from different spits and/or different squares, but the patterns of their disposal and joining usually suggest that this was due to the manner of their deposition as opposed to later disturbances. This is demonstrated by re-fitting sherds usually lying immediately adjacent to each other, or in two or three discrete clusters at some distance from each other. This suggests that the displacement of the different parts was caused by the deposition of fragments broken prior to the deposition rather than by post-depositional disturbance. Displacement of single sherds can, in a few cases, be argued to have happened after the deposition, but the positions of the single sherds do then suggest that this was caused by the flattening effect of an overburden. With the mounting pressure from above pot fragments with a good curvature would break and the different parts become relocated on the surface, while the material accumulated around the fragment would still preserve the relative position of joining sherds, as illustrated in Fig.11.2. As the curvature increases and a smaller part of the fragment actually rested on the surface, individual sherds might become superimposed upon each other as opposed to being pushed apart.

The implications from the study of the pot-groups are:
1) there were only limited post-depositional disturbances;
2) there are two different types of activity involved in the deposition of pottery in the bulk of the midden deposit, and one type of activity (whole pots) limited to the lowest levels;
3) the fragments were in several instances placed on a soft soggy surface sloping slightly towards the east and containing localised dips and peaks;
4) trampling or other means of localised fragmentation seems generally negligible.

On this basis we must conclude that most of these groups are composed of pots, which were broken *away* from the location of the midden, but which

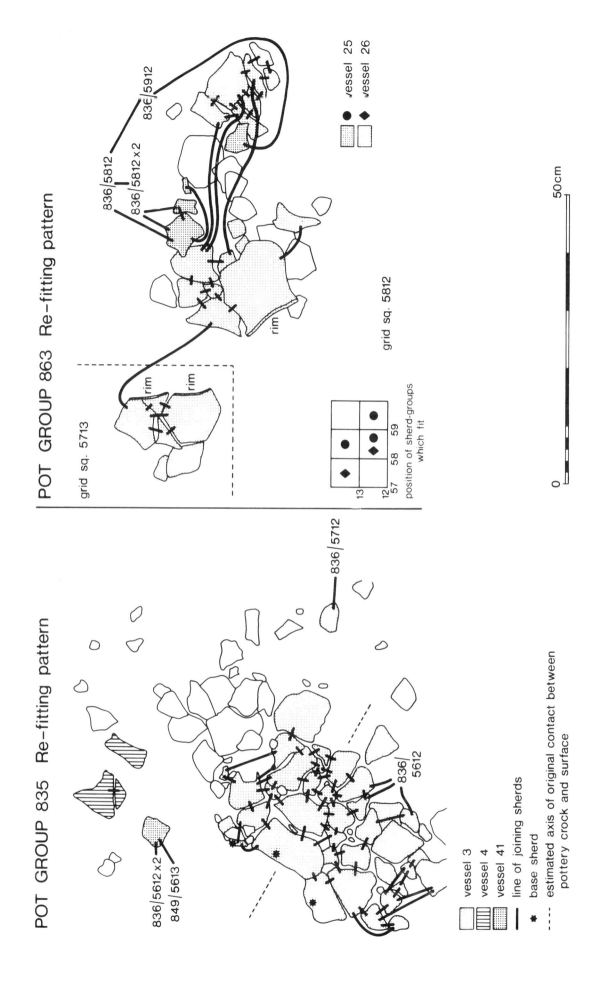

POT GROUP 835 Re-fitting pattern

POT GROUP 863 Re-fitting pattern

grid sq. 5713

grid sq. 5812

836/5912

836/5812
836/5812 x 2

rim

rim

rim

vessel 25
vessel 26

position of sherd-groups
which fit

13

12

57   58   59

836/5712

836/5612 x 2
849/5613

836/
5612

vessel 3
vessel 4
vessel 41

line of joining sherds

base sherd

estimated axis of original contact between
pottery crock and surface

0   50cm

Fig.11.2 Two examples of planned pot groups from Area 16 East showing re-fit patterns.

121

were then quickly incorporated in the midden deposit while still in relatively big fragments.

Analysis of Abrasion

All the sherds from Area 16 East, more than 9,000, have been individually assessed with respect to abrasion. The size of the sample and the fractured condition of many sherds meant that the abrasion was considered according to a coarse division into 3 stages, low, medium, and high (Sørensen forthcoming). In this study it was decided to use the lowest degree of abrasion observed on any individual sherd since this seemed to be the best signature of the formation of the deposits as opposed to the processes through which the sherds went prior to deposition.

A complex picture is emerging from the study of abrasion. There is considerable variation in the levels and in the uniformity of abrasion from context to context. The most obvious patterns emerging from the analysis of abrasion are:
1) The deposits are neither uniformly composed with respect to the levels of abrasion nor are there any simple gradual horizontal or vertical changes.
2) There is a high variability between the individual squares of each context/spit with respect to the proportion of the 3 levels of abrasion. This was measured in terms of population standard deviation which was found to range from 3.5 to 35.5.

The general trend is that there is an increase downwards of low abraded sherds combined with a rather uniform presence of medium abraded sherds seen against a decrease in highly abraded ones. Against this trend, however, peaks and falls in the distribution of the 3 levels of abrasion throughout the deposit demand further consideration. These irregularities are primarily found in the contexts 814, 834, 836 and 849, which constitute the middle of the vertical sequence, see Fig.11.3. Before conclusive comments are made about these irregularities they must be correlated with the mean deviation within each context in order to evaluate the extent to which the pattern is spatially consistent within a given level.

The mean deviation in the classification of abrasion was established across the $13m^2$ of Area 16 East. This showed that the deviation is especially high in the top layers. This is possibly caused by differential degree of disturbances (e.g. machining) and weathering combined with the partial erosion of original concentrations at this level. Thus, the homogeneity of the 'upper zone' is not absolute, and it can be seen to be the result of post-depositional processes resulting in higher abrasion and greater fragmentation of the single sherds. Meanwhile, although these processes have diffused the original differences within the levels, it can be argued that they were not sufficient to have erased entirely these original variations. As opposed to this level with high deviation the greatest 'trench-uniformity' (i.e. the contexts with less deviation in sherd abrasion pattern across the trench) is found in the middle contexts 819 to 829 with a peak in 820–824. Hence,

variations are limited within these contexts; and they are likely to have accumulated in a comparable manner as well as consisting of a similar range of materials and/or they have been affected by a similar set of post-depositional abrading factors and to a comparable extent. Such uniformity is absent from context 834 to 849 and decreases even further in the lowest contexts (865–872). This suggests that the 'beginning' of the deposit was caused by a different range of activities and, that it was little affected by post-depositional mechanisms.

These changes in the uniformity of contexts across the trench correspond with peaks in abrasion so that, for example, a high degree of low abraded sherds will correspond with a high level of deviation within that context. The combination of the two variables suggests that the levels underneath context 829, as opposed to the contexts above, do not consist of uniformly built-up deposits composed of similar assemblages. Rather, we see the accumulation of distinct deposits covering a limited area of the trench resulting in heaps whose central peak and sloping peripheries are marked by high percentages of low abraded sherds and other materials. This suggests that separate depositional events were either superimposed on or juxtaposed to the rubbish heaps created by previous depositions, and that the single heaps might at one time have been separated from one another by differentially composed materials, constituting the surfaces of previous deposits.

Analysis of Size and Weight

The analysis of average weight and size of the sherds adds to the patterns produced by the pot-groups and by the analysis of abrasion, and will be presented briefly here. The most important result is that there is neither uniformity in average weight or size throughout the context nor are there obvious gradual horizontal or vertical changes. High average weight and large size appear to cluster at certain levels and in various locations within the trench. It is furthermore the case that there may be a marked change from one spit to the next in the size distribution, whereas one might expect more gradual changes. Moreover, the highest readings shift around within the trench — a characteristic which supports the interpretation that we are studying the accumulation of discrete dumpings rather than homogeneous horizontal layers.

Formation of the Refuse Deposit

With respect to the formation of a midden deposit one can suggest that various dumpings of refuse would 'naturally' have been placed next to each other — possibly reflecting the direction of behavioural patterns dictated by structures and activity areas. With time this would result in an extremely mixed deposit with respect to activity units but one which might superficially appear even and homogeneous. At Runnymede, the evidence provided by the pot-groups furthermore demons-

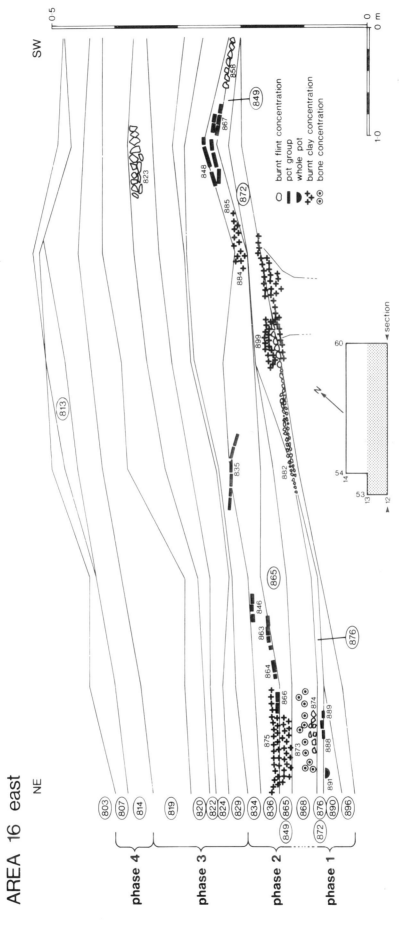

Fig.11.3 Schematic section south through the late Bronze Age deposits in Area 16 East on to which have been projected all *in situ* groups from the adjacent one metre strip. The vertical scale is exaggerated six times.

123

trates that although various types of disposal activities were involved in forming the midden, the material dumped in any one episode would often only consist of what a single person could carry. We can therefore expect that various dumpings might often have happened in quick succession; and these repeated dumpings would mean that the surface continuously changed its nature, appearance, and configuration.

The possibility of phasing these apparently homogenous deposits of late Bronze Age material has emerged from the case study. Although the original duration and the intervals between different phases can not be reconstructed, it is possible to argue for 'passive' and 'active' stages in the accumulation of the midden. This has severe implications for our understanding of the site since it implies change either in the use of the areas adjacent to the study area or changes in the types and amount of debris coming from given living quarters. Apart from such 'phasing' of the intensity of use, it is also possible to establish horizontal differences within the trench, which allow us to identify the contribution of many single events which belie the concept of a single continuous process. It is therefore possible at this stage to demonstrate that the build-up of late Bronze Age deposits in Area 16 East resulted from a changing set of activities rather than being formed by steady accumulation or an 'organic' growth.

At this point we can suggest three basic phases (1–3) in the lower zone and describe in further detail the upper zone (phase 4). In the lowest phase (phase 1) the trench reflects a midden deposit very much dominated by rich domestic refuse, notably including whole pots one of which appeared to contain a cremated/burnt lamb. At this stage the deposits are distinctly clustered and have only a limited soil component. The deposits are placed directly upon the surface of the alluvial silt sealing part of a row of post-holes, which must therefore have belonged to an already defunct structure. In the next stage of active accumulation we see a number of single events in which considerable amounts of rejected domestic ware, burnt daub and clay, and concentrations of crushed burnt flint are dumped in discrete heaps. Mixed amongst this material are a number of tools which seem to be specifically concerned with the preparation of pottery temper. These are lower 'quernstones' and large pebble hammers used to fragment the burnt flint to a size suitable for pot temper. This activity seems to have taken place *in situ* simultaneously with phase 2 midden accumulation. Most of the discernible post-depositional disturbances of phase 2 contexts seem best explained in terms of fragmentation caused by a quickly accumulated overburden. This may account for the large sized sherds, the medium abrasion, the existence of pot-groups within these levels, and the apparent absence of dog-gnawing, coprolites and trampling as well as the lack of surfaces within the contexts in question. Phase 3 seems to begin in quick succession but is distinct. The material is less narrowly focussed upon the domestic sphere and contains the remains of various activities at different removes from their initial discard. This third phase

may have been of some duration with surfaces open to post-depositional influences of various kinds. The overall character (i.e. high abrasion, trench uniformity) of phase 3 might point to the midden now being on the outskirts of an occupation unit. Finally, in the upper zone it seems that we originally had a material which was comparable to phase 3, but altered by additional post-depositional processes.

The Nature of 'Middens'

We can now conclude that the deposit is composed of a mixture of materials at different refuse stages. The appearance of this accumulation merits the name 'midden'. However, when naming an activity it is important to realise the extent to which the nature of that activity depends on the particular context in which it takes place. This is certainly the case for middening, which has different socio-economic functions in different contexts depending on the organisation of the particular society and its attitudes towards rubbish (e.g. Moore 1982). The problems currently considered with respect to Runnymede are tied in with the problem of anticipating what might be the nature of 'midden-type' activities within a late Bronze Age society, and in particular of understanding the scale of the activity. It is therefore worthwhile, as a final exercise in this paper, to consider the nature of middens. This must relate both to the functions which middens have within a settlement or settlement hierarchy and to the practical archaeological problem of identifying differences in midden formation.

The processes through which different types of material pass onto a midden will vary and consequently so will the disposal pattern created by their deposition. It is therefore possible to supplement the interpretation of the formation processes reached through one type of material by study of the deposition of other artefacts in the same levels. One of the most important classifications in this respect is that between primary and secondary refuse — or between waste products and rubbish (Schiffer 1976) — although we found the division too coarse for analysing the secondary refuse at Runnymede.

Secondary refuse, such as pottery and precious materials, when found as rubbish are most commonly discarded broken objects or accidentally lost pieces, which may have been produced and functioned at considerable distances from the midden deposit and which could easily have passed through many different stages of use, each potentially in a different location, before finally entering the archaeological record as 'rubbish'. With respect to pottery we can attempt to predict correlations between size or abrasion and the distance or the length of time they have been moved around (Bradley and Fulford 1980); but it is not possible to establish absolute measures for these relationships. With respect to primary refuse, such as waste from flint or bone working or metallurgical manufacturing, we can on the other hand, usually expect the refuse to be close to the production unit or that it was moved from there directly to a rubbish heap. Of course, if an area within the site changed function through time different discrete activities or activity areas become superimposed upon each other (see for example discussion by Kvall and Issacs 1984). On this basis it is worth noting that the various materials do not show the same vertical and horizontal patterns within excavated areas at Runnymede.

The midden material we have considered in detail here mainly constitutes *secondary refuse* (Schiffer 1976), yet it contains some variety in its structure. To comprehend this variation better it is useful to consider different practical reasons for the accumulation and movement of 'refuse' after its initial discard. These can be put under four broad headings:

1) *Rubbish Clearance* of certain types from the working and dwelling quarters, and the consequent dumping in available (redundant?) features, in permissible areas within the settlement (including specially reserved areas) and beyond the settled area.

2) *Expedient Uses* of rubbish, such as, for example, consolidation of damp ground or filling-in irregularities in the ground, used as infill amongst buildings, or used in rituals as 'killed objects' or as representation of, for example fertility.

3) *Midden as Resource*. This can for example be organic refuse for manuring, dung heaps for leather tanning, or pot dumps to provide grog temper or pit linings.

4) *Incidental Movement*, where the refuse is no longer recognisable as a discrete body and is merely a constituent of the soil/deposit it lies in, and therefore is likely only to be disturbed incidentally if and when the soil deposit is transported.

It must be recognised that there might, at any stage, be a conscious separation of materials to be retained or thrown out, to be dumped as unwanted refuse, or as potentially useful material. Moreover, refuse would on occasion have moved through a 'chain' of processes, each of a different nature. One such chain might, for example, start with refuse clearance to a designated midden location, then to be followed by the separation and discrete dumping of material considered to be useful, only later to become relegated to an expedient use as infill of irregular ground and ultimately come to be thrown up as part of a bank which gradually eroded back into its ditch. Obviously, such chains could be of any duration and complexity, but broadly speaking overt refuse management will have been a feature of the earlier part of the sequence. The passage of events will generally take the refuse progressively towards a retrieval threshold, beyond which the refuse as an entity (rather than rare individual discards amongst it) was no longer recognisable as a specific resource for any purpose. This is not to say that we are less interested in the later stages of the sequence, but simply that it will be rather important to discriminate between 'early' and 'late' deposits within such chains. The labels early and late need not be treated as precise measurements of the number of events particular refuse has passed through, but should rather be applied on the basis of a combined assessment of the constituent elements and the nature of the context itself with special reference to

the mechanisms by which the refuse became incorporated. Context and constituents are inextricably linked. For example, if a group of small trampled pot sherds, accompanied by negligible organic matter, was swept up from a house floor and dumped directly down the slope of a bank into a newly cut ditch, then this group would have immediately reached a terminal stage in terms of refuse management. Any further disturbance of the material would almost certainly be *incidental*.

The same argument would apply to green midden material once it had been spread on fields as manure (Crowther 1983). At Runnymede and comparable sites attention has to be directed to the beginning of the manure chain. All too often middens have been associated solely with manuring, and we must be aware of the cultural implications we impose upon the past by assuming this synonym. Assessing the relationship between on-site refuse and manure is not, however, easy. Let us suppose firstly that there was no systematic practice of manure removal to the fields. Being above the water table on the occupied surface, the organic components making up such manure would have quickly decayed on the spot, thus conflating the midden layers. On the other hand, if regular manuring took place, this would have been sensibly based on an effective separation of manure from the mass of durables — potsherds, burnt flint and big bones. Either way there would have been (and clearly at Runnymede there were) large quantities of durable refuse left behind to be dealt with on site. Possible ways of extrapolating back from the observed refuse deposits at Runnymede might be to assess the evidence for conflation in the midden layers, or consider the phosphate levels. Needless to say both factors are likely to depend also on unknown variables and we cannot at present see a way through to establishing the presence or absence of a manuring policy. We can say with some assurance, however, that the material we are studying in such quantities at sites such as Runnymede has no bearing on the manure issue, and relates more directly to the practice of refuse management.

To turn now to the positive side, the deposits from Runnymede Area 16 East are, in part at least, the result of refuse management and the changes through time imply alterations in site lay-out or organisation which determined the maintenance of space. In terms of our proposed refuse chain the above described changes in the character of the refuse reflects a transition from 'early' stages in phase 1 and 2 to 'late' stages in phase 3. Certain elements of the phase 1 material could be *de facto* refuse from a possible preceding dwelling phase or an adjacent structure. More certainly, in phase 2 some primary refuse relating to the preparation of pottery temper is superimposed on the bulk of early stage secondary refuse. Pot groups tend to occur at certain horizons within phase 2, whilst the condition of sherds is not consistent from context to context. These factors point to minor fluctuations in the rate of accumulation and/or the sources of the rubbish, and it may herald a transition to a new refuse status whereby more diffuse 'background' deposition took precedence. This phase of deposition is best understood as incidental rather than specific, with a good proportion of the material having had a lengthy refuse history and hence being classified as late stage secondary refuse. Given this interpretation, the duration of phase 3 is likely to have been relatively long and slight fluctuations in the rate of accumulation could explain changes in the condition of the sherd assemblage through the phase 3 contexts. Of phase 4 we can say rather less. Indications are that, prior to alteration, the deposits had echoed the patterns of phase 3.

Middens or rubbish heaps are well known in different archaeological, historical and ethnographic contexts. The scale of the phenomena at Runnymede and the unknown structural relationships do, however, make comparisons difficult and the deposits appear at present distinct from other contemporary phenomena. Thus, we lack any analogues to help in the interpretation of our deposit. It has, however, been possible to emphasise some of the characteristics in the treatment of rubbish at Runnymede which can help to illustrate the cultural attitude involved. With future research, we hope to expand this preliminary picture of refuse management at Runnymede, and thus to provide new insight into settlement activities in the late Bronze Age.

Acknowledgements

Illuminating ideas about refuse have come through discussions with John Barrett, Christopher Evans, Andrew Herne, and Martin Trott, to whom we are grateful. The illustrations are the work of Stephen Crummy.

References

Bradley R. 1984 *The Social Foundations of Prehistoric Britain: themes and variations in the archaeology of power*. Longman: London.

Bradley R. and Fulford M. 1980. Sherd size in the analysis of occupation debris. *Bull. Inst. Archaeol. London* 17:85–94.

Crowther D. 1983. Old land surfaces and modern ploughsoil: implications of recent work at Maxey, Camb. *Scottish Archaeological Review* 2-1:31–44.

Evans C. 1986. *Haddenham Site V* Unpublished archive Report.

Gingell C. and Lawson A.J. 1983 The Potterne project: excavation and research at a major settlement of the Late Bronze Age. *Wilts. Archaeol. and Nat. Hist. Magazine* 78:31–34.

Gingell C. and Lawson A.J. 1985 Excavations at Potterne, 1984. *Wilts. Archaeol. and Nat. Hist. Magazine* 79:101–108.

Halstead P., Hodder I. and Jones G. 1978 Behavioural archaeology and refuse patterns: a case study. *Norwegian Archaeological Review* 11–2:118–131.

Hietala H.J. (ed) 1984 *Intrasite Spatial Analysis in Archaeology* Cambridge University Press, Cambridge.

Kvall E.M. and Issac G.L. 1984 Configuration of artefacts and bones at early Pleistocene sites in East Africa. In H.J. Hietala (ed) 1984:4–31.

Longley D. 1980 *Runnymede Bridge: excavations on the site of a late Bronze Age settlement*. Surrey Archaeological Society Research no. 6.

Moore H.L. 1982 The interpretation of spatial patterning in settlement residues. In I. Hodder (ed) *Symbolic and Structural Archaeology*. 74–79. Cambridge University Press, Cambridge.

Needham S.P. 1985 Neolithic and Bronze Age settlement on the buried floodplains of Runnymede. *Oxford Journal of Archaeology* 4-2:125–137.

Needham S.P. and Longley D. 1980 Runnymede Bridge, Egham: a late bronze age riverside settlement. In J. Barrett and R. Bradley (eds) *Settlement and Society in the British Later Bronze Age* Oxford, BAR 83:397–436.

Schiffer M.B. 1976 *Behavioural Archaeology*. Academic Press, New York.

Sørensen, M.L.S. forthcoming. Sherds as keys to refuse management. A case study from Area 16 East at Runnymede.

Thomas R. *et al.*. 1986 A late Bronze Age riverside settlement at Wallingford, Oxon. *Archaeol. J.* 143:174–200.

12. Production, Circulation and Exchange: Problems in the Interpretation of Bronze Age Bronzework

John C. Barrett and Stuart P. Needham

Introduction

The study of copper and bronze working from the late third to the mid first millennia bc has always extended beyond the material itself to the wider social and economic implications. Recent studies differ not so much in a newly found desire to write 'social' or 'economic' archaeology, but in the realisation that many of the traditional conceptual categories (such as *trade, wealth, class* or *merchants*) are highly problematic. To use them demonstrates an ethnocentrism towards the working of the ancient world. The emphasis is now to rethink the way small-scale, pre-modern societies functioned, and to understand the nature of the broader geographical and historical systems of which they were a part.

Amongst British authors Rowlands' work best exemplifies these recent concerns. He has explored the way the cycle of production, circulation and consumption of certain classes of material would have been essential for maintaining local, and at times highly competitive, political systems. He has argued that we have to understand the way these local political systems functioned within conditions determined by the larger 'world system' of which they were a part.

Given this approach it is worth considering for a moment the contrast between the perspective established by Rowlands and others in the study of metalwork, and the model originally developed by Childe for the European Bronze Age (cf. Rowlands 1984). Childe saw the Bronze Age representing a quite distinct step in European social and economic evolution (Childe 1957 & 1962). For him metallurgy represented the establishment of an original and inventive science within Europe. Innovatory skills were in the hands of itinerant metalworkers who always appeared on the fringes of the agricultural societies they served. It was the "itinerancy and far flung contacts" of these "non-tribal smiths" which helped to promote their own inventive capabilities (Childe 1947:161 & 1962:169).

It is less easy today to maintain the unity of the European Bronze Age in either time or space. Sherratt has demonstrated how the role of early metals can be overemphasised; they were but one element in the widespread exchange of non-utilitarian objects and materials established by the mature Neolithic. These networks of exchange extended from southeast to central Europe and beyond. Sherratt's work emphasises the unity of that period which contains the earliest metalworking but is not necessarily defined by it. He is also able to specify the particular regional character of these exchange networks without losing sight of the wider systems to which they ultimately contributed (Sher-

ratt 1976 & 1984). Finally he integrates the circulation of such non-utilitarian materials with cycles of agricultural production and consumption (Sherratt 1976 & 1982). The importance of this point has been echoed by other writers for, as Rowlands states, we cannot assume "that there is something called a subsistence sector (i.e. food/agriculture) and something else called production for exchange (i.e. craft production). Such differentiation ignores completely the often highly symbolic value that is attached to the consumption of particular kinds of foodstuffs in these ceremonial exchange systems." (Rowlands 1984:150).

Rowlands argues that it is during the Bronze Age, rather than at its inception or at its close, that a major social transformation can be traced. In temperate Europe this is characterised by the replacement of traditional and relatively stable hierarchies of the late Neolithic and early Bronze Age by highly competitive systems of status procurement (Rowlands 1980 & 1984:152). Rowlands rejects the idea that these later hierarchies were based upon the control of land, or in the case of southern Europe by investment in irrigation or polyculture (*contra* Gilman 1981). Instead he argues that the minimum political unit was determined by the form of the kinship system whereby labour was accumulated. Indeed it is possible to envisage a form of kinship system which would allow for the establishment of numerous far flung and competitive alliance networks.

The networks which carried marriage partners and certain prestige items were the means by which local political authority could be extended via 'ceremonial displays, feasting and fighting' (Rowlands 1980). In this model local surplus is produced to claim entry into the wider exchange network. Certain agricultural products might be exchanged, others would be used in displays of feasting. Local surpluses would be accumulated through the control of labour products. Different circuits of exchange would have existed, for local products could not be exchanged directly for prestige items. Instead each cycle of exchange was used to establish and maintain certain forms of political status, and it was through the accumulation of political statuses that the entire system was integrated. Thus local production might be dominated by a political authority which was itself based upon the control of exotic items (cf. Frankenstein & Rowlands 1978). This model shifts the emphasis away from Childe's concern with production to the control of circulation and consumption. This does not deny that production, circulation and consumption represent a unified cycle, but we have to understand the way the entire cycle was structured. In the case of metal, consumption normally refers to the deliberate deposition of objects in hoards, graves and 'wet places' which effectively removes them from circulation. We will comment further upon this model below.

These ideas have two important implications. First, no distinction can be made between economic and political spheres, and whilst different spheres of material circulation would have existed we have to consider the functioning of the entire system. Studies of metalwork alone are of questionable validity, and it becomes an urgent priority to evaluate the place of metal in specific regional strategies of political reproduction. Second, growth in systems such as these has to be understood in terms of the growth of *political* authority. That authority does not depend upon the accumulation of what we would today regard as 'wealth' but rather in maintaining control of a network of social obligations and alliances. This brings us to a point central to this whole argument; the difference between commodity and gift exchanges.

Gregory has discussed the distinction in detail. He has surveyed the failure of neo-classical economics in its belief that the principles of commodity economics are universally applicable (Gregory 1982). Gregory's empirical study was on the indigenous economy of Papua New Guinea, and his basic analytical principle was to direct analysis at the economic and social practices which established "the conditions necessary for the replacement of both things and people." (Gregory 1982:29). His emphasis has therefore been upon understanding processes of social and economic *reproduction* which "must weld eight elements—the production, consumption, distribution and exchange of things on one hand; the production, consumption, distribution and exchange of people on the other—into a structural whole." (Gregory 1982:30).

Gregory identifies two forms of exchange. Gift exchange maintains an obligation over the period which elapses between the gift being received and a gift of similar or greater value being returned (Mauss 1969). This circulates different categories of material in a given rank order. Commodity exchange however establishes an equivalence of value between things at the moment of exchange, whereby the obligations of that exchange are cancelled out. Thus in Gregory's terms gift exchange establishes "a relation of equality between homogeneous things at a different point of time" whilst commodity exchange "establishes a relation of equality between heterogeneous things at a given point in time" (Gregory 1982:47).

Commodity exchange includes barter and the monetary economics of our contemporary world. It facilitates no lasting obligations between the transactors, different kinds of commodity can be exchanged for each other (money is today a medium of conversion), and the accumulation of commodities represents wealth because it acts as an investment for future exchanges.

Gift exchange functions differently because an obligation exists between transactors until a cycle of gift giving, involving objects of an equivalent rank order, cancels these obligations out. However gift giving can become competitive as each transactor attempts to outdo the other.

We have emphasised the importance of re-thinking processes of production, exchange and consumption in terms of political strategies rather than in traditional terms of economic adaptation. Political authority results in some form of control being established over people and materials. Such authority is built out of these different forms of exchange in different ways. In the ancient world we face forms of authority which derived from differences in age, gender, kinship relations and genealogical status, itself calculated in relation to ancestors or gods. Other forms of authority may arise through obligations accumulated by conspicuous displays of gift giving and feasting.

The social changes Rowlands sees having occurred during the Bronze Age can be represented as a shift in some of the dominant forms of political authority; away from the relatively stable reckoning of genealogical and ritual status to more openly competitive systems concerned with kinship alliances, gift giving, feasting and warfares. Commodity exchanges play little or no part in such transformations. We are not dealing here with societies within which the *ownership* of critical resources is the basis of social control. Where commodity type exchanges did occur they would have been at the margins of these larger political strategies. They were the transactions of barter established between relative strangers (Sahlins 1974:185ff.).

Emphasis upon political authority adds another dimension to our understanding of social reproduction, an element not recognised by Gregory. We are concerned not only to understand processes of material and biological reproduction (the reproduction of things and of people), but also the reproduction of the systems of authority whereby people recognised and accepted obligations and demands made upon them. In short we must accept that particular classes of object and the way they were used and exchanged carried a form of meaning which in turn determined the way those objects were further treated.

All these ideas represent some very general concepts. It would be wrong to use them, or models such as that proposed by Rowlands, as once and for all explanations for the nature of our archaeological evidence. These ideas certainly prevent glib comparisons between the ancient and the modern world, and we cannot go on talking about 'merchants', 'wealth' or 'bronze industries'. They should therefore be drawn upon as a form of underlying guidance when we come to look at the detail of our archaeological evidence. It is our contention that the full complexity of the archaeological evidence available to us today has hardly been realised. Some writers have begun to apply these ideas to Bronze Age material (Kristiansen 1978; Bradley 1982, 1985b) and we will now look at three particular kinds of evidence which raise some of the issues introduced here.

First, if different cycles of exchange carried different forms of meaning and maintained particular types of authority then the objects used would have been treated in specific ways. This will be true for the circulation of artefacts (largely invisible archaeologically), as it will when artefacts are used in other forms of ritual display which are archaeologically visible such as in grave deposits or in hoards.

Second, if we are to understand the way a system of production and consumption works, thus integrating all forms of agricultural and craft activity, we need to establish detailed programmes of regional analyses. Britain has a long tradition of settlement archaeology, and it is one area in Europe where it should be possible to begin this kind of work. The aim must be to examine the way metal and other products circulated and were consumed in terms of different kinds of social practices.

Third, it is no longer possible to use the range and distribution of the various types of metal objects found in hoards as an indication of the organisation of production. Comparisons between the increasing amounts of mould debris being recovered, the types of artefacts found on settlements, and the remarkable wreck finds at Moor Sand, Salcombe, and Langdon Bay, Dover, demonstrate that the processes of deposition which produced the hoard and 'single-find' record are selective. Indeed we can now realise that a cycle of production and consumption may hardly register archaeologically, and that hoarding is itself a particular process which needs explaining.

Early Bronze Age Depositional Practices: Their Inception and Demise

Our first study concerns early Bronze Age metalwork. Elsewhere this has been separated into two sets of equipment with different contextual identities (Needham 1988). One set, comprising daggers, most ornaments and small tools, prevails in the funerary record. These objects are taken to be symbols which it was permissable to send into the afterworld. The second set features halberds, spearheads, lunulae and, above all, axes, types which almost invariably occur in hoards or as single finds, although rarely mixed together. These belong to a broader background of deliberate deposition, possibly having more than one explanation, but generally of ritual and specifically non-funerary significance (Needham 1988).

In order to achieve a greater understanding of these contextual distinctions we must investigate how the system evolved out of late Neolithic practices, how it interacted with contemporary practices relating to non-metal goods, and the nature of change at the early/middle Bronze Age transition. In this way we might identify whether metalwork had a particular importance, and added a new dimension to ritual practices.

'Hoard' deposition, which we take to include most single finds, is considered first. Although on a regional level fluctuating fortunes may be discerned, these deposits are numerous and appear to present a continuous record since the early stages of metallurgy. A general umbrella term, 'community deposits', has been applied to these finds (Needham 1988). A case can be made for their involvement in ceremony and visual display, explaining for instance the phenomenon of axe decoration. While such deposits are patently not to do with burial, this does not exclude them from pre-burial mortuary rites. Another possibility however is that they were used to mark other critical events or transitions outside the realm of death. These might include bonds of obligation amongst the living, the establishment of relationships between groups or of authority within a group. If we assume that these deposits had no part in funerary rituals, but were important in structuring social relations, this makes sense of the continuing hoard/single find record after the loss of the burial metalwork record. We will argue that the latter are in fact supplanted by wet deposits.

The occurrence of selective deposition in a 'ritual' sphere is not unique to the age of metal. The later Neolithic of Britain shows signs of growing assemblage differentiation to suit different non-utilitarian needs. This includes the development of a specialised artefact range, used in part as grave accompaniments, including jet sliders, bone pins, antler and stone maceheads, lozenge arrowheads, edge-polished knives, axes and adzes, or the unique pottery flask from Liff's Low (Kinnes 1979:46). Most of these types also occur in non-funerary contexts and Wickham-Jones has recently made the case that these contexts may include deliberate lithic deposits (1985:170–2).

Selective deposition also affects the various pottery styles of the later Neolithic and early Bronze Age. Traditionally Peterborough Ware, Grooved Ware and Beakers, were thought to identify distinct cultures. Emphasis is now put on different hierarchical elements of a single community. In this way the discrete contextualisation of different styles relates ultimately to different levels of prestige exchange (Bradley 1982b). Braithwaite (1984) and Thorpe and Richards (1984) have suggested that the distinction between Grooved Ware assemblages and contexts, and Beaker deposits lies in their use in different and competing spheres of social exchange and consumption. Complex distinctions in the way various artefact types were employed therefore prevailed before the development of metal in the insular economy. On a general level we can claim that the appropriate preconditions existed for a rapid partition of metalwork into two or more spheres of circulation. It is understandable that a material as scarce, intrinsically beautiful and durable, yet highly manipulative through its recyclability, should not only be quickly promoted to positions of prime importance, but might also create its own terms of ritual expression. This is perhaps more likely for objects which had no antecedent in the Neolithic, such as daggers and halberds. Local communities would have the choice between simply slotting the type into a pre-existing strategy, absorbing artefact and role united from the immediate source area, or formulating specific roles for it. In this respect it is worth contrasting distinct regional uses of tanged daggers. In southern Britain they appear tied to an early Beaker funerary package apparently prescribed by an introduced ideology (Burgess and Shennan 1976). Taking this further, Braithwaite (1984) implies that this package was drawn upon to effect a challenge on the existing social order, in Wessex at least. This provides a plausible rationale for the acceptance of a new burial custom and makes the initial introduction of metal into the local economy almost incidental, merely a spoke in a wheel. On the other hand we cannot identify a like process in Ireland where tanged daggers occur as bog finds, usually single, thus epitomising their acceptance by that society on its own terms (Needham 1988).

The leading metal type contrasting with the daggers are the axes. In Britain they occur in different contexts and are considered to have fulfilled different roles. Whether the lengthy background of the axe as part of a basic tool kit had a bearing on its treatment is difficult to determine. Undoubtedly on occasions Neolithic stone and flint axes were accorded special treatment. In addition to the limited numbers of grave-deposited axes, there are probably a greater number in burial mound material (e.g. Piggott, in Jessup 1939; Manby 1979:81; Laing 1983). It is possible that the Greenbrae find (Aberdeenshire), with jet and amber beads and an edge-polished axe, belongs in this context category (Kenworthy 1976–7), while Thorpe and Richards suggest that the Seamer flint hoard, placed again in a mound, was deposited with just a token human bone deposit (1984:71). There may be increasing evidence for the special use of axes outside the funerary sphere. Most jadeite axes should have non-utilitarian and ritual connotations, a point driven home by the pristine example buried under the Neolithic Sweet Track (Coles 1979). Meanwhile, still usable axes of stone and flint occur in pit deposits in causewayed enclosures (e.g. Wheeler 1943:164–171; Mercer 1980:22–3) hinting again at deliberate depositional practices.

With the development at the end of the Neolithic of two series of shaft-hole stone implements we find more scope for contrasting patterns of deposition. Axe-hammers and battle axes are in many respects alike. They are made of durable stone, are labour-intensive in their production and well fashioned (although not necessarily with the same degree of finish). Both types have limitations on their practical use, (e.g. axe-hammers for ore crushing, battle axes in warfare) and it is not unreasonable to suppose a major if not exclusive role in a non-utilitarian sphere. Despite the obvious parallelism between these two shaft-hole implement series, their contextual patterning is quite different; there are almost twice as many axe-hammers as battle-axes, yet none of the former are known from secure burial contexts (Roe 1979:26–30). About one sixth of all battle axe finds come from graves (Roe 1966:218–27). Although their geographical distributions have rather different emphases, there is sufficient overlap to suggest that many areas had access to both types of implement yet stuck to different rules governing their respective treatment. In particular axe-

hammers were inadmissable as grave goods.

To summarise so far, we have shown by considering shaft-hole implements and ceramics that metalwork was by no means alone in the late Neolithic and early Bronze Age in being separated into different contextual compartments. Given the nature of the artefacts, it is logical to suppose that compartmentalisation in the archaeological record stems from cycles of use in the systemic context. What has been more difficult to determine is whether the patterning seen in the metalwork merely perpetuates existing late Neolithic practices. We would suspect not; metallurgy brought new methods of working and recycling material and new artefact types possibly in tandem with new roles. Type and function (utilitarian or not) may have been inseparable. A new input such as suggested might well alter the balance of different cycles of exchange, and even increase polarisation. Furthermore the very versalility and convertibility of copper alloys would tend to change attitudes to deposition and artefact renewal. We must conclude then that the metalwork did indeed introduce new elements to an existing circumstance of selective circulation and deposition.

The Paradox of the Demise of Grave Goods

Past notions that relative wealth or relative status are mirrored in grave goods may now be questioned. An analysis of the significance of grave goods, formulated by one of us (Barrett, this volume), demands that we pay more attention to the understanding of mortuary process, particularly its variability and the effects on archaeologically visible evidence. The presence of grave goods have more to do with the *structure* of the funerary rituals, than the social station of the individual interred. It is argued that in general primary inhumation burial presupposes a short mortuary period which gives scope for specific artefacts to be incorporated with the body in the grave. In contrast cremation rites may allow greater temporal and spatial distance between the rites of *liminality* and the rites of *incorporation*. By the time of the burial all necessary transactions between the living, the dead and the ancestors may have been effected and it may no longer have been necessary to accompany the burial with artefacts. Given these general observations, it is hardly surprising that for much of the early Bronze Age grave goods tend to accompany inhumations rather than cremations (secondary burial of inhumed bones, although present, does not have the predominance it had in Neolithic practices). Exceptions occur, the most obvious being the elaborate terminal deposits of early Bronze Age cremation traditions of the Wessex 2 group. We shall return to this point.

The perversity of the British Bronze Age record has always been the lapse of 'rich' grave goods at a time when, according to all indicators, more prestige equipment and particularly metalwork was in circulation. To suggest that a process of devaluation, due to more abundant metal stocks, made the use of metalwork in grave goods sacrilegious would contradict much clear evidence that bronze remained an

Table 12.1. Predominant trends in metalwork deposition in the British earlier Bronze Age (excluding Wessex).

Metalwork Assemblage	Context		
	Funerary	Non-Funerary	Wet-Places
MA III-IV (Butterwick/Aylesford) (Migdale)	**dagger graves widespread**	many single axes; axe and halberd hoards concentrated in the north	a few axes
MA V (Bush Barrow) (Willerby Wold)	dagger graves in localised pockets only	many single axes; axe hoards concentrated in the centre	several axes and one dagger
MA VI/MBA 1 (Camerton Snowshill) (Arreton/Acton)	sporadic dagger graves	many single axes and a few spearheads; hoards (some mixed) concentrated in the south	**many finds: particularly daggers, also axes**
MBA 2 (Taunton)	no dagger/rapier graves	many single axes; tool hoards; a few single weapons* and discrete weapon hoards	**many rapiers and spearheads ; some tools**

* excluding side-looped spearheads, regarded by some as hunting implements.

important manipulative resource throughout the Bronze Age. The instrinsic value of the metal *itself* was doubtless only a minor component of total *perceived* value (e.g. Barrett 1985:98–100), so that the presumed growing abundance of the metal stock during the Bronze Age need not have adversely affected its importance.

The switch from opulent funerary disposal in the early Bronze Age to other forms of disposal, particularly in wet places, has in recent studies been seen in terms of an eclipse in the control over critical resources (Barrett 1980a:84–90; Bradley 1980:59–64). The eclipse involved a geographical shift in the capacity of communities to retain surpluses and this was tied to changes in depositional practice, themselves perhaps signalling acceptance of new ideologies and rejection of the old. It has to be borne in mind that these changes take place against a solid and continuous background of hoard and single find deposition which more than spans the entire period. The actual changes observable in the metalwork record therefore appear more specific. It is also vital to look at a broader geographical perspective within which to set the regional identities of Wessex, the lower Thames and other zones. In other words, understanding the transition from early to middle Bronze Age practices should be less Wessex-oriented and should pay more attention to long-term trajectories.

Daggers and dirks are central to our enquiry into the nature of the early/middle Bronze Age transition. They are a key type in the 'richer' grave assemblages of the early Bronze Age, while in their evolved middle Bronze Age form they are almost universally single finds. The way they behave may therefore shed light on the important change in funerary ideology.

The parameters of our study material must first be defined. It comprises a range of dagger/dirk types which in broad temporal terms post-date the Armorico-British range and pre-date the developed triple-arris rapiers of the mature middle Bronze Age (Taunton Stage). The range contains two broad classes defined on the basis of complex or lozenge-shaped blade sections, groups I and II (Burgess and Gerloff 1981), both of which have broadish proportions and usually two or three rivets. We regard the Camerton-Snowshill weapons as a homogeneous sub-set of the group I spectrum which also includes other nominally early Bronze Age types such as Hammersmith (Gerloff 1975). The basis for any gross chronological distinction between these and the group I and II weapons, as defined by Burgess and Gerloff, has been eroded by successive writers (e.g. Needham 1979:290; O'Connor 1980:39–40, 42–3; Burgess and Gerloff 1981:15–19, 42–5) and this paves the way for the whole set being treated as broadly contemporaneous during the period *c.* 1600–1350BC (1350–1100bc).

Although we should re-attribute some daggers within the existing classification, the long recognised contextual difference between the Camerton-Snowshill type and more variable remainder of group I and II weapons stands unchallenged. The bulk of the former type occur in grave contexts, while the latter material is almost invariably found singly and is predominantly from rivers and other watery contexts (Burgess and Gerloff 1981:15, 41). There are rather few finds which cut across these typological-contextual correlations. A few of the Camerton-Snowshill daggers are river finds, as from Bermondsey, Sandford-on-Thames(2), Datchet and Egham (Gerloff 1975, nos 158, 162 A and B, 168, 185). Meanwhile several group I daggers come from graves: Winterborne Came, possibly Cranborne, Roke Down, Huntshaw, St Brides, Mullion, (Gerloff 1975, nos 143, 144, 152, 157, 200, 201) with a noteworthy distribution in the southwest of Britain barely impinging on Wessex. In two cases, though, the dagger appears to be associated with a Camerton-Snowshill example (Winterborne Came, Cranborne). In addition, two group II implements, from Harlyn Bay and Waterhouse (Gerloff 1975, nos 202, 293) are burial finds. To emphasise the distriction, some of these non-Wessex type daggers were associated with urn burials which is not a rite proper to the Wessex 2 series (*pace* Burgess and Gerloff 1981, 15—group I examples from 'Wessex burials').

With these exceptions in mind we can nevertheless identify two complementary dagger groups by typological-contextual definition and, moreover, with good geographical demarcations. It is worth reflecting also on their hoard occurrence, which is generally infrequent in the contemporary Arreton and Acton Park assemblages. The daggers included prove to be extremely diverse in type (Acton Park, Ebnal, Totland, Arreton, Plymstock and a new hoard from Bridgemere, Cheshire) thus, if anything, echoing the varied character of daggers in Britain as a whole at this stage.

While there is a danger that local comparisons may well be invalid through different recovery patterns (e.g. barrow-diggers in Wessex versus dredging of Thames), on a broader scale this risk diminishes. For example, in Scotland many cists have yielded earlier dagger types, while none have group I–II dirks which are instead single finds. What we can suggest is the emergence late in the early Bronze Age of a frequent practice of single deposition in rivers/bogs which is exceptionally rare for any earlier metal material in Britain. Earlier daggers were almost universally put in graves (tanged copper, flat bronze, Armorico-British). It is not clear whether these very different practices are in any degree contemporary. Current dating would suggest that parts of the country, especially those lacking Armorico-British weapons, saw a lull in any form of dagger deposition (Gerloff 1975, plate 34).

Wessex differs radically from this general model. Firstly it is largely devoid of hoards and single finds and secondly we see a strong continuation of dagger graves through Metalwork Assemblages V and VI, even making allowance for enhanced recovery in the region (which has incidentally brought into prominence a regional group I dagger variant, Camerton-Snowshill). Elsewhere in the country the enduring patterns of middle Bronze Age water deposition were already being set in Metalwork Assemblage VI, while sporadic dagger graves employed a variety of dagger types in a variety of rites.

In addition to the group I and II weapons noted above, Camerton-Snowshill blades occurred at several sites (e.g. Earl's Barton, Northants; Butterbumps, Lincs; Hammeldon, Devon; Rillaton, Cornwall; Chippenham, Cambs; Hove, Sussex). On the last two sites they accompany inhumations, not the classic cremated remains, and mention has already been made of other daggers with urn burials. Outside Wessex therefore we see a greater diversity in the depositional record.

It is understandable that gross substitution of grave-deposited metalwork for wet-place deposition might be regarded as a switch within one sphere of activity, namely funerary and burial. Indeed some have suggested that some river metalwork could actually represent the grave goods of watery burials (Burgess 1980:351; Bradley 1984:110-4). This is difficult to validate, but it may be relevant that no bog burials are known in association with metalwork in either Britain or Ireland.

If we are to pursue a 'concept of equivalence' between the dagger graves and wet context daggers, we need to ask two questions. Firstly, was there development or dislocation in funerary ideology over the transition and secondly, how do the river deposits relate to the continuing background of simple cremation during the middle Bronze Age? On the first point, the contrasts observed in artefact typology, context and distribution might at first encourage the view that wet place deposits belong to a completely new order of burial and religion (Ellison 1981:442) competing with the established traditions (c.f. Braithwaite's model, 1984). However, an alternative sequence allowing greater continuity is rooted in the prolongation of the mortuary process.

By this hypothesis the river finds and some of the contemporary 'poor' cremation burials on land belong to different stages of one extended funerary process, in effect a sequence in which emphasis is placed upon a complex liminal period rather than the burial act (rite of incorporation) and the two have become separated in time and/or function in a more extreme form than hitherto encountered in the metal age. The all-important transfer of authority occurred away from the burial grounds and was validated by (inter alia) the deposition of daggers or rapiers in rivers or bogs. The choice of wet places could merely have been to underline the spiritual, if not always physical, inaccessibility of the deposited materials; recovery would have invalidated the whole operation. We can speculate further that once the community was satisfied as to the succession of authority, the deceased was no longer conferred with visible symbols of his or her position in life. As the final act of distancing, i.e. removal to the other world, the cremated body was consigned to the ancestral burial ground, with or without an urn. It is possible that, on the adoption of new practices, the former grave set (daggers, ornaments, small tools) became split and that only the dagger retained its major symbolic importance, while the other components might still accompany the deceased. Occasionally a small trinket, personal implement (e.g. razor) or a fragmentary hunting implement accompanied a cremation.

We still have not answered the question of *why* the depositional practices changed. To search for indigenous development is perhaps logical, since Britain stands apart in deposition terms from much of Europe after the early/middle Bronze Age transition. One possibility is that flamboyant disposal into a river or bog, a captivating spectacle, was just another manifestation of a concern for the *display* of fine metalwork inferred in other ritual spheres during the early Bronze Age (Needham 1988). This had involved other types of object, probably in non-funerary roles, but display might perhaps have become a dynamic force in its own right which eventually impinged on long-lived and stable funerary traditions. When display and flamboyant disposal became the signals of the all-important transfer of authority, then the scene was set for the greater geographic partition of the rites of separation, liminality and incorporation.

We must emphasise at this point that our hypothetical model above is applicable only to a minority of burials. In such cases we identify a major change of funerary practice, but this has to be seen against a substratum of unaccompanied or minimally accompanied burials which we might assume to continue across the transition. In particular one would point to the continuity of urned and unurned cremations beginning with early Collared Urn currency, probably as early as the first *bronze* working (*c.* 2000 BC), and doubtless having its antecedents in later Neolithic cremation cemeteries. Superimposed upon this, and too complex for discussion here, are the numerous Beaker and Food Vessel accompanied inhumations, as well as the 'richer' burials we have been considering.

It is against this background that we need to view the anomalous Wessex 2 practices. While in one respect they conform to the countrywide resurgence of dominant cremation rites after *c.* 1600 BC (1350 bc), they are otherwise unique in the regularity with which a set of grave goods, but no urn, is associated. The protraction and segmentation of the funerary process which, as postulated above, occurred elsewhere may have been obstructed by beliefs held in Wessex. Contrary to the general model outlined, cremations need not always imply significant time lapse between death and burial; at Edmondsham, Dorset, for example a pyre was identified under the burial mound itself (Proudfoot 1963, 400). Nevertheless, whatever the form and duration of the funerary sequence in Wessex 2, it is clear that certain important acts were reserved until the end, namely the deposition of artefacts of fine workmanship and the subsequent erection of a mound, for many of the burials are primary deposits. There was therefore greater conceptual proximity between symbolism of grave goods and the final entry of the deceased to the world of the ancestors.

The distinctiveness of Wessex burial rites at this time cannot therefore be put down to a different economy, or a different level of wealth or surplus. Although any of these things are possible, the burial rite itself tells us only of a basic difference in the business of conducting important personages to the afterworld and in the process of conferring authority on new shoulders. This might or might not have been due to an alternative social structure of the living. It is possible however that it was social reorganisation which precipitated the demise of this erstwhile stable funerary system sometime around 1100 bc. There is little evidence to characterise this demise, but we should not necessarily assume catastrophic models.

Agricultural Production and the Circulation of Metalwork

We have already observed that attempts to rethink the role of metalwork in the reproduction of social relations involve adopting conceptual categories which break with twentieth century economic models. Central to this is the realisation that the gifting (including votive deposition) of certain artefacts is a strategy of social control, for it captures obligations and confirms alliances.

What we will do here is to reflect upon the problems inherent in some contemporary ideas concerning the nature of Bronze Age social reproduction by looking in particular at the work of Rowlands (1980) and of Kristiansen (1978 & 1984). The most important problems arise from the general theory employed in this work, but it is obviously beyond the scope of this paper to undertake a detailed critique. However a cursory examination of the relationship between the general model and the empirical evidence may raise issues which do have both theoretical and methodological implications.

Rowlands' (1980) model for the later Bronze Age draws obliquely upon a theory of social evolution established by Friedman (1975) and himself (Friedman & Rowland 1977). The model specifies the kind of structures (kinship systems and residence rules) which might have organised local production. However these local conditions were also part of a larger system. "As production for exchange seems a constant factor in evolution we must deal with a system larger than the local political unit,..., if we are to understand the conditions of its existence and transformation." (Friedman & Rowlands 1977:204).

Rowlands is thus able to model the evolution of local political systems which controlled the surplus product of local (agricultural) production. Emergent elites established long distance contacts by which certain exotic, sumptuary, items circulated (e.g. weaponry). These items would have been used to increase local political prestige through ritual display, gifting and consumption. In such a system local products would have been exchanged as debt payments in social obligations and some exotic objects may have been passed down as gifts. The circulation and consumption of bronzes can thus be integrated within the organisation of agricultural production. The latter is itself partly dependent upon local ecological factors. "Thus the specific evolution of social formations depends on the internal properties of local systems, upon the local constraints and upon their place in a larger system." (Friedman & Rowlands 1977:205).

Kristiansen's original study set out to look at exactly this kind of relationship. All bronze in Denmark ultimately derived from communities in central Europe, a process which Kristiansen argues would have been linked in some way to the success of the local Danish systems of agricultural production. The amount of metal consumed in grave or votive deposits would have been determined by the nature of particular ritual requirements (Kristiansen 1984:91), but the availability of material to be consumed would itself have depended upon the success of procurement strategies. The latter is archaeologically attested by comparing the use-wear observable on the variously deposited bronze items. Kristiansen examined, for five different geographical zones in Denmark, degrees of wear on sword hilts which indicate circulation time, and compared these data to population sizes and settlement location (given by grave numbers and location), and the productive potential of soils. He argued that he was able to observe, over time, competition between the zones for metal supplies and the ultimate 'success' of eastern Denmark in maintaining local production and securing bronze supplies from those communities to the south.

Whilst the detailed empirical work of Kristiansen is important, it remains difficult to specify with any precision the workings of the local system, a problem which reflects the almost total lack of contemporary settlement evidence. However it would be possible, if naïve, to adopt Rowland's model to 'explain' the processes at work. Would such an approach be viable, given the very limited empirical data currently available?

The example we wish to consider here is the seemingly short lived group of settlements recognisable on the chalk downland of Sussex. Until recently these sites represented some of the clearest and best preserved settlement archaeology of the period in Britain. The sites are recognisable as house platforms and enclosures, where the enclosures may be embanked and fenced, and are associated with field lynchets and cremation cemeteries (although there are in fact only a few such cemeteries from Sussex). In Sussex and elsewhere these Deverel-Rimbury settlements have, in the past, been presented in terms of a cultural dislocation and colonisation of the uplands. This view is in some need of revision. Two points can be made. Firstly, the pottery found on the settlements seems to be part of a longer tradition predating the appearance of these particular settlements (Barrett 1976 & 1980b). Secondly the settlement and cultivation traces recorded on the uplands are a final phase of Bronze Age land-use. This means that earlier settlements are likely to have been ploughed away or to be sealed beneath colluvium whilst abandonment has preserved the final phase of settlement.

Rowlands uses the southern British Deverel-Rimbury material, and Ellison's analysis of it, to support some of his basic propositions regarding settlement organisation (Rowlands 1980; Ellison 1978, 1980a & 1980b). However what is more important is the historical interpretation given to these upland settlements (followed also in Barrett &

Bradley 1980a & 1980b). These, he suggests, are a particular geographical modification of the basic structural model. Thus the underlying determinants are the rules of kinship and residence which under the ecological conditions of an isolated chalk upland give rise to a specific form of economic reproduction. He suggests that the accumulation of local agricultural surpluses can be recognised on certain sites, and that these surpluses are unlikely to be meant for local consumption. "In fact it seems more fruitful to view these upland settlements as forming one sector within a larger regional division of labour. Perhaps their location would be best understood as the result of a demand for upland products by communities situated in lowland river valleys or on the coast?" (Rowlands 1980:34). He goes on to repeat that "access to external trade is vital for local political development" and thus the procurement of exotic material would again have been a source of elite exchange and competition.

In his analysis of the 'domestic mode of production' Sahlins emphasises that "to speak of '*the* economy' of a primitive society is an exercise in unreality. Structurally 'the economy' does not exist." Instead economic procedures are "something that generalised social groups and relations, notably kinship groups and relations, *do.*" (Sahlins 1974:76). He then characterises the three basic elements of the domestic mode of production as a "small labor force differentiated essentially by sex, simple technology, and finite production objectives" (Sahlins 1974:87). Production for exchange value is not a feature of these objectives and the domestic mode of production appears "underproductive". By this Sahlins means that reproductive procedures do not maximise the productive potential of the land. Growth of agriculturally intensive systems are not inherent to the domestic mode of production. Rowlands on the other hand specifies conditions under which increased production can occur when the circulation and consumption of local products are carried along in competitive systems of political growth. The point of the contrast is that we must demonstrate and not assume growth in the productive forces.

On the area of the Sussex downland between the rivers Ouse and Cuckmere lie two extensively excavated Deverel-Rimbury settlements. These are Itford Hill (Burstow & Holleyman 1957) and Blackpatch (Drewett 1982). Both sites were identifiable as a series of house terraces and slight embanked enclosures, and both lie within or above field lynchets. At Itford Hill a contemporary cremation cemetery has also been excavated (Holden 1972). Burstow and Holleyman regarded Itford Hill as representing a 'nucleated village', a view discounted by Ellison (1978) who has shown that it is unlikely all the enclosures were contemporary. What we have on both sites is a series of buildings which show little sign of renewal. However different enclosure and platforms may have been constructed at different times, and platform 4 at Black Patch seems to show the consecutive addition of two further buildings (Huts 4 & 5) (Drewett 1982, Fig.9). Where fenced enclosures exist they define a small area, containing ponds, around the front of the buildings. Storage pits occur within some of the buildings but there is no extensive provision for grain storage, nor for the corralling of stock. Indeed these sites are some distance from permanent water (Drewett 1982, Table 12). One of the more notable tasks undertaken within these settlements seems to have been textile production.

It is difficult to understand why such sites are constantly regarded as self sufficient (Drewett 1982:341). It seems more than likely that the labour for cultivation would have been drawn from more than an individual settlement, and the numbers of stock required to maintain viable herds and flocks must have represented another inter-communal resource. People are also likely to have been more mobile than is often allowed, moving between the upland sites, and between the uplands and lowlands. Such movement would have maintained the communal obligations of agricultural labour and the residential demands of marriage and inheritance.

We would therefore see these residential sites functioning within a larger open system of social reproduction rather than representing the atomised, relatively autonomous units of an economic system (c.f. Drewett 1982). The reproduction of any social system depends upon the biological reproduction of people, the production, circulation and consumption of materials (including animal and grain), and the maintenance of structures of knowledge and authority. Here and elsewhere all these were united within the routine patterns of daily activity. If we are to talk about 'growth' in such systems then we are discussing the accumulation of political authority by certain groups or individuals. We may therefore ask if such political accumulation can be recognised, and look particularly at the role of metal in such strategies. The point at issue is to demonstrate that certain metal items did play a central part in establishing political authority through their use as gifts and their display in ritual consumption. We would contend that this cannot be demonstrated. Instead we would argue that the dominant sources of authority were reproduced with reference to the settlements themselves. Indeed one of the most notable features of the middle Bronze Age is the construction of settlement enclosures (Barrett 1988). The social distinctions maintained within these sites are likely to be precisely those identified by Sahlins, namely distinctions of age, gender and kin, and these would have structured the organisation of residential activity and of agricultural labour. However, apart from these distinctions it is difficult to argue for the development of other political structures.

In this area we cannot, for example, locate centres for the accumulation of an agricultural surplus. There are also few metal finds from this area of chalk upland. A small group of bronzes do come from the Black Patch site, but if the circulation of exotic metal artefacts were a means of political control it is not recognisable archaeologically; such material was not consumed in either burials or in large votive deposits. This alone implies that such circulation systems did not become the focus for conspicuous consumption and thus the means of extending political domination.

In turning to the metal from Black Patch it is important to recognise that it comes from a variety of contexts on that site. It is certainly wrong to assume that each house platform was associated with a single set of activities (*contra* Drewett 1979). For example an awl or tracer came from the porch post-hole of Hut 3, Hut Platform 4, presumably reflecting not an 'activity area' but a foundation deposit similar in context to the chalk phallus from the porch post-hole of Hut D at Itford Hill (Drewett 1982:361; Burstow and Holleyman 1957:202). The remaining material from the buildings is unlikely to represent the casual discard of material during the routine use of the domestic space but, instead, the casual discard and the deliberate deposition of material within the buildings at the period of their abandonment. Such processes of abandonment are likely to have been complex and difficult to unravel. Abandoned platforms may also have been reused for activities unconnected with their original function.

In Hut 3, Hut Platform 4, 21kg of threshed and burnt grain were deposited in one of the internal storage pits along with a bronze razor. A similar 19.5kg deposit of burnt grain was placed in the internal storage pit of Hut 1, Hut Platform 1. Both deposits are comparable in their nature to the *c.* 5kg deposit of burnt barley from the internal storage pit 26 in Hut D at Itford Hill (Drewett 1982:382; Burstow & Holleyman 1957:177). Such deposits are clearly deliberate and it is difficult to see them resulting from accidental burning. The idea that abandoned buildings may form the focus for some votive deposits is supported by the occurrence of a human cremation placed outside Huts 1 and 2, Hut Platform 1, at Black Patch. It is interesting that such votive deposits include the consumption of considerable quantities of grain, but little metal.

The other metal finds from Black Patch all come from within the buildings and were found on the floors of Huts 1, 3 and 4, Hut platform 4. They include two finger rings placed together on the floor of Hut 1. Whilst all such material need not be votively deposited there is certainly enough evidence of the settlement becoming the stage for a limited amount of votive activity to reinforce our view that acts of enclosure themselves indicate that settlements were increasingly the focus of political conflict (Barrett 1988).

In this, metal appears to have played a limited and secondary role in the establishment of political authority. It would be wrong to assume that this was because the uplands were isolated and unable to procure such material; the barrow cemeteries of an earlier period certainly indicate that a range of exotica could be put into graves high on the chalk downland. It is surely more likely that the strategies of social reproduction turned upon the relations of the domestic mode of production discussed by Sahlins; relations of age and gender where political/economic growth was not inherent in the system and where metal circulated as tools, ornaments and dress decoration in a quite secondary role to social statuses established by other means.

Later Metalwork: The Distance Between Production and Deposition

We have already argued that most early Bronze Age single finds and hoards can be regarded as the results of deliberate deposition. In due course it will be shown that such a premise also accords well with the later metalwork evidence, although it should be stressed that this does not imply uniformity in the reasons for deposition. In accepting these explanations, we have to face up to the very real possibility that the extant evidence is partial and unrepresentative, that where regional traditions did not involve consigning certain material to the ground, such material present in the systemic context may not be represented at all in the archaeological record. This means that, using the traditional forms of metalwork evidence—hoards and stray finds, we are unlikely to comprehend the diversity of the material in circulation. This is a point of concern, for in order to see regional and contextual deposition strategies in perspective we need to characterise the pool from which material is selected. A related issue is the 'distance' between production and deposition, this defined as 1) the typical course an object type follows in circulation, and 2) the extent to which production was instigated in anticipation of an ultimate destiny, which might be funerary accompaniment, river disposal, or another archaeologically visible context.

Certain types of context may help us out of this impasse, but each has its own limitations urging care in interpretation. Three key context types have come to the forefront as a result of recent discoveries: settlement assemblages, clay mould assemblages, and cargoes. Formerly such finds were either completely unknown or wholly exceptional; even now they are rare when compared with the multitudinous hoards and single finds. Many more are needed to verify the existing deductions from comparisons between assemblages.

We will start by treating the metal casting debris, which is at the base of the whole utilisation cycle. The identification of the bronze types that would have been cast in mould finds continues to throw up surprises. Sometimes the precise form is hard to match amongst known bronze objects, as for Dainton type i spearheads (Needham 1980b:201–3), or two of the matrices on the New Mills, Powys, stone mould (Green 1985). More often it is the question of distributional anomaly, such as the presence of Wilburton type casting debris at Fimber, north Humberside, which is beyond the concentrations of the appropriate bronze types (Burgess 1968:29). Again the Dainton assemblage occurred in a region sparse in any contemporary weaponry (Needham 1980b:211), while some have been puzzled that several stone moulds for 'south Welsh' socketed axes all come from well away from the 'core' area in southeast Wales (but see Needham 1981).

However, when discrepancies occur at the local or site level, there is a more ready acceptance of the effects of efficient recycling. For instance, it is not considered to be an embarrassment to have metal-lurgical debris yet no bronze finds at Aldermaston (Bradley *et al* 1980) or more spectacularly at Springfield, Essex (D. Buckley—pers. comm.). At Springfield total excavation of a ring-fort yielded not a single scrap of bronze, whereas the ditch terminals at opposing entrances produced two large dumps of clay casting debris. Clearly, we may argue, we have efficient collection and recycling of the metalwork produced and used on the site. To accept such a hypothesis on a regional scale demands a rejection of the idea that the bronze record largely comprises casual losses, since this would, across a broader landscape, negate the marked inconsistency between products and moulds. So we must reject the idea of casual loss if we are to make sense of the inconsistencies repeatedly being observed.

When many more metalworking assemblages are recognised, moulds could ultimately give us a fairly balanced view of relative production. Still, there may never be a direct equation between the number of mould finds and original production levels for a given bronze type, since the use of different mould materials (stone, bronze and clay), each with its own survival potential, will introduce complicating variables. Nevertheless, there is the prospect that, in time, moulds will attest to all but the most exceptional of metalwork types; at least then a near complete inventory of types might be attained.

Such a prospect is far less likely for other new contexts namely cargoes and settlement assemblages. Potential cargoes, although few in number in British waters, are already showing unexpected components, such as types unknown or extremely rare on land sites, or types in earlier contexts than anticipated (e.g. Needham and Dean 1987). Clearly therefore they are not respecting the patterns set for land deposition in Britain, nor indeed on neighbouring continental shores. If we are correct to view the sea-bed scatters as shipwrecked cargoes, then these may be exceptional instances of truly accidental loss. This effectively excludes selection at the time of deposition. However marine erosion may work differentially on each object type, a transformation for which allowance must be made, and we still have to consider the source of the 'cargoes' (which may incorporate ship's arms etc), for selection will have been at work at various earlier points in the history of the material. For example, take the hypothetical case that the large Langdon Bay assemblage was drawn from just a single reserve stock in northern France and transported to another region merely as a metal source, that is as a 'commodity' in Gregory's terms (1982). The cargo might well be representative of the source stock, but the composition of the stock itself will have been conditioned by local economic and social factors and is unlikely to be fully representative of that region's stock in circulation. On the other hand, if we envisage the Langdon Bay cargo as the accumulation of many piecemeal exchanges with different parties, new implications arise. Some or all of the exchanges may have been honourable, prestigious or obligatory transactions. Suitable material would have been selected from stock by the giver thus making the aggregate

assemblage unrepresentative of the total pool of metal types. This may seem a fine distinction in terms of interpretation, but it is vital to an understanding of the relationship of hoard deposits to stock in the source area, in this case believed to be northern France. Under the first hypothesis we infer a stock (in reserve and/or circulation), which in composition is not unlike the Langdon Bay assemblage itself, yet contemporary hoards in the source area do not include Taunton-Hademarschen socketed axes nor tanged and collared chisels, both types reasonably well represented at Langdon Bay. The logical implication is that certain available object types were not being chosen for inclusion in hoard deposits. It is possible to avoid this conclusion given the second, piecemeal exchange hypothesis, but to do so we must invoke a supra-regional collection policy to allow certain types to come direct from other regions. Thus we might accommodate the socketed axes as a consignment picked up in northern Germany, or Britain itself. But this still will not explain the tanged and collared chisels, which cannot be found anywhere at this date (Penard/Bronze Final 1/Hallstatt A). Even hypothesis 2 does not therefore wholly remove our predicament for Langdon Bay and we might do better to face up to the implications of the first line of deduction.

Bradley (1985a & b) has recently applied the contrast between gift and commodity exchanges to explaining the different contexts of hoards and single river finds. He rightly observes that bronzes may have circulated as gifts or have been exchanged as commodities, accepting the point made by Godelier concerning the different contexts of exchange for 'salt money' amongst the Baruya of New Guinea (Godelier 1977). These different kinds of exchange will have functioned in quite different social contexts (Gregory 1982); they will also have involved a transformation of some sort as the bronze moved from one sphere of circulation to another. Bradley contends that these different kinds of exchange will be matched by different contexts of deposition containing different assemblages of material. He repeats, for example, his argument that weapon finds from rivers and other wet places are 'gifts to gods' (Bradley 1982). He goes on to argue that metal bartered as a commodity will take a particular form, either as broken and fragmentary material, or as a particular artefact type such as the axe (or perhaps as sickles in central Europe). He notes that axes are the most common feature of the 'industrial' or 'scrap' hoards in southern Britain, and that some appear in an 'as-cast' state as well as in fragmentary form.

Bradley's ideas emphasise the complexity of the exchange systems, but we would hesitate in applying a straight equation between type of deposit and type of exchange. There are a number of reasons for this. Firstly we are not told why barter/commodity exchanges should result in a hoard record in the first place. Hoards are after all material which has not been recovered, and we argue here that for the most part it was not intended for retrieval. The problem is further complicated by the argument that the hoards actually fall at distinct chronological horizons (Burgess and Coombs 1979 *versus* Bradley 1985b:39), although the evidence for this is far from conclusive. It is also the case that one area where barter may be expected is along river systems, which would run counter to some aspects of Bradley's geographical model.

Again, if we are correct in regarding the Langdon Bay and other sea-bed assemblages as representing commodity shipments, then it is telling that certain of the artefact types are not represented in land-based hoards. Indeed it seems logical to assume that material acquired through balanced transactions, some of it alien to the recipients, would not be suitable for permanent deposition in hoards especially if, as Bradley himself intimates, they were deposited at boundaries in the course of group rivalry. Surely in such circumstances it would be important for a community to deposit objects which unambiguously identified their group and thereby their territory, prowess and resistance.

Deposition, as we continue to stress, is a transformation of other processes which are hardly registered in the archaeological record. And the formal nature of that transformation may be similar for quite dissimilar social processes. For example if a sword is to be gifted to a god then the transition from the human to supernatural worlds requires some form of transformation, symbolised by throwing the sword into water or by bending and smashing it before deposition. The transformation of metal into a commodity may also require a physical transformation of the object, the smashing of a sword for example. Thus two quite different social strategies may lead to very similar deposits of material. Can we simply 'read off' from the archaeological record to social processes? When we look at the Blackmoor hoard (Colquhoun 1979) with its large number of swords, all broken and many fragmentary, and its spearheads, we may feel confident that here the selection is such that we are seeing some kind of votive deposit and not a hoard of bronze for barter. But how do we treat the recurrent inclusion of sword fragments in the Carp's Tongue hoards of southern Britain. Are these deposits really no more than bronze collected and stored, but never recovered, for barter?

Let us make one final point. If we accept that some hoards may be connected with the process of metalworking then should we not confront the question of social position of the smith (c.f. Rowlands 1972)? It is often stated that the position of the smith in traditional societies is highly ambiguous, both dangerous and powerful. The person who can make the signs of adult status is often also a person involved in 'making' rites of political transition. The relationship between community and smith is likely to be complex and surrounded by taboos. We rarely find hammers, tongs and anvils (Ehrenberg 1981) amongst our 'industrial' hoards, and perhaps the storage and supply of raw materials to the smith will be controlled through certain prescribed cultural procedures of selection and exclusion. So while we may admit that the character of certain hoards reflects various parts of the production cycle, we should perhaps be more chary of assuming that they are simply metalworkers stock-piles, left unretrieved due to some unforeseen disaster.

The recent growth of Bronze Age settlement excavation has brought to light a reasonable number of metalwork assemblages for the middle and late Bronze Ages. As a generalisation we may state that such assemblages are not representative of the artefacts present in the hoard record. Apart from significant differences in mean size/weight (Needham and Burgess 1980:440, Fig.1), which might be determined by economic factors, the compositions in terms of the artefact types represented do not match up between hoards and settlement contexts. It is possible to explain such patterns as a direct product of casual losses and discards on the settlement sites contrasting with material in scrap hoards being of a size worth recycling (Needham 1980a:24–6). This is a purely economic model which may nevertheless underpin other arguments incorporating other forms of deposition. We must be careful to isolate different levels of the production/circulation/deposition network. Let us suppose that a weight threshold existed on material accepted for recycling; axes and swords, even when broken, would normally be accepted while pins and buttons might not. The axes and swords would become incorporated into a scrap metal stock; at this point they do not *exit* the systemic record, they merely move from a stock in circulation to a stock in metallurgical reserve. On the other hand smaller items, once expended, might be discarded immediately, thus directly entering the archaeological record. Only at a subsequent stage might the scrap stock, or a part thereof, reach an equivalent position and the reason for such a transfer may be utterly at variance with that for its initial removal from circulation.

There are two things we must be clear about in our consideration of settlement assemblages. The first is that the 'loss and discard' component may often be 'contaminated' by hoard deposition (including single pieces) on the site itself. The second is that we cannot take a pure 'loss and discard' assemblage as representative of the systemic metalwork assemblage. Settlement assemblages are themselves formed by selection processes; in other words what got deposited was a direct result of other deliberate actions, particularly ritual disposal and the return of material to reserve stocks. Settlement assemblages are therefore as partial as hoards or grave groups, but they illuminate another facet of the metalwork in circulation.

The character of late Bronze Age settlement assemblages has been summarized elsewhere (Needham 1980a). Those of middle Bronze Age date are somewhat less common and one or two deserve comment to reinforce certain points made. At Grimes Graves, in addition to pins and awls, a bronze saw was recovered; this unusual item has only two parallels in the middle/late Bronze Age hoard record. Unusual items also occurred on the Plumpton Plain sites (Holleyman and Curwen 1935:32–3): on site A a conical fitting without precise parallel, on site B a fragmentary axe which best corresponds to the median-winged type so common in the Langdon Bay cargo (Muckelroy 1981:281), yet absolutely rare in any British context. It is surely significant that the only secure British land find of this alien type is a lost or discarded fragment amongst occupation refuse. Meanwhile the large numbers arriving in cargoes such as Langdon were systematically excluded from the south coast palstave hoards and were presumably normally recycled before *or after* a period of use. It is tempting, though more difficult to argue, to view the Bohemian type palstave from Horridge Common, Devon, in the same light. Its casual loss in a contemporary field, as suggested by Fox and Britton (1969), may alone account for the survival of the type in the archaeological record for Britain.

Although many of the ideas generated in this section remain as yet unsupported by quantified data, they point unequivocally to a complex system, of which we only see limited representation in any given archaeological context. Understanding production, circulation and deposition does not depend on the consideration of gross distributions alone, even if contextual differences are highlighted. We must rigorously analyse the constituents of each context type and tabulate their differences. We may then proceed, always taking into account recovery biases, to pursue logical chains of deduction through the life-cycle of our study material. If necessary we examine two or more contradictory chains simultaneously; eventually internal inconsistencies in relation to the recovered evidence should eliminate certain chains to leave us with tested models. These may illuminate the behaviour and identity of Metal Age Societies far better than literal interpretations of technology, style, and regionality.

Conclusion

This paper has been no more than a series of observations upon the problems inherent in our current interpretations of bronze age bronzeworking. It has certainly not been our intention to provide a comprehensive review, and we have not dealt at all with the important work on metal analysis. Nor has it been our intention to stipulate answers to the problems raised. Instead this is an appeal to begin to rethink current assumptions and to recognise the rich and complex data which are available for investigation. As Bradley has noted (1985:21), too much is said about the "limitations of the archaeological record"; when the limitations derive more from our own intellectual engagement with the past than with some inbuilt failing in the nature of archaeological evidence.

References

Barrett J.C. 1976 Deverel-Rimbury: problems of chronology and interpretation. In C. Burgess and R. Miket (eds) *Settlement and Economy in the Third and Second Millennia BC*. Oxford, BAR 33:289–307.

Barrett J.C. 1980a The evolution of later bronze age settlement. In J.C. Barrett & R.J. Bradley (eds) *Settlement and Society in Later Bronze Age Britain*. Oxford, BAR 83:77–100.

Barrett J.C. 1980b The pottery of the later bronze age in lowland England, *Proc. Prehist. Soc.* 46:297–319.

Barrett J.C. 1985 Hoards and related metalwork. In D.V. Clarke, T.G. Cowie & A. Foxon (eds) *Symbols of Power*. Edinburgh, HMSO, pp. 95–106.

Barrett J.C. 1988 Food, gender and metal: questions of social reproduction In M.L.S. Sørensen & R. Thomas (eds) *The End of the Bronze Age in Europe*. Oxford:,BAR.

Barrett J.C. & Bradley R.J. 1980a Later bronze age settlement in south Wessex and Cranborne Chase. In J.C. Barrett & R.J. Bradley (eds) *Settlement and Society in the British Later Bronze Age*. Oxford, BAR 83:181–208.

Barrett J.C. & Bradley R.J. 1980b The later bronze age in the Thames valley. In J.C. Barrett & R.J. Bradley (eds) *Settlement and Society in the British Later Bronze Age*. Oxford, BAR 83:247–270.

Bradley R.J. 1980 Subsistence, exchange and technology: a social framework for the Bronze Age in southern Britain c. 1400–700 bc. In J.C. Barrett & R.J. Bradley (eds) *Settlement and Society in the British Later Bronze Age*. Oxford, BAR 83:57–75.

Bradley R.J. 1982a The destruction of wealth in later prehistory. *Man* 17:108–122.

Bradley R.J. 1982b Position and possession: assemblage variation in the British Neolithic. *Oxford J. Archaeol.* 1:27–37.

Bradley R.J. 1984 *The Social Foundations of Prehistoric Britain*, London: Longman.

Bradley R.J. 1985a Exchange and social distance: the structure of bronze artefact distributions. *Man* 20:692–704.

Bradley R.J. 1985b *Consumption, Change and the Archaeological Record*. Edinburgh: University Department of Archaeology.

Bradley R.J., Lobb S., Richards J. & Robinson M. 1980 Two late bronze age settlements on the Kennet gravels: excavations at Aldermaston Wharf and Knight's Farm, Burghfield, Berkshire. *Proc. Prehist. Soc.* 46:217–295.

Braithwaite M. 1984 Ritual and prestige in the prehistory of Wessex. c. 2200–1400 BC: a new dimension to the archaeological evidence. In D. Miller & C. Tilley (eds) *Ideology, Power and Prehistory*, Cambridge University Press, pp. 93–110.

Burgess C. 1968 *Bronze Age Metalwork in Northern England c. 1000 to 700 BC*. Newcastle upon Tyne: Oriel.

Burgess C. 1980 *The Age of Stonehenge*. London: Dent.

Burgess C. & Coombs, D. 1979 Preface. In C. Burgess & D. Coombs (eds) *Bronze Age Hoards*. Oxford, BAR 99:i-vii.

Burgess C.B. & Gerloff S. 1981 *The Dirks and Rapiers of Great Britain and Ireland*. Munich, PBF. Abb. IV, Band 7.

Burgess C. & Shennan S. 1976 The Beaker phenomenon; some suggestions. In C. Burgess & R. Miket (eds) *Settlement and Economy in the Third and Second Millennium BC*. Oxford, BAR 33:309–331.

Burstow G.P. & Holleyman G.A. 1957 Late bronze age settlement on Itford Hill, Sussex. *Proc. Prehist. Soc.* 23:167–212.

Childe V.G. 1947 *Prehistoric Communities of the British Isles*, London.

Childe V.G. 1957 The Bronze Age. *Past and Present* 12:2–15.

Childe V.G. 1962 *The Prehistory of European Society*. London.

Coles J.M. 1979 A jade axe from the Somerset Levels. *Antiquity* 48:216–220.

Colquhoun I. 1979 The late bronze age hoard from Blackmoor, Hampshire. In C. Burgess & D. Coombs (eds) *Bronze Age Hoards*. Oxford, BAR 67:99–115.

Drewett P.L. 1979 New evidence for the structure and function of middle bronze age round houses in Sussex. *Archaeol. J.* 136:3–11.

Drewett P.L. 1982 Later bronze age downland economy and excavations at Black Patch, East Sussex. *Proc. Prehist. Soc.* 48:321–400.

Ehrenberg M.R. 1981 The anvils of bronze age Europe. *Antiqu. J.* 61:14–28.

Ellison A. 1978 The Bronze Age of Sussex. In P.L. Drewett (ed) *Archaeology in Sussex to AD 1500*. London, CBA Research Report pp. 30–37.

Ellison A. 1980a Deverel Rimbury urn cemeteries: the evidence for social organisation. In J.C. Barrett & R.J. Bradley (eds) *Settlement and Society in the British Later Bronze Age*. Oxford, BAR 83:115–126.

Ellison A. 1980b Settlements and regional exchange. In J.C. Barrett & R.J. Bradley (eds) *Settlement and Society in the British Later Bronze Age*. Oxford, BAR 83:127–140.

Ellison A. 1981 Towards a socioeconomic model for the middle bronze age in southern England. In I. Hodder, G. Issac, N. Hammond (eds) *Pattern of the Past*. Cambridge University Press, pp. 413–438.

Fox A. & Britton D. 1969 A continental palstave from the ancient field system on Horridge Common, Dartmoor. *Proc. Prehist. Soc.* 35:220–228.

Frankenstein S. & Rowlands M.J. 1978 The internal structure and regional context of early iron age society in southwestern Germany. *Bull. Inst. Archaeol.* 15:73–112.

Friedman J. 1975 Tribes, states and transformations. In M. Bloch (ed) *Marxist Analysis and Social Anthropology*. London, pp. 161–202.

Friedman J. and Rowlands M.J. 1977 Notes towards an epigenetic model of the evolution of civilisation. In J. Friedman & M.J. Rowlands (eds) *The Evolution of Social Systems*. London, pp. 201–276.

Gerloff S. 1975 *The Early Bronze Age Daggers in Great Britain, and a Reconsideration of the Wessex Culture*. Munich, PBF, Abt. VI, Band 2.

Gilman A. 1981 The development of social stratification in bronze age Europe. *Current Anthrop.* 22:1–23.

Godelier M. 1977 'Salt money' and the circulation of commodities among the Baruya of New Guinea. In M. Godelier (ed) *Perspectives in Marxist Anthropology*. Cambridge University Press, pp. 127–151.

Green H.S. 1985 A bronze age stone mould from New Mills, Newtown, Powys. *Arch. Cambr.* 32:273–274.

Gregory C.A. 1982 *Gifts and Commodities*. London: Academic Press.

Holden E.W. 1972 A bronze age cemetery barrow on Itford Hill, Beddingham, Sussex. *Sussex Archaeol. Collect.* 60:70–117.

Holleyman G.A. & Curwen E.C. 1935 Late bronze age lynchet-settlements on Plumpton Plain, Sussex. *Proc. Prehist. Soc.* 1:16–38.

Jessup R.F. 1939 Further excavations at Julliberie's Grave, Chilham. *Antiqu. J.* 19:259–281.

Kenworthy J.B. 1976–7, A reconsideration of the 'Ardiffery' finds, Cruden, Aberdeenshire. *Proc. Soc. Antiqu. Scot.* 108:80–93.

Kinnes I.A. 1979 *Round Barrows and Ring-ditches in the British Neolithic*. London, British Museum.

Kristiansen K. 1978 The consumption process in tribal societies. In K. Kristiansen & C. Paludan-Muller (eds) *New Directions in Scandinavian Archaeology*. Copenhagen, pp. 158–190.

Kristiansen K. 1984 Ideology and material culture: an archaeological perspective. In M. Spriggs (ed) *Marxist Perspectives in Archaeology*. Cambridge University Press, pp. 72–100.

Manby T. 1979 Typology, materials and distribution of flint and stone axes in Yorkshire. In T.C. McK. Clough & W.A. Cummins (eds) Stone Axe Studies. London: CBA Research Report pp. 23–48.

Mauss M. 1969 *The Gift*. London.

Mercer R. 1980 *Hambledon Hill: a neolithic landscape*. Edinburgh University Press.

Muckelroy K. 1981 Middle bronze age trade between Britain and Europe: a maritime perspective. *Proc. Prehist. Soc.* 47:275–297.

Needham S.P. 1979 The effect of foreign influence on early bronze age axe development in southern Britain. In M. Ryan (ed) *The Origins of Metallurgy in Atlantic Europe*, pp. 265–293.

Needham S.P. 1980a The bronzes. In D. Longley, *Runnymede Bridge 1976: Excavations of a Late Bronze Age Settlement*. Surrey Archaeol. Soc. Research Rept., Vol. 6:13–27.

Needham S.P. 1980b An assemblage of late bronze age metalworking debris from Dainton, Devon. *Proc. Prehist. Soc.* 46:7–215.

Needham S.P. 1981 *The Bulford-Helsbury Manufacturing Tradition*. London: British Museum.

Needham, S.P. 1988 Selective deposition in the British Early Bronze Age, *World Arch.* 20:229–48.

Needham S.P. & Burgess C. 1980 The Later Bronze Age in the lower Thames valley: the metalwork evidence. In J.C. Barrett & R.J. Bradley (eds) *Settlement and Society in the British Later Bronze Age*. Oxford, BAR 83:437–69.

Needham S.P. & Dean M. 1987 La cargaison de Langdon Bay à Douvres (Grande-Bretagne): la signification pour les èchanges à travers la Manche *in* J.-C. Blanchet (ed) *Les Relations entre le Continent et les Iles Britanniques à l'Age du Bronze*, Supplement á Revue Archèologique de Picardie Amiens, pp. 119–24.

O'Connor B. 1980 *Cross-channel Relations in the Later Bronze Age*, Oxford, BAR S91.

Proudfoot E.V.W. 1963 Report on the excavation of a bell barrow in the parish of Edmondsham, Dorset, England, 1959. *Proc. Prehist. Soc.* 29:395–425.

Roe F.E.S. 1966 The battle-axe series in Britain. *Proc. Prehist. Soc.* 32:199–245.

Roe F.E.S. 1979 Typology of stone implements with shaftholes. In T.H. McK. Clough & W.A. Cummins (eds) *Stone Axe Studies*. London, CBA Research Reports, pp. 23–48.

Rowlands M.J. 1972 The archaeological interpretation of prehistoric metalworking. *World Archaeol.* 3:210–223.

Rowlands M.J. 1980 Kinship, alliance and exchange in the European Bronze Age. In J.C. Barrett & R.J. Bradley (eds) *Settlement and Society in the British Later Bronze Age*. Oxford, BAR 83:15–55.

Rowlands M.J. 1984 Conceptualising the European Bronze and Early Iron Ages, In J. Bintliff (ed) *European Social Evolution*. Bradford University, pp. 147–156.

Sahlins M. 1974 *Stone Age Economics*. London.

Sherratt A.G. 1976 Resources, technology and trade. In G. de G. Sieveking, I.H. Longworth & K.E. Wilson (eds) *Problems in Economic and Social Archaeology*. London, pp. 557–581.

Sherratt A.G. 1982 Mobile resources: settlement and exchange in early agricultural Europe. In C. Renfrew & S. Shennan (eds) *Ranking, Resource and Exchange*. Cambridge University Press, pp. 13–26.

Sherratt A.G. 1984 Social evolution: Europe in the Later Neolithic and Copper Ages. In J. Bintliff (ed) *European Social Evolution*. Bradford University, pp. 123–134.

Thorpe I.J. & Richards C. 1984 The decline of ritual authority and the introduction of Beakers into Britain. In R. Bradley & J. Gardiner (eds) *Neolithic Studies*. Oxford, BAR 133:67–84.

Wheeler R.E.M. 1943 *Maiden Castle, Dorset*. London, Society of Antiquaries.

Wickham-Jones C.R. 1985 Stone. In D.V. Clarke, T.G. Cowie & A. Foxon (eds) *Symbols of Power*. Edinburgh, HMSO, pp. 164–175.

INDEX OF SITE NAMES